THE COLONIAL OFFICE AND CANADA, 1867-1887

THE OLD COLONIAL OFFICE, NO. 14, DOWNING STREET, IN THE 1870's
(By permission of the Colonial Office)

THE COLONIAL OFFICE
AND CANADA, 1867-1887

David M. L. Farr

University of Toronto Press : 1955

FOR JOAN

PREFACE

OVER TWO DECADES AGO Professor A. R. M. Lower, in discussing some of the neglected aspects of Canadian history, suggested that an investigation of the "middle period" in Canada's relations with Great Britain, the period stretching from Confederation to the Colonial Conference of 1897, might profitably be undertaken. The present work represents a belated attempt to shed some light on part of this broad subject. It is primarily a study in the making of British policy towards Canada during the first twenty years after the creation of the Dominion. In this time the attitude of the United Kingdom towards Canadian problems was largely the attitude of the Colonial Office, and, more specifically, the attitude of the permanent officials at the Office. These men, such as Sir Frederic Rogers and Sir Robert Herbert, exercised a continuous influence in the determination of policy relating to Canada which was more important than the views of any individual Secretary of State. Their role in maintaining a satisfactory relationship with Canada, and their position against the background of the general English attitude towards the autonomous colonies in the late Victorian age is here defined. Yet in this period, as in earlier ones, it is unrealistic to discuss British colonial policy exclusively in terms of the Colonial Office. Other departments in Whitehall maintained an interest in specialized subjects, so that most decisions which were reached represented an amalgam of several, often distinct, viewpoints. Thus the special function of the Office consisted in discovering courses of action which would be acceptable to other British departments of state as well as to the Government of Canada. This was an exacting role, which inevitably earned the Office censure and misunderstanding, both in London and Ottawa. It was, however, honestly and, on the whole, competently performed, with the result that it allowed a relationship between Great Britain and Canada to emerge that was neither jeopardized through Imperial restriction nor vitiated by British official indifference.

The dates chosen for the limits of this study are not entirely arbitrary. The year 1867 witnessed the appearance, in North America, of a nascent colonial state, born into an Empire that seemed destined to an inevitable dissolution. By 1887 the first Colonial Conference had occurred, tentatively applying the principles of consultation and alliance that were to transform the mid-Victorian Empire into a coherent and viable structure. The years between 1867 and 1887 saw "Little England" sentiment replaced by a strong faith in continued unity and were, in effect, the beginning of a transition period in which the British Empire was to be changed into the Commonwealth of Nations. In this momentous political experiment the experience of Canada was to be decisive. As the senior Colony the Dominion was enabled to take the lead in asserting colonial aspirations, so that her unique status became the model for the association of sovereign states comprising the modern Commonwealth.

The working of the imperial connection, at any point, can only be discussed in terms of the specific issues which go to make up its content. The present book presents, therefore, a group of "case studies" in the relations between the United Kingdom and Canada in the period 1867-87. It does not purport to include all the issues that arose between the two countries during these years, but only to review selected questions which seemed both significant and representative of the general course of events. The questions considered throw light on financial and judicial aspects of the imperial connection, on the British view of the nature of Canadian federalism, and on the conflict between the commercial and diplomatic aspirations of Canada and the requirements of imperial unity. Some notable problems of the period have been deliberately omitted from the book: the final withdrawal of the Imperial troops from Canada, which has been adequately studied elsewhere; the mediation by Lord Carnarvon in the Pacific railway controversy, which is a subject extensive enough to warrant separate treatment; and the transfer of the Hudson's Bay Company territories to Canada, in which the role of the Colonial Office has already been examined. There are other topics, such as the Lepine case or Blake's revision of the Governor-General's Commission and Instructions, which are of great importance in imperial constitutional development, but which have had to be omitted because the original materials bearing on them are missing from the records of the Colonial Office.

The sensitive student of Commonwealth affairs will notice that the questionable word "Dominion" appears throughout this book. In explanation it may be said that I have tried to use this word as the Colonial Office and many Canadian statesmen used it in the latter part of the nineteenth century--to describe the special <u>kind</u> of advanced colony which Canada had become after 1867--and not necessarily as part of a national title which has no justification in constitutional law.

I have to acknowledge generous assistance from many quarters in the preparation of this volume. To the Canadian Social Science Research Council, which first awarded me a fellowship for research in Great Britain and later provided a grant in aid of the publication of this book, I would like to express a deep sense of gratitude. The work of the Council over the past decade has put every student of Canadian history and politics irrevocably in its debt. I would like also to thank the President and Board of Governors of Carleton College for granting me leave of absence to undertake research abroad, and the Warden and Fellows of Nuffield College, Oxford, for electing me to a Studentship which enabled me to spend a further year in England. Professor Vincent Harlow supervised the work in its original form when it was being prepared for an Oxford degree; his extensive knowledge of British imperial history and his generous counsel proved a constant encouragement to me. Professor K. C. Wheare furnished valuable comments on chapter V; Dr. A. F. Madden assisted me from his special knowledge of the early history of the Colonial Office, while Mr. K. C. Robinson of Nuffield College kindly undertook to read chapter IV of the manuscript. In Canada I would like to acknowledge the co-operation of Professor F. H. Underhill and Professor F. H. Soward, who read the whole of the work; of Dr. W. Kaye Lamb, who led me, in the first place, to an aspect of this subject; of Dr. R. O. MacFarlane, who read and criticized chapter V; and of Dr. James A. Gibson, for help and encouragement throughout. I would like to make clear that these persons are in no way responsible for the shortcomings of the book, although they may very well take credit for any merits it may be found to possess.

I am under obligation also to Mr. B. Cheeseman, Librarian of the Colonial Office, for his kindness in arranging for the photographs of the old Colonial Office building and the bust of Sir Robert Herbert; these are reproduced by permission of the Colonial Office and the Commonwealth Relations Office, respectively. John Murray (Publishers) Ltd. have allowed me to include in the volume a drawing of Sir Frederic Rogers done by George Richmond, which originally appeared in G. E. Marindin's collection of Rogers's letters. I have to acknowledge the assistance of the staffs of the following libraries and institutions: the Bodleian Library, the Library of New College, and the Library of Rhodes House, Oxford; the Public Record Office and the Institute of Historical Research, London; the Public Archives of Canada, the Library of Parliament, and the Library of Carleton College, Ottawa; and the University of Toronto Library. Finally, Miss M. Jean Houston of the University of Toronto Press has saved me from many pitfalls in preparing the manuscript for publication and I would like to express my thanks to her for much valuable aid.

My greatest debt, however, is to my wife, who not only assisted at the launching of the project contained in this volume but served manfully in numberless ways during the course of a long and sometimes arduous voyage. Now that the ship has come safely into port I would like to record my gratitude, however inadequately, by inscribing this book to her. This I do, with sincere appreciation.

D.M.L.F.

Carleton College, Ottawa
December, 1954

ABBREVIATIONS

CO, Records of the Colonial Office, Public Record Office, London
FO, Records of the Foreign Office, Public Record Office
T, Records of the Treasury, Public Record Office
PRO, Gifts and Deposits Series, Public Record Office
PP, Parliamentary Papers, House of Commons (United Kingdom)
SP, Sessional Papers, Parliament of Canada (Province and Dominion)

CONTENTS

ILLUSTRATIONS

THE COLONIAL OFFICE AND CANADA, 1867-1887

"The real problem of politics is to distinguish
between that which you have a right to do and
that which it is right you should do. That the
Imperial Legislature has a right to legislate for
the colonies cannot be disputed: how far it is
right that it should do so is a matter of policy
and discretion. "

Sir W. Vernon Harcourt, 1876

CHAPTER ONE

THE BRITISH EMPIRE AND THE CONFEDERATION OF CANADA

"I have felt an interest in this confederation scheme (in British North America) because I thought it was a step in the direction of an amicable separation." Richard
Cobden, 1865

THE UNION of three British colonies in North America in 1867 may be considered to
have inaugurated a new era in the long historical process by which Great Britain's colonial Empire has become transformed into the modern Commonwealth. By the middle
of the nineteenth century the foundations of the Old Empire had been irrevocably destroyed and a new imperium created into which it was possible (and necessary) for the
first colonial state to emerge. The imperial organization in 1867 was animated by
three forces: the compelling support possessed by laissez-faire principles in economic
activity; the policy of granting the larger settlement colonies local autonomy; and the
growing realization that the defence of the Empire must rest, essentially, on the inhabitants of the various colonial territories. The victory of free trade brought about,
in the long run, the liberty of the self-governing colonies to frame their own commercial policies. It also made easier the concession of responsible government, which
marked the beginning of an unexampled diversification among the parts of the imperial system. The military reorganization which Cardwell carried out in 1868-74 removed a perennial element of friction from the colonial relationship and enabled it to
be infused with new principles of co-operation and voluntaryism. To many these tendencies seemed strongly centrifugal in nature; a fact which accounted for the prevalence, among influential circles in England in the sixties, of separatist and pessimist
views about the prospects of the Empire. Yet in spite of the lack of faith, the consolidation of Canada was approved and indeed supported by the British Government.
The result was a unique and remarkable polity: a federation "with a Constitution similar in Principle to that of the United Kingdom";[1] a dependency which governed colonial areas of its own; a colony which was also the first "Dominion." During the following decades Canada's relationship with the mother country came to form the decisive model for the evolution of the Commonwealth.

Adam Smith described the Old Empire as founded for the purpose "of raising up a
nation of customers."[2] The judgment may have been coloured but it was none the less
true that in neither Great Britain nor the colonies did the first Empire inspire sentiments
of disinterested and lasting affection. The American Revolution, although it must be
ranked as the greatest tragedy in British imperial history, at least made possible a fresh
start. For a time the opportunity of a new beginning was not taken. The memory of

---

1. For references to chapter I see pages 25-7.

the insurrection in North America, and of the alarming catastrophe a few years later in France, impressed themselves deeply upon the statesmen charged with the task of re-constructing the imperial structure. The result was a policy which buttressed the con-servative elements in colonial society, strengthened the executive power in govern-ment, dismembered the larger administrative units overseas, and drew tighter the bonds of economic control. The nineteenth century, in short, ushered in an age of forebod-ings about the prospects of empire; a period in which Turgot's celebrated analogy rep-resented the predominant expression of the imperial vision.

But even as they were being reapplied, the economic principles which had sup-ported the first Empire were suffering the loss of their vitality. The new theories of laissez-faire, which rose to favour as an aspect of the industrial transformation of Great Britain, represented the complete antithesis of the Old Colonial System. Their victory, by the middle of the nineteenth century, meant that it was utterly impossible to con-tinue, even in a much modified form, the economic organization of the first Empire. For laissez-faire abhorred monopoly, particularly monopoly of trade. The practice of restrictive trading, declared Adam Smith in 1776, "like all the other mean.and malig-nant expedients of the mercantile system, depresses the industry of all other countries, but chiefly that of the colonies, without in the least increasing, but on the contrary diminishing, that of the country in whose favour it is established."3 From this con-clusion it followed that the new economic doctrine was fundamentally anti-imperial in tone. Postulating a natural order dominated by enlightened self-interest, it laid down that it was now essential for the British manufacturer to secure the largest possible mar-ket for his products and to purchase his raw materials in whatever corner of the globe they might be most cheaply found. To confine one's trade to the limited colonial mar-ket was to negate completely the validity of the new theories. The subject of mercan-tile transportation, also, required a new approach, determined by considerations of economy and efficiency rather than by national or strategic interests. In addition, the rising industrial and commercial classes of the United Kingdom looked with suspicion upon other and incidental aspects of the imperial system. The Empire was an expen-sive luxury, the expenditure on its defence and administration causing higher taxation in the mother country which in turn reacted unfavourably on English costs of production. Colonies provided comfortable posts for the representatives of privilege in British so-ciety: the aristocratic and military classes. Colonial territories were a source of dis-agreement with foreign countries; and the new industrialist was at heart a pacifist and an internationalist. As the Industrial Revolution advanced, the proponents of laissez-faire came to justify their system less by economic theory and more by economic in-terest. From Smith to Malthus, however, they continued to emphasize one constant element in their teaching: the conviction that in the British Empire of that day there was to be found little economic justification.

The influence of this anti-imperial opinion might have been greater than it was but for the efforts of a small knot of individuals who drew their inspiration from the liberalism of the French Revolution. The "Philosophical Radicals"--Durham, Buller, Wakefield, and Molesworth--young men of ill-starred lives, also found reason to attack the workings of the Old Colonial System. But, unlike the adherents of laissez-faire, they progressed from purely negative criticism to specific proposals for the welfare of Great Britain and her colonies. Concede the larger settlement territories local autonomy, assist a planned migration from the mother country that would be closely related to the economic and social requirements of the colonies, attempt to establish overseas the beneficial features of English society, and the Empire would remain linked to Great Britain by the invincible bonds of sentiment and affection. In an age which lacked conviction about the permanence of the imperial tie, Durham and his associates contributed not only the practical solution to the problem of imperial government but the faith that was needed to transform an anachronism into a viable organization.

The rising sentiment in favour of laissez-faire principles was responsible for extensive modifications in the old pattern of British economic regulation. The first changes occurred in the terrible years of depression and reaction that followed Waterloo, when the pressure of economic distress contributed to a liberalization of the United Kingdom's commercial policy. In 1820 the London merchants presented their famous petition in favour of free trade to Parliament, and two years later, the "Wallace-Robinson code" took a long step towards simplifying the complicated structure of over 2,000 laws which regulated commerce and navigation. Shortly afterwards William Huskisson assumed the direction of the Board of Trade, with momentous consequences for British overseas commerce. To Huskisson, who was a practical man of business, free trade meant relaxing the prohibitions that had so far governed commercial intercourse within the Empire. It did not mean that trade should be unregulated by the state. In his four years in office Huskisson worked towards the establishment of a system of preferential duties on imports both in England and in the colonies. His measures represented a halfway house on the road to free trade and foreshadowed the changes that were to come.

Under Peel the system of imperial preference was continued and extended. The Canada Corn Law, for instance, gave Canadian flour a special entry into the British market and had as its result a significant expansion of the milling industry of Canada. All the time, however, the leaven of free trade sentiment was working, to influence Peel as well as many lesser men. The bad harvests of the middle forties gave the Prime Minister an opportunity to announce his conversion, and, in 1846, the blow fell. The Corn Law replaced the sliding scale of grain duties, which had protected British agriculture, with, after 1849, a purely nominal duty on foreign wheat. It was the decisive victory in the triumph of laissez-faire economics, and it spelled the doom of the Old Colonial System. The Wealth of Nations and the Industrial Revolution had combined to overthrow the most important symbol of the mercantilist age.

From June, 1846, when the new Corn Law was placed on the statute books, the system of imperial preference, and the regulation of colonial trade which was contained within it, disintegrated rapidly. The process caused shocks and dislocations in the economies of the important British colonies, such as the dissatisfaction which in 1849 reached a sudden and perilous height in North America, but in the end the transition to free trade was accomplished without a rupture of the Empire. Before he left office

Peel reduced the long-standing preference on Canadian timber, and when in opposition he supported Russell's measures to diminish the duty on foreign sugar. The Enabling Act, by allowing the colonies to abolish the element of British preference in their tariffs, became a virtual charter of colonial fiscal autonomy. Later, in 1849, the Russell Ministry repealed the Navigation Act of 1845, which had consolidated the complex code of laws relating to the protection of British shipping. Throughout the decade of the fifties the remaining vestiges of protection were swept away. The last colonial preference, that on timber, was repealed in 1860 by Gladstone, as a consequence of the liberal tariff policy inaugurated by the Cobden Treaty with France. Nine years later Lowe removed the nominal duty on foreign grain and for the first time since the seventeenth century this basic foodstuff entered England untaxed. It was truly the end of an era.

The destruction of the economic organization of the Old Empire was not, by itself, enough to make possible the establishment of a new British imperium. The political principles on which the Empire had been governed since the American Revolution had also to be adapted to meet the changed conditions of the Victorian age. This adaptation took place primarily through the mother country's relations with the remaining British colonies in North America. It was slow in coming, for the Imperial Government at first attempted to found a political system in these territories that would deny to the local assemblies the independence which their counterparts in the Thirteen Colonies had assumed. Consequently the personal authority of the Governor was increased, appointive Legislative Councils were continued, and the safeguard of reservation made a prominent part of Imperial control. The Canadas possessed representative government after 1791, it is true, but it was a government akin to the English constitution under the Tudors.4 The result of this policy was to bring about a deadlock between the executive and the legislature, complicated in Lower Canada by racial antagonisms and in Upper Canada by the unyielding attitude of a governing oligarchy. In 1837 the failure of the policy was emphatically proclaimed when armed rebellion broke out in each of the colonies. The revolts, although abortive, were an inauspicious prelude to the reign of a new Queen. Special measures were clearly demanded, and in the following year Lord Durham, accompanied by his advisers Buller and Wakefield, landed in North America as Governor-General and Lord High Commissioner.

Durham's few months in the Canadas produced his celebrated Report on the Affairs of British North America, which contains the political assumptions on which the new Empire was to be created. Stimulated by talks with Robert Baldwin, the leading Canadian reformer, Durham submitted as his most important recommendation the principle that representative government must be complemented by the device of responsible government. By the latter term he meant the convention by which the executive is required to possess the confidence of the popular branch of the legislature; a relationship which was largely unrecognized at the time as being the unique strength of British parliamentary institutions. From it has grown the modern cabinet system which forms the mainspring of administration throughout the countries of the Commonwealth. Durham did not, however, advance the proposal that responsible government necessarily meant a complete colonial autonomy. In his view certain topics--"the constitution of the form of government, the regulation of foreign relations, and of trade with the mother country, the other British Colonies, and foreign nations, --and the disposal of the public lands"--should continue to be fields for Imperial legislation.[5] The Governor-General's far-reaching proposals were unacceptable to the Melbourne Ministry, and the Act of 1840, designed to deal with the situation caused by the rebellions, simply united the Canadas without meeting this fundamental problem of political responsibility.

For almost a decade after the publication of the Durham Report English statesmen struggled to grasp the implications of responsible government. The maintenance of the solidarity of the Empire seemed totally incompatible with a colonial executive dependent on a local legislature, for the indivisible nature of the Crown meant that it was impossible for the Sovereign to have at once two sets of advisers. Lord John Russell's long and subtle introspections on this point reflect the difficulty with which the mind trained in the Austinian theory of the state approached the question of reconciling autonomy with imperial unity. Successive Governors-General of Canada faced the problem according to their own lights and with varying degrees of achievement. Finally a situation was reached in which the Governor was forced to enter the public arena in support of his principles, thus creating the anomalous spectacle of the representative of the Crown leading a political party in an atmosphere of bitter controversy. Clearly the problem of colonial government was very far from being solved.

In 1846, with the dissolution of Peel's power, Lord John Russell led the waiting Whigs to office. Lord Grey, connected by family ties with Durham and sympathetic with his views, became Colonial Secretary. Resolved to apply the principles of responsible government in Canada, he appointed Lord Elgin, Durham's son-in-law, as Governor-General. Secretary of State and Governor now commenced that fruitful partnership which has made Russell's Administration so notable in British colonial history. A new election returned a Reform majority in the Canadian Assembly and Elgin installed a one-party ministry dependent on this majority. There could be no turning back of the hands of the clock now, and in the spring of 1849 came the test by which responsible government was confirmed. The Rebellion Losses Bill, so detestable to the conservative element in the colony, was presented by the Baldwin-La Fontaine Ministry to Elgin for his approval. Although met with rioting and personal abuse he signed the Bill, the Russell Government refused to disallow it, and it became law. The principle of effective ministerial advice had at last been vindicated. A few months before these exciting events, responsible government had been applied in the older Colony of Nova Scotia, but the Canadian experience made the achievement decisive. From these territories the theory and practice of responsible government were to be taken to other provinces in British North America, to Australasia, and to the settlement colonies in Africa. The process of transplanting the institutions of colonial autonomy occupied the remainder of the nineteenth century and is still one of the vital forces shaping the development of the British dependent Empire.

A new era opened in imperial relations when Elgin made the momentous decision to allow his Canadian Ministers to exercise final responsibility in domestic matters. In a sense this era has only recently closed, for self-government has proved, in the Canadian experience, to be a theme capable of almost indefinite expansion. Ultimately its range has been determined solely by "the legitimate interests of the Canadian people."[6] Durham's conception of responsible government as merely self-government on the municipal level meant that he never associated autonomy with the formation of a colonial nationality. But Canadian statesmen who followed him saw in autonomy the germ of nationhood and worked to nourish this growth. Similarly, the empirical manner by which the British Empire has been created helped to forward the development of colonial home rule. Limited self-government could only represent a temporary status, containing within itself the source of future desires. Requests were made piecemeal in the light of practical requirements, and once they were conceded, their consequences formed a basis for further action. Granted ministerial responsibility in the colonies, an expanding self-government was a result as inevitable as the disintegration of mercantilism following the victory of free trade.

Durham's formula for the political organization of the Empire--a division of authority between the United Kingdom and colonial governments--broke down almost as soon as it was elaborated. The fact that it had never been defined by Imperial statute obviously rendered it the more vulnerable to attack from the colonies. The British Government's control over the public lands of Canada was given up by the Act of Union of 1840, and similarly relinquished in Australia by Sir John Pakington in 1852. The power of colonial assemblies to modify their own constitutions was partly conceded to Canada by the Act of Union and then granted in a general fashion to all colonies by the Colonial Laws Validity Act of 1865. The Imperial regulation of colonial tariff policies also lapsed into desuetude, although the machinery of control was not completely abandoned until the end of the nineteenth century. By that time as well the autonomous colonies had gained the right to assume a leading role in the negotiation of commercial treaties affecting their interests. Only in the field of foreign political relations was their autonomy seriously limited by 1900. The last of the Durham reservations did not pass into the realm of disuse until after the World War of 1914-18.

The roots of the modern Commonwealth are also to be found in the transformation of the imperial defence system that occurred after the revolt of the American colonies. The problem of defence, central to the background of the American Revolution, was one stubborn of solution. From the bitter experience in North America in 1775-83, however, emerged a valuable approach to the basic issue. In 1778 Parliament pledged that never again would the colonies be taxed from London for defence expenditure. This promise Great Britain faithfully honoured during the remaining days of the Old Empire. Its inescapable implication, which became increasingly distasteful to the British Government and public, was that the mother country must bear the entire burden of imperial defence. Thus it was that British North America, during the crises of the Napoleonic Wars and the War of 1812, benefited from large defence projects undertaken at the cost of the British taxpayer. The Rideau Canal, for instance, the most ambitious defence measure which Great Britain ever undertook in North America, dates from shortly after this period. It is true that in the War of 1812 Canada formed a small militia force of indifferent quality, but the principal responsibility for the defence of the Colony rested with the body of British regulars permanently stationed along the border.

With the rise of anti-imperial sentiment in Great Britain critics of the Empire joined in pointing out the huge annual charges for defence, expended on an Empire from which the mother country drew no commercial advantage. The early Radicals made this complaint, Colonial Reformers like Wakefield, Adderley, and Molesworth echoed it, and later Goldwin Smith and the mighty voices of the Manchester School impressed it deeply on the public mind. Lord Grey believed that as commercial and political freedom were awarded the colonies, they must assume a larger share of their defence costs. Following this argument, he would have reduced the garrisons in Canada but for the truculent nature of the United States after the Mexican War. Under his successors the British regulars in North America were steadily brought home until by 1861 there were only 2,000 troops left in Canada.

Parliament was clearly coming to believe at this time that, unless the self-governing colonies were prepared to shoulder part of their defence expenditure, the policy of withdrawal must be carried to its final stages. In 1861 the Mills resolution made this point, thus throwing the challenge to the settlement territories. But there was no response from Canada. For a time the overwhelming crisis of the American Civil War reversed British thinking with the result that troops were dispatched to North America in larger numbers than had ever crossed the Atlantic before. The Confederation negotiations provided a final opportunity to discuss the question of Canadian defence. Macdonald and his associates were, however, unenthusiastic. There was a promise given to construct fortifications on the St. Lawrence, but nothing resembling a participation in defence costs could be elicited from the new Dominion. Thus in 1868 when Gladstone and the first Liberal Ministry came to power the seal was set on the policy of withdrawal. The reforming zeal of Edward Cardwell at the War Office had as its twin objectives the achievement of economy in the Army Estimates, and the promotion of strategic efficiency in the disposition of the regulars. Both these results were dependent on a concentration of Imperial troops at home, and as a consequence the process of withdrawal was carried into its culminating phase. In 1869-70 the troops were evacuated from New Zealand and Australia, and in 1871 from Canada, with the exception of small garrisons left at naval bases. The Canadian people were critical of the operation but in the long run the movement was a salutary one. For, in the words of the historian of the British Army in Canada, "it put an end to the one concrete grievance which the British taxpayer and his representatives in Parliament could present against the overseas empire; and the removal of that grievance infinitely strengthened the whole Imperial structure."[7] The recall of the legions permitted a new association to be formed between Great Britain and her self-governing colonies, one that was looser and less burdensome than the one that had existed before.

The year 1867, when the Bill for uniting the British North American provinces

was presented to the United Kingdom Parliament, came in the midst of a period dominated by anti-colonial sentiment in the mother country. The "Little England" outlook
of this age can be mainly attributed to the powerful influence of the Manchester School.
Since the days of the Colonial Reformers there had been no body in England with as systematic an approach to colonial questions as the Manchester School and none as forthright in the expression of its views. The tragedy of the individual Colonial Reformers
was that they died before their work was done. Beginning with Durham in 1840 and
ending with Molesworth, possessing the seals of the Colonial Office for a final moment
in 1855, the principal members of the group passed from the realm of active political
life. The new radicalism in colonial subjects which succeeded their teachings came
from the leaders of the Manchester School. It was to make a strong impression upon
all the political groups in Parliament. The Colonial Reformers had been Whigs in their
party allegiance, but their influence in the Whig and Liberal factions was not destined
to be permanent. Ten years after Durham's death Cobden and Bright had assumed much
of his role as the imperial educator of the Whig party. Through his association with
Peel, Cobden gained an authority sufficiently strong to convert the majority of the
Peelites to the colonial opinions of the Manchester School. The Tories offered only
bleak forebodings to any discussion of the colonial question. In their minds the development of colonial autonomy must lead inevitably to the disintegration of the Empire. Politically the party, enfeebled by the debâcle of free trade, was unable to offer any effective opposition to the increasing adherence of Whigs and Peelites to the
"Little England" attitude. By the middle of the century Derby, no less than Granville
or Gladstone, was really a follower of Cobden. Lord Grey, as early as 1849, noted the
impression which the anti-colonial viewpoint was making on responsible politicians.

> There begins to prevail in the House of Commons, and I am sorry to say in
> the highest quarters, an opinion (which I believe to be utterly erroneous) that
> we have no interest in preserving our colonies and ought therefore to make no
> sacrifice for that purpose. Peel, Graham and Gladstone, if they do not avow
> this opinion as openly as Cobden and his friends, yet betray very clearly that
> they entertain it, nor do I find some members of the Cabinet free from it.[8]

Although but few of the statesmen who held influential positions in Great Britain from
1837 to 1870 could be described as extreme separatists, the majority of them held pessimistic views about the prospects of the Empire.

The men of the Manchester School represented the new forces in English society.
They were the agents and spokesmen of the great secular change that had occurred in
Great Britain since the advent of the Industrial Revolution. In them the ideas of Adam
Smith were made incarnate and laissez-faire was elevated to the status of a divine law.
Free trade, for England and for the world, was their supreme objective. And, in the
middle of the nineteenth century, when the Anglo-French Commercial Treaty had
crowned the hopes of all free traders, it seemed as if the golden age of unrestricted
commerce was about to be ushered in. In these circumstances what was an empire but

an offence against the natural laws of economics? Based on "a thorough-going devotion
to material profits,"[9] the philosophy of the group assumed a standard of values which
could not but reflect unfavourably on the British overseas Empire. A concern for the
burdens which empire entailed comprised the strongest motive behind all the protesta-
tions of the Manchester School. Disraeli's observations to Derby in 1866 represented
an attitude which the "Little Englanders" of any party could have been expected to endorse.

> Leave the Canadians to defend themselves; recall the African squadron; give up the
> settlements on the west coast of Africa; and we shall make a saving which will, at
> the same time, enable us to build ships and have a good Budget.
> What is more, we shall have accomplished something definite, tangible, for
> the good of the country. In these days, more than ever, the people look to re-
> sults....[10]

Although Cobden and Bright gave adequate expression to the views of the Manchester School, the most brilliant and suggestive of the anti-imperial group remained
outside Parliament all his life. Goldwin Smith, journalist, Oxford professor, pamph-
leteer, and social lion, living successively in England, the United States, and Canada,
embodied in his writings most of the aspects of separatist opinion. In The Empire, a
series of letters written in 1862-3 at the height of Anglo-American tension over the
Civil War, he developed the anti-colonial argument of the Manchester School with
matchless persuasion. A change had occurred in the world since the foundation of the
British Empire; a change so far-reaching that it must inevitably modify British policy.
In what direction? The logic of the answer was remorseless.

> The time was when the universal prevalence of commercial monopoly made it
> well worth our while to hold Colonies in dependence for the sake of commanding
> their trade. But that time is gone. Trade is everywhere free, or becoming free;
> and this expensive and perilous connexion has entirely survived its sole legitimate
> cause. It is time that we should recognise the change that has come over the world.
> We have, in fact, long felt that the Colonies did nothing for us. We now are
> very naturally beginning to grumble at being put to the expense of doing anything
> for them. If they are to do nothing for us, and we are to do nothing for them,
> where is the use of continuing the connexion?[11]

Among the greatest evils which the colonial status produced Smith placed the
habit of mind which favoured a protective tariff policy. The propensity of the settlement colonies to the "commercial vice of Protection" was the result of "ignorant cupid-
ity" and of a society which was "intensely commercial and wanting in education."[12]
This inclination might be cured by emancipation, which would bring maturity and a
sense of responsibility in its train. Separation would also confer a special benefit in
North America, where it would ease the tension between Great Britain and the United

States. Through an independent existence Canada would learn self-reliance and the necessity of observing moderation in her dealings with the American republic. "Leave the Canadians to themselves, and experience will soon teach them to struggle against their own political infirmities, to take care of their own money, to provide for their own defence, and to avoid giving unnecessary provocation to a powerful neighbour when she is (not unnaturally) in a rather irritable mood."[13]

Smith anticipated the Cardwell policy of military concentration by pointing out that separation would allow Imperial troops to be withdrawn from the autonomous colonies. Through this movement the British Isles could be turned into an invulnerable fortress and the nation's public expenditure enormously reduced. Nor would separation diminish the United Kingdom's prestige, claimed Smith, for "the greatness of England really lies not in her Empire, but in herself."[14] And yet Smith would have been indignant at being termed a "Little Englander," for he possessed a large vision of a new empire which he hoped would succeed the old. It was to be a moral association of the English-speaking nations all over the world. "That connexion with the Colonies, which is really a part of our greatness--the connexion of blood, sympathy and ideas--will not be affected by political separation. And when our Colonies are nations, something in the nature of a great Anglo-Saxon federation may, in substance if not in form, spontaneously arise out of affinity and mutual affection."[15]

The tremendous response which Goldwin Smith's views evoked illustrates how adequately they portrayed the state of much English opinion towards the self-governing colonies in the early sixties. Smith's uncompromising style and some specific recommendations which he made excited criticism, but in the main his reasoning was accepted by the influential circles of his day. He earned the high distinction of a lampoon by Disraeli in Lothair, was offered the nomination for a safe Liberal seat in London, and secured the reputation which was to make him a controversial but respected figure for over half a century.

The literature dealing with imperial topics in mid-Victorian England, although comparatively limited, shows the prevalence of separatist opinion among a wide range of groups. Beginning with Sir George Cornewall Lewis's Essay on the Government of Dependencies and Herman Merivale's Lectures on Colonization and Colonies, both published in 1841, it is possible to discern authoritative expression of the idea that Great Britain should be prepared to give her colonies political independence whenever they could stand alone. That the separation of the North American colonies was both desirable and inevitable was suggested by Anthony Trollope in an excellent travel book on the New World, published in 1862, and by Viscount Bury in his Exodus of the Western Nations, written in 1865. The literature of separatism was impressively strengthened by the publication in 1868 of Sir Charles Dilke's Greater Britain. In a sense this book occupied a transitional position in the evolution of imperial thinking, for although it reached separatist conclusions about some British colonies, it was also concerned to increase the mother country's interest in backward areas of the Empire. Dilke decided, after touring Canada, that the Colony was indefensible and that it should, therefore, be written off the list of British possessions. Its secession from the Empire would enable

Great Britain to turn to the task of cultivating a lasting friendship with the United States.

The anti-imperial attitude in Great Britain at the middle of the nineteenth century was reinforced by the traditional indifference in which the colonies had been held ever since the American Revolution. Parliament's attention to colonial topics throughout this period was almost always episodic. Colonial debates were generally sparsely attended and Cabinet Ministers speaking on imperial matters tended to deprecate the value of their subject. Governments placed colonial legislation at the end of a busy session, with the result that measures were either passed precipitately or abandoned. In the constituencies and in political life outside Parliament colonial topics were similarly disregarded. Indeed it is doubtful whether any general election in Great Britain in the nineteenth century, or the return of any individual member to Parliament, turned on a colonial question.[16] The Canadian rebellions of 1837 played a significant part in the defeat of President Van Buren in the American election of 1840, but it had almost no effect in the downfall of the Melbourne Ministry in the following year. The truth is that the British public were only indifferently interested in the self-governing colonies during the first three-quarters of the nineteenth century, and that the parliamentarians who concerned themselves with colonial matters were a small and devoted group. The reporters of the House of Commons had a favourite toast which they proposed on social occasions, "Joseph Hume getting up and George Canning sitting down."[17] It was possible to abridge the report of a speech on colonial subjects by the indefatigable Hume, but a statement by Canning must be covered verbatim.

It may appear remarkable that at a time when anti-colonial sentiment in Great Britain was reaching its climax, a great scheme of imperial consolidation--the union of the British North American provinces--should have been carried through to a successful conclusion. Further examination indicates, however, that the Confederation of Canada was directly related to the prevalence of separatist opinion in the mother country and was probably promoted by it. The connection between the two sets of circumstances lies, of course, in the wider aspects of British policy as they were assessed in the mid-Victorian period. British North America, which had always been a vital factor in the conduct of Anglo-American relations, had become a dangerous commitment to Great Britain by the decade of the sixties. The American Civil War, with its attendant problems of neutrality and belligerency, had imposed an almost intolerable strain upon the relations between the two countries. The British recognition of the Southern Confederacy as a belligerent power in 1861 caused intense dissatisfaction in the Northern states, while the Trent affair seemed to the United Kingdom a gross violation of the rights of a neutral. Similarly the servicing of Confederate raiders in British ports gave the North a legitimate cause of complaint which was to become a burning issue between the two nations for years after the last shot of the Civil War had been fired. Canada showed a negligence in allowing Confederate forces to raid Union territory from bases in the Colony, while the state governments of the North turned an equally blind eye towards Fenian preparations to invade British North America. Once begun, the train of disagreement between Great Britain and the United States increased in intensity. With the ending of hostilities, relations passed into a second and more critical phase. By 1865 the Union armies numbered over one million men and formed the strongest military force in the world. They rested at the disposal of the American Executive and Congress, both of whom had taken no pains to conceal a hostility towards Great Britain. W. H. Seward, the Secretary of State, made speeches proclaiming the expansionist aims of the United States; Charles Sumner, the Chairman of the Senate Foreign Relations Committee, hinted darkly that American designs on Canada should be accepted by the United Kingdom as the price of peace. In 1866 a measure, introduced into Congress, provided for the admission of the North American colonies into the republic.

These circumstances revealed more sharply than ever the liability which Great Britain possessed in her North American territories. The Trent affair had been responsible for a strengthening of the Imperial garrison in Canada but military opinion was extremely doubtful of the ability of these, or any troops, to withstand an invasion from south of the frontier. Colonel Jervois in 1864 reported definitively that Canada was indefensible. It was not surprising, therefore, that when certain of the North American colonies expressed a desire to be joined together in a federal union, Great Britain should have given the project its support. Divided, the colonies in North America were entirely at the mercy of the American colossus; united, they might develop a strength and self-reliance which would enable them to withstand the advances of their great neighbour. Independence seemed to be the destiny of these settlement colonies in any event, and there were many in England who did not see that this consummation differed markedly from annexation into the United States. But above all, consolidation in North America would have the supreme virtue of simplifying Great Britain's defence problems. As The Times expressed it: "We look to Confederation as the means of relieving this country from much expense and much embarrassment.... We appreciate the goodwill of the Canadians and their desire to maintain their relations with the British Crown. But a people of four millions ought to be able to keep up their own defences."[18]

Thus British influence, powerful both on the official level and among the population of the North American colonies, was introduced into the discussion of the federation proposals. In the Maritime colonies it proved decisive in tipping the scales in favour of union; in Canada it provided strong support to a movement which had already a wide popular backing. The Civil War, which saved the American union, probably created the Canadian one. Without it the campaign for federation would have followed a long and protracted course which might have arrived too late at the moment of decision. Without the compelling urgency of the international situation after 1865 British support for the plan of federation would never have proved as prompt and effective as it turned out to be.

This estimate is not intended to depreciate the importance of the purely Canadian motives in the federation movement. Obviously they were of direct and incalculable significance. The abrogation of the Reciprocity Treaty in 1866 forced British

North America back upon itself as an economic unit, causing the commercial and manufacturing groups of Canada to look eastward to the Maritime colonies and westward to the prairies for an extension of their economic activities. The desire to prevent the North West from becoming yet another field of colonization for American settlers also exerted great influence in the older regions of British North America. Lincoln's Homestead Act and the chartering of the first transcontinental railway in the United States announced that the American frontier was on the march and could not long be expected to leave unexploited a vast area of fertile land ruled by a fur trading company. Without quick action by Canada the disintegration of the Hudson's Bay Company's domain would occur, and the pattern of the occupation and concession of the Oregon territories would be repeated. The political deadlock in the Province of Canada meant that federation came to represent the only expedient which would provide a satisfactory system of government for the two racial groups existing in an unharmonious association within one colony. Thus Canada gave the federation movement the most enthusiastic support of any of the colonies of North America. It contributed both the leaders of the campaign and the men who assumed control over the destinies of the new state. Without the genius of Macdonald and his associates the magnificent opportunity for constructive achievement which the Charlottetown Conference offered would never have been realized.

There remains but one factor to be noticed in the British attitude towards North American union. Why was the federation of Canada carried through without an attempt being made to cut the new state loose from its connection with the United Kingdom? The answer must be found partly in the fact that the North American colonies failed to express any desire to separate from the mother country. Without the consent of the colonies, no responsible statesman would have forced a break between Great Britain and her overseas territories. This is a constant pledge throughout all the official pronouncements of the period. There was also another, and more obscure force working for the continued association of Canada with the United Kingdom: the factor which Professor Brebner has described as that of "financial imperialism."[19] It was founded on the investments which Great Britain possessed in her North American colonies--provincial securities, Hudson's Bay Company stock, and railway and canal shares. The interests behind the International Financial Society, a holding company formed in the early sixties to consolidate the ownership of the Grand Trunk Railway and the Hudson's Bay Company, and many other smaller investors, formed a group whose influence upon the political parties, although difficult to assess, was increasing throughout the mid-Victorian era. Holders of railway bonds in particular favoured Confederation because it offered an enlargement of the existing railway systems in Canada and a chance to tap the resources of the rich interior of the continent. They and other financial elements composed a vested interest in the preservation of the connection between British North America and the mother country. This is not to suggest that they necessarily represented a sinister force working behind the apparatus of government but merely to draw attention to a new factor whose role in the formulation of British policy became more important as the century progressed.

It was in a mood of pronounced indifference that the Imperial Parliament took up the consideration of the British North America Act. Members were hardly inclined to tarry long over the 147 clauses of the Bill, embodying the complex federal arrangements hammered out by Canadian delegates and the Colonial Office during months of conference. Nor were they prepared to discuss the destiny of the new state to which they were giving life. The first "Dominion" emerged into being with cursory parliamentary attention, accompanied by few significant expressions of the imperial vision. In the Commons the British North America Bill was disposed of in four short sessions; in the Lords in one meeting of the Committee of the House. To one resident of British North America, who watched the proceedings of the Commons on this memorable occasion, the fate of the measure seemed to represent the last twilight of the England of Burke and Chatham.

The great body of the House was utterly indifferent, even the delegates seemed chagrined at the lazy contempt with which a thin House suffered their bill to pass unnoticed through Committee.

A clerk at the table gabbled on not the clauses even but the numbers of the clauses and as if that were not a quick enough mode of rushing through a disagreeably dull measure which did not affect anybodys [sic] seat, and which therefore could not be listened to, he used to read a whole batch of numbers at once, for example saying "Moved that clauses 73, 74, 75 pass" and they passed sure enough, without anybody worrying himself about their contents. . . .

The House got livelier and better filled when a dog tax bill came up--for you see the country gentlemen who could not maybe point out Nova Scotia on the map keep fox hounds subject to tax which interests them more keenly than a Canadian tariff.

I confess this utter indifference was more mortifying to me than positive opposition. . . . when I saw English gentlemen sitting where Burke once sat framing his indignant sentences against the Government's disregard for the popular wish in the old American colonies I felt that their changed policy, contrasting so remarkably with his was one of the worst signs of the time. It showed that they considered Colonists beings so little related to them as the inhabitants of some nameless Chinese mud village. . . .20

If the episode expressed the mood of the age it also foreshadowed the appearance of a new spirit in imperial relations, when tolerance would be substituted for indifference and mutual trust take the place of recrimination.

The men at the head of the Government of Canada during the first twenty years after Confederation were largely those who had planned and executed the scheme of union. Among this group the figure of Sir John Macdonald is pre-eminent. From almost the year of his entry into public life in 1844 until his death as Prime Minister in 1891, Macdonald can be said to have dominated the Canadian political scene. His career spanned the winning of responsible government, the achievement of federation, and the consolidation and expansion of the new Dominion. In the history of Canada Macdonald is the chief architect of nationhood: the man who above all others shaped its structure and established firmly its foundations.

First and foremost, then, Macdonald was a nationalist. His nationalism was to a large extent the product of geography. Raised in Kingston, situated at the foot of the Great Lakes and the head of the St. Lawrence River, he was very conscious of the unity of the St. Lawrence basin. He realized that upon the preservation, in an undivided condition, of this geographical region rested the basis of British power in North America. The St. Lawrence, which had been an economic system ever since the French first colonized its banks, represented the key to the problem of creating a new state on the American continent. Thus to Macdonald the great river and its domain formed the ultimate reality of Canada.

His conception of the new Canadian state was Hamiltonian in its origin. It embodied support for all those forces and agencies which would contribute power to the central authority: a conservative upper class, a strong executive, a nominated upper house, a constitution which left the residuum of responsibility to the federal government, centralized financial institutions, industrialism, and tariff protection. In Macdonald's view the local units in the Canadian federation were to exist as distinctly inferior adjuncts to the central government, whose control would be all-pervading throughout the Dominion. A new spirit had of necessity to be created; a national spirit which would look to Ottawa rather than to Toronto or Halifax for its inspiration. This in turn presupposed the existence of a national party to sustain the edifice of Confederation. In the skill with which he set about the task of constructing this party resides one of Macdonald's chief claims to fame. The party's foundations rested on an alliance between French and English conservatives, but it also drew support from the outlying sections of Canada, from financial and manufacturing interests, and from powerful religious bodies. The elements in its composition, seemingly irreconcilable, worked together in effective harmony during Macdonald's lifetime. This circumstance provides the best possible indication of the measure of the man.

Macdonald's views on foreign policy were similarly dictated by his intense faith in Canadian nationality. The only enemy to that nationality, after 1867, was the expansive force of the United States. Thus the essence of Canadian nationhood consisted in remaining distinct from the American union, in resisting those tendencies towards continentalism which were at times so compelling. Canada was too weak and too young to accomplish this feat unaided. She needed an ally, and Macdonald looked to Great Britain to fill this role. The British connection to Macdonald was thus not mere sentiment but the formal expression of an Anglo-Canadian entente. It assumed the existence of Canada as an autonomous nation within the British Empire, linked to the United Kingdom by ties of interest as well as by a common Crown. For Great Britain provided the traditional market for exports from British North America; her investment capital represented the chief source of Canadian public loans; she possessed an unrivalled consular service freely placed at the disposal of Canadian commerce; and her Navy afforded valuable protection to the young state in the disputed conduct of the North Atlantic fisheries. In the Judicial Committee of the Privy Council functioned an impartial tribunal willing to act as a court of final appeal for Canada. All these factors, together with the more intangible benefits of being associated with the leading world power, made Macdonald confident that in alliance with Great Britain lay the true destiny of Canada.

His vision of the Anglo-Canadian relationship emerged most clearly at the time of the founding of the Dominion, when the new state's external alignments had to be charted. Although something of what Macdonald said in the period 1864-7 can be classed as rhetorical gesture inspired by the emotion of the occasion, there remained in his utterances a concrete expression of Canada's role within the Empire. His proposal that the new federation be called the "Kingdom of Canada" suggested immediately that to his mind partnership and not subordination should form the character of the revised imperial tie after 1867. Confederation had been accomplished, he said, for "the noble object of founding a great British Monarchy, in connection with the British Empire, and under the British Queen."[21] It would inaugurate a new era in imperial relations:

When this union takes place we will be at the outset no inconsiderable people... our alliance will be worthy of being sought by the great nations of the earth. I am proud to believe that our desire for a permanent alliance will be reciprocated in England... The colonies are now in a transition state. Gradually a different colonial system is being developed--and it will become, year by year, less a case of dependence on our part, and of overruling protection on the part of the Mother Country, and more a case of healthy and cordial alliance. Instead of looking upon us as a merely dependent colony, England will have in us a friendly nation ... to stand by her in North America in peace or in war.[22]

The goal which he laid down in 1867 he kept before him for the rest of his life. American economic influence in Canada must be resisted, he affirmed, and at a time of financial depression, when his political position was insecure, he strongly opposed a plan to enter into intimate commercial relations with the United States. Protection for native industry, combined with a British preference, embodied his ideal of a desirable tariff policy for Canada. He rejoiced in co-operation with Great Britain, whether expressed in a joint Anglo-Canadian expedition to quell the uprising in 1870 on the Red River or in the building of a national transcontinental railroad which was at the same time a valuable link in the Empire's communications. The project of alliance did not mean, however, unlimited commitments from one partner. Its burdens and obligations should be deliberately negotiated and defined by permanent treaty. Thus in 1885 he rejected a suggestion that Canada send an expeditionary force to assist Great Britain in the troubles in the Sudan. This was not a proper subject for imperial co-operation, he told Tupper. "The Suez Canal is nothing to us, and we do not ask England to quarrel with France or Germany for our sakes.... Why should we waste

money and men in this wretched business? England is not at war, but merely helping
the Khedive to put down an insurrection.... Our men and money would therefore be
sacrificed to get Gladstone and Co. out of the hole they have plunged themselves into
by their own imbecility. "[23]   Canadian interests must be consulted and respected before co-operation in imperial relations could become fruitful, he always believed.

Personally Macdonald's most valuable characteristic was his ability to reconcile
the diverse elements forming the Canadian nation. This facility required a strong ad-
mixture of opportunism: a cast of mind which Macdonald never hesitated to adopt.
Much may be excused, however, because in welding together the English and French
racial groups Macdonald performed the most valuable service possible for the Canadian state. Compromise sometimes meant postponement and Macdonald, nicknamed
"Old Tomorrow," knew well the worth of time as a useful political ally. Allied to
this knowledge was Macdonald's ability to judge men, to turn foes into supporters, to
divide the refractory into futile factions. In the art of managing men Macdonald has
had no equal in Canadian life. His casual air, his bonhomie, his human qualities,
his uncanny trick of recognition, made him known from end to end of his vast Dominion. His standard of political ethics was, to say the least, undistinguished, but that
was the price he paid for maintaining the structure of Canadian unity over almost a
quarter of a century. By the 1880's, when he had become a virtual legend in British
North America, "it could almost be said that Macdonald was Canada and Canada was
Macdonald. "[24]

In creating a national Conservative party Macdonald gathered about him a number of able colleagues. Sir Alexander Galt, although never an orthodox Conservative,
was the Prime Minister's counterpart in the field of finance. One of the promoters of
the Grand Trunk Railway, Galt remained closely identified with the financial interests
of Montreal during his lifetime. His advocacy of the scheme in 1858 first brought federation into the arena of practical politics and during the negotiations which led to the
drafting of the British North America Act he served as the chief expert on the financial
aspects of union. Like Macdonald he was a centralist whose efforts were devoted to
providing the Dominion Government with the fiscal powers necessary for it to exercise
an overriding authority throughout the country. In Galt's eyes Confederation, besides
founding a new nation, made it possible for Montreal finance to extend its operations
over several colonies and a vast area of unexploited territory. He remained always the
promoter, whether in the sphere of railway or canal transportation or in land development.

Vigorous and outspoken in the expression of his views, Galt left the Macdonald
Ministry in 1867 after holding office as the first Minister of Finance for Canada. He
retired from Parliament and spent much of the remainder of his life in diplomatic pursuits. In negotiations with France and Spain he attempted to increase Canadian external trade; earlier he had served as a member of the commission established to ad-
judicate the value of Canadian fisheries to the United States; and he was to end his
career as the first High Commissioner of the Dominion in London. In the latter post
he steadfastly impressed upon all with whom he dealt the freedom of action which the

new state was determined to assume in foreign commercial transactions. Galt's personal views on Canada's place within the Empire were always somewhat erratic. Immediately after Confederation he had confidently pronounced that the Dominion's future lay in complete independence from Great Britain; a decade later he was just as firmly convinced that the best interests of the Colony resided in its becoming a unit in a federated Empire. As High Commissioner Galt took an active part in the work of the Royal Colonial Institute and spoke and wrote in favour of imperial federation several years before the project received general attention. Imperial unity assumed specific forms to Galt, with the result that he urged state-aided emigration, tariff preferences, and an imperial defence tax as subsidiary measures which might precede political federation. Throughout the two decades following 1867 Galt played a leading part in defining the practical basis of the relationship between Canada and Great Britain. Essentially an independent at heart, he was enabled by the respect which his great ability afforded him both in Canada and Great Britain to assert Canadian autonomy without fear or favour.

A more dependable colleague of Macdonald's was Sir Charles Tupper, the Premier of Nova Scotia at the time of Confederation. Through Tupper's skill Nova Scotia was brought into the union and (an even more remarkable feat) the leader of the malcontents who had opposed the arrangements of 1867, Joseph Howe, induced to join the Conservative Administration at Ottawa. Thereafter Tupper served as Macdonald's right hand man among his English-speaking colleagues, playing an important role in the construction of the Canadian Pacific Railway and in the establishment of Dominion representation in London. He succeeded Galt as High Commissioner in 1883 and soon showed that he was more adroit than his predecessor in gaining concessions from the British Government. During his régime in England notable advances were made in the Canadian treaty-making power and in the procedure of communication between Ottawa and London. Like the later Galt, Tupper was a strong believer in the concept of imperial unity, favouring a constitutional change by which the Agents-General of the autonomous colonies would form a permanent body sitting in London to advise the British Government on foreign policy. He definitely did not support the idea of colonial contributions for an imperial defence force, however. Tupper became a leading figure in the councils of the Imperial Federation League, although he envisaged the League as an agency by which his personal faith in schemes of protection and tariff preference could be disseminated. After thirteen years in London as High Commissioner Tupper became known in the mother country in a manner which few other Canadians have achieved. His social charm, energy, and determination to promote Canadian ends made him an ideal ambassador of the Dominion during a formative period.

The final member of Macdonald's circle who was of importance in the conduct of Anglo-Canadian relations during the period 1867 to 1887 was Sir John Rose. Not connected with the movement for Confederation, Rose was nevertheless one of Macdonald's most intimate associates. A lawyer, with a large commercial practice in Montreal, he possessed only a limited acquaintance with public life before becoming Minister of Finance in 1867. He resigned two years later to take up a position as an

investment banker in London. Having already performed several diplomatic missions
for Macdonald, it was but natural that Rose should have been asked to undertake the
duties of a quasi-official representative of the Canadian Government in Great Britain.
He carried out this role for over a decade with conspicuous success.[25] Rose's ability
was quickly recognized by the Gladstone Government, which entrusted to him the delicate negotiations leading up to the appointment of the commissioners for the Treaty of
Washington. In later life he served on various British royal commissions and filled posts
in the household of the Prince of Wales, whom he had first met in Canada in 1860. His
position during his years in London was hardly exclusively Canadian, therefore, and he
represents a unique example of a statesman holding a genuinely imperial point of view.
Appreciating the existing colonial relationship from the standpoint of both London and
Ottawa, Rose was enabled to offer a substantial contribution towards its cordial maintenance. His personal views, even in the mood of uncertainty about the Empire which
characterized the early seventies, were those of a moderate exponent of imperial solidarity. In a letter to The Times he asserted that nothing must be done to disturb the
political balance between England and her self-governing colonies. The noble benefits
of empire could only be achieved by continuing the connection in its present form. The
imperial atmosphere must be cleared of suspicion and ill will and the responsibilities of
empire resolutely taken up:

> [It is our task to assert] ... the unity of the empire--to discountenance op-
> posite views, and to mould all our policy in accordance with that conception; to
> remove any fears which exist in England with reference to the danger resulting from
> the possession of any colony; to ascertain, with as much precision as possible, the
> real extent of burdens they severally entail; to get rid of the idea of the supposed
> readiness of the colonies to palm these burdens on England, and of their unwilling-
> ness from time to time to revise the relations or place them on a footing which
> shall be just to both; and to dispel the idea that Colonial Governments are ready to
> enter into commercial treaties with foreign Powers adverse to English interests.
> There is great need, too, that the colonies should be disabused of the impression
> that there exists on the part of England a desire to throw them off. The appearance
> of unrequited love, with communities as with individuals, sometimes leads to un-
> reasonable resentment.[26]

The Liberal party controlled the Government of Canada for only five years during
the period covered by this study. Macdonald's fall from power, occasioned by the rev-
elations of political corruption in the awarding of the Pacific Railway contract, was
not, in the end, destined to be a permanent check to his fortunes. The Liberal interregnum was not without significance in the development of Canadian relations with the
United Kingdom. Whereas the nationalism of the Conservatives tended to assume an
anti-American character, that of the Liberals was based on the conviction that Canadian interests must be protected against the overriding authority of the Imperial Government. Thus the Liberal Administration of 1873-8 laid great store on the task of

defining the constitutional position of Canada within the Empire. Several constructive achievements were recorded during this period. The Governor-General's Commission and Instructions were revised to bring the office into accord with current practices; the Supreme Court of the Dominion was established; and vice-admiralty courts exercising civil jurisdiction upon the Great Lakes were placed in operation. In domestic matters the Liberals were far less successful. Although the commercial depression of the mid-seventies undoubtedly increased the difficulties of administration, the Government showed that it had no real programme for internal development. The Prime Minister and leader of the party, Alexander Mackenzie, proved to be politically inept and incapable of providing dynamic direction to the efforts of his supporters. He concentrated on a careful supervision of the Department of Public Works and neglected to form the Liberals into an organization comprising a variety of sectional attitudes. Until the time of Laurier the party remained, essentially, a modern expression of the old Grit faction of Canada West, representing mainly agrarian interests.

The most outstanding Liberal in Canadian politics before 1887 was not Mackenzie but his principal lieutenant, Edward Blake. Spending most of his career in public life at Ottawa, Blake became thoroughly identified with the promotion of Canadian national aspirations rather than with the wishes of a particular region. He was attracted, immediately after Confederation, by the doctrines of independence and self-determination put forward by Goldwin Smith and the "Canada First" group, and these ideas coloured his subsequent thinking about Canada's position within the Empire. He became an uncompromising advocate of the autonomy of the Dominion in imperial matters; "a stickler ... for Canadian rights as against the Crown," as a member of the Colonial Office described him. [27] Not only did he attempt to promote Canadian self-government in all his official dealings with Great Britain, but he sketched a scheme of nationhood for the new Dominion that went beyond the current requirements of imperial relations. Dufferin remarked once that Blake was fundamentally a Celt, possessed of the Celtic inclination for logical symmetry in constitutional forms. [28] This is a valid judgment, for Blake was never satisfied by merely reaching agreement on an ad hoc basis. He retained always in his mind the grand design of Canadian autonomy, the conception of the abiding principles underlying Canada's relations with the Imperial power.

Blake's personal characteristics are of some importance in estimating the strength and the limitations of his approach. Like many brilliant men he was unstable by temperament: aware of his abilities and morbidly suspicious of any fancied slight; arrogant and inconciliable in nature; subject to alternate moods of exultation and depression; intensely ambitious, restless, and independent. Yet withal he was urbane and high-principled, a man who could display great social charm if he were so inclined. Dufferin warned Carnarvon about this outward aspect of Blake's personality on the occasion of the Canadian's momentous visit to London in the summer of 1876. "You will find him very gentlemanlike in his manner, but you must not be misled by his amiable 'allures' for the pot boils over without giving any warning, though as far as I am concerned, I have always taken care never to light a match beneath it."[29] The

following incident which occurred on one of Blake's trips to London was related by
Dufferin. With an ordinary man it might h ave been passed over without notice, but
with Blake it became one more factor which "put him out of temper with British Dom-
ination."

> One day at the Colonial Office he sent in his card to the Secretary of State, and
> was extremely displeased the officials did not at once know who he was. He was
> also put out by Hugessen [Parliamentary Under-Secretary, 1871-4] coming into
> the waiting room, and saying by way of an agreeable opening to the conversation,
> --"Well I hope our friend Sir John Macdonald is getting along all right." Blake
> being at the time his most bitter opponent.[30]

Blake's nationalism differed markedly from Macdonald's in that Blake emphasized political factors while Macdonald gained his greatest success in attracting economic interests to the development of Canada. Like his contemporaries in the United
States Government, Macdonald freely distributed public subsidies and favours to economic groups which could contribute to the building of the country. Blake, the political theorist and disinterested professional man, felt nothing but suspicion for this government assistance to business activity. He was alarmed at the influence which it
could give large corporations in the state and distressed with the thought that the practice might lead to a lowering of the moral standards of the community. Unlike Macdonald he was cautious and pessimistic in his approach to the material development of
Canada, an attitude which caused him to commit the blind error of opposing the Canadian Pacific Railway. As a Liberal he believed in a low tariff and fought Macdonald's
"National Policy" through years of opposition after 1878. Yet when the Liberals decided to espouse the idea of closer economic relations with the United States and pressed for what they called "unrestricted reciprocity," he drew back in alarm. To his
mind a Commercial Union between the United States and Canada would ultimately result in political association, which would represent the negation of all that he had advocated. In the end he left the Liberal party and retired from Canadian politics over
the question.

On the broader issue of Canada's relations with the United Kingdom Blake showed
himself to be in touch with the deep historical trends of the time. In the early years of
the Dominion, indignant at what he felt was the sacrifice of Canadian interests in the
Treaty of Washington, he took up the project of imperial federation and made several
vague gestures towards it. His reasoning was that unless Canada preferred simply to accept British control in her foreign relations she must demand a greater share in their
making, and at the same time be prepared to shoulder some of the responsibilities of
imperial policy. Although he soon abandoned this dream his original antagonism to
Imperial authority remained a guiding principle throughout his life. It was an essential
concomitant to the nationalism he advocated in his celebrated and "disturbing" Aurora
speech of 1874.

... our Government should not present the anomaly which it now presents--a Government the freest, perhaps the most democratic in the world with reference to local and domestic matters, in which you rule yourselves as fully as any people in the world, while in your foreign affairs, your relations with other countries whether peaceful or warlike, commercial or financial, or otherwise, you may have no more voice than the people of Japan.... It is impossible to foster a national spirit unless you have national interests to attend to.... the time will come when that national spirit which has been spoken of will be truly felt among us, when we shall realize that we are four millions of Britons who are not free.... Tomorrow, by the policy of England, in which you have no voice or control, this country might be plunged into the horrors of a war.... The future of Canada, I believe, depends ... upon the cultivation of a national spirit.[31]

While rejecting closer association with the United Kingdom, Blake did not support Goldwin Smith's arguments that nationalism for Canada should mean an end to the imperial connection. In the early seventies, when separatist doctrines were fashionable on both sides of the Atlantic, he deprecated such reasoning.[32] His faith in the permanence of the imperial tie became stronger as the years passed. In 1900, as a member of the British Parliament, he showed that he realized, more clearly than Joseph Chamberlain and the centralists of the day, that it was in the intangibles that the durable links of empire were to be found. Chamberlain had criticized these factors as being too "slight and slender," but Blake echoed Burke's words in suggesting that it was the concrete forms of association which were, in the long run, unimportant.

But I believe [the ultimate aspects of the relationship] to be absolutely impalpable, not founded on costly appeals, not on your clauses of reservation, not on your powers of disallowance, and not on the paramount legislative power of this Parliament. I am not complaining of these things. But they are not the real links that bind the whole.... They are links of good will, founded on local freedoms.[33]

In making this claim, says the foremost student of his work, Blake expressed "the quintessence of the spirit of Canadian liberal nationalism."[34] It was also, as it happened, the fundamental assumption upon which the structure of the modern Commonwealth has been erected.

1. 30 and 31 Vict., c.3, preamble.

2. Quoted in E. A. Benians, "The Beginnings of the New Empire, 1783-93," The Cambridge History of the British Empire, II (Cambridge, 1940), 2.

3. Quoted in R. L. Schuyler, The Fall of the Old Colonial System: A Study in British Free Trade, 1770-1870 (New York, 1945), 53.

4. V. Harlow, "The New Imperial System, 1783-1815." Cambridge History of the British Empire, II, 139.

5. Sir R. Coupland, ed., The Durham Report (Oxford, 1945), 144.

6. Chester Martin, "The United States and Canadian Nationality," Canadian Historical Review, XVIII (March, 1937), 10.

7. C. P. Stacey, Canada and the British Army, 1846-71: A Study in the Practice of Responsible Government (London, 1936), 257.

8. Grey to Elgin, May 18, 1849, quoted in J. L. Morison, British Supremacy and Canadian Self-Government, 1839-1854 (Glasgow, 1919), 266-7.

9. Stacey, Canada and the British Army, 35.

10. Disraeli to Derby, Sept. 30, 1866, quoted in W. F. Monypenny and G. E. Buckle, The Life of Benjamin Disraeli, Earl of Beaconsfield (London, 1910-20), IV, 476-7.

11. Goldwin Smith, The Empire: A Series of Letters Published in "The Daily News," 1862, 1863 (Oxford, 1863), 2-3.

12. Ibid., 90.

13. Ibid., 109.

14. Ibid., 8.

15. Ibid., 6.

16. There is a possible qualification of this statement in the general election of 1880, in which the colonial policies of the Beaconsfield Government undoubtedly contributed towards its downfall.

17. S. C. Hall, Retrospect of a Long Life, quoted in E. Porritt, The Fiscal and Diplomatic Freedom of the British Oversea Dominions (Oxford, 1922), 308.

18. The Times, March 1, 1867, quoted in Stacey, Canada and the British Army, 179.

19. J. B. Brebner, North Atlantic Triangle: The Interplay of Canada, the United States and Great Britain (New Haven, 1945), 174-7.

20. Report by William Garvie, March 15, 1867, in L. J. Burpee, ed., "Joseph Howe and the Anti-Confederation League," Transactions of the Royal Society of Canada, series III, X (May, 1916), 462-3.

21. Edward Whelan, ed., The Union of the British Provinces, quoted in J. S. Ewart, The Kingdom of Canada and Other Essays (Toronto, 1908), 2.

22. Macdonald in the Confederation Debates in the Legislature of Canada, Feb. 6, 1865. Printed in W. P. M. Kennedy, ed., Statutes, Treaties and Documents of the Canadian Constitution, 1713-1929 (Toronto, 2nd ed., 1930), 568.

23. Macdonald to Tupper, March 12, 1885, printed in J. Pope, ed., Correspondence of Sir John Macdonald (Toronto, 1921), 338.
It may be noted that Macdonald, although strongly persuaded of the necessity of preserving Canada's freedom of action in respect of imperial obligations, was not above accepting (and soliciting) help from the United Kingdom on a number of occasions after 1867. There would seem to be a hiatus here between the Prime Minister's speeches and his deeds as they related to the subject of imperial solidarity. However, on this, as on all other questions in Macdonald's career, the deeds afford the truer measure of the man.

24. A. R. M. Lower, Colony to Nation: A History of Canada (Toronto, 1946), 379.

25. See below, pages 256-7 for an examination of Rose's work in London, 1869-80.

26. The Times, Jan. 20, 1870.
See my article, "Sir John Rose and Imperial Relations: An Episode in Gladstone's First Administration," Canadian Historical Review, XXXIII (March, 1952), 21-4, for a fuller account of Rose's attitude towards the Empire.

27. Minute by Malcolm, March 12, 1877, on Dufferin to Carnarvon, telegram, March 9, 1877: CO 42/748.

28. Dufferin to Carnarvon, private, June 1, 1876: PRO 30/6/29.

29. Ibid.

30. Dufferin to Carnarvon, private, Oct. 10, 1874: PRO 30/6/27. Herbert confirmed the truth of this anecdote.

31. Edward Blake, Oct. 3, 1874, printed in W. S. Wallace, ed., "Edward Blake's Aurora Speech," Canadian Historical Review, II (Sept., 1921), 255-6.

32. See Dufferin to Kimberley, confidential, Nov. 14, 1872: CO 42/709, for an illustration of Blake's sentiments on this point.

33. Edward Blake in the British Parliament, 1900, quoted in F. H. Underhill, "Edward Blake and Canadian Liberal Nationalism," in R. Flenley, ed., Essays in Canadian History (Toronto, 1939), 153.

34. Ibid.

CHAPTER TWO

THE COLONIAL OFFICE, 1867-1887

"I believe that very rarely has any department in the State had the good fortune to be guided by a series of permanent civil officers so able. " Lord Carnarvon, 1878

IN 1867 the Colonial Office occupied, as it had done for many years, a large Restoration house standing at the end of the cul-de-sac of Downing Street. Beside this building, which was No. 14, stood the Foreign Office; both structures were equally unpretentious and dilapidated. The house used by the Foreign Office had been condemned as early as 1839, while in 1860 the physical state of the Colonial Office was so alarming as to cause the Duke of Newcastle to write: "It is to be hoped the building will fall (for fall I believe it will) at night."[1] Thus assessed in 1860, the accommodation in Downing Street continued to be the administrative centre of the British colonial Empire until 1876, when the Office transferred to spacious new quarters in the Foreign Office quadrangle in Whitehall. (Except for No. 10 and No. 11, the houses in Downing Street were demolished and the steps leading into St. James's Park now mark the site of the old Colonial Office.) The original building, which to Sir Henry Taylor resembled nothing so much as a "decent lodging-house,"[2] was cramped, unhealthful, and totally inadequate for the increasing responsibilities of a great public department. In itself it suggested something of the empirical and casual manner in which the British Empire had been created. For in England, observed Taylor complacently, "we have not cared much to keep up appearances, wearing the star of our order within."[3]

The initial stages in the shaping of a system of administration for the British Empire were pre-eminently experimental and indecisive. In the seventeenth century the long struggle between King and Parliament, resulting in the Civil War, and the effects of the Revolution of 1688, following so closely upon James II's attempts to establish royal authority, made for an inconsistent attitude towards the colonies. Colonial affairs during this period were supervised by the various departments of the English Government concerned in them: the Admiralty, the Treasury, and the Privy Council. The latter body, originally the chief advisory agency to the Crown, exercised both administrative and judicial functions in the regulation of the colonies. Administrative duties were assigned to a sub-committee of the Privy Council--the first "Council" of Trade and Plantations--established in 1660; appeals from the colonies were originally heard by the whole Privy Council, but later delegated to a smaller section--the Judicial Committee. The Board of Trade and Plantations, created to enforce the operation of the Navigation Acts, functioned intermittently and under different titles until 1782, taking as the years passed an increasingly advisory role in the administration of the overseas

---

1. For references to chapter II see pages 56-63.

Empire. The Secretary of State for the Southern Department, one of the two principal Secretaries of State, tended to assume executive responsibility for colonial affairs until in 1768 it was judged desirable to appoint a third Secretary of State for the American or Colonial Department. But control also remained vested among a number of governmental offices, and it is not surprising that under the strain of the American Revolution the entire system collapsed.

By Burke's Act of 1782[4] the old Board of Trade and Plantations and the Secretary of State for the Colonial Department were abolished. Executive duties in connection with the colonies were transferred to the two remaining Secretaries of State, although in practice colonial matters fell under the care of the Secretary for the Southern (or Home) Department. Here for some years these duties were performed by one permanent clerk in the Department. Two years later the dual system of control was re-established when a standing committee of the Privy Council, the Committee for Trade and Plantations, was appointed to deal with such pressing colonial subjects as the regulation of trade after the American Revolution and the disposition of the Loyalists. In the division of work which ensued the Home Secretary took over responsibility for the drafting of instructions for Governors, the preparation of colonial estimates, and correspondence with other departments about the colonies. The Committee, for its part, reported on problems laid before it by the Privy Council, supervised colonial administration generally, and examined colonial acts, particularly those relating to trade and commerce. This latter function was emphasized by the Committee under the presidency of the first Earl of Liverpool (1786-1804) when a strong effort was made to maintain the mercantilist system in the face of the loss of the American colonies. As a body primarily concerned in regulating commerce the Committee was gradually transformed into the modern Board of Trade which emerged as a separate Department in the British Government in 1861.

In 1794, at the time of the wars with Revolutionary France, a new Secretary of State, for War, was created. The colonies were turned over to him in 1801, possibly because of their strategic value, or possibly simply to provide him with duties in the period of peace that was anticipated. His title became the Secretary of State for War and the Colonies and as the chief executive officer concerned with the Empire he soon succeeded in occupying a central position in colonial administration.[5] As long as the warfare with France continued the colonial activity of the Secretary was naturally subordinated and it was not until the first years after Waterloo, under the regime of Lord Bathurst, that an effective organization was created within the general Department for the management of colonial affairs. With the aid of capable Under-Secretaries, Henry Goulburn (1812-21) and R. J. Wilmot-Horton (1821-8), Bathurst worked industriously to introduce order and efficient methods into the administration of the overseas colonies. Under him the term "Colonial Department" came into general use and it is probable that after 1815 he and most of the permanent clerks in the Department of War and the Colonies were spending the greater part of their time on colonial matters. (The Secretary-at-War, a post dating from the period of Charles I, was concerned solely with military topics.) Bathurst held the seals of the Department until 1827, leaving

behind him a core of able officials who were to dominate the Colonial Office for the
next two generations--men like James Stephen, Henry Taylor, and T. W. C. Murdoch.

The sphere of authority of the Colonial Office, involving particularly its relationship with the Board of Trade, was adumbrated by Sir James Stephen during the thirty
years in which he was associated with the Office.[6] Stephen entered the Department in
1813 as a part-time counsel to advise on colonial legislation and twelve years later became permanent counsel to both the Colonial Office and the Board of Trade. In the
interim the Board had virtually ceased to concern itself with colonial administration or
the supervision of colonial laws unless they affected trade or navigation. The practice
of an earlier age was still followed, however, and colonial acts, after having been reported on by Stephen at the Colonial Office, were sent to the Board of Trade, which formally advised the Sovereign in Council whether to assent to, or reject, the legislation.
The Colonial Secretary was supposedly present at these meetings of the Board of Trade
but normally he was represented only by his minutes, which had been written by Steph-
en. These minutes usually constituted the Board's report to the Privy Council. It was
not until the fifties that this absurd arrangement was eliminated and laws that were of
a political nature were allowed to be sanctioned by the Secretary of State for the Colonies in the name of the Privy Council. Commercial and financial legislation continued to be referred to the Board of Trade and the Treasury until late in the century, although the necessity of gaining the Board's approval for laws of this type had passed by
1867.[7]

As Permanent Under-Secretary, a post he assumed in 1836, Stephen shaped the
character of the nineteenth century Colonial Office. A brilliant man, with a sympathetic approach to colonial autonomy and a hater of privilege, whether religious or economic, in the colonies, he was a product of the humanitarian circle of Wilberforce
and Macaulay. In the organization of the Colonial Office he showed the same zeal
and thoroughness that marked his advocacy of liberal social causes. When he became
the permanent head of the Office he found many archaic procedures in force which he
simplified, thereby reducing the element of "red tape" and inefficiency in departmental business. (For instance, he reduced the volume of private unofficial correspondence
with colonial Governors--a cause of much administrative confusion in earlier years.)
Throughout his official career he was handicapped, in an era before competitive examinations, by a lack of good subordinates, and frustrated by exasperating delays with
other departments which continued to plague the Office despite his best efforts to reduce them. Secretaries of State, during his association with the Office, tended to be
numerous and often mediocre, and inevitably Stephen became the target for charges
that he wielded irresponsible power. Even his friend Taylor could declare that for a
generation he "ruled the Colonial Empire."[8] The easy judgments made by the Colonial Reformers regarding "Mr. Oversecretary Stephen" must be reassessed, however.
A closer study of his work has revealed that Stephen was extremely amenable to direction from his parliamentary superiors and conscientious in seeking their opinion on important colonial issues. The administrative processes of the Colonial Office were complicated, though, and it naturally took some time for a new Secretary of State to un-

derstand them. This meant that in the absence of specific direction, or sometimes in the face of the neglect of Department responsibilities by a Minister, Stephen was forced to take decisions. Even when this qualification has been recorded it is still true that Stephen's constructive steps in organizing the work of the Colonial Office make him the prototype of the perfect Under-Secretary and one of the most distinguished figures in the history of British administration in the nineteenth century.

In the years following Stephen's retirement, as the Empire increased in size and colonial problems became more pressing, it was necessary to enlarge the staff of the Colonial Department. Assistant Under-Secretaries were appointed and, after the Northcote-Trevelyan reforms in the civil service in the fifties, able university-trained men were brought in, by examination after nomination, to fill the junior ranks in the Office.[9] Thus the form of the Department had been firmly established by 1854 when, at the outbreak of the Crimean War, the logical step was taken to divide the administration of war and the colonies. A separate Secretary of State for the Colonies was created in that year; the change had probably little effect on the Colonial Office, which already had its own traditions of service, but it certainly improved the administration of the War Department. From 1854 until 1925 the fourth principal Secretary of State, for the Colonies, was responsible for the relations between Great Britain and the large settlement colonies overseas.

The general indifference with which the colonies were regarded in the first half of the nineteenth century reflected unfavourably on the prestige of the Colonial Office as a government department. During this period the portfolio of Secretary of State for the Colonies was not considered an important post; the surprise occasioned in 1895 when a leading politician like Joseph Chamberlain deliberately selected the Colonial Office reveals how late this attitude persisted. Compared to the Foreign Office or the Treasury the Colonial Office was considered a second-rate department.[10] In the face of this low regard, it is the more remarkable that the Office secured the services of able men at all, and certainly statesmen of the type of Huskisson, Gladstone, Derby, Grey, Cardwell, Carnarvon, and Hicks Beach would be regarded as outstanding men in any company. On the whole, however, it was not until the twentieth century that the Colonial Office established itself as one of the major government departments and the post of Colonial Secretary became something more than a convenient resting place for a Minister of the second rank or a temporary perch for an aspiring young politician.

The estimation in which the Office was held in public reached its lowest point in the thirties and forties, when the energetic Colonial Reformers waged violent warfare against the Department and the system which it administered. Charles Buller painted in 1840 his classic picture of "Mr. Mother-Country," the bureaucrat arbitrarily exercising authority over the colonial Empire, while Molesworth ridiculed, in a celebrated passage, the ubiquitous activities of the Secretary of State.[11] Even the size of the staff at the Colonial Office came in for attack. "Look at the map, with our possessions dotted or sprawling over the globe, and compare their demands with the capabilities of that dingy small building in Downing Street, with five superiors and sixteen clerks therein. Many a union workhouse has a stronger administrative machinery."[12]

These are but the high-lights in a literature of criticism which found its inspiration in the work of the Colonial Office during these decades. Some of the abuse was unjustified; some of it should have been directed against other departments; much of it should have been aimed at the principles of British colonial rule, particularly in the period before 1846-9. Throughout the nineteenth century the Office found itself continually handicapped by the fact that a large part of its business had to be referred to other departments. Some of these offices, like the Treasury or the Board of Trade, were notoriously dilatory in attending to correspondence, and had to be continually prodded by the Colonial Office for an answer to dispatches. When the reply did come it often revealed a lack of knowledge of colonial conditions which might necessitate a further consultation. These circumstances inevitably caused delay and inefficiency, which in turn served to discredit the Office still further. The result was that, in the opinion of many Englishmen and colonials of the mid-century, Molesworth's indignant judgment of the rule of the Office, "government by the misinformed with responsibility to the ignorant."[13] was allowed to stand.

The Colonial Office was also discredited, in the popular eye, by its connection with the Colonial Land and Emigration Commission. This body, which had grown out of the official organization set up to promote emigration to the Colony of South Australia, had supervised emigration to all parts of the Empire since 1840. Inevitably it was forced to concern itself with Irish relief measures, the poor law, and pauper institutions, in carrying out its chosen duties. Its relationship with the Colonial Office, which it advised, caused these and other unsavoury features of English society in the nineteenth century to be connected by the general public, with the Department. It was not until 1872 that the control of emigrant ocean transport was transferred to the Board of Trade, and the Colonial Office was able to face its critics free from the taint of pauper emigration.

In 1867 the Colonial Office still had about it something of the sedate, unhurried atmosphere that the pens of Dickens and Trollope have associated with the unreformed civil service of Victorian England. Certainly the nature of Office life had changed significantly from the informal existence of the 1820's portrayed in the pages of Sir Henry Taylor's Autobiography. But among the versatile young men who made up the junior staff of the Department there was still much of the attitude of the dilettante and the amateur, which had characterized Taylor and his contemporaries. Literary, military, or scholarly pursuits were to be frequently encountered among the private interests of the clerks; administration was not so much a profession as a craft and an intellectual exercise.[14] The observations of Sir William Baillie Hamilton, who entered the Office straight from Harrow in 1864, reveal the fact that at this time the occupations of the junior staff of the Office were far from being wholly constructive.[15] Supervision was inadequate and periods of intense activity, such as after the colonial mails came in, were often succeeded by days of comparative idleness. When Hamilton began his official career one clerk was in the habit of offering a wager that he could undertake singly the entire business of the Department in a normal day, but no one could be found who would accept the bet! "It can hardly be said," notes Hamilton, "that the work of the Colonial Office was in those days heavy. "[16]   There was little encouragement for individual initiative, the activities of the juniors being dominated by a discipline which employed them for hours at copying into ledgers drafts of dispatches that were always retained in the Office anyway.   There was no compulsory retirement age and chances of advancement were limited because of the practice of bringing in men from outside, as in the case of Herman Merivale, to fill important positions.   There were some sine-cure posts on the staff; some officials, like Taylor, were allowed to do their work at home; everyone enjoyed a two-month holiday during the year and a varying number of free days.   The atmosphere of the Office, for the junior clerks at least, resembled a comfortable social club, with its placid and well-ordered routine.   The truth was, how-ever, that the activities of the Office were not well distributed: the senior men, like Rogers and Elliot, were overworked, while the younger men were generally not given enough to do.   The improved internal organization of the Department that Rogers in-stituted had, in time, a salutary effect in correcting these conditions.

From about 1870 as well, far-reaching changes in technology and in English so-ciety radically altered the practices of the great departments of Whitehall.   With the establishment of open competitive examinations, which became general in most de-partments in the seventies, the civil service ceased to be a prerogative of the English governing classes.   In the case of the Colonial Office the first entrance examination of 1856 was succeeded after 1877 by a formal set of papers and an interview, open to all qualified candidates.   From about this time it can fairly be said that hard work became the normal state of the routine of all grades of clerks in the Department.

In the wider sense one of the principal factors in the transformation of the Colon-ial Office was the establishment and improvement of telegraphic communication.   The first permanent cable was laid to North America in 1866, and during the seventies tele-graphic services were extended to the Indian Ocean area, Australia, and the West Indies. Whereas previously a dispatch had taken four months to reach Hong Kong, on the other side of the world from London, by the early seventies a message could be sent and an answer obtained in as many days.   With this development the tempo of government busi-ness was naturally hastened and the requirements of administration made more pressing. Moreover, the revival of interest in imperial affairs which coincided with Great Britain's increasing insecurity during the last part of the nineteenth century brought about an en-largement in the number of colonies administered by the Colonial Office.   In South, East, and West Africa new areas were brought under British rule or influence; in the Near East, in Malaya and Borneo, in the Pacific islands, colonies and protectorates were established.   It is estimated that in the period between 1870 and 1900 the popu-lation of the British Empire doubled.   By 1895 the Colonial Office had the task of ad-ministering a world-wide Empire linked together by modern means of communication and transportation.   The concern which the Office had shown in 1837 for the colonies of white settlement and representative institutions was replaced sixty years later by an absorbing interest in the dependent and non-European portions of the Empire.

The metamorphosis of the Colonial Office after 1870 is, of course, reflected in the volume of correspondence handled by the Department.   In 1870, states Sir John

Bramston, the Office dealt with about 25,000 letters, divided almost equally between dispatches received and dispatches sent out. In 1880 the correspondence amounted to 38,000 letters, or 20,000 letters received and 18,000 dispatched. By 1890 the figure was 46,000: 25,000 received and 21,000 sent out. By 1900 the total correspondence of the Office came to 84,000 letters and dispatches; the fact that there had been five years of Joseph Chamberlain's vigorous leadership helps to explain this prodigious enlargement in the volume of correspondence.[17] Hall states that the number of telegrams handled in the Department increased from 800 in 1870 to 2,800 in 1880 and 3,500 in 1890. (And 10,000 in 1900!)[18] A similar growth can also be observed in the number of Parliamentary Papers, Confidential Prints, and private memoranda printed for the use of the Department. Rather curiously, the staff of the Office does not seem to have kept pace with this enlargement of official duties. In 1862, when the first Colonial Office List appeared to provide an accurate record of the personnel of the Office, the total staff numbered fifty-nine.[19] In 1870 Bramston gives the entire staff, from the Secretary of State down to Office keepers and messengers, as sixty-seven people.[20] Ten years later the staff was only sixty-five, a figure which also obtained in 1890. Not until 1900, when the staff was numbered at ninety-nine, did the modern tendency of the public service reveal itself. The only explanations for this stationary condition in the personnel of the Department in the years between 1870 and 1890 would seem to be that either the staff as a whole became more efficient, or incompetents were weeded out and replaced by new men of ability and energy. Probably both reasons applied. The numbers in the different administrative grades also remained fairly constant during these years. The Assistant Under-Secretaries increased from one to three by 1874; the upper division clerks decreased their ranks by one in twenty years; the supplementary clerks by four; while the second division clerks showed an increase of thirteen. On the other hand the fifteen copyists that were on the establishment in 1870 had disappeared by 1890, their work taken over by junior clerks and typists. The minor functionaries of the Office also existed in the same force in 1890 as they had done in 1870.[21]

The basic procedure of the Colonial Office changed very slightly over the years described in this study. The essential business of the Office was, and remained, "getting off the mails," as Stephen once said. The dispatches from the colonial Governors, "full, reasoned, and expository, ... supported by confirmatory reports and documents,"[22] were received in the Registry, opened, entered, and the minute papers attached. A reference would be appended about their contents and the preceding correspondence, and they would be sent on their way through the Office organization. The habit of writing minutes began under Stephen about 1836 and had become fully established by the forties.[23] At first only the heads of divisions and their superiors were allowed to minute a paper, but in the period 1870-2 the practice was extended to include all grades of clerks in the Office. A directive by the Permanent Under-Secretary in September, 1872, established this custom beyond doubt.[24] The system was an extremely valuable one, especially when the minuting was first done by the junior clerks and the whole group of minutes, each written without fear or favour, passed on to the Under-Secretary. In

1880 almost all dispatches reached the desk of the Permanent Under-Secretary, while about three-quarters of the correspondence was seen by the Colonial Secretary himself. Naturally general supervision at this level became impracticable and had to be abandoned as Office business grew during the last part of the nineteenth century. After a decision had been reached, at some point in the hierarchy of the Department, the matter would be referred back to the section concerned for the drafting of the Colonial Secretary's reply. The importance of the subject would determine the official who would prepare the draft dispatch, which would then follow the same path back to the heads of the Office. After it was passed for signature the dispatch would be copied and, if going to the Governor-General of Canada, for instance, signed by the Secretary of State. Domestic and inter-departmental letters were signed by the Permanent Under-Secretary or an Assistant Under-Secretary. Great care was taken over the drafts of Office dispatches, which, in the words of one commentator, strove to be "brief and concise in form, ... distinguished alike by reserve and lucidity, at once considerate and conclusive."[25] Any student of Colonial Office correspondence during the late nineteenth century will have been impressed at the number of times these exacting conditions were fulfilled in letters from the Secretary of State.

The modern organization of the Colonial Office dates from 1860, when Sir Frederic Rogers assumed the post of Permanent Under-Secretary. There was at this time only one other Under-Secretary on the permanent staff of the Department. He was Sir Thomas F. Elliot, a man of thirty-five years' experience in the public service, who possessed a special knowledge of North American affairs. Rogers decided to divide, in a systematic manner, the supervision of the work of the Office between himself and Elliot. This idea was not new, for the Office had been separated into "departments," each dealing with a contiguous group of colonies, for many years, perhaps ever since the thirties. It was the practice for these departments to be supervised by Under-Secretaries or senior clerks, although the precise distribution of work is obscure for the early years. An official like Taylor, however, concentrated exclusively on the West Indies, and there must have been other areas of specialization in the case of other men. Rogers made definite this informal supervision of the preceding period and confined it to the Under-Secretary level. In the reorganization of 1860 he took over the Australian, West Indian, and Eastern colonies, and all the legal matters, as his special responsibility. Elliot, for his part, undertook to supervise the business relating to the North American, African, and Mediterranean colonies, as well as military and convict topics.[26] Thus it was arranged that one superintending Under-Secretary dealt with colonies at all stages of constitutional development and no distinction was made either on the basis of colour or social maturity, between the inhabitants of different territories. This division presented difficulties of a special and rather subtle nature. How far the attitude of mind which an official would assume in dealing with Sierra Leone might be carried over to a consideration of the affairs of Nova Scotia is a question which can only be answered by a detailed study of the respective policies. The geographical division confirmed in 1860 was typical of the organization of the Colonial Office throughout the period under review, although, with the appointment of ad-

ditional Assistant Under-Secretaries, the Permanent Under-Secretary ceased to be directly responsible for the affairs of particular regions. Rogers introduced this further departure in 1868 - "a horizontal instead of vertical" arrangement of the work of the Permanent Under-Secretary[27] --but it was more logically developed by his successors.

The first issue of the Colonial Office List shows the following divisions within the
Department in 1862: Domestic and Financial, West Indian, North American, Mediterranean, Australian and Eastern, and, after 1865, Registry. The North American Department in its original form included the colonies of Canada, Nova Scotia, New Brunswick, Prince Edward Island, Newfoundland, Vancouver Island, British Columbia, and
the Falkland Islands. In 1867, when the federation of Canada seemed to promise a
diminution of the labours of the division, for the correspondence of three colonies was
now to be channelled through a single agency, the Australian colonies were added to it.
It then became the North American and Australian Department, including Canada and
the North American colonies that remained outside the Dominion, together with Bermuda, the six Australian colonies, and New Zealand. Five years later, after Herbert
became Permanent Under-Secretary, a reorganization reduced the territorial departments to two, the North American, Australian, African, and Mediterranean Department, which included an incongruous group of colonies ranging from Canada to the
Gold Coast and St. Helena, and the West Indian and Eastern Department, which included the remaining colonies; two general departments were set up to handle financial and registry matters. This arrangement was soon found too cumbersome to be successful and after three years' trial it was abandoned in 1875. The North American and
Australian Department was reconstituted and remained the unit through which Canadian
affairs were handled until well into the twentieth century. In 1875, Newfoundland and
Canada were the only North American colonies under the Department's charge, but in
later years British Guiana, Bermuda, the Bahamas, British Honduras, and the Falkland
Islands were added. Eventually Fiji and the Western Pacific colonies (presumably because of their proximity to Australia), together with Gibraltar and Cyprus, were also
placed under the Department, so that by 1903 it had again assumed a rather motley
character. In practice certain officials in the division concentrated on Canadian affairs, but the arrangement threw a heavy burden on the senior clerk in charge of the
Department and the Assistant Under-Secretary who superintended its work.

II

Among the permanent staff of a public department the most important figure is
normally the Under-Secretary. Sir Henry Taylor, after almost fifty years' experience
in the Colonial Office, emphasized the special and paramount significance of this post
in the colonial service.

The choice of a Permanent Under-Secretary is, in my estimation, by far the
most important function which it can devolve upon a Secretary of State to exercise.
The direct consequences of that one act extend far and wide through the whole Col-

onial Empire, and last in all probability for a long series of years. A bad appointment to this office is the deadliest blow that can be dealt to the Colonial Service,
and a good one is the greatest blessing that can be bestowed upon it. [28]

In the making of Imperial policy towards Canada in the mid-nineteenth century, the
Permanent Under-Secretary was the dominant factor. His advice was accepted by the
Secretary of State in almost every major problem which arose between the two coun-
tries for at least twenty years after Confederation. In a very real sense the official
British attitude towards Canada in these years was the personal attitude of the Perma-
nent Under-Secretary of State for the Colonies.

It is doubtful whether today any member of the higher civil service exercises the
same authority as did the permanent heads of departments in the nineteenth century.
In the Victorian age the leaders of the civil service enjoyed a position in the governing classes independent of their offices. Indeed it has been suggested that some heads
of departments, such as Sir Robert Herbert at the Colonial Office, were appointed partly because of that position. [29] Coming from the same social class as the Minister under whom he served, usually educated with him, often a personal friend or relative,
the civil servant of the nineteenth century spoke to his parliamentary chief with the
easy assurance of an equal. Today the relationship between the public servant and his
Minister is one of subordination, and such intercourse as exists between the two is usually only on an official level. The great civil servants of the last century--Hammond,
Welby, Farrer, Mallet, Rogers--moved in an atmosphere where this separation of the
political and permanent heads of a department was unknown. Its absence made possible the remarkable influence which these men and their counterparts wielded in every
branch of British administrative life.

The Colonial Office was singularly fortunate in the Under-Secretaries that headed its permanent organization in the nineteenth century. Stephen, as the first effective Under-Secretary, set distinguished standards of achievement and character which
his successors very largely managed to emulate. He was followed at the Colonial Office in 1847 by Herman Merivale, who as Professor of Political Economy at Oxford had
published his celebrated Lectures on Colonization and Colonies six years before. Merivale has been compared to Macaulay in the range of his intellectual powers, but his
administrative competence was not especially marked. He failed to impart the same
abiding impression to the work of the Department as did Stephen. Merivale left the
Colonial Office in 1860, to be succeeded by Sir Frederic Rogers, [30] who served as Permanent Under-Secretary during the early years covered by the course of this study.

For twelve years Rogers occupied the highest permanent post at the Colonial Office. They were eventful years for those responsible for governing the British Empire.
The criticism of the Manchester School had to be countered and great schemes of imperial consolidation, such as the union of the British North American colonies, implemented in the face of indifference and hostility. The period saw the initiation of the
plan for recalling the troops from the autonomous colonies and witnessed the shock of
the Governor Eyre case and the riots in Jamaica. It ended with the Red River insurrec-

tion in Canada and the discontent roused in New Zealand by the military policy of
Gladstone's first Administration. Through all these major occurrences and a host of
minor ones Rogers presided over the Colonial Office: forthright, rational, and discerning, with a strong philosophical bent to his mind.

　　He was not stirred by the imaginative or emotional aspects of empire. He did not
wish to see the responsibilities of the British Empire increased, nor great imperial projects like the Canadian Pacific Railway encouraged. He never really trusted the free
and undisciplined political systems of the larger British colonies; colonial democracy,
with its "suicidal jealousy"[31] produced a succession of untried and aimless ministries.
Even in England the masses were capable of licence, and in 1877 he expressed to Gladstone his apprehension of the new popular organization of the Liberal party which Joseph
Chamberlain was creating at Birmingham.[32] He felt concern over the welfare of native peoples, but he was more interested in the establishment of a colonial bishopric.
Questions of ethics or politics fascinated him, and he tended to discuss issues extensively and in the abstract whenever possible. Thus when giving his views on the vital problem as to whether an amnesty should be granted to Louis Riel in 1870-1, he filled many
pages of minute paper with a discussion of the virtues of the amnesty as a political act.
He spent, perhaps, too much of his time in detailing again the facts of a case for presentation to the Colonial Secretary; the Secretary of State invariably got Rogers's version even though the matter had been outlined adequately by junior officials. He was
extremely tactful in his dealings with responsible colonial ministries, and generous to
a fault in accommodating colonies with what might be called "the amenities of imperial membership." (These can be taken to include, among other things, the provision
of services to visitors from the colonies staying in England, the distribution of government publications and maps, and the supply of technical assistance.) He followed the
salutary rule of his great predecessor, Stephen, in recommending that the machinery of
disallowance be used with great caution. Faulty drafting was not, in itself, to be a sufficient reason for vetoing a colonial act; the principle of the measure must be the primary object of the Imperial Government's attention. Unless it was manifestly unjust to
some group or obviously ultra vires, a local act should be left to its operation. Weaknesses in it would soon be discovered, and remedied, by those who suffered from its in-
adequacies.

　　Rogers was always independent in his views. He insisted, for instance, that English precedents were not necessarily of value in developing a colonial legal system and
that political considerations alone should influence the application of the English code
of law to a colonial environment. His belief in the institution of private property did
not blind him to the manner in which land could be abused in a new settlement, and
he inveighed strongly against both the idle absentee proprietor and the land speculator.[33]
His greatest fault was a bluntness of expression, and an official style which was often ex-
cessively formal and prone to ignore explanation and elucidation. This deficienty was
strikingly revealed in the crisis with New Zealand in 1869-70, in which Rogers strongly
supported Granville's policy of withdrawing the British troops from the Colony. The tone
and style of the dispatches used on that occasion certainly did not contribute to the

SIR FREDERIC ROGERS (LORD BLACHFORD), THE DRAWING BY GEORGE RICHMOND
(By permission of John Murray (Publishers) Ltd.)

speedy settlement of the controversy. All things considered, Rogers presents a picture of a successful and competent administrator, combining "force with circumspection," as Sir Henry Taylor once aptly observed. [34]   Taylor went on to pay a tribute to Rogers which was founded on a close official and personal association. "I think I can now say that, looking back through forty-eight years of official experience, in the course of which I served under twenty-six Secretaries of State and a somewhat larger number of Under Secretaries, I have not known anyone of either class who was a greater adminis-trator, and, I think, only two who were on a par with him in their intellectual range and powers. "[35]

The consideration which influenced Rogers most strongly in his dealings with the autonomous colonies, particularly the North American ones, was his belief that "[the] great establishment of colonial independence cannot (as I think) be justly or wisely or possibly arrested. "[36]   The following exposition of his faith in this consummation can be taken as the epitome of the anti-imperial viewpoint of the mid-Victorian period.

I had always believed--and the belief has so confirmed and consolidated itself that I can hardly realise the possibility of any one seriously thinking the contrary-- that the destiny of our colonies is independence; and that, in this point of view, the function of the Colonial Office is to secure that our connexion, while it lasts, shall be as profitable to both parties, and our separation, when it comes, as amic- able as possible. This opinion is founded first on the general principle that a spir-ited nation (and a colony becomes a nation) will not submit to be governed in its internal affairs by a distant Government, and that nations geographically remote have no such common interests as will bind them permanently together in foreign policy, with all its details and mutations. [37]

Rogers was not one, however, who would surrender colonies simply because they were a source of danger to England. A gulf, although narrow, separated him from Lowe and Bright and the Manchester School. To let Canada fall into American hands by default he considered "chicken-hearted," and a sign that the English spirit was becoming deca-dent. Canadian desires should be respected and the connection defended even if it meant fighting the United States on ground that was disadvantageous to Great Britain. For, after all, there were nobler questions than even English prestige bound up in the issue. [38]

After Rogers's retirement from office, his views are seen more distinctly as they stand out in relief against the background of the rising imperial sentiment of the seven-ties and eighties. He had no sympathy for the new imperialism as it expressed itself in a crude desire to acquire more tropical dependencies for the British Crown. It induced in him, he confessed, "that state of disgust which one feels at a thing which you find to your surprise is not too stupid to be formidable.... "[39]   In 1876, as Lord Blachford, he spoke in the House of Lords about certain proposed territorial transfers with France in West Africa, coming out strongly, alone among all the speakers in the debate, he said rather proudly, in urging that certain outlying districts in the area be abandoned. [40]

In articles on colonial topics which he wrote for the Edinburgh Review and the Nineteenth Century,[41] as well as in private correspondence, he revealed this consistent distaste for imperial expansion. Thus, in 1878, in discussing the Near Eastern crisis, he
said, "Of the past history of Russia I know next to nothing. I only see with my eyes on
maps the respective annexations of England and Russia during the last century and a
quarter, and am astounded at the fact that England should assume the position of ac-
cuser in this respect. "[42]   The justification for airing these views in public he found in
the conviction that the revived enthusiasm for imperial objects was encountering meagre
resistance from the older Gladstonian liberals. Writing to Taylor in 1877 he observed
that he had a special responsibility to stand out against the new tendency:

> I think that the notion of Empire is really gaining ground, and that as political peo-
> ple like Lord Kimberley do not like to take up a ground against it which is unpopu-
> lar, and gives opponents an advantage at the hustings, it is likely to establish itself
> in John Bull's mind as a principle of policy, unless somebody or other can get a
> hearing on the other side. And it appeared to me that an old official who had noth-
> ing to hope or fear was the kind of animal that might be expected to bray aloud on
> the subject. [43]

Imperial Federation, which had become a popular cause by 1885, excited his bit-
terest strictures. "I totally disbelieve in the possibility of Federation, into which the
world is running with its eyes shut, and really think that the question ought not to go' by
default.' The cat wants belling. "[44]   In the same year he attacked a proposal for a
Colonial Board of Advice, which the aged Lord Grey had put forward.[45]   Composed of
colonial Privy Councillors, or the Agents-General, this body would tender advice to the
British Government on imperial foreign policy. Blachford felt that the proposed Board
would seriously hamper the work of the Colonial Office by allowing intervention in the
making of imperial policy from persons whom the Office was normally accustomed to
consult only on specialized matters. He discounted the idea that a common foreign
policy for the Empire was possible and seriously questioned whether the imperial tie
could be long maintained if the colonies were given a share in the shaping of Great Britain's external relations. For the connection, which in its present form served mainly to
produce "mutual contentment, " was probably only a temporary link anyway. To submit it to the strain of working out a consultative arrangement would be to snap it instant-
ly. His demoded views were plainly enunciated when he went on to deprecate the motives behind a federated English-speaking union.

> The notion of a great Anglo-Saxon alliance, not formed with a specific object, as
> to arrest the supremacy of some overgrown power or immoral principle, but on a
> general understanding (as I conclude) that all shall join in furthering the wishes and
> interests of each, seems to me likely, if, per impossibile, it should last long enough,
> to degenerate into a successful or unsuccessful contrivance for bullying the rest of the
> world. To contend for such an alliance on the grounds that Anglo-Saxons--the great

exterminators of aborigines in the temperate zone--would, when confederated, set a
new and exceptional example of justice and humanity, seems to me a somewhat
transcendental expectation.[46]

There can be no doubt that Rogers's independence of mind, the remorseless logic of his
opinions, and his critical attitude to empire, resulted in his being isolated from the
main body of his countrymen during the last years of the Victorian era. This judgment
does not, however, diminish a later generation's appreciation of his great intellectual
and administrative powers.

Rogers's successor as Permanent Under-Secretary of State for the Colonies was a
man whose distinction has always been recognized but who has remained somewhat obscure to historians. Robert G. W. Herbert,[47] who was appointed to the post in 1871,
remained Permanent Under-Secretary until 1892, the longest period during which anyone has ever held that high office. Herbert's personality was singularly attractive.
One who served under him in the last days of his official career has described him as an
urbane, gracious individual, courteous and gentle in all his actions.[48] Herbert, indeed, represents a social type which is becoming rare today; the refined product of
birth in one of the great families of England, combined with a sound classical education, a wide knowledge of foreign countries, and throughout his life an impeccable social position. He was a civilized man, in the sense that recalls some of the cultured
Whig noblemen of the eighteenth century. As early as 1879, long before the world realized that the conditions of English life capable of producing such exquisite blooms
were fast disappearing, one of Herbert's contemporaries remarked on the auspicious
train of circumstances which had shaped his personality. "[Lord Carnarvon's] cousin,
Mr. Robert Herbert, Permanent Under-Secretary of State, was facile princeps among
all his contemporaries for elegant and accurate classical scholarship at Eton and at Balliol. Polite learning, a devotion to the scenes and countries which classical antiquity
has hallowed, unsullied integrity and a consistent elevation of aim, may be described
as the traditions of the House of Herbert."[49]

The bust at the Colonial Office portrays a rather imperious attitude, which apparently was far from his usual mien. Herbert was the type of administrator who would invite the views of all his colleagues, and would carefully weigh those opinions before
coming to his own decision. He did not defer to rank and the contribution of a junior
clerk was entitled, in his estimation, to the same amount of serious attention as that of
an Assistant Under-Secretary.[50] Such an ideal arrangement may not always have been
possible, but Herbert was undoubtedly esteemed among his staff for his sympathetic consideration of every member's point of view. Under his leadership the Colonial Office
continued to hold, as he himself described in 1870, "a high character in the service,
as being an office in which the work is well done, and the men work well together with
a gentlemanly good feeling which is not the universal rule."[51] Physically Herbert
was a small man, just over five feet tall, with a general demeanour that is best described by the old-fashioned word 'courtly.' He was an excellent conversationalist, a
polite listener, the possessor of a good wit, and a bachelor. It is no wonder that he was

apparently often in London society!

His charm of manner and freedom from pretension were celebrated. To representatives from the Empire he was always extremely affable; it was said that a colonial
Minister who went in to see the Permanent Under-Secretary never failed to come out
feeling more contented than when he entered. His residence in Australia[52] (he was
the first Permanent Under-Secretary since Stephen to have had any direct experience
of colonial territories) made him sympathetic to the colonial point of view on innumerable questions. It provided him with an individual and salutary approach to the framing of British imperial policy. His colonial experience was also of great value to him
in the task of selecting personnel for service appointments, always a major responsibility of the Permanent Under-Secretary, and his years in office witnessed some happy
choices. Finally there was about Herbert a placid quality which has been described by
many who knew him. Perhaps it was the result of his thorough classical training, perhaps an aspect of personality, but he never showed himself greatly moved or discom-
posed. He worked at a pace that rarely varied and which might seem more suited to
the scholar's study than to the demands of a complex administrative organization. But
he invariably got through his day's work and retained his contentment of mind as well.
"Tidings of Colonial revolution might arrive without causing him visible excitement,
and would simply suggest themselves as incidents--all coming in the day's work--each to
be dealt with in its proper turn. "[53]   The unruffled appearance which he presented to
the world is probably related to another quality, also discerned by several of his colleagues. He maintained always an attitude of "amused tolerance" towards the activities of mankind, a sort of "genial cynicism" which suggested that he had no great faith
in human nature. [54]   A journalist, describing Herbert's "disbelief in the doctrine of
human perfectibility," suggested acutely that the Permanent Under-Secretary "does not
think that everything is for the best in this best of all possible worlds. "[55]   It was a trait
which was perhaps inevitable in the personality of so rare and gifted an individual as
Sir Robert Herbert. While denying him the constructive advances of the statesman it
allowed him to perform admirably the duties of the administrator. It was the most valuable qualification that he could bring to his work at the Colonial Office in the twenty-
one years in which he served as Permanent Under-Secretary.

Notwithstanding our knowledge of his character and manner, Herbert remains a
somewhat remote figure. In particular, his personal views on the questions of his day
have very largely failed to survive his death. It is only from minutes on official correspondence and from the occasional letter in private collections of papers that any picture of the outlook of the man can be painted. [56]   Fundamentally he appears to have
been only a moderate exponent of the growing imperial sentiment which influenced
most of the period in which he headed the Colonial Office. However, unlike Rogers,
who in this respect represented accurately an earlier age, Herbert was prepared to take
vigorous measures for the expansion of the British Empire. He foresaw that the nascent
state in South Africa would eventually demand an extension to the northward along the
west coast of the continent and as early as 1875 he favoured claiming that coast as far
as Delagoa Bay. He earnestly advised Carnarvon in 1876 to annex the Transvaal[57] and

in later years was convinced that its retrocession had been a serious mistake. He supported Carnarvon's scheme of federation in South Africa and would have pressed forward with it under succeeding Secretaries of State. He was sympathetic towards the expansionist pressures in the Australasian colonies and realized that if they were resisted by the Home Government there would be a severe strain on the colonies' relations with the United Kingdom.

For all his belief in enlarging the Empire, Herbert was, however, curiously cautious about the prospects of new territories. He could not become enthusiastic over the future of the Canadian Pacific Railway, because he felt the project would never recoup the money spent on it. On the other hand he was not insensitive to material development generally, as the number of chartered companies licensed to operate in various parts of the Empire during his period at the Colonial Office bears testimony. The Director of the Royal Botanic Gardens at Kew once stated that Herbert anticipated Chamberlain in his interest in the economic development of the overseas Empire, and in his encouragement of the scientific study of colonial health and agriculture. Hall provides several examples of this attitude of Herbert's,[58] but it did not figure, in even the slightest fashion, in his thinking on Canadian economic growth. The absence of responsibility for this subject was, perhaps, a determining factor. He was interested in the welfare of native peoples, but in a distant, rational manner. There was little opportunity for the Colonial Office to concern itself with the condition of the aborigines in Canada after 1860 and Herbert did not possess the nature which would regret this circumstance.

The most important element in Herbert's outlook towards Canadian problems was a full recognition of the dynamic nature of Canadian autonomy. He respected the Dominion's self-government and was not prepared to cabin it within artificial bounds. Domestic affairs must be left to the exclusive control of the Canadian Ministry and Parliament, and Herbert always interpreted the content of "domestic affairs" in a very generous manner. A little conciliation in the present would prevent awkwardness and independent action in the future, he believed; a demand granted in one case might forestall an impossible request in another. The relationship depended for its permanence more on cordiality than on compulsion. Probably no imperial administrator since responsible government was conceded realized more clearly than Herbert that the connection between Great Britain and the self-governing colonies was gradually assuming more of a diplomatic, and less of a colonial, character. The extreme delicacy of the relations between the United Kingdom and Canada, for instance, required that they should be managed primarily by the Colonial Office, or, if this were not possible, that the views of the Office should guide other departments in their dealings with the Dominion. Herbert's struggle to have this principle recognized in Whitehall, although not completely successful, was motivated by the sincere conviction that the Colonial Office understood the aspirations of the Canadian nation more adequately than any other branch of the Imperial Government. And, in surveying the course of Anglo-Canadian relations in the period from 1867 to 1887, it would appear that this contention was well founded.

Towards the subject of commercial policy, his attitude was remarkably liberal.

He was wise enough to realize that the free trade system was not of universal validity, and he depreciated attempts to convert Canada to it, either by coercion or propaganda. He did not take affront at the Dominion's imposition of differential duties, even when they operated against Great Britain, and he thought that retaliatory tariff measures were also justified on occasion. By intellectual conviction he was, for many years, a free trader and a believer in laissez-faire, but his brand of the dogma was woefully diluted when compared to the principles of Bright. In 1887 he was prepared to accept, although with regret, the fact that Canada might desire to establish a Commercial Union with the United States. After his retirement from the Colonial Office Herbert took up the cause of imperial preference and was active in the formation of the British Empire League, one of the bodies working for imperial unity that emerged from the wreckage of the Imperial Federation League. In 1903 Joseph Chamberlain appointed him Chairman of the Tariff Commission instituted to enquire into the movement of imperial trade, and he took a limited part, before his death in 1905, in the campaign for "Tariff Reform." Herbert was not, however, a bold and imaginative architect of empire, and it would have been alien to his nature to have become deeply involved in controversial issues of this magnitude.

In the light of these preliminary considerations, what, then, was Herbert's philosophy of empire? The available evidence necessitates an answer which must be primarily in administrative terms. First of all, he believed fervently in the unity of the British Empire. To his mind the forms of unity existed in the supreme power of the Imperial Parliament to legislate for the whole Empire, and in the authority of the common Crown. The first of these, he recognized, must be asserted with extreme discretion; the second was vital and could not be abridged without weakening the imperial structure. There were a few fields of legislation, such as naturalization and merchant shipping, in which British and colonial practice should be complementary. Through developments of this nature links other than those of race and culture would be forged. He would have liked to have seen some of the colonies contribute towards imperial defence works situated within their own boundaries, but it is significant that the territories he had in mind were Crown colonies.[59] He seems never to have expressed an opinion on a joint Anglo-Canadian defence scheme, at least not in the years before 1887. There is no evidence of his outlook towards the project of imperial federation, but it is altogether unlikely that so great a disturbance of the status quo would have been attractive to him. This comment contains the key to Herbert's conception of the Empire. Unfitted by temperament or position to be a visionary, he worked for the maintenance of the status quo in the imperial organization. His handling of the problems of the Empire was based firmly on an empirical approach and on the intuitive common sense of his class and generation. He realized thoroughly his own capacities and within his appointed limits sought to discharge an enormous and increasing responsibility. In the end his achievement was all that any administrator could desire.

The remainder of the senior permanent staff of the Colonial Office who were concerned with Canadian affairs during the period 1867 to 1887 can be more briefly noted.[60] Sir Thomas Frederick Elliot[61] had been an Assistant Under-Secretary superintending the work of the North American Department of the Office since 1847. His unrivalled knowledge of Canadian affairs, for which he had been especially appointed to this post under Merivale, was of immense importance during the movement for federation in British North America. With the federal union achieved, Elliot retired in December, 1868. He was definitely not a separatist. "The more united, flourishing, and power-ful that are the British provinces in America, the more durable, as the writer of this paper firmly believes, will be their connection with the mother country," he wrote in 1858. [62]   Thus he showed great sympathy towards the efforts of the British North Amer-ican colonies to promote their economic development (he favoured Galt's scheme of interprovincial free trade in 1859-60), and would have been prepared to extend Im-perial assistance in 1858 for the abortive project of an intercolonial railway. After Confederation he became nettled over the "encroaching" spirit shown by the Canadian Ministers and Parliament in the question of honours and titles, but the role of Downing Street in that exhausting and graceless controversy would have tried the patience of a saint. Elliot's departure meant that the Office never again possessed an Assistant Un-der-Secretary as thoroughly conversant in North American affairs, and it is significant that his aid had to be solicited on more than one occasion after his retirement. [63]

Elliot's place was taken by a succession of men, mostly lawyers, who concerned themselves in varying degree with the problems arising from the relationship between Great Britain and Canada. Among the more important of these Under-Secretaries was Henry T. Holland, [64] a barrister whom Carnarvon appointed to the Department in Jan-uary, 1867, to relieve Rogers of some of the burden of legal business. Holland was given the rank of Assistant Under-Secretary in 1870, and a year later became a super-intending Under-Secretary, taking Herbert's place after his promotion. For the remain-der of his period in the Office, Holland looked after the affairs of the North American colonies. In 1873 he succeeded to a baronetcy and, in August of the following year, financially independent, he resigned his official place to stand for Parliament. Thir-teen years later he was to return to the Department as Secretary of State in Salisbury's second Administration. Holland's resignation in 1874 necessitated a successor, and at the time it was decided to increase the number of Assistant Under-Secretaries to three. Among the new men appointed was William Rolle Malcolm. [65]   Like Herbert, Mal-colm came to the Colonial Office from the Board of Trade. He superintended relations with the North American colonies from 1874 until his resignation in June, 1878. In the interim John Bramston, [66] an intimate friend of Herbert's, whose career closely paral-leled Herbert's, was appointed an Assistant Under-Secretary. When Malcolm left the Office Bramston became superintending Under-Secretary for North American affairs, and held this post until he retired in 1897. He does not seem to have had any personal experience in British North America until the nineties, when he went out to Newfound-land to inquire into the French treaty rights in that Colony.

There were also a handful of clerks in the North American Department who con-cerned themselves specifically with Canadian affairs. Arthur Blackwood was succeed-ed in 1867, as clerk in charge of the division, by William Dealtry, who was educated at Eton and Trinity College, Cambridge. Dealtry retained the post until he retired in

June, 1879, with the rank of Chief Clerk. His successor was Edmund Burke Pennell, who had entered the North American Department as early as 1862. With the exception of a few years, Pennell spent all his official life in the North American Department, and during much of the period covered in this study was the first or second person in the Office to read the incoming dispatches from Canada. He had a gift for lucid exposition which served him well in this post. As a Principal Clerk he presided over the junior members of the North American Department from 1879 until his death in 1895. Pennell, as well as Bramston, became an expert on the complicated question of the French treaty rights in Newfoundland, and paid several official visits to the island in the eighties.

It will be readily observed that there is a remarkable similarity in the background of the more important permanent officials who managed Great Britain's relations with Canada in the two decades after 1867. All these men came from the higher middle classes or the upper classes of English society. Elliot and Herbert belonged to ancient noble families; Rogers and Holland were the sons of baronets; all the Under-Secretaries were knighted or ennobled before the conclusion of their official career. Of the higher permanent staff all except Elliot and Taylor, who belonged to an earlier generation, were university men; most of the later group were lawyers. The majority of them were men of considerable academic distinction, there being three Fellows of All Souls--Herbert, Malcolm, and Bramston--among them. This was no ordinary group of administrators, but an outstanding body of men, even when judged by the exacting intellectual standards of the English public service in the late Victorian age. The Colonial Office has probably never in its history been served by men of greater ability than during the period 1867 to 1887. In addition to their intellectual capabilities some of these permanent officials possessed another valuable requisite for the administration of overseas territories: they had lived and worked in various parts of the Empire. Herbert is the outstanding example of this class, but a large proportion of the senior officials during these years had undergone some experience of colonial life. It would be unrealistic to contend that this familiarity with overseas areas had not made them better administrators. Many of the group, as far as can be learned, had Liberal political sympathies. Rogers and Herbert, for instance, had both come under the personal influence of Gladstone, while Sir Robert Meade, another Under-Secretary, had been closely attached to Granville. Taken collectively, the permanent staff of the Colonial Office in the Victorian age was splendidly representative of the great English professional and administrative tradition. If it possessed some of the limitations of the well-born element in Victorian society it also revealed the critical intelligence, the fairness, and the magnanimity which are associated with the period and its leaders.

III

The twenty years which followed 1867 are notable in English political history for the appearance, as disciplined groups, of the two great parties which controlled the British Government until the World War of 1914-18. The Gladstone Ministry of 1868 can be considered as the first truly Liberal Government, relying as it did mainly on the

support of the industrial and commercial classes. The Liberal party possessed two substantial advantages in the struggle for power of these years. In the principles of laissez-faire, personal liberty, and free trade it enjoyed a cogent philosophy, and in Gladstone it had a leader whose source of authority was more than simple considerations of
personal loyalty. In addition, it was soon to have a dynamic popular organization
rooted in the great municipalities of England and Scotland. The Conservative party,
similarly, established itself as a political entity when Derby's gout finally forced him
to retire and Benjamin Disraeli, the fabulous Jew, became its principal leader. The
second Reform Bill marked Disraeli's overture to the new social order from which the
Conservative party was to draw its strength, and although he had to wait seven years
for the realization of the vision, the result justified his expectations. The decade of
the seventies witnessed new currents in English public opinion which Disraeli was quick
to adapt to his own purposes. Out of the wreck of the Tory party, in the face of suspicion within and disparagement outside, Disraeli succeeded in associating the landed
proprietor and the workingman as the basis of a viable organization. Salisbury and
Balfour even more than himself were to reap the harvest from this extraordinary achievement.

      During the years 1867 to 1887, the responsibility for conducting Her Majesty's
Government rested with the two parties for almost equal periods. The Derby-Disraeli
Ministry of 1866-8 inaugurated the era by sponsoring the Act of British North American
confederation; the next Conservative Government came with the six years of Beaconsfield's authority during the latter seventies; and the period ended with the two ministries of Salisbury in 1885-6 and 1886-92. The latter governments began what was to
become, with one brief Liberal interlude, almost twenty years of Conservative rule.
During the second of these administrations the first Colonial Conference was held, foreshadowing the emergence of a new system of imperial relations. Although the two decades encompassed by this study opened and closed on a Conservative note, there were
important Liberal variations within the whole. The first Gladstone Government was a
constructive one in British domestic history; it was no less energetic in its approach to
the problems of the Empire. Gladstone's second Ministry, from 1880 to 1885, was
faced by more arduous conditions in imperial administration and any success it attained was distinctly limited. The Government which Gladstone formed in 1886 was so
dominated by the Home Rule Bill and so brief that it can be dismissed from this record.

      Generally speaking, the political transformations of the two decades, 1867 to
1887, did not depend on the vicissitudes of colonial affairs. Until the late eighties and
even the nineties the colonies, with the exception of areas like South Africa, played
but a small part in English domestic politics. The advent of Gladstone in 1868 was
principally due to the demand for domestic reform, so long forestalled by Palmerston,
and resulted in a government which provided Great Britain with modern institutions and
services. Disraeli invoked the new consciousness of imperial and foreign responsibilities to turn Gladstone out of office, but his success was not dependent on specific colonial issues. During his Ministry, however, episodes like the purchase of the Suez
Canal shares, the acquisition of Cyprus, and the Sovereign's identification with India

were spectacular anticipations of the new climate of opinion. When Gladstone returned to power in 1880 he was obliged to take up complex imperial problems concerning
which his political philosophy afforded him very meagre counsel. The pace of domestic reform went regularly forward, but Majuba and Khartoum showed how unsteady was
the Liberal grasp in the realm of colonial policy. After 1885 Irish affairs dominated
the British political scene, until the defeat of the first Home Rule Bill relaxed the tension. Then the Salisbury Government proceeded, most capably, to sponsor a new programme of domestic legislation while at the same time officiating at the partition of
Africa.

There were nine Secretaries of State for the Colonies during the period 1867 to
1887.[67] In birth and background they formed a typical group of public men drawn
from the governing classes of the United Kingdom. Six were peers, two were baronets
(later ennobled), and one was the son of a peer. Their careers were strikingly similar.
Of their number five had been successively at Eton and Christ Church, while the remainder had gone to Harrow or Rugby and then on to either of the ancient universities.
Only one, F. A. Stanley, was not a university man. (He had left Eton to join the
Grenadier Guards.) Most of them had entered Parliament early in life and had held
junior posts, mainly at the Foreign Office, soon after. Two, perhaps three, were influential in the counsels of their party; the rest were what might be called politicians
of the second rank. Some, like Hicks Beach, had the promise of brilliant careers before them when they assumed the post of Colonial Secretary, while others, like Derby,
had already witnessed their most active period. Their average term in office was just
over two years, a fact which provides a further explanation for the influence which the
Permanent Under-Secretary exercised in the Department at this time. On the whole
they concerned themselves only occasionally with the problems of the new Canadian
state.

Of the six Secretaries of State for the Colonies which the Conservative party contributed to this period, the name of the fourth Earl of Carnarvon[68] is easily the most
outstanding. Carnarvon was a high-principled, generous, and idealistic man, a conscientious administrator and an imaginative statesman. He recommended himself to
Rogers because he was interested in ecclesiastical matters, and his warmth of feeling
made him a more attractive chief than Cardwell, who had been his predecessor. His
greatest handicap was an excitable temperament, unfortunately never disciplined,
which earned him the nickname of "Twitters" from Disraeli. Carnarvon's relations
with Herbert were of "the greatest intimacy," his biographer noting that the Permanent
Under-Secretary was at all times much more than an official adviser on colonial affairs.[69] Carnarvon's concern with colonial problems showed itself not only in his public activities but in his personal life as well. Herbert is the authority for the statement
that he took a greater individual interest in the progress of the colonies than almost any
of his predecessors in office. Unlike most Colonial Secretaries of this period, he understood the colonial background from having travelled extensively in the self-governing parts of the Empire. British North America and the Australian territories had each
seen him for lengthy visits. He wisely appreciated the value of hospitality and social

kindnesses and almost every colonial Minister who came to England was entertained by
him at Highclere, his Hampshire home. This practice was similarly in marked contrast to the attitude of other Colonial Secretaries, who were careful not to allow their
official lives to intrude upon their personal habits.

Like Grey, Carnarvon possessed what might be called an "imperial consciousness."
He recognized the British Empire as a living organism, capable of making an enormous
contribution to human brotherhood and welfare. Almost his first speech in Parliament
was to urge that a gesture of appreciation be provided the colonies for their assistance
in the relief of Crimean War veterans; some of his last public utterances discussed sympathetically the idea of imperial federation. In company with the Colonial Reformers
he believed fervently in the importance of sympathy and co-operation as the foundation of imperial policy. When he attacked Lord Granville's attitude towards New Zealand in 1869-70, Carnarvon was doing more than engaging in partisan controversy; he
was vindicating a life long conviction. His second term at the Colonial Office witnessed a notable enlargement of the Empire that anticipated the spectacular acquisitions of
the succeeding decade. When he became Colonial Secretary in 1874 he urged that the
Cardwell policy be immediately reversed, a suggestion with which Disraeli found favour. Showing "the bearskin," as the Prime Minister put it, would serve the dual purpose of strengthening the military position of the Empire while at the same time reassert-
ing its unity. [70] But Gathorne-Hardy at the War Office interposed the problem of re-
cruiting and Carnarvon saw his project killed in Cabinet discussion in 1876. In spite of
this set-back, the realization of a scheme of joint imperial defence remained his aim,
and although it has never been made public, the report of a committee on military
security which he headed from 1879 to 1882 almost certainly recommended such an arrangement. It is, perhaps, contradictory that an individual who found imperial defence a fascinating subject should have also been vitally interested in the reform of
prisons and in the regulation of vivisection, but such was the measure of the man.

Carnarvon's greatest significance in the history of the British Empire lies, however, in his advocacy of what Rogers called "showy schemes."[71] These were the great
acts of imperial consolidation and construction; the foundations on which colonial nationhood has been erected. Carnarvon was fortunate enough to be in power when the scheme
of Canadian federation came to fruition. As Secretary of State he led the later stages
of the discussions with the British North American delegates in the winter of 1866-7 and
then introduced the Act of Union in the Lords with a masterly speech. Thereafter federation became to him a rational goal of colonial progress, sometimes outweighing
sounder considerations, as in the case of his South African policy. In spite of its relative failure it may be said, however, that Carnarvon's work in South Africa entitles
him, as the preliminary architect of union, to the same place as Cardwell holds in
Canadian history. And federation did not comprise the whole of his vision of colonial
development. As early as 1859, when the licence under which the Hudson's Bay Company operated in the western part of North America expired, he urged that the area be
brought under the direct control of the Crown. Already he was conscious of the value
of the prairie region and concerned with its orderly development. He saw that a rail-

way to link the empty lands to the settled parts of British North America was indispensable and at that time favoured the granting of an Imperial subsidy for this purpose.
Years later, when he was Colonial Secretary and the railway was under construction,
he intervened in Canadian domestic affairs when there seemed a possibility that the
project might be abandoned. It was one of the most dramatic and hazardous acts of
his career, but it successfully kept the plan of a transcontinental railway from becoming the plaything of sectional interests in Canada. The hopes which he expressed in
1867 for a united Canada were still present in his mind in 1883, when he spoke of a
nation which should some day dwarf Europe in achievement.

In the period 1867-87 there were only three Colonial Secretaries in the ten years
during which the Liberal party held power. None of them were as able or large-mind-
ed as Carnarvon in their dealings with the self-governing colonies. The second Earl
Granville[72] twice held the seals of the Colonial Office, in Gladstone's first and third
Administrations. Rogers thought very highly of Granville as the head of a department
and the two men developed extremely cordial relations.[73] In temperament and in opinion they were remarkably similar. Of Granville, Rogers later wrote:

> ... the pleasantest and most satisfactory chief of those under whom I served. His
> merits as a chief were, that he trusted his subordinates in matters of detail, that he
> saw his way clearly and would act vigorously in what may be called ministerial as
> distinguished from departmental policy, and he was ready to act with promptitude
> and authority in matters which none but a chief could handle, matters requiring ac-
> tion in the House of Lords or the Cabinet or the Treasury. And in a diplomatic kind
> of way he thoroughly enjoyed the characteristic and amusing side of business.[74]

There is a more revealing sentence about the state of his relations with Lord Granville
dating from the period when Granville first came to the Colonial Office. "I like my
chief very much. He is very pleasant and friendly, and I think will not meddle beyond
what is required to keep us clear of political slips."[75] Rogers's expectation was borne
out by events, a fact which was bound to influence his attitude towards the Secretary of
State.

"Lord Granville was by birth and breeding a Whig of Whigs, but in his economic
and political convictions he will be found the fine flower and product of the Manchester
School."[76] This background and outlook naturally did not commend him to the democratic and protectionist governments of the self-governing colonies, and the policies
which he was obliged to implement served to make the estrangement more complete.
Upon Granville's shoulders fell the task of withdrawing the Imperial troops from the
autonomous colonies, a movement which was widely misunderstood both in England
and overseas. Granville's separatist views, which he barely troubled to conceal, did
not make his stand any less ambiguous. During the two years in which he headed the
Office his handling of colonial problems, particularly in relation to the self-governing
colonies, was, to say the least, indecisive. In extenuation it must be admitted that
Granville was unable to give consistent attention to the affairs of the Colonial Office

during these critical years, for his best efforts were directed to the difficult task of piloting Gladstone's Irish measures through the House of Lords. [77]

On Clarendon's death Granville went to the Foreign Office, where his conciliatory approach to the Alabama claims dispute, and his scrupulous care over the Franco-Prussian War, showed wisdom and judgment. When Gladstone formed his second Administration in 1880, Granville was again appointed Foreign Secretary. His inability during this second term of office to cope with powerful European statesmen makes his nickname of "Puss" Granville[78] at least credible. In addition, a rather easy-going nature caused him to be quite overcome by the vast increase in Foreign Office business which occurred during the eighties. In 1886, on the formation of Gladstone's third Ministry, he refrained from taking the Foreign Office again and returned as Colonial Secretary. The greater part of this final period at the Office was occupied with the bitter and hopeless struggle over Gladstone's Home Rule Bill. Sir Robert Meade, who was Granville's private secretary on a number of occasions, thought that he was a man whose capabilities had never been realized by his contemporaries.

> Justice has not been done him in many respects. It is the fashion to speak of him as a pleasure-loving man who sacrificed business to pleasure. Never was a greater mistake. He enjoyed amusements, but never neglected business. He was an excellent administrator, because when he had a good man under him, he trusted him while holding all the threads in his hands. His judgment was sounder than that of any other man I ever came across. [79]

Granville's successor, as Colonial Secretary and then as leader of the Liberal peers, was the first Earl of Kimberley. [80] Kimberley was a Norfolk landowner who embodied the free trade views and anti-imperial bias characteristic of many of the prominent Liberals of his day. Indeed, in some of its deeper convictions his mind recalled the mental attitude of a Whig magnate of several generations earlier. He had, as one observer noted, the customary Whig reserve and abhorrence of precipitate action. "Nor was Lord Kimberley the man to create events as some men can create them. If he is free from the Whig laissez faire, which was so conspicuous in Lord Melbourne, he has to the full the exceeding caution and the almost nervous dislike of undertaking any responsibility which can be possibly avoided, that are, above all things, Whig traditions."[81] He was cool to the idea of imperial expansion. Great Britain had more than enough territory scattered around the world to govern and protect, he considered. "If we multiply our stations too much, we really weaken ourselves by multiplying the points open to attack beyond our power to defend."[82] The notion that Great Britain should annex an area simply to prevent it from passing under the control of a foreign power he considered ridiculous. He would have liked to have seen the important colonies contributing in imperial defence measures, but he never raised the issue. In the long dispute with the Australian colonies over differential duties, he took a more conciliatory line than Gladstone, although he shared to the full his chief's faith in the necessity of upholding international agreements and in the wisdom of universal free trade. He endorsed the proposal of a general amnesty for the participants in the Red River insurrection, a step which, when taken in 1875, contributed largely to the domestic peace of Canada. His period at the Colonial Office, like Granville's, was interrupted by duties in the House of Lords, where he had the task, for instance, of introducing Bruce's controversial licensing bill in 1872.

When Gladstone formed his second Government in 1880, Kimberley went naturally to the Colonial Office, where he spent two more years. This period at the Office was less successful than his first, the stormy current of South African affairs proving a constant source of worry. His handling of the Transvaal Boers was irresolute, and the proclamation of the South African Republic, the British defeat at Majuba Hill, and the Convention of Pretoria marked successive stages in the weakening of the British position in South Africa. In 1882 he followed Hartington to the India Office, where he was to spend a great part of the remainder of his official life. He was responsible for the passage of the third Reform Bill through the House of Lords in 1884-5. Among Liberal leaders, Kimberley was always largely unknown to the general public. As a personality he possessed little of the warmth and colour of Carnarvon and seemed incapable of appreciating the importance of the human relationship in the technique of administration. He is said never to have entertained a colonial Minister at his home during six years of office. In spite of these limitations there was probably never a Colonial Secretary who was more conscientious in attention to his work or who laboured longer at the composition of dispatches suited to the sensibilities of the self-governing colonies than Lord Kimberley. If he was too honest to be completely agreeable he was a man of too much integrity to be negligent or cavalier. The most accurate designation of Kimberley would be to enumerate the qualities of a country squire: the sense of responsibility, the diligent and hard-working attitude, the unwavering concern with practicable aims.

For the most part, the Parliamentary Under-Secretaries attached to the Colonial Office during the twenty years after 1867 concerned themselves only slightly in the affairs of Canada, and exercised little influence in the determination of policy towards the Dominion. There were eleven of them in the period under review, so that their individual tenure of office was even shorter than that of the Secretaries of State. The arrangement by which the Parliamentary Under-Secretary was appointed to secure representation for a department in the other House from his chief was followed, and some of these men performed useful services in the Commons in answering questions or defending governmental policy. The departmental responsibilities of a Parliamentary Under-Secretary have always tended to be undefined, a situation which caused Lord Buxton to describe the position as "neither fish nor flesh nor fowl nor good red herring."[83] The Parliamentary Under-Secretaries read all the important Canadian dispatches before 1887, and, in fact, Knatchbull-Hugessen once complained when he was not furnished in good time with certain Canadian correspondence. But this perusal resulted in few comments or suggestions. For the most part they simply minuted the papers before passing them on to the Secretary of State. An examination of the Canadian correspondence received in the Office during this period assigns to the Parliamentary Under-

Secretaries a minor role in the formulation of British policy.

There were exceptions, of course, to this general conclusion. Sir Charles Adderley (Lord Norton), [84] who served as Parliamentary Under-Secretary under both Carnarvon and Buckingham from 1866 to 1868, was a well-known expert on colonial questions who made his views felt in the Office. Adderley had been an associate of Wakefield and Godley in the founding of Canterbury and was active in the work of the Colonial Reform Society in its early years. He allied with an interest in the Empire a systematic attention to problems of social reform and education. The most distinctive feature of his public life, however, was his long advocacy for the withdrawal of the garrisons from the autonomous colonies. The presence of British troops in overseas territories was to him a thoroughly discreditable aspect of imperial administration. It thwarted the expression of the principle of colonial self-government, in which he fervently believed, and prevented the growth of a spirit of self-reliance. Vigorous and independent in his opinions, Adderley consistently attacked the garrison system over a period of many years, notwithstanding the political complexion of the government in power. The implementation, in the early seventies, of the Cardwell programme of strategic concentration was partly attributable to Adderley's efforts in preparing Parliament for this major change in policy. As Under-Secretary Adderley introduced and piloted the British North America Bill through the House of Commons and handled the controversial discussions on the Governor Eyre case. Always tolerant of Canadian pretensions, he remained nevertheless a firm believer in the unity of the British Empire under the Crown. His views were not very compatible with Rogers's, but he worked well with Carnarvon. He is distinguished among the Parliamentary Under-Secretaries of the period for his interest in Canadian questions and for the constructive way in which he participated in the work of the North American Department.

IV

A discussion of the administrative machinery by which the Imperial Government conducted relations with Canada after 1867 would not be complete without a brief reference to the post of Governor-General. For in addition to being the executive head of the Government of Canada, the Governor-General also served as the agent-in-chief of the Colonial Office in the Dominion. The two aspects of the position combined to make it one of peculiar difficulty and delicacy. The concessions of responsible government had produced the anomaly of the irresponsible governor in a responsible colony and it was to take many years of experience in administration before the dilemma could be resolved. In the meantime the Governor-General of Canada, to use a phrase coined by a distinguished holder of the office, walked "inevitably on a razor edge."[85]

The ultimate solution of the problem of the Governor-General's role in an autonomous colony was one which few could have foreseen in 1849. It was brought about by the steady enlargement of Canadian self-government, a process which, domestically, occurred largely at the expense of the powers of the Governor-General. It left him, by the twentieth century, as the constitutional head of the Canadian state with a position largely analogous to that of his Sovereign in England. This trend secured its most spectacular achievements in 1878, when important alterations took place in the Commission and Instructions of the Governor-General. These changes, besides having the effect of recognizing existing practices on the part of the holders of the office, also resulted in the sphere of independent action open to the Governor-General being restricted still further. The section in the Instructions requiring the Governor to reserve various types of bills was abandoned, as were other clauses allowing him to preside at Council meetings and to exercise a personal discretionary power. The principle that the Governor-General must perform executive acts only on advice was steadily applied through the years that followed these modifications in the formal instruments of the office. The power to disallow provincial legislation, to exercise the prerogative of mercy, to grant or refuse dissolution, to dismiss a Lieutenant-Governor, to reject appointments suggested by the Prime Minister--the responsibility for all these functions came to lie with the Cabinet and not with the person of the Governor-General. In the same way the Governor's right to reserve or withhold assent from bills of the Canadian Parliament passed into desuetude. Throughout the entire evolution it was the requirements of Canadian autonomy that determined the process. Behind the concessions and the compromises loomed Grey's precept of 1846: "... it cannot be too distinctly acknowledged that it is neither possible nor desirable to carry on the government of any of the British Provinces in North America in opposition to the opinion of the inhabitants."[86] The Imperial Conference of 1926 made a formal recognition of the change which had occurred in the position of the Governor-General by divesting him of his obligation to act as the representative of the United Kingdom. Today, although his powers have gone the way of his Sovereign's, he retains, like the Crown, residual privileges which may be of great importance during a constitutional crisis. For the most part, however, he now relies on influence where once he exercised authority. He is, as Professor Dawson has stated, "a legal survivor who has contrived to remain a political necessity."[87]

This transformation of the vice regal office was already well under way by the time of Canadian Confederation. It is for this reason that the Governor-General occupied a secondary position in the conduct of Anglo-Canadian relations after 1867. In most of the episodes discussed in the present work he served merely as the channel through which communication was maintained between the Canadian Cabinet and the Colonial Office. This does not mean that the Governor-General played a purely neutral role in all the issues that arose between the United Kingdom and Canada in these years. Monck, for instance, was instrumental in completing the arrangements for the withdrawal of the Imperial garrisons. Dufferin undertook an ill-advised and ultimately unsuccessful intervention in the railway dispute with British Columbia. Lorne blundered in acting beyond his constitutional authority in the Atalaya affair and again when he was forced to assume an unwanted responsibility for the dismissal of Lieutenant-Governor Letellier. There are many other instances which show that the Governor-General occasionally exercised independent powers during this period.[88]

Since it is mainly as a cypher that the Governor-General figures in the topics making up this study, it is appropriate to examine the procedure of communication which linked London and Ottawa. Most of the Colonial Office correspondence with Canada was carried on by means of numbered dispatches which the Governor could show without restraint to his Canadian advisers and which could be published without difficulty. The Canadian Cabinet corresponded directly with the Secretary of State by memoranda and reports, approved by the Cabinet and transmitted to London by the Governor-General. The majority of these communications were either written by the Cabinet for the Governor or were merely formal covering letters. Dufferin and Lansdowne wrote their own numbered dispatches but in this display of initiative they were unique among the occupants of Rideau Hall at this time. The Governor-General also received at irregular intervals dispatches marked "Secret" or "Confidential," which might be shown to the Prime Minister and Cabinet under special conditions. His replies to these communications were, of course, drafted personally, although he usually discussed the subject with his advisers beforehand. This type of dispatch accounted for only a small part of the official correspondence to which he affixed his signature. There appears to have been only scattered and episodic private correspondence between the Governor-General and the Colonial Secretary after 1867, although Carnarvon and Dufferin were close friends and maintained an extensive exchange of letters. [89] Dufferin is outstanding among Canadian Governors of his time for the personal interest which he took in official correspondence and for the careful way in which he kept the Secretary of State informed of the background to events in the Dominion. On several occasions he assisted Carnarvon by writing draft dispatches for Canada which were used to meet problems about which the Governor-General possessed expert knowledge.

The success which a Governor-General of Canada achieves depends largely upon his personality and his conception of his position. This statement is certainly true today; it is no less accurate when applied to the period following Confederation. Viscount Monck, the first Governor-General of the Dominion, possessed experience gained from English political life and from a term as Governor-General of the united Province of Canada. Macdonald thought very highly of him and relied on his knowledge of constitutional practice in the difficult early days of the Dominion. Monck's successor, Sir John Young (Lord Lisgar), who was of a reserved disposition, proved to be an indolent individual who took little part in the affairs of his Government. Lord Dufferin assumed the position of Governor-General in June, 1872. With a nature diametrically opposed to Young's, from the outset he evinced a great interest, and a desire to participate, in the political life of Canada. He requested information on every decision which the Government made and would have presided over the meetings of the Privy Council if his Ministers had been agreeable. He came to British North America to be a governor, with the result that the life of a constitutional monarch proved a source of constant vexation to him. "The Governorship of a Colony with Constitutional advisers does not admit of much real control over its affairs, and I miss the stimulus of responsibility," he told Carnarvon. [90] During his period in office the Canadian Executive was mainly under the control of the Liberals, a circumstance which meant that he was forced to work with men who resented his manner and were suspicious of his outlook on national questions. The inevitable consequence was a long series of disputes and misunderstandings between the Governor-General and his principal advisers. Possessed of great charm and sophistication, Dufferin was always extremely popular among the people of Canada, and but for his unhappy relations with the Mackenzie Cabinet, his governorship might have been one of the most successful in the history of the Dominion. He was succeeded by Lord Lorne, a son-in-law of Queen Victoria. Young and inexperienced, with no real political ability, Lorne was powerless in the hands of Macdonald, now back in office. His period at Rideau Hall was distinguished socially but marred by several errors of judgment in the field of administration. The last Governor-General of the period, Lord Lansdowne, maintained dealings with the Macdonald Cabinet that were both competent and harmonious. His tenure of the post entitles him to be described as a model Governor-General, whom future holders of the position could profitably emulate.

Individually, the political capacities of the Governor-Generals of Canada varied markedly, but collectively the holders of the post performed an indispensable role in the working of the imperial relationship. "Acting as shock absorber between colonial autonomy and imperial control, the function of a governor might not be spectacular; it was none the less essential."[91] The constitutional authority of an impartial Governor to warn and advise became as important an attribute of the position as any formal or ceremonial aspect. The office of Governor-General, like that of the Sovereign in England, provided an element of continuity in the political life of Canada and, in the Empire, became the symbol of a higher loyalty for the separate colonial nationalisms. In the conduct of imperial relations after 1867 the Governor-General may not have occupied the centre of the stage but he was always close at hand in the wings. From this situation the United Kingdom's representative in Canada was able to make his own distinctive contribution to the achievement of the Commonwealth form of association.

REFERENCES

1. Quoted in H. L. Hall, The Colonial Office: A History (London, 1937), 48-9.

2. Sir Henry Taylor, Autobiography, 1800-75 (London, 1885), II, 34.

3. Ibid.

4. 22 Geo. III, c. 82.

5. A very useful discussion of the formative years of the Colonial Office is contained in J. C. Beaglehole, "The Colonial Office, 1782-1854," Historical Studies, Australia and New Zealand, I (April, 1941), 170-89. See also H. T. Manning, British Colonial Government after the American Revolution, 1782-1820 (New Haven, 1933),

chap. XV, and, for a sketch of the Office in the thirties, W. L. Burn, Emancipation and Apprenticeship in the British West Indies (London, 1937), chap. III.

6. The fullest study of Stephen as an administrator is by Paul Knaplund: James Stephen and the British Colonial System, 1813-47 (Madison, 1953).

7. A clear account of the procedure for handling colonial laws is given in Paul Knaplund, "Mr. Oversecretary Stephen," Journal of Modern History, I (March, 1929), 47-8.

8. Taylor, Autobiography, I, 123.

9. Hall, The Colonial Office, 74-5.

10. See, for example, the comment of the Prince of Wales in 1886 on the occasion of Lord Granville's appointment to the Colonial Office; quoted in ibid., 52.

11. Molesworth's attack was directed against the system of colonial administration rather than a particular Secretary. It is quoted in W. P. Morrell, British Colonial Policy in the Age of Peel and Russell (Oxford, 1930), 486.

12. Examiner (London), April 21, 1849, quoted in Porritt, The Diplomatic Freedom of the British Dominions, 304.

13. Mrs. Fawcett, Life of the Rt. Hon. Sir William Molesworth, quoted in ibid., 291.

14. Taylor's treatise, The Statesman, published in 1836, is one of the best expositions in English political literature of the art of the administrator. The assumptions underlying it and its treatment of the subject afford a clear indication of the mind of the gifted permanent official in the early part of the nineteenth century. There is a modern edition of The Statesman, with an introductory essay by H. J. Laski, available (Cambridge, 1927).

15. Sir William Baillie Hamilton, "Forty-four Years at the Colonial Office," Nineteenth Century, CCCLXXXVI (April, 1909), 599-613.

16. Ibid., 600.

17. Sir John Bramston, "The Colonial Office from Within," Empire Review, I (April, 1901), 280.

18. Hall, The Colonial Office, 24. Bramston provides the more cautious estimate

that the expenditure on telegrams rose fivefold in the period 1870 to 1900. (Bramston, "The Colonial Office from Within," 281-2.) By the end of the century the Colonial Office maintained a staff of resident clerks to answer telegrams.

19. Colonial Office List, 1862, 2.

20. Bramston, "The Colonial Office from Within," 283. The Colonial Office List for 1872 gives sixty-two names.

21. These figures are taken from Bramston, "The Colonial Office from Within," 283, and from successive editions of the Colonial Office List.

22. Sir Anton Bertram, The Colonial Service (Cambridge, 1930), 26.

23. Hall, The Colonial Office, 6.

24. Ibid., 19.

25. Bertram, The Colonial Service, 26-7.

26. Rogers to Miss Rogers, May 4, 1860, quoted in Lord Blachford (Sir Frederic Rogers), Letters, ed. by G. E. Marindin (London, 1896), 226.

27. Rogers to Miss Rogers, Dec. 20, 1868, quoted in ibid., 276.

28. Taylor, Autobiography, II, 158-9.

29. H. E. Dale, The Higher Civil Service of Great Britain (Oxford, 1941), 134.

30. Born in 1811, the son of a baronet. Educated at Eton and Oriel College, Oxford. Took a double first in classics and mathematics, 1832. Elected to a fellowship at Oriel, 1833. Called to the bar, 1837. An intimate friend of J. H. Newman and active in the Tractarian movement, although never converted to Roman Catholicism. Practiced law in London and wrote leaders for The Times after leaving Oxford. In 1844 became the first Registrar of Joint Stock Companies. Two years later appointed a Colonial Land and Emigration Commissioner, which brought him into touch with the work of the Colonial Office. Performed some of the duties of a legal draftsman for the Office before being made Permanent Under-Secretary in May, 1860. See Blachford, Letters, for a personal account of Rogers's life and opinions.

31. Hall, The Colonial Office, 223.

32. Rogers to Gladstone, Jan. 11, 1877, quoted in Blachford, Letters, 374-5.

Rogers's views on the extension of democracy in his own day are to be found, by implication, in his review of Sir Thomas Erskine May's Democracy in Europe, in Edinburgh Review, CXLVII (April, 1878), 301-33. See also Blachford, Letters, 388.

33. Hall, The Colonial Office, 83.

34. Taylor, Autobiography, II, 161.

35. Ibid.

36. Sir Frederic Rogers, "Notes of Autobiography," 1885, quoted in Blachford, Letters, 297. See below, chapter IX, for other expressions of Rogers's separatist opinions.

37. Rogers, "Notes of Autobiography," 1885, quoted in Blachford, Letters, 299-300.

For an earlier expression of this opinion, written at the time when Rogers was drafting the constitutions for some of the Australian colonies, see Rogers to R. W. Church, Sept. 15, 1854, quoted in ibid., 157-8.

38. Rogers to Taylor, 1865, quoted in Taylor, Autobiography, II, 241-2.

39. Rogers to Taylor, Feb. 26, 1870, quoted in Blachford, Letters, 394.

40. Rogers to Taylor, Feb. 19, 1876, quoted in ibid., 367.

41. See especially "Native Policy in South Africa," Edinburgh Review, CXLV (April, 1877), 447-87; "The Causes of the Zulu War," Nineteenth Century, XXV (March, 1879), 564-74.

42. Rogers to G. E. Marindin, May 15, 1878, quoted in Blachford, Letters, 389.

43. Rogers to Taylor, Oct. 26, 1877, quoted in ibid., 381.

44. Rogers to Taylor, Jan. 20, 1885, quoted in ibid., 423.

45. Grey's proposals are found in the Pall Mall Gazette, January 7, 9, 1885. They are foreshadowed in his article, "How Shall We Retain the Colonies?" Nineteenth Century, XXVIII (June, 1879), 952-4.

The Pall Mall Gazette, under the editorship of W. T. Stead, was engaged at this time in a vigorous campaign for imperial consolidation. On January 19, 1885, it invited Rogers's comments on Grey's scheme, but repudiated them completely in a leader in the same issue.

46. Rogers in Pall Mall Gazette, Jan. 19, 1885, quoted in Blachford, Letters, 425-6.

47. Herbert was born in 1831, a member of the Carnarvon branch of the Herbert family. (He was related to the fourth Earl of Carnarvon, the Colonial Secretary, who was also an intimate friend.) Educated at Eton and Balliol College, Oxford. Won many academic distinctions, crowned by election to a fellowship to All Souls College in 1854. (He was a Fellow of All Souls all his life, for he never married.) Private secretary to Gladstone in 1855, called to the bar in 1858. In 1859 went out to Australia as secretary to Sir George Bowen, the first Governor of Queensland. Became successively Colonial Secretary of the Colony, a member of the Legislative Council, and Premier. For five years served as Premier, the key figure in the initial development of Queensland. Returning to England, appointed an assistant secretary at the Board of Trade in 1868, and transferred to the Colonial Office in February, 1870, as an Assistant Under-Secretary.

48. H. E. Dale, who entered the Colonial Office in 1898, supplied personal reminiscences of Herbert to the author in a conversation at New College, May 1, 1951. Herbert returned to the Colonial Office by request for a short period in 1900, thus enabling Mr. Dale to observe him in his former official capacity.

49. T. H. S. Escott, Pillars of the Empire (London, 1879), 17.

50. Hall provides an illustration of this habit of Herbert's in The Colonial Office, 22-3.

51. A minute by Herbert, July 9, 1870, quoted in ibid., 76.

52. Herbert also visited Canada and the United States in the mid-eighties, travelling on some of the recently completed railway lines in the American West.

53. Escott, Pillars of the Empire, 121.

54. The expressions in quotation are those of Mr. Dale.

55. Escott, Pillars of the Empire, 121.

56. Herbert left no corpus of private letters and memoranda, as did Rogers, and it is extremely doubtful whether any such collection of material exists. There is no biography of Herbert in print, no memoir, no fragment of an autobiography. His obituary appeared in The Times, May 8, 1905. See also The Times, May 11, 1905.

57. Sir Arthur Hardinge, Life of the Fourth Earl of Carnarvon (Oxford, 1925), II, 232-3.

58. Hall, The Colonial Office, 257-8.

59. Ibid., 39.

60. See Appendix A, 320-1, for a chart, The Organization of the Colonial Office, 1867-87, which gives the senior permanent staff of the Office for these years.

61. Born in 1808, educated at Harrow. Entered the Colonial Office as a boy of seventeen. Secretary to the Earl of Gosford's Commission investigating the political difficulties of Lower Canada in 1835-7. Chairman of the Colonial Land and Emigration Commission, 1840-7.

62. Minute by Elliot, Nov. 4, 1858, quoted in Hall, The Colonial Office, 77.

63. It is interesting to note that Elliot belonged to the Minto family, who contributed the fourth Earl as Governor-General of Canada in 1898.

64. Born in 1825, educated at Harrow, University of Durham, and Trinity College, Cambridge. A barrister in the northern circuit. Assisted a royal commission on the reform of the common law in 1850, but possessed no official experience before coming to the Colonial Office.

65. Malcolm's career touched Herbert's at several points. He was educated at Eton and Balliol College, elected to a fellowship at All Souls, and called to the bar. Secretary to a commission investigating the public schools in 1868, and then entered the Board of Trade as an assistant secretary in 1870.

66. Educated at Balliol College, Oxford, elected to a fellowship at All Souls College in the year following Herbert, went out to Queensland with Bowen and Herbert. Member of the Legislative Council and Executive Council for Queensland, Attorney-General for Queensland. Attorney-General of Hong Kong and later a judge on the Supreme Court of the Colony, 1873-6.

67. The political staff of the Colonial Office during these years is given in Appendix A.

68. Born in 1831, educated at Eton and Christ Church, Oxford. Parliamentary Under-Secretary at the Colonial Office under Stanley and Lytton, 1858-9. Secretary of State for the Colonies, 1866-7, and 1874-8. Resigned from the Office on both occasions because of disagreements with Disraeli. Lord Lieutenant of Ireland, 1885-6.

69. Hardinge, Life of Carnarvon, III, 318.

70. Ibid., 37.

71. Blachford, Letters, 263.

72. Born in 1815, educated at Eton and Christ Church, Oxford. Parliamentary Under-Secretary for Foreign Affairs, 1840-1. Held minor offices in Lord John Russell's Administration before becoming Foreign Secretary in 1851-2. Lord President of the Council under Aberdeen and again under Palmerston in 1859.

73. On Rogers's retirement from the Colonial Office in 1871 Granville invited him to come to the Foreign Office as Permanent Under-Secretary. Blachford, Letters, 295.

74. Ibid., 264.

75. Rogers to Miss S. Rogers, Dec. 20, 1868, quoted in ibid., 275.

76. H. E. Egerton, A Short History of British Colonial Policy, 1606-1909 (London, 9th ed., 1932), 316.

77. Lord E. Fitzmaurice, Life of the Second Earl Granville (London, 1905), II, 2-20.

78. Goldwin Smith, Reminiscences (New York, 1910), 208.

79. Notes on Granville by Meade, quoted in Fitzmaurice, Life of Granville, II, 500.

80. Born in 1826, educated at Eton and Christ Church. Parliamentary Under-Secretary for Foreign Affairs under Aberdeen and Palmerston, 1852-6. British Minister in Russia, 1856-8. Parliamentary Under-Secretary for Foreign Affairs, 1859-61. Parliamentary Under-Secretary for India, 1864. Lord Lieutenant of Ireland, 1864-6. Lord Privy Seal, 1868-70. Secretary of State for India, 1882-5, 1885-6, 1892-4. Foreign Secretary, 1894-5.

81. Escott, Pillars of the Empire, 172-3.

82. Hall, The Colonial Office, 184. See also ibid., 181, for another expression of this point of view by Kimberley.

83. Lucien Wolf, Life of the First Marquess of Ripon, quoted in ibid., 51.

84. Born in 1814, educated at Christ Church, Oxford. Vice-President of the Committee of the Privy Council for Education and President of the Board of Health, 1858-9. President of the Board of Trade in Disraeli's second Administration, 1874-8.

85. John Buchan, Lord Minto, a Memoir, quoted in Gwen Neuendorff, Studies in the Evolution of Dominion Status (London, 1942), 71.

86. Grey to Sir John Harvey (Lieutenant-Governor of Nova Scotia), Nov. 3, 1846, quoted in Earl Grey, The Colonial Policy of Lord John Russell's Administration (London, 2nd ed., 1853), I, 212.

87. R. M. Dawson, The Government of Canada (Toronto, 1948), 165.

88. The development of the office of Governor-General of Canada, with copious illustrations of the exercise of the Governor-General's powers, is provided in Neuendorff, Evolution of Dominion Status.

89. These letters are now available in a collection edited by F. H. Underhill, The Dufferin-Carnarvon Correspondence, 1874-8 (Toronto, 1955).

90. Dufferin to Carnarvon, private, March 18, 1874: PRO 30/6/26.

91. W. M. Whitelaw, "Responsible Government and the Irresponsible Governor," Canadian Historical Review, XIII (Dec., 1932), 370.

CHAPTER THREE

THE TREASURY AND IMPERIAL GUARANTEES ON CANADIAN LOANS

"As the Treasury are unfortunately wrong both in law and in policy I do not see how
we can fail to support Canada." Sir Robert Herbert, 1877

AMONG ALL THE MATTERS which went to make up the official intercourse between Great Britain and her self-governing colonies during the nineteenth century, there
is none which can be more accurately called an "imperial" subject than the provision of
guarantees by Great Britain on colonial loans. For this service by the United Kingdom
had simultaneously a joint and an individual significance. To many of the British colonies the grant of a guarantee by the British Government on the interest and principal of
a loan which they desired to raise was one of the substantial privileges of imperial membership. It facilitated the placing of their loan on the money markets of the world; it
gained them better terms and considerably easier interest rates; and it afforded them a
marked advantage over small independent nations in the highly competitive world of
international finance. Thus the guarantee, so highly esteemed by colonies whose economy was still in a primary stage, became an instrument of British colonial policy.[1]
It was used, as in New Zealand, as a bargaining measure to render Imperial decisions
more acceptable to a recalcitrant colony, or in North America, as a concession designed to promote the achievement of difficult objects. But, although employed in the
conduct of broad Imperial policy, the guarantee had also a specific bearing on the interests of the parties concerned in the arrangement. In the last resort the guarantee of
interest and principal had to be redeemed from the Consolidated Fund of Great Britain,
which meant that ultimately it was a direct charge on the British taxpayer. Supposedly, the guarantee was granted for projects which possessed an importance for the whole
Empire; in reality, in many cases, such projects affected only the colony requiring the
money. Under responsible government that colony was vitally concerned, therefore,
in superintending the appropriation and expenditure of the loan funds. Once the guarantee had been given, the interests of Great Britain and the colony so favoured often
tended to diverge in an alarming manner.

The device of issuing Imperial guarantees for colonial loans was open to the same
objections as those directed against the maintenance of British troops in the self-governing colonies. And, like the garrison system, which was attacked almost every year
in Parliament when the Army Estimates were taken up, the Imperial guarantee was subject to full parliamentary scrutiny. An act had to be passed in each case to authorize
the Lords Commissioners of the Treasury to extend the guarantee. The debate on this
act provided an opportunity for the opponents of the principle of Imperial guarantees

---

1. For references to chapter III see pages 97-106.

to state their case, and they often stated it in the same terms as did the critics of the garrison system. A guarantee by the British Treasury, they said, was a financial commitment which must be regarded as yet another charge on the revenues of the nation. It weakened the financial standing of the country and depressed England's credit among the states of the world. It had an injurious effect on the colonies as well, for it encouraged them in extravagant expenditure and unsound development and inhibited that spirit of self-reliance which ideally should be the goal of fiscal as well as political growth in colonial territories. It is not surprising that the men of the Manchester School, who provided most of the criticism of the garrison system, were also responsible for the public dissatisfaction with the practice of colonial guarantees.

The system of guarantees illustrates, in a striking fashion, the important fact that British colonial policy was never exclusively controlled by the Colonial Office but was often formed in a number of the great departments in Whitehall. In the case of guarantees for the colonies the Colonial Office obviously shared a responsibility with the Treasury; it was often apparent, however, that the two departments differed widely in their conception of the guarantee as an element in official policy. The Treasury, naturally concerned with the inescapable reality that British money was involved in a colonial guarantee, sought to safeguard the position of the loan by imposing sound borrowing practices, by a strict accounting of expenditure under the loan, and by careful management of the sinking fund. This direction, although usually purely financial, sometimes affected considerations relating to the political connection between Great Britain and her Empire: a sphere of action which the Secretary of State for the Colonies was charged to administer. That measures which the Treasury considered as financial were viewed by the Colonial Office as influencing political questions is revealed by the acrimonious exchanges which occurred between the two departments on the subject of governmental economy. The Treasury's predilections in this direction often hampered the Office in the provision of information and services to the colonies. These "little amenities," as the Office called them, were regarded as extremely useful in fostering sound relations, especially in the days before the autonomous colonies established permanent agents in London. In 1871, for instance, Lord Kimberley complained of a Treasury decision to stop the gratuitous distribution of certain United Kingdom publications among the Canadian governments. "Their Lordships are naturally not as well able to appreciate the bad effects which refusals in small matters of this kind which are attributed in the colonies to a want of friendship on the part of the Imperial govt. have on our relations with the Colonial govts., as the Secretary of State who has to watch over those relations, and I feel bound to bring the subject again under their notice and to urge its reconsideration."[2]   The Colonial Office had constantly before it, as its principal aim, the formation and maintenance of mutually beneficial relations between the United Kingdom and her colonies. With Canada and the other territories which enjoyed responsible government, this task was occasionally difficult and always delicate. Canadian fiscal freedom was a basic attribute of local autonomy and successive Colonial Secretaries after 1867 were extremely reluctant to appear to exercise any interference in the management of Canadian public finance. Thus the political considerations which the Colonial Office looked to for guidance in administering an Imperial guarantee were often far removed from the narrower interests of the Treasury in the same measure. This administrative dualism, observable over large areas of British colonial policy, is admirably illustrated by the history of United Kingdom guarantees on Canadian loans during the early years of the Dominion.

I

The first Imperial guarantee granted to Canada after 1867 was intimately connected with the achievement of federal union in British North America. It was given to promote the construction of a railway to link the Maritime colonies of Nova Scotia and New Brunswick with the new provinces of central Canada. Ever since George Stephenson had begun railway transportation in England in 1825, this project had been mooted by public men in British North America. A communication route by land between the old colonies by the Atlantic and the settlements of the St. Lawrence valley had obvious economic and military advantages, particularly in the winter season, when ice made the estuary of the St. Lawrence unnavigable. After having suffered frustration and failure for several decades, the plan for an intercolonial railway was given fresh impetus when it became merged in the general scheme for the federation of British North America. The Maritime colonies came to regard it as a sine qua non of union, and Canada, in the resolutions adopted at the Quebec Conference of 1864, committed herself to the completion of the railway immediately federation was achieved.[3] Cardwell at the Colonial Office promised an Imperial guarantee for the loan which would be necessary to construct the railway, and Carnarvon adhered to this pledge in his discussions with the British North American delegates at the Westminster Palace Hotel Conference in 1866-7. It was fortunate for the project that Disraeli, the Chancellor of the Exchequer, was deeply immersed in his Reform Bill at the time, for he was indifferent to the guarantee and assented to it by default rather than by conviction. When the Colonial Secretary called on him to discuss the matter, Disraeli, Carnarvon relates, "soon threw the Railway papers aside and opened the question of Reform."[4]

The debates in the Imperial Parliament on The Canada Railway Loan Act, 1867 provide an excellent illustration of the attitude assumed by British public men at this time towards the grant of colonial guarantees.[5] Sir Charles Adderley, Carnarvon's Parliamentary Under-Secretary, who introduced the measure into the Commons, was an old opponent of the garrison system who found it difficult to conceal his dislike of the provision of guarantees by the mother country. He frankly admitted that he hoped this would be the last request for a guarantee to come before Parliament. There were, however, circumstances which rendered this Canadian guarantee exceptional and worthy of the approval of the House. The Bill authorized the Treasury to guarantee the interest on a loan of £3,000,000 to be raised by Canada for the construction of the Intercolonial Railway. This railway, by ensuring the security of Canada in North America, was the key to the success of the Confederation scheme. The endorsation of the project by the Imperial Government would have a very beneficial effect on the relations between Great Britain and British North America. "If England desired that Canada should remain with her--and he, for his part, hoped that the two would long be connected--the way to bind their interests was by taking a liberal view of any common enterprize."[6]

Adderley was followed closely by the opponents of the Imperial guarantee. The Intercolonial Railway line was economically unsound, they said; was situated too close to the border to be of any value during a war, and would only involve Great Britain in heavy and futile expense. The whole undertaking was simply the price which Great Britain had to pay in order to bring about the union of the North American colonies. The guarantee was "nothing more nor less than hush-money," one member declared.[7] In their eyes, the provision of guarantees was clearly an unattractive feature of Imperial sovereignty which should be discontinued. Robert Lowe was warmly applauded when he uttered a dramatic warning against the financial burden guarantees imposed on the Imperial Exchequer. "In the time of the American Revolution the colonies separated from England because she insisted on taxing them. What I apprehend as likely to happen now is that England will separate from her colonies because they insist on taxing her."[8] The Manchester School attitude, so adequately expressed by John Bright in the debates on the British North America Act, seemed to underlie much of the criticism of this Canadian guarantee. A month earlier Bright had diagnosed the causes of the dissatisfaction with colonial guarantees and suggested a remedy.

> But if they [the British North American colonies] are to be constantly applying to us for guarantees for railways and for fortresses and for works of defence; if everything is to be given a nation independent in everything except Lord Monck and his successors, and except in the contributions we make for these public objects, then I think it would be far better for them and for us--cheaper for us and less demoralizing for them--that they should become an independent State--and maintain their own fortresses, fight their own cause, and build up their own future without relying on us.[9]

In the end it was Gladstone, who, though not a member of the Government, did more than any Government spokesman to secure the approval of the Intercolonial Railway guarantee. In the course of his remarks Gladstone gave characteristic expression to his current opinions on colonial questions. He took, for instance, the broadest possible view of the subject: the Intercolonial Railway was much more than a proposition for investors. It was ancillary to the great work of Confederation itself. By promoting the economic growth of Canada it would ensure the preservation of the Canadian nation on the North American continent. Self-reliance and responsibility for domestic affairs had for long been Gladstone's principal aims in colonial development and to his mind the plan of Confederation represented a long step towards these ends. He saw no disparagement to Canada in the speed in which Parliament had approved the British North America Act, but rather a tribute to Canadian political competency.

I must say we are in the path of reason and precedence as well as equity and liber-
ality. We have passed a measure by the unanimous assent of the House, and with
a promptitude which if it had been a matter of legislation affecting ourselves would
have been precipitancy. But when one thinks it was an acknowledgment of the title
of these colonies to deal practically with their own affairs--with a speed of which
there is hardly an example--we have passed a measure for uniting these colonies
together, and we hope ... that the result of that measure will be the development
along that great extent of territory of a stronger sense of political existence, more
self-reliance, and more self-relying habits. [10]

The connection between Great Britain and Canada was one of mutual interest and feeling, he said. The House's approval of the British North America Act and of this Bill,
which was inseparably connected with it, would go far towards continuing the relationship in this happy form. Gladstone's liberal interpretation of the Canadian guarantee
was accepted by the House, which gave leave to bring in the Bill by a handsome majority. [11]

        Canada fulfilled the duty laid upon her by the British North America Act by pass-
ing, in December, 1867, a measure for the construction of the Intercolonial Railway.
This piece of legislation also authorized the raising of a loan of Ł8,000,000, partly
under Imperial guarantee, for the expenses of the project. [12]   With the authority for
the railway and the guarantee contained in these acts of the Imperial and Canadian
Parliaments, the Colonial Office and Treasury could undertake the task of approving
the details of the scheme. This phase of the work was accomplished swiftly and without incident. By the spring of 1868 a route running close to the Gulf of St. Lawrence
and the Bay of Chaleur had been selected by the Canadian Government for the proposed
railway, estimates had been prepared for the cost of construction, and the United Kingdom had shown itself perfectly satisfied with the Canadian arrangements.   John Rose,
the Canadian Minister of Finance, visited England in the summer of 1868 to take advantage of a favourable state of the United Kingdom money market to place the Canadian loan. He submitted to the Treasury the terms on which the loan would be raised
by the Canadian financial agents in London, Messrs. Baring Brothers and Glyn, Mills
and Currie. These terms were approved, trustees for the sinking fund to represent both
the United Kingdom and Canadian Governments were appointed, and the loan was placed in July, 1868. It was successfully taken up on terms that were very favourable to
the Canadian Government. Until this point the arrangements for the guarantee seemed
to have been conducted with exemplary ease. [13]

        In August, 1868, Rose reported to the Canadian Cabinet that the loan had been
satisfactorily placed and paid tribute to the Treasury and the Colonial Office for the
co-operation shown him during the transactions. A fortnight later, on August 27, he
submitted suggestions for the temporary use of the proceeds of the loan; suggestions
that were the cause of the disagreement which presently arose between the two governments. Rose had raised Ł2,000,000 (of which Ł1,500,000 were guaranteed by Great
Britain) in this first venture of the Dominion into the English money market, and yet,

because of the fact that necessary surveys for the railway occupied most of 1868, he was not able to expend immediately the sum gained by the loan. He discovered that if he left the proceeds on deposit with the Canadian bankers in London he would only be credited with interest of one per cent on them. On the other hand the new Dominion had large floating debts outstanding to the United Kingdom, the Bank of Montreal in Canada, and the Province of Ontario, on which she was paying interest that ranged from five to seven per cent. The proposal which Rose made to the Canadian Privy Council was simply to use the proceeds of the Intercolonial Railway loan to pay off these obligations, at the same time issuing Exchequer Bills of the Dominion for the amount expended. He anticipated that the flourishing state of the Canadian revenue, together with certain investment payments which the country was due to receive in the coming year, would ensure that funds would be readily available for the construction charges of the Intercolonial Railway. The Dominion would save a substantial sum in interest payments while at the same time its excellent financial position would render the whole manipulation perfectly justifiable. These proposals were accepted by the Privy Council and approved by the Governor-General, although the Minute of Council endorsing this unconventional appropriation of funds raised under a British guarantee was not transmitted to the Colonial Office at this time.[14] The temporary investment of the loan funds was accordingly carried out; the Colonial Office, together with the Canadian and British public, remaining ignorant of the matter until the following spring.

Then, in May, 1869, on the occasion of Rose's Budget speech in the Canadian House of Commons, the whole affair was suddenly and dramatically revealed. It appears that the leaders of the Liberal Opposition, Alexander Mackenzie and L. H. Holton, had obtained word of the transaction and had indulged in unfavourable comment on it. Rose decided that the most sensible course was to anticipate their objections and he therefore inserted a defence of his proceedings in the Budget message. This explanation was the first news that most Canadians outside the Macdonald Cabinet received of the entire episode. The placing of the loan so far ahead of the time when the money would be required for construction he justified as a move demanded by the exigencies of the London money market. In contrast to earlier loans raised under British guarantee, such as the one associated with Lord Sydenham's name in 1842, the Intercolonial Railway loan had been handled exclusively by Canada, which had the responsibility of selecting a favourable time to place the loan before the public. The summer of 1868 had seen a number of large loan offerings in London by various European countries, but Canada had managed to place her loan ahead of the others and had secured even more favourable rates than Russia, which had a very good record as a debtor. Rose went on to state that the loan had of necessity to be for a large sum (perhaps a greater sum than was required at once), since only a substantial offering would attract competitive tenders. Then he came to the most serious criticism of his actions: that the loan funds had been temporarily employed in a manner that was contrary to the spirit of the Imperial guarantee. Here Rose adopted a lofty tone and while admitting the duty of the House of Commons to scrutinize the Government's financial actions, stated that any other course than the one he had taken would have justly earned him the censure of the House. By using the proceeds of the loan Canada had been able to retire old debts to the value of over $5,500,000, thus saving the country an annual interest payment of $350,000.[15] The Government had set aside, in the form of securities/ and bank deposits, a sum of over $10,000,000 to recoup the loan. This amount would amply redeem the entire £3,000,000 which would eventually be raised under the Imperial guarantee. The more orthodox course, which would have been to leave the loan funds on deposit in London at one per cent interest until they were needed, while the Government carried a debt on which it was paying between five and seven per cent, would have been a "gross, wanton, and deliberate disregard of the public interest" of Canada.[16] To claim that the Government was in financial straits at the time and raised the Intercolonial Railway loan simply to pay off obligations which it could not otherwise meet was to state a travesty of the situation. The whole operation was conceived as a piece of sound financing and had proved eminently successful. The Opposition sat silent and Rose continued his Budget speech in a spirit of triumphant virtue.

As soon as the Canadian newspapers were received in England, the critics of Imperial guarantees, understandably enough, raised the matter in the British Parliament. Sinclair Aytoun, Liberal member for Kirkcaldy, asked whether the Canadian action in using the loan money for the general payment of debts was not in contravention of the Imperial Act granting the guarantee. He also asked for the correspondence bearing on the topic. Monsell, the Parliamentary Under-Secretary, showed himself at a loss for precise information on the point and admitted that the Colonial Office possessed no correspondence which could be published. He stated that on the face of the matter there seemed nothing illegal in the transaction as the Imperial Act did not specify what was to be done with the loan money between its receipt and its application for the purposes of the railway. However, he assured the House that the Colonial Office was studying the question and was aware of the possibility that the Canadian transaction might not be in accordance with the spirit of the guarantee authorized by Parliament.[17] As it happened the Office had received private notice of the temporary appropriation of the loan funds a fortnight before Aytoun's question was asked, so that Monsell's reluctance to enter into a discussion of the matter arose from design rather than from ignorance. On May 10, Rose himself, who was in England on public and private business, left for Lord Granville a collection of papers which had been printed for the Canadian Parliament on the raising of the railway loan.[18] It contained the Privy Council Minute of August 27, 1868. Aytoun's question prompted the Office to an action which was certainly timely, although the manner in which it was undertaken might have been more tactful. A dispatch, resembling in tone the unfortunate communications which Lord Granville sent to New Zealand during the same year, was prepared to admonish the Canadian Privy Council. The Governor-General was instructed to refuse his concurrence in further plans to use the proceeds of the loan other than those "of investment properly so called" and to supply immediately a full report of the transaction. The Privy Council was told that the proceedings were "not ... justifiable"; Rose was singled out in the dispatch for criticism and requested to provide a defence of his actions.[19] This attitude, although certainly appropriate in the circumstances, was to cause displeasure to the Canadian Ministry and had the effect of ruffling violently the then smooth waters of the relations between the Colonial Office and Canada.

The Office had to wait until the middle of June before an official communication was received from Canada about the disposition of the loan funds. Then, in the documents that were forwarded, it was apparent that the Canadian Government wished to state its case in the event that the Imperial Parliament should call for papers regarding the transaction. The correspondence included a long memorandum by the Minister of Finance, endorsed by a Minute of Council dated May 29, 1869. Rose's paper, which follows narrowly the arguments he advanced in his Budget speech, is an extremely able defence of his actions in disposing of the loan funds for the welfare of the Canadian Treasury. He was impelled to invest the money temporarily, he stated, by the very low rate of interest which Messrs. Baring and Glyn offered for the use of the Canadian funds. If this return had been larger, the funds would not have been employed for an intermediate purpose. There could be no question that Canada was not sincere in her desire to build the Intercolonial Railway, for the work, subsidized regularly by the Canadian Exchequer, was now proceeding as rapidly as circumstances would permit. The inquiry in the House of Commons had insinuated that the railway money had been used under the pressure of financial necessity and that Canada had really deceived Great Britain in obtaining the guarantee in the first place. This charge could be easily repudiated by a glance at the favourable fiscal and economic position of Canada. The most important consideration which arose from the Canadian action was one of principle, Rose went on. The trust which Great Britain had placed in Canada by virtue of extending a guarantee must be accompanied by a similar confidence in the Colony's ability to manage any technical arrangements arising out of that guarantee. In other words the provision of an Imperial guarantee should not be incompatible with a full recognition of Canadian fiscal autonomy.

The credit of the Dominion of Canada stands too well to render the recourse to any indirect or unworthy means for the payment of her debts necessary, and she prizes her reputation for good faith too highly to resort to them. Canada has but to offer her own securities to her own people, or on the London money market ... to find whatever means are needed for the maintenance of the public credit, or for the prosecution of enterprises which her people think can be prudently and advantageously undertaken ... she claims the right of making such subsidiary arrangements, whether in regard to the Loan on the works themselves, as her own interests may require.

Her Majesty's Government has hitherto extended a most generous confidence to Canada in connection with all the antecedent negotiations on this subject, and there is no reason to believe that in future that confidence will be abridged. This feeling induced the Minister of Finance to recommend to His Excellency the propriety of making the extraordinary and unwonted provisions already referred to....

It is the duty of Canada to see that the amount of the loan is faithfully expended on a work in which Her Majesty's Government and the Dominion have confessedly a common interest. Of that duty Canada is fully sensible, and it will be performed with the most exact integrity.[20]

Sir Frederic Rogers endorsed Rose's statement of principle with a characteristically vigorous and independent opinion. It was an indisputable fact that there was no statutory prohibition to preclude the Canadian Government from using the loan funds as it desired in an intermediate period. The sole obligation to which Canada was committed was to build the railway, and only a violation of that agreement would afford an opportunity for the United Kingdom to complain of the Canadian course of action.

> I confess I go very much with the Colony--i.e. --viewing the matter as one of mere common sense, and apart from conventional rules. I think the Canadian Govt. was justified in treating the bargain betw. them and the Imperial Govt. as simply this "We the Col. Govt. will at our entire expense and without delay and without costing you a farthing accomplish an object which you consider valuable to yourself, if you on your part will lend us your credit in order to raise on cheap terms 3/4 or so of the sum necessary for that object. "...
> We may think their mode of using such deposits loose or speculative--as they no doubt think our mode of using such deposits narrow and pedantic. But there is nothing in the letter or spirit of the agreement to bind them to adopt our principles in the treatment of their money.
> For it must be steadily borne in mind that it is theirs. They will have to pay the interest and they will have to repay the capital. We are not [making a contribution but only a guarantee]. [21]

It was not until July, 1869, that the Colonial Office received an answer to the critical dispatch which had been sent to the Governor-General. Then Sir John Young replied in the time-honoured fashion associated in official correspondence with moments of crisis. He sent two dispatches, one simply forwarding another Minute of the Canadian Privy Council; the other a confidential letter explaining his own position. The Canadian Cabinet reacted strongly to Granville's attempts to supervise the disposition of the guaranteed loan. They stoutly asserted the principle of cabinet solidarity by refusing to let Rose be called to account for actions which they as a body approved. They stated that the British Government had not raised a single objection to the details of Canada's plan to raise the loan (which was true), and that joint control over the appropriation of the loan money had never been contemplated by the Colony. If it had been suggested, Canada would not have accepted the guarantee on such terms. They regretted that the Colonial Office should show a distrust of Canadian integrity in financial matters so shortly after the achievement of federation. "... your Excellency's advisers feel that it is no light thing at the outset of the new career on which Canada is entering, that any suspicion should attach to its reputation for financial integrity and upright dealing; and they cannot but express their deep regret that ... expressions should have been publicly used, having a tendency to throw doubt on the scrupulous

exactitude of the Government in its financial dealings. "22   They concluded that the
Canadian Privy Council had a constitutional right and duty to manage the loan to the
exclusion of all other considerations and hoped that the Colonial Office would see fit
to recognize this right by recalling the opinions and instructions contained in Granville's
dispatch of June 1. Never has a Canadian Ministry, being found out in an irregular proceeding, shown itself more sensitive and more inclined to fall back on constitutional
dignities!

The substance of this Minute was sufficiently disturbing to the calm of the North
American Department of the Colonial Office, but worse was to follow in Sir John Young's
private dispatch. Young reported that the words "not justifiable" which Lord Granville
had used in referring to the provisional use of the loan funds had caused the gravest offence to the Canadian Cabinet. The Prime Minister, Sir John Macdonald, who could
certainly not be described as prejudiced against Great Britain in any way, although temperamentally somewhat cool towards a Liberal Secretary of State, had described Granville's words as "harsh and insulting." In his opinion the Imperial Government had no
right to use such discourteous language, which would have been out of place even if addressed to the ministers of the pettiest state in Europe. Diplomatic courtesy did not permit the use of such terms, Macdonald significantly told Young. The Finance Minister
had apparently been even more pained than Macdonald, for Rose had at once threatened
to resign. This had been prevented but Young expressed the belief that it would be a
great loss to Canadian public affairs if Rose decided to give up his post through a sense
of grievance. There was considerable public excitement in the country over the episode, Young reported, and Macdonald had gained the support of the entire Canadian
House when he asserted that the Imperial Government had no right to seek any form of
control over the appropriation of the loan funds. All in all, Young said, he had had
"rather a stormy week" over the issue. Personally he felt that the Canadian position
was reasonable, especially since the Government would have been able to give him a
cheque for the entire amount of the loan (and had indeed recently offered to do so) at
any point during the last year. 23

Attacked on the one side by the self-righteous indignation of the Canadian Government, the Colonial Office was also to experience a storm from another quarter.
The Treasury, the "omnipotent guardians of the Public Purse," as a Parliamentary Under-Secretary once described them, had up to this point taken no part in the discussions between the Office and Canada over the temporary appropriation of the Intercolonial Railway funds. Now, in a letter which one of their own officials described as being of "unusual vehemence, "24 the Lords Commissioners of the Treasury plunged heavily into the fray. The Canadian Government was really in the same position as a trustee in a marriage settlement in respect to the funds from the guaranteed loan, My
Lords said, which meant that it was expressly forbidden to apply the funds to its own
"use or advantage." But what had it done? Out of L1,500,000 of the first issue of the
guaranteed loan, the Government of Canada had spent about L1,000,000 "in payment
of the Debts of the Colony." Canada had called the transaction a "temporary investment," but it was scarcely temporary, for the money was now spent, and scarcely an

investment, for there existed no security which could be sold to realize the money. The Treasury had only the word of the Canadian Government as a security for their guarantee, a bond hardly formal enough to sustain a legal claim for indemnity. My Lords concluded that they would never have issued the guarantee if the Canadian transaction had been imagined, and they would not proceed to guarantee the remainder of the loan until the whole sum had been expended on the construction of the railway or placed in securities approved by themselves.[25]

On this dispatch Rogers dryly minuted, "Strong meat for Canadian digestion,"[26] while Granville tactfully directed that the opinions of the Treasury should be sent to Canada without the arguments. At the same time, the Colonial Office obtained the advice of the Law Officers of the Crown, who were quite definite in their opinion that the temporary investment arranged by Rose was not in conformity with the Imperial Act guaranteeing the loan. The Law Officers went on to indulge in a commercial disquisition on the difference between an investment and an appropriation.

We think that it was not the intention of the Imperial Legislature that the money should be invested at all. It was to be appropriated or set aside. The only sort of investment within the provisions of the Imperial Act would be, we think, an investment (if any such exists or can be conceived), the value of which does not fluctuate and which is convertible at any moment without loss. Paying off with the Railway Loan, Canadian Government debts, bearing a high rate of interest, may be perhaps an useful investment of the money raised, but does not seem to us to be an appropriation of it, and we think therefore the spirit and intention of the Canada Railway Loan Act, 1867, has not been complied with.[27]

In the dispatch that was ultimately sent to Canada, based on the opinions of the Treasury and the Law Officers, it is important to notice that the Colonial Office chose a more moderate approach to the subject than that expressed by the other two branches of the Government. Granville, in his opening remarks, was almost apologetic about the effect of his dispatch of June 1. His sole desire in that communication, he said, had been to obtain information from the Canadian Government, and not to fasten a responsibility on anyone. "You will assure your advisers, that I have never had any intention to call in question the financial integrity and upright dealings of the Dominion of Canada, still less the personal honor of Mr. Rose and his colleagues."[28] The spirit of the Act providing the guarantee required that the loan money should be placed in a distinct fund, applicable "in its entirety, and at any moment, to the object for which it is destined." "You will observe," he continued, "that the first of [the Law Officers'] opinions more than bears out the conclusion at which I had arrived." Could this be a hint that the Colonial Office was not prepared to insist on the strict interpretation of "appropriation" given by the Law Officers? Granville ended by saying that Her Majesty's Government had full confidence in the ability of the Canadian Government to replace the loan funds. The Colonial Office had thus steered between the Scylla of the Treasury and the Charybdis of the Law Officers on this question; it had not transmitted to Canada the harsh conditions which the Treasury would have required for a further issue of the guarantee, and it had not been as specific as the Law Officers in their definition of a lawful use of the money.

On the same day on which this communication was dispatched, the entire subject of the Canadian application of the loan funds was aired in Parliament. [29] Sinclair Aytoun, the member who had questioned Monsell on the subject over a month before, moved a resolution condemning the Canadian Government in the strongest terms for misappropriating the proceeds of a loan guaranteed by the Imperial Exchequer for a specific purpose. In his motion Aytoun took the opportunity to criticize the Governor-General for assenting to the operation, and Rose for initiating it. He urged that no further issue of the loan be guaranteed until the Treasury was perfectly satisfied that the first portion had been directly applied to the building of the railway. He also demanded that the statement of accounts regarding the position of the loan should be laid before Parliament, as the Act provided. This, it happened, had not been done for the session 1869. George Ward Hunt, Disraeli's Chancellor of the Exchequer, defended the policy of the late Government in the matter of the guarantee, and he was followed by T. Baring, the head of the great banking house. Baring, who had been nominated by the Canadian Government as one of the trustees for the management of the sinking fund set up under the guarantee, paid an expert tribute to Rose for his skill in the investment of the funds. Gladstone wound up the brief debate in a speech which showed his consummate ability in the technique of reconciling divergent opinion. The House had a right to watch over the execution of acts of Parliament, he admitted, but in this case all the information was not yet available and there was reason to dispute the proposition that the Canadian Government had acted unwisely. He therefore asked the House not to take a vote on the motion since a division might be understood as impugning the good faith of Canada. Perhaps if the original guarantee Act had been more precisely drawn the situation might not have arisen, but he would not like to be thought of as critical of the late Government in this matter! The Prime Minister's plea was heeded and the motion, by permission of the House, withdrawn. A parliamentary inquiry, distasteful alike to Canada and to the Government, had been forestalled.

The Treasury's dissatisfaction with the Canadian use of the Intercolonial Railway loan funds now reached out to influence two other Imperial guarantees that were associated with the arrangements for the achievement of Confederation. One guarantee concerned the transfer of Rupert's Land to Canadian sovereignty; the other was designed to promote the construction of a system of fortifications in Canada. Rupert's Land lay expectant for settlement in the sixties, and one of the first objects of Canada was to incorporate it into the new Confederation. The Hudson's Bay Company demanded compensation for the surrender of its rights and it was the Colonial Office, during 1868-9, which brought the parties together, and negotiated an agreement between them. It was decided that the Hudson's Bay Company would be allowed to retain certain desirable lands in the district, and that Canada would pay to the Company a compensation amounting to £300,000. The actual transfer of sovereignty was to be accomplished in two stages. First, by the Rupert's Land Act, 1868, the Crown was authorized to accept the surrender of the Company's charter rights in western North America. The deed of surrender was to be drawn up at the same moment that the Company received the payment of compensation from Canada, and the territory was to be formally transferred to the Dominion as soon as possible thereafter.[30] To facilitate these arrangements the Gladstone Government promised to extend a guarantee on a loan of ₺300,000 which Canada proposed to raise to reimburse the Company for their surrendered rights.

The other guarantee related to the vital question of the defence of British North America. In negotiations preceding Confederation, held in the anxious months after Appomattox, Great Britain and the province of Canada had sketched an ambitious programme of fortifications for the St. Lawrence valley. The mother country had agreed to strengthen the defensive works about the great bastion of Quebec, while Canada had promised to commence fortifications at Montreal valued at over ₺1,000,000. The money for the latter operation was to be raised by loan in England, backed by an Imperial guarantee. The United Kingdom commenced her part of the arrangement with vigour and three large installations were erected on Point Lévis, opposite Quebec. The Canadian effort was delayed by the country's traditionally dilatory attitude towards questions of defence and it was not until the session of 1868 that an Act[31] was passed authorizing the raising of a loan for the construction of defensive works.

In the year 1869, therefore, the Gladstone Government, in fulfilment of pledges made by themselves and by their predecessors, had to ask Parliament to approve two more guarantees for Canada. Coming hard on the heels of the unorthodox use which the Canadian Ministry had made of the Intercolonial Railway loan funds, these additional guarantees might be expected to arouse strong opposition in the House of Commons. It was a difficult position for the Treasury, on whom fell the responsibility of proposing the guarantees to Parliament. The Department showed that it intended to anticipate criticism from the Commons by making much more stringent the terms on which the guarantees were to be extended to Canada. The Parliamentary Counsel was instructed to insert clauses in the draft bills providing that the loans were not to be raised until needed and that when raised, their proceeds were to be paid over to four trustees, nominated by the Treasury and Canada, who would apply the money to the purposes designated in the statutes. The Treasury also fell back on the services of a clause first used in 1854 in extending a loan to Jamaica: that any colonial act which affected the charge made by this loan on the revenues of the colony would be invalid until confirmed by the British Government. These safeguards, the Treasury hoped, would not only mollify parliamentary opposition to the guarantees, but would prevent a repetition of the troubles over the Intercolonial Railway loan.[32]

The Colonial Office received news of this intention with displeasure, Rogers stating that in the case of the Rupert's Land loan guarantee, he did not see the necessity for extra caution. It would only make more difficult British relations with Canada.

> I confess I wd. much rather have made it a matter of specific agreement between the Lds. of the Treasury and the Colony that [the loan] wd. not be raised till the Company put out their hand to receive it.

If the Address were strictly followed and the money paid <u>at the Transfer</u>, ie. on the day on wh. the Order in Council was issued, I shd. have thought proper certainty could be attained witht. increasing the risk of quarrelling with Canada and throwing our relations with them, or by natural consequence, theirs with Nova Scotia, into confusion--and so undoing all that we have been about for the last two years. [33]

Monsell agreed with him: "... in this case, raising and paying may be made to synchronize. "[34]   Accordingly, Rogers told the Treasury that the Colonial Office saw no need to resort to any special precautions about the Rupert's Land loan guarantee, as the payment of the loan funds resembled a simple business transaction between a vendor and a purchaser.   The mode of payment was a matter between the Government of Canada and the Hudson's Bay Company, in which the United Kingdom had no legitimate concern.   Action such as the Treasury contemplated would have an unfortunate effect on the sensitive regard which the Canadian Ministry possessed for its financial integrity. "Lord Granville therefore thinks that the present occasion would be an inopportune one for raising the question of intermediate custody by inserting in the Act of Parliament a clause to which the Canadian Govt. and their friends will probably object. "[35]

But the Treasury, as any student of British administration during the nineteenth century knows, could be as tenacious in its adherence to a principle it considered desirable as any department in Whitehall.   Brushing aside the Colonial Office objections to the plan of intermediate custody, it sent the Office a draft bill amalgamating the two guarantees and retaining the precautionary provisions.   Rogers, in a long minute, exploded when he received this latest Treasury proposal.   The scheme by which trustees would be appointed to control the expenditure of the guaranteed loan funds was unnecessary and unworkable, he felt.   There was no clear definition of the function of the trustees in the bill and he foresaw with apprehension a long series of controversial exchanges between Canada and the Treasury (with the Colonial Office in the unfortunate intermediate position) before the question might be settled.   He admitted that there was some justification for the Treasury seeking to exercise a closer control over the guaranteed loan for the fortifications, as this would inevitably be a lengthy undertaking, but he resented the Treasury's overruling so summarily the Colonial Office point of view in applying this same principle to the guarantee for the Hudson's Bay Company loan.   For if the Treasury gained its way, the precautionary machinery would undoubtedly relate to both loans.   This might very well prejudice the success of the entire agreement which the Office had so laboriously achieved between the Colony and the Hudson's Bay Company.

For myself, I shd. certainly have [preferred] that the operation of settling the HBC. question, should stand clear of the controversies likely to arise about the Fortification Act.   It appears to me not very wise to hamper an operation which is really of great political importance with respect to the consolidation of the Dominion as an independent or quasi independent power, with what I wd. venture to call an attorney's question--by which I mean, not a question as to what is to be done, but as to the nature of the security to be exacted for the doing of a thing, about the doing of which there is in fact not the slightest reasonable doubt.[36]

The Permanent Under-Secretary of State reveals in this comment a conception of the new status of Canada after 1867 which Sir John Macdonald and some of his collegaues would have endorsed with hearty approval. It helps to explain why Rogers tended to regard the conduct of Anglo-Canadian relations as a problem in diplomacy rather than as an aspect of Imperial control.

Rogers's views controlled the answer which the Office returned to the Treasury. It was desirable to have separate bills for the two guarantees because of the different procedures envisaged in expending the loan funds. The "direction" which the trustees were to exercise was vaguely defined in the draft bill, and might provoke controversy. Finally the provision requiring a suspending clause in any Canadian act affecting the general revenue fund of the Colony was, in Rogers's private opinion, "such a mischief that Canada ought not to be subjected to it."[37] It might mean invalidating an entire act because of the weaknesses of one clause; a result which had on occasion caused great inconvenience to particular colonies. The provision also revealed, the Colonial Office implied, the Treasury's ignorance of Canadian legislative practices. The British North America Act provided for the reservation by the Governor-General, for the Queen's pleasure, of doubtful bills, and as a consequence the suspending clause was rarely used in Canadian legislation. The Office proposed instead a milder version of section 5 of the draft bill which had the effect of distinctly protecting the charges which British guaranteed loans would make upon the general revenue fund of the Dominion without interfering in the drafting of Canadian financial legislation.[38]

Thus the plan of a dual guarantee for the Canadian projects was dropped, and the Government went ahead instead to introduce, in the session of 1869, a Bill merely authorizing the smaller of the two guarantees. Parliament's hostility to the principle of colonial guarantees, together with the lateness of the session, made it expedient to abandon the plan of a large guarantee for Canadian fortifications until a more opportune moment.[39] In the Commons the Rupert's Land loan guarantee Bill was obstructed in its passage by a solid phalanx of the opponents of Canadian guarantees. C. J. Monk, Liberal member for Gloucester, an indefatigable critic of colonial guarantees, moved that the Bill be read a month later, on the slightly inconsistent grounds that the principle of colonial guarantees was unsound and that there was insufficient time to consider this particular measure. Sir Charles Dilke seconded Monk in a speech which revealed his growing impatience with the guarantee system, and Aytoun supplemented Dilke's remarks with a few jibes at the financial incompetence of Canada. Other members purported to speak for the British taxpayer in regretting the number of Imperial guarantees in force at the moment.

In the end, Gladstone was forced to interpose his great authority to overwhelm these malcontents. The House would observe, he said, that the wording governing the appropriation of the Rupert's Land loan funds had been made much stricter than that

used in the Intercolonial Railway guarantee. This was true, for the Treasury had gained its way over the appointment of trustees to handle the funds during the intermediate
period.[40] This point made, the Prime Minister passed rapidly on to more congenial
considerations of high policy. The Rupert's Land guarantee was an example of the type
of financial assistance which it was desirable that Great Britain should extend to her colonies, for it promoted an object of "broad Imperial policy."[41] That aim was to give
the North American colonies financial independence, which meant that they must be
extricated from the old system of relying on Great Britain for protection and support.
Here was an allusion, albeit undeveloped, to the impending changes which the Cardwell programme would contain for the security of the self-governing colonies. The
Rupert's Land guarantee, by facilitating the consolidation of Canada, would prepare
the way for a new imperial relationship. It was not a continuance of financial dependence, but a step marking the end of the period of transition. "Neither in public nor
in private life could one escape the consequences of former errors without some cost.
To put an end to the old system once and for all, the Government made arrangements
with Canada which bound them to ask Parliament to assist the North American Provinces with the Imperial credit.... That was not to be a beginning, but an end."[42]

Monk's motion was defeated in a thin House which actually mustered only ten
opponents of the Canadian guarantee, and the bill passed second reading.[43]   In the
six days which remained of the session the guarantee was perfunctorily approved by the
Lords and received the Royal Assent on the last day of Parliament. Its experience in
the Commons was typical of the manner in which Canadian questions were treated during the busy years of the first Gladstone Administration. Parliament, engrossed in domestic matters, still remained strongly influenced by the anti-colonial theories of the
Manchester School. The Rupert's Land loan guarantee, accompanied by its Treasury
safeguards, failed to create any difficulties with Canada. But it was always a guarantee endorsing a special and uncomplicated type of arrangement, so that the Colonial
Office apprehension was not entirely vitiated.[44]

In the summer of 1869, the dispute over the Canadian appropriation of the Intercolonial Railway loan funds was, however, far from being concluded. The Treasury
still cherished a suspicion of Canadian financial methods--a suspicion from which they
could not rid themselves in considering future guarantees--while the Canadian Government continued stubbornly to justify the course of action which it had taken. The Colonial Office had yet to receive an answer to Granville's dispatch transmitting the Law
Officers' reports, and this reply did not reach London until well into November.[45]   It
consisted of another long and reasoned statement of the Canadian case, this time based
on the strictures which the Law Officers had directed against the Dominion's proceedings. The Canadian Treasury Board pointed out that whereas the United Kingdom Act
of 1867 was silent about the custody of the money raised under the guarantee, the Canadian Act had distinctly mentioned the "appropriation" of the loan. The Treasury had
approved the grant of the guarantee, so presumably they must have been satisfied with
the details of the Canadian statute. The Board went on to consider the Colonial Office
suggestion that the money should have been placed in a distinct fund and used only for

the purposes of the railway. This arrangement could only have been achieved by physical ly putting away the money in packages; even if the funds had been left in a bank, they would have been merged into its general holdings and probably invested. The United Kingdom Parliament surely did not have this sort of an operation in view when they provided the guarantee. The Law Officers had mentioned that an investment which possessed an unfluctuating rate, and was freely convertible, was the only medium by which the funds could have been used, and the Canadian Ministers answered by declaring, supported by a mass of technical evidence, that this was exactly the sort of investment which had been made. The Parliament of Canada had undertaken the responsibility of managing the fund, and the Cabinet's readiness to make good any loss ensured the very conditions which the Law Officers proposed. The final point made by the Attorney-General and Solicitor-General--their criticism of the Canadian action in using the loan funds to redeem a part of the Dominion's general debt--could be answered succinctly by recalling the existence of Canadian autonomy in financial matters. The Government possessed a constitutional obligation to the Canadian Parliament to guard the country's Exchequer from unnecessary loss and this required a complete control over domestic financial policies. [46]

While asserting their unlimited right to deal with the loan funds as they wished, the Macdonald Cabinet at the same time adopted a plan which went a long way towards meeting the Secretary of State's request of July 8. This had been for the creation of a separate fund corresponding to the amount of the guaranteed loan and really represented the minimum arrangement which would have satisfied the Treasury. The Canadian Government now set up a separate account with its bankers for over £1,000,000, which, together with what had already been spent on the railway, more than covered the amount of the guaranteed loan. The Governor-General informed the Colonial Office that his Ministers were very anxious that this operation should not appear as having been done under pressure from the United Kingdom. It must be regarded, in Canada at least, as a spontaneous proceeding! [47]

The Colonial Office, in sending these Canadian papers to the Treasury, virtually abdicated any duty in teaching the colonial Ministry the error of its ways. The clerk who wrote, "The Treasury may I suppose be left to fight their own way out of it," expressed the general feeling of the Department. [48]   The Treasury duly noted this lack of enthusiasm for the cause of imperial financial orthodoxy on the part of their sister Department. It had been present in the Colonial Office attitude, minuted one Treasury official, ever since Lord Granville's dispatch of July 8. In that communication the Office had criticized Canada for not complying with the Imperial Act providing the guarantee, whereas there was a much better argument to be found in the non-fulfilment of the Canadian Act authorizing the loan. This simple statement of Treasury opinion reveals how wide a gulf separated them from the Colonial Office in their interpretation of the revised status of Canada after 1867. The Office would not have dreamt of remonstrating with the Canadian Government on the basis of its non-compliance with an act of the Dominion Legislature. But to the Treasury an argument of this nature was quite "within court" and they chided the Office for not having used it against Canada. "Tha

Department had gone out to battle, if I may borrow a joke, with its breastplate buckled carefully on behind instead of before, and the Canadian Ministry found no difficulty in piercing its buckram doublet."[49]   The concensus of opinion in the Department seemed to be that it was futile to prolong the controversy, and that the Canadian arrangement in setting up a separate account for the loan funds provided a convenient opportunity to abandon the discussion.[50]

The penultimate move in this controversy came from Canada, where once more an alert Opposition, and the occasion of a Budget speech, brought the whole matter into the full light of publicity. On April 7, 1870, Sir Francis Hincks, who had succeeded Rose as Minister of Finance in September of the previous year, introduced his first Budget into the House of Commons. He delicately avoided the subject of the Intercolonial Railway loan until in the evening, after the recess, the persistent questioning of the Opposition forced him to take it up. Then Hincks was nothing if not frank in his treatment of the subject. In answer to Galt and Holton, who asked about the instructions which Granville had sent to Young in the previous year, Hincks replied that there had been no change in the investment of the funds raised under the Intercolonial Railway guarantee. The instructions had then been disregarded, queried Holton? The money was in the same position as it was last year, Hincks replied. He went on to say that "no man was more loyal than he, but he would say that the Government would not be dictated to by anybody as to their actions in a matter purely affecting Canadian interests. (Hear, hear) With these they would deal as they saw fit."[51]   The opinion of the Law Officers was "illogical" and if it had been followed it would have made it impossible to have done anything with the funds.[52]   There was now no difference between the two governments on the matter, Hincks continued, as the United Kingdom had ceased to press their views and had accepted the Canadian explanation. (The Canadian Hansard inserts a "Hear, hear" from Sir John Macdonald at this point.) The Prime Minister, who had entered the chamber at the height of the exchange, supplemented Hincks's remarks by making the startling disclosure that the entire controversy had been touched off by a mischievous private person who had written a letter to the Treasury full of manufactured charges.[53]   Macdonald warmly defended the conduct of his former colleague and close personal friend, Rose, and ended with a type of counter-attack in which he excelled: a charge that the Opposition was being unpatriotic in criticizing the Government on this issue.

It is significant to note that the Opposition was unconcerned about the propriety of the Government's use of the loan funds. In the first decades after Confederation the Liberal party was more assertive of Canada's autonomy inside the British Empire than was Macdonald's group, and on this instance they criticized the Law Officers as severely as the Government for venturing to advise on Canadian financial practices. But they did charge Macdonald with being inconsistent in his reception of Imperial legal advice; sometimes adopting it, when it benefited his interests, and at other times rejecting it. Here, the Opposition referred to a recent dispute between the Dominion Government and the Province of Ontario over respective fields of domestic legislation. Macdonald, as Minister of Justice, had taken strong exception to several acts of the Ontario Legis-

lature, passed in 1868, which touched on subjects within the exclusive jurisdiction of
the Dominion Parliament.   He went to the trouble of obtaining the opinion of the
United Kingdom Law Officers on the measures in question.   This opinion was favourable to the Dominion Government's claims, and after using it unsuccessfully in an effort to compel Ontario to repeal the acts, the Canadian Privy Council advised the Governor-General to exercise his power of disallowance over them. [54]   The whole affair
had concerned subjects of purely domestic legislation, and the Opposition recalled it to
point out that now, in a field where large British obligations were affected, legal opinion from the United Kingdom had been airily disregarded.   Macdonald appealed glibly
to their loyalty, but at the same time was prepared to repudiate Imperial direction if
it suited his interests.   The charge possessed substance but the Liberals were too unskill-
ed in the techniques of public advocacy to use it to inflict any serious harm on the majorities of Macdonald, in his lifetime the consummate master of Canadian political
manoeuvring.

    Hincks's interesting revelations in the Canadian Parliament could not fail to come
to the attention of the critics of the system of Imperial guarantees in the mother country.   The Times, four days after it was made, carried a bald report of Hincks's statement that the Law Officers' opinions had been disregarded, and on the following day
the irrepressible Monk rose in the Commons to ask Monsell if he had seen the notice in
the newspaper.   Monsell had, but the Colonial Office possessed no official information
on the statement. [55]   Thereupon Monk called for papers containing the Law Officers'
opinions and other correspondence, [56] and a little later gave notice of a resolution which
he would move bearing upon the Intercolonial Railway Loan.

    In the meantime, the Colonial Office had not been idle.   Upon Monk's question,
a telegram had been sent to Young asking for an explanation of Hincks's statement, and
the Governor-General's reply arrived in London early in May.   Sir John Young stated that
he considered himself to be still bound by Lord Granville's instructions of June 1, 1869,
which forbade him to give his assent to any further measures regarding the investment
of Intercolonial Railway loan funds.   He had followed those instructions faithfully, he
said, although as a matter of fact no proposition about the employment of the money
had been submitted to him since he wrote to the Colonial Office on October 30. [57]   The
Governor-General went on to say that he had never received an answer to this dispatch
and that he interpreted the Colonial Office silence as meaning that the differences between Great Britain and Canada had been happily adjusted. [58]   Sir John's assumption
would have certainly been correct but for the contingencies of parliamentary questioning!

    The most important document among the Canadian papers was a memorandum by
the Minister of Finance, in which all the Canadian arguments for the soundness and propriety of their transaction were assembled once again.   Hincks made at the outset the
very telling point that Canada had received no reply to the Privy Council Minute of
August 12, 1869, in which the impracticability of acting in accordance with the Law
Officers' opinions had been set forth, and that the Cabinet had therefore assumed that

the Imperial Government was satisfied with its explanations. He went on to lay bare
the dilemma which had paralysed the Colonial Office in its conduct of the controversy
with Canada ever since the early summer of 1869. Hincks submitted that there was a
wide divergence between the opinions of the Law Officers and the instructions of Lord
Granville. Granville had recognized the propriety of "investment properly so called"
in temporarily disposing of the loan funds, provided that they could quickly be made
available for the construction of the Intercolonial Railway. The Law Officers had stated,
in effect, that no investment would be satisfactory unless it fulfilled impossible standards of unfluctuating value and immediate convertibility. Hincks pointed out that
even English securities of the most gilt-edged variety did not meet these conditions.
Rose also, in a memorandum he wrote for the Colonial Office in May, 1870, condemned the Law Officers' recommendations as impracticable and "utterly at variance with
the system of monetary affairs throughout the commercial world." "The system of payment by Cheques and through Clearing Houses, --of depositing money with Bankers, --
the use which it is notorious all bankers make of their deposits, must all be set aside if
the critical interpretation contended for, is to be given to this wording of the Act."[59]
Canada had, in fact, complied with Lord Granville's instructions to place the money
in a distinct fund; in addition the country possessed large bank deposits and holdings of
securities which were sufficient to meet any obligations arising out of the Intercolonial
Railway project. Finally, Hincks stated that Lord Granville had never directly instructed the Governor-General to carry out the opinions of the Law Officers, which was perhaps the last word that could be said on the subject![60] Rogers made the same point in
another way when, in May, he was asked whether the correspondence could be printed
in response to Monk's request. "It is rather disagreeable to print it--as it is not com-
plimentary to the Law Officer's opinions, and brings out into [bright] light the fact that
Lord Granville did not feel confident enough in the validity of that opinion to[demand]
the Canadian Govt. to act upon it."[61]

    After the crisis (if crisis it can be called) had been passed at the administrative
level, the inquiry in Parliament resembled something of an anticlimax. Monk, in
moving his resolution, drew attention to the correspondence that had been printed on
the Intercolonial Railway loan guarantee and recalled the earlier criticisms that had
been made in the House about the Canadian appropriation of the funds. He felt that
the Canadian Act authorizing the loan had been too vague in its provisions for the custody of the money and attacked the Treasury for granting the guarantee on the basis of
an inadequate statutory undertaking from the Colony. He recognized that Rose's proceedings had been competent and successful, but insisted that they were hardly in accordance with the intentions of Parliament when granting this guarantee. His resolution was to the effect that the Canadian Act of 1867 did not fulfil the requirements of
the Imperial Act of the same year, authorizing the guarantee.[62] Monsell replied for
the Government with an unqualified defence of the Canadian action. The zeal of
some members for the security of loans guaranteed by the Treasury had led them to
take an unfair view of the conduct of the Canadian Government. Canada had faithfully discharged its obligations to Great Britain in the matter of the Intercolonial Rail-

way and he was happy to be able to report that it was expected that the whole line would be completed by 1872. The Canadian Act of 1867 went pari passu with the Imperial Act, and both the Law Officers and the Colonial Office were convinced that no divergence existed between the two statutes. In the light of Canada's recent gallant conduct (in repelling the Fenian raids from Vermont in the previous month) he thought the motion injudicious and asked that it be withdrawn. [63] This was done, although one member, who had closely read the correspondence, had the temerity to ask the Attorney-General what he would have considered a "safe investment" for the Canadian loan funds. Sir Robert Porrett Collier gave him short reply: the opinions of the Law Officers about a "safe investment" referred to a "suppositious case" and had no bearing on the present motion. In any event, he did not feel it was wise to publish the opinions of the Law Officers, since they were the Government's private advisers on law, and not on policy. [64]

After the inconsequential inquiry in Parliament, the subject of the Canadian use of the first moiety of the Intercolonial Railway loan funds may be said to have been closed. It had been settled, in the true spirit of British political practice, by a compromise. The Canadian Government's creation of a separate Railway loan fund had satisfied the minimum technical objections of the Treasury and convinced the Colonial Office that the matter might be safely dropped. At the same time, however, the Canadian Ministry had asserted, without contradiction, the doctrine that they possessed the power to make whatever disposition they felt desirable of funds raised under an Imperial guarantee. In the minds of Macdonald and his colleagues the most important aspect of the issue had been the vindication of this principle, an opinion in which they were supported by the majority of the Canadian Parliament. The indirect acceptance of such a rule of action by the Colonial Office contributed powerfully to its ultimate establishment. The Treasury, as the history of a later Canadian guarantee was to show, did not completely mark the implications of the Intercolonial Railway loan controversy. That Department had been sheltered from the full force of the storm raised by this episode, since the opinions of the Law Officers had attracted most of the Canadian criticism. Soon, through the preparations for a later guarantee, the Treasury was to be brought face to face with the insistent and somewhat uncourteous disposition of Canadian financial autonomy.

The assumptions on which a self-governing colony rests a claim for an unlimited freedom to manage the custody and appropriation of Imperial guaranteed funds have never been better expressed than in the words of the Canadian Minister whose financial perspicacity was responsible for initiating the controversy over the Intercolonial Railway loan. In a memorandum[65] which he drew up for the Office in 1870 Rose touched on the broad issues behind that dispute.

> The good faith and credit of Canada have never hitherto been questioned. She has met all her engagements with punctuality, and the only other amount guaranteed by England has been paid off long ago. Her revenues are ample for all her expenditure. The Imperial Government was satisfied of this fact, because before

the Guarantee was authorized an examination was made into her affairs, and the Treasury reported their entire satisfaction with them.

The Guarantee being given it surely ought to suffice, after this admitted ability to repay the Loan, if the money raised is expended on the work as rapidly as its nature will warrant, and it would be time enough to complain when the work is delayed or left undone. Surely intermediate applications by any one, who had sufficient confidence to endorse a Bill for another, as to what the latter is doing with the money would, even as between individuals, be somewhat out of place, and as between Governments should not be made except on the clearest proof of permanent misapplication.

Do any of the many States, whether European or American, who guarantee the Bonds of Railway Corporations, enquire into their application of the amounts deposited during the construction of the Works provided these are prosecuted with diligence and good faith?

It is obviously for the interest of the Surety that the debtor should so employ the money as to derive a benefit from it, rather than add to his liabilities by the amount of interest unnecessarily lost. [66]

II

There were eventually four guarantees authorized by Great Britain for the purpose of facilitating the consolidation of the British North American colonies. The first of these, that for the Intercolonial Railway loan, brought into sharp focus the divergent interests of the Treasury and the Canadian Government in the management of funds raised under an Imperial guarantee. The Rupert's Land loan guarantee, although its form was modified as a consequence of the Intercolonial Railway loan episode, presented no difficulties in its application. The remaining guarantees of this group illustrate significant features. Once again the Treasury tends to give financial considerations a wider interpretation than the Colonial Office is prepared to accept. At the same time the guarantee is seen in its most useful capacity as a means of securing political decisions of the highest importance.

The guarantee of a loan for the construction of Canadian fortifications, projected in 1869, was not submitted to the Imperial Parliament until July, 1870. In the Commons the opponents of the system of guarantees were becoming distinctly restless by this date. They had reluctantly acquiesced in the two previous guarantees on the understanding that they were to be the last presented to Parliament, and yet a third commitment was now before them! It was not surprising, therefore, that the Fortifications Loan Bill was the subject of a motion for the three months' hoist when it was introduced in Parliament. The measure was described as representative of a system which was "pernicious and dangerous, if not futile."[67] Monk's criticisms of colonial guarantees were supplemented by the ironic remarks of William Vernon Harcourt, who asked the Chancellor of the Exchequer to explain his attitude to this Bill in view of the objections he had taken to the Intercolonial Railway loan guarantee in 1867.[68]   Apparently Lowe was not in the House, and amidst cries of "The Chancellor of the Exchequer" Gladstone rose to defend once more a colonial guarantee. He insisted that the House had a duty to approve this guarantee, since it had in effect underwritten the entire fortifications scheme by sponsoring new works at Quebec. The Bill was a means of getting rid of "that demoralizing system, the burden of supporting troops in our Colonies."[69] In the end, the motion was defeated by a majority of forty-eight votes in a House which was certainly not crowded.[70] The Canada Defence Loan Act, 1870, authorized the Treasury to guarantee the interest and principal of a loan of Ł1,100,000 for Canadian fortifications. It contained a clause which stated that the guarantee would not be extended until provisions for "the due payment, custody, and application of the money raised by the loan" had been approved by the Treasury.[71] The insertion of the word "custody" marked a not unforeseeable consequence of the difference of opinion over the Intercolonial Railway loan guarantee.

The early years of Canadian federation were disturbed by the pressing difficulties which the American Civil War bequeathed to the three members of the "North Atlantic triangle"--Great Britain, the United States, and Canada. There was, for instance, the large question of compensation to the United States for Great Britain's failure to observe a strict neutrality during the War. There was also a host of problems requiring settlement between the United States and British North America: the question of American participation in the inshore fisheries of the British colonies; the future commercial relations between the two areas after the abrogation of the Reciprocity Treaty in 1866; the Canadian desire for redress for the losses sustained in repelling the Fenian raids; the difficulties over the navigation of inland waterways. The truculent tone assumed by American spokesmen, official and private, in the years immediately after 1865 continued the diplomatic tension of the war years and made any settlement impossible. It was not until the autumn of 1870 that Hamilton Fish, the American Secretary of State, came to the realization that Great Britain had no intention of abandoning Canada and that the Colony could not be used as a pawn in a larger settlement between Great Britain and the United States. This discovery, although belated, was the first step towards easing the strain under which the three countries had laboured since 1861, and it resulted in the appointment of a Joint High Commission to examine and adjust existing differences. Expediency dictated a Canadian member of the Commission, and Sir John Macdonald became the first colonial minister to be given a part in the negotiation of a major agreement in British diplomacy.

The Commission, which met at Washington in 1871, worked out, partly at Canada's expense, a far-reaching settlement between the great powers. The Alabama and Florida claims were referred to international arbitration; while the Canadian fisheries were opened to American participation in return for a cash compensation, a rather meaningless right of entrance for Canadian fishermen into American waters, and certain tariff concessions. The American delegates resolutely refused to discuss their country's breaches of neutrality in allowing Fenian raiders to assemble in the United States for attacks on British North America. Historically the Treaty of Washington is of immense importance, for it showed that for the first time the United States recognized, as an unalterable fact, the existence to the north of her borders of a British American nation of trans-continental extent. From 1871 Canada became a distinct entity in the eyes of the United States and not just a field for possible territorial expansion. But at the time Canadians, with an immersion in contemporary circumstances that has not been confined to the year 1871, failed to see this significance in the Treaty.   Loud was the cry that Canadian interests had been sacrificed to Anglo-American friendship, and Macdonald himself was unhappy as he put his signature to the document. It soon became apparent that to pass an Act through the Canadian Parliament giving effect to the fisheries provisions of the Treaty of Washington would be a difficult undertaking. Macdonald therefore played for time. He delayed introducing the Act until the session of 1872, not only to let the opposition to the Treaty exhaust itself and its arguments, but also to secure from Great Britain some concession that might smooth the passage of the enabling legislation. The nature of this concession was revealed to the United Kingdom, after appropriate preliminary overtures by Canada, to be in the guise of a large Imperial guarantee. [72]

This proposition was put forward in a dispatch from the Governor-General (now Lord Lisgar) which reached London early in February, 1872. The Canadian Privy Council introduced the request with the delicacy befitting such an important object. Canada had, the Cabinet felt, a just claim for compensation for the expenses which the country had incurred over the Fenian raids. Furthermore, they sincerely regretted that the British Commissioners in Washington had not seen fit to press this claim on the American Government. The Privy Council also refused to accept the British view, expressed in earlier correspondence, that Canada had received adequate consideration for the concessions granted in inshore fisheries. They had hoped that the United Kingdom Government would suggest a plan which would enable the Canadian Ministry to submit the Treaty of Washington Bill to Parliament with a fair prospect of success, but no proposal had been made. A direct financial grant to Canada in lieu of compensation would not be entirely satisfactory. There was, however, another type of assistance which might be suitable.

> There is, in the opinion of the Committee of Council, a mode by which their hands might be so materially strengthened that they would be enabled not only to abandon all claims on account of the Fenian raids, but likewise to propose, with a fair prospect of success, the measures necessary to give effect to those clauses in the Treaty of Washington which require the concurrence of the Dominion Parliament.
>
> That mode is by an Imperial guarantee to a portion of the loan which it will be necessary for Canada to raise in order to procure the construction of certain important public works, which will be highly beneficial to the United Kingdom as well as to Canada. [73]

The projects contemplated were two in number. There was the construction of the transcontinental railway, agreed upon when the Colony of British Columbia, on the

Pacific slope of North America, entered Confederation in 1871. This was to be built
by a private company, but the magnitude of the undertaking meant that the Canadian
Pacific Railway Company would require a subsidy of approximately Ł5,000,000 from
the Government of Canada. Secondly, there was the deepening and improvement of
parts of the Canadian canal system in the Great Lakes--St. Lawrence region. Both these
projects were imperial in scope, the Privy Council stated, since they would assist in
opening the western prairies to British immigration, and would provide a quick "all-
red route" for communications with the Pacific and the Far East. The announcement
of a British guarantee on a loan for Ł4,000,000, to be raised by Canada for these projects, would make a strong contribution towards overcoming the difficulties which
would be raised in the Canadian Parliament over legislation to give effect to the Treaty
of Washington.

After discussion in Cabinet the Canadian proposal was accepted,[74] although the
Gladstone Government balked at the figure of Ł4,000,000 and scaled it down to a more
modest Ł2,500,000. They were specific in the conditions which they laid down regarding the issue of the guarantee. "On their part, Her Majesty's Government will engage
that when the Treaty shall have taken effect by the issue of such Proclamation, they
will propose to Parliament to guarantee a Canadian loan of Ł2,500,000, such loan to
be applied to the purposes indicated by the Council..., on the understanding that Canada abandon all claims on this country on account of the Fenian raids."[75]   Fortified
by this assurance Macdonald introduced the Treaty of Washington Bill into the Canadian
House on May 3, 1872, in a masterly speech. The measure passed second reading on
May 16, after a division in which the Government obtained a majority in every province in the Dominion. This does not mean that Macdonald deliberately over-estimated the strength of the opposition to the Bill, but is rather a tribute to the Prime Minister's parliamentary dexterity and his dominance within the Conservative party. Lisgar assented to the Bill just before he left Canada, in what was to be one of the last official acts of an undistinguished governorship.

In Great Britain the news of the agreement on this latest guarantee was first released by those newspapers which had correspondents in Canada; an unfortunate occurrence which had created misunderstanding about colonial guarantees long before 1872.
To a questioner in the House on April 29, Gladstone was obliged to admit that the guarantee had been arranged by the two governments and promised to table the correspondence regarding it.[76]   The opponents of the principle of colonial guarantees showed
their dissatisfaction with the new commitment to Canada long before the actual measure came before Parliament. They found an occasion in July, 1872, when Parliament
was asked to provide legislation[77] to implement the fishery clauses of the Treaty of
Washington. In the Lords a few peers criticized the Government for giving in too easily
to the Canadian demands, while Lord Salisbury contended strongly that a hazardous
guarantee for several million pounds was a substantial cost for Great Britain to pay for
the Treaty.[78]   On the second reading of the Bill in the Commons Sir Charles Dilke
asked whether, if the House assented to this measure, it would be bound to give favourable consideration to the Canadian guarantee.[79]   Gladstone, with the following com-

ments before him from the Colonial Office, had no difficulty in answering this question. Herbert had said, in minuting the notice of Dilke's question: "Parliament and the people having offered no opposition to the guarantee since they have been aware of its existence, have adopted the action of the Government, and it is only a peculiar class of intellect and judgment that would ask such a question in such a form."[80] Kimberley had added: "The guarantee is not a matter contained within the four corners of the Treaty. Parliament by giving effect to the Treaty does not bind itself to the guarantee. The Govt. is bound by Canada to propose to Parliament the guarantee as soon as the Treaty comes into effect. But the discretion of Parliament to grant or refuse the guarantee remains unfettered."[81]

The terms of the new Imperial guarantee were settled upon by Canada and Great Britain at such a late date in the session of 1872 that it was impossible to present legislation, even guarantee legislation, to Parliament in that year. It was just as well, for further proposals were pending from Canada. On September 20, Lord Dufferin (Lisgar's successor) sent a secret dispatch to the Colonial Office enclosing a further Minute by the Canadian Privy Council on the subject of the Public Works guarantee. The Canadian Cabinet now asked that the guarantee of £1,100,000 which Great Britain had authorized for Canadian fortifications in 1870 be transferred to the new undertaking, together with an additional sum which had been promised for armaments for the Canadian defence system. These supplements would bring the total Imperial guarantee to £4,000,000, which, by coincidence, was precisely the figure suggested in the first Canadian request. It was further stated that the request for a transfer of the military guarantee would have been made earlier, but that the controversy between Great Britain and the United States over the "indirect claims" resulting from the Alabama depredations had rendered it unfeasible to raise any question about the abandonment of fortifications. Now that this dispute was happily settled, it was fitting and expedient to transfer a guarantee for military works to one for the more peaceful purposes of economic development. If the need arose, of course, Canada would not hesitate to erect the fortifications she considered desirable.[82]

After consultations with Gladstone and the Cabinet, Lord Kimberley replied to the Canadian suggestion on December 5. In the interval he had conferred with Sir George Cartier, the Canadian Minister of Militia and Defence, who made a journey to England to explain the Canadian proposals. Cartier's assurances were satisfactory, for the Secretary of State approved the Canadian plan for the transfer of the fortifications guarantee. Kimberley also issued a mild admonition that Canada must not delay her share of the defensive works indefinitely (a hope which has never been fulfilled), and made the statement that the United Kingdom did not favour providing guarantees for public works which would be of primary benefit to the people of a particular colony. However, in view of the fact that Canada was about to be called upon, in the construction of the Pacific Railway, to incur expenditures greater than had ever before been undertaken by a colonial government, the Secretary of State felt justified in recommending the new guarantee to Parliament. He could not, at the same time, suggest that the total sum be increased by £400,000, as desired by the Canadian Govern-

ment, since he felt that Parliament would raise serious objections to such a proposal.
The maximum sum which the United Kingdom would be prepared to endorse was, therefore, Ł3,600,000. Kimberley's final words expressed a useful caution, born in the Colonial Office after years of bitter experience in assisting colonial undertakings: "I have
only to add that it must be distinctly understood that H.M.'s Govt. take upon themselves no responsibility for the success of the Pacific railroad nor of any other works
which the Canadian Govt. may construct with the proceeds of the loans in question."[83]

The Canada (Public Works) Loan Bill came before the Imperial Parliament in the
early summer of 1873. It was an ambitious measure which invited substantial criticism.
Knatchbull-Hugessen, who spoke for the Bill in the Commons, tried to forestall some of
the objections by pointing out that Parliament was not being asked to guarantee the success of the Pacific Railway, and therefore a discussion of routes or of the line's economic soundness was irrelevant. The guarantee would result in a great saving of interest to Canada (over Ł500,000 a year)[84] and would make possible the completion of a
work designed as an object of broad imperial policy. Canada was not really being
weakened by the transfer of the fortifications guarantee, for a country's true strength
lay in its internal resources, its population, and its communications, all of which were
being promoted by this new measure. The critics of the guarantee made great play of
the fact that each of the three measures which had been presented to the House since
1867 had been defended by the Government as necessary to end a discreditable system.
It was now six years since the federation of the North American colonies and guarantees
were still being sought from Parliament for Canada. It seemed as if the old system was,
like Charles II, an unconscionably long time in dying! Dilke was bitter in his condemnation of this latest guarantee. It was simply "hush money" to get Canada to ratify the
Treaty of Washington, he said, and exposed our utter weakness in dealing with the
United States. The plain fact was that we preferred to bribe Canada over the subject
of the Fenian raids rather than ask compensation from the American republic. In spite
of the imaginative flights in Greater Britain Dilke showed himself narrow and pedestrian
in his vision of North American material development. To his mind the Pacific Railway was quite impracticable and would turn out to be a gigantic failure.[85]

Gladstone again replied to the challenge of the critics of the guarantee. He insisted that his references to past guarantees had been sincere and, in fact, well-founded.
The loans which the United Kingdom had endorsed for Canada in 1867, 1869 and 1870
were "the price which we had had to pay for extricating ourselves from a false and mischievous colonial policy, and those guarantees had most vitally and essentially aided
us in getting rid of that policy."[86] Canada had suffered pecuniary losses in the Fenian
raids through her connection with Great Britain, and he felt that these circumstances
gave her a just claim on the mother country. The motion to give the Bill second reading was passed by a majority of over one hundred votes, which showed that the Common's interest in Canadian guarantees was at last becoming more marked.[87]

The Canada (Public Works) Loan Act was more stringent than earlier guarantees
in its provisions for Treasury approval of the expenditure of the loan funds. It stated
that the "application" of the money raised by the loan must be in a manner sanctioned

by the Treasury[88] and that the Treasury need not guarantee succeeding moieties of the loan until earlier portions, consisting equally of both guaranteed and unguaranteed funds, had been spent by Canada on the railway or canals. It was supplemented in the following year by a Canadian measure[89] authorizing the raising of a loan of £8,000,000, of which a part was to be guaranteed by the British Treasury. Another statute passed in the same session, The Canadian Pacific Railway Act, 1874, [90] provided for the construction of the railway. Section 21 of this Act stated that the Governor in Council might apply to railway purposes sums not exceeding £2,500,000 out of the loan raised under the Imperial guarantee.

When, in the summer of 1874, this Canadian legislation was transmitted to England for the approval of the Imperial Government, the subject of the Pacific Railway had become a burning issue in Canadian public affairs. It will be recalled that in 1872 the Macdonald Government had awarded a charter to build the railway to a group of Canadian capitalists headed by Sir Hugh Allan of Montreal. Early in 1873 charges were made that the Conservative party had accepted campaign contributions from Allan's syndicate and the Macdonald Government was forced to submit to a full investigation of its relationship with the Allan interests. This investigation was so damaging that Macdonald and his colleagues resigned office in November, 1873, before a vote of censure could be moved in the House. The new administration, headed by Alexander Mackenzie, proceeded with marked caution to implement the railway project of its predecessors. While in opposition the Liberals had criticized as rash and impracticable Macdonald's promise to British Columbia to begin the railway within two years and to complete it within ten. In office they determined to construct the railway only as rapidly as the finances of the country would permit, taking advantage of the lengths of water communication along the route to reduce the cost of the enterprise. Furthermore, the decade of the seventies was a period of commercial depression in Canada which forced the Mackenzie Government to observe a strict economy in public expenditure. A portion of the line was built as a government work, but the project as a whole went forward with discouraging slowness. British Columbia became restless and appealed to the Dominion Government to fulfil literally the terms of the contract under which it had entered Confederation. The Mackenzie Government, however, refusing to comprehend the national importance of the work, made no effort to allay British Columbia's apprehensions by modifying its railway policy. A serious quarrel developed and hardened between the two governments.

It was against the background of this dispute that the Colonial Office and the Treasury began a consideration of this latest Canadian guarantee. The Colonial Office felt that the legislation authorizing the railway loan was in conformity with the Act providing the Imperial guarantee, but they wondered whether an undertaking about the rate of construction should not be extracted from Canada before the guarantee was granted. A reference to the Law Officers to determine the United Kingdom's capability to impose such a condition was suggested. [91] In making this request the Department initiated a more extended attempt at the Imperial supervision of a guarantee than it had ever intended. The Law Officers of the Disraeli Ministry, Sir Richard

Baggallay and Sir John Holker, gave it as their opinion that the Mackenzie Government was not in earnest over its plans to build the Pacific Railway. They anticipated that the loan of Ł8,000,000 would not be raised, or if raised, would be used exclusively for canal improvements. To disallow the Canadian acts would not solve the problem, however, and they therefore suggested that the Treasury should attach the following condition to the guarantee. It should be required of Canada that the Ł3,600,000 guaranteed loan be <u>entirely</u> expended on the Pacific Railway and that no part of the funds be used for canal projects until the railway was completed.[92]   The Canada (Public Works) Loan Act established no order of priority for the two Canadian undertakings, nor did it fix a division of the funds between them. Indeed, as the Colonial Office later proved, the opinion of the Law Officers had no foundation in law, and represented simply an excursion into the field of policy. True, it was not an entirely gratuitous excursion, but it was none the less unwarranted and improper, an <u>obiter dictum.</u>   There can be no question that it represented a well-intentioned desire to force Canada to use the guaranteed loan funds to fulfil the railway agreement with British Columbia.

The Colonial Office at once realized that the Attorney-General and Solicitor-General had strayed far from the law in making this suggestion. The Department's legal adviser, Sir H. T. Holland, said that as sections 2 and 3 of the United Kingdom Act clearly stated that the loan was to be used for the two purposes of the railway and the canals, the Law Officers were not at liberty to recommend such a qualification.[93] As to the question of imposing regulations upon Canada at all, the Office revealed varying shades of opinion. Lord Carnarvon felt that the conditions which the Treasury were empowered to lay down under the Imperial Act were financial rather than political. He went on, "... on the other hand the [terms] are wide and the case is so peculiar that it may not be inexpedient to take advantage of any power that we may possess, and circes. may take a turn which may make it desirable to exercise them though not altogether in the direction indicated by the Law Offr."[94]   He suggested a division of the loan funds that would allot Ł3,000,000 to the Canadian Pacific Railway and Ł600,000 to canal purposes. Herbert was more cautious than the Secretary of State in his approach to the matter. He felt that the Colonial Office should endeavour to persuade the Treasury against taking up an unwarranted construction of the Imperial Act and that if this failed, the Office should frame its policy without reference to the Law Officers' suggestions. "It would be inexpedient, if we have the power, to interfere with local politics to the extent suggested. But I am not aware that if we followed the Law Officers' suggestion we should inconvenience Canada or help British Columbia. Would not Canada cheerfully reply that if it suited this Government to dictate that the Guaranteed Ł3,600,000 should all be spent upon the Railway they would accept the condition protesting formally against any such dictation?"[95]

The Treasury was asked to consult the Law Officers again on the specific question of whether the guaranteed loan must be used entirely for the Pacific Railway and whether Great Britain might decline to issue the guarantee unless this condition was accepted. The Colonial Office letter concluded, on Herbert's suggestion: "It would of course remain a further question whether if the Imperial Government has the power of prescrib-

ing that the guaranteed loan shall be expended on the Railway, it would be expedient
to exercise any such interference. "96   It was not until November, 1874, that the
Treasury sent the outcome of this further reference to the Colonial Office.   The Law
Officers retained their opinion of the previous July, although they stated that they left
to the Treasury to decide whether it would be politic to impose such a condition. 97
The Treasury apparently did not think so, for they now announced to the Colonial Office that they proposed to divide the Canadian loan in the proportion of ₤2,500,000
for railway construction and ₤1,100,000 for canal works.   They also were prepared to
insist upon the Canadian Government raising and appropriating independently an equal
sum of money for these purposes. 98   These two conditions represented the basic position which the Treasury assumed throughout the entire controversy.

The matter was brought to a head in the summer of 1875, when the Canadian
Government showed itself desirous of negotiating the first moiety of the guaranteed
loan.   The Canadian proposals for raising the loan at first proved unacceptable to the
Treasury and it was Sir John Rose, the Dominion's agent in London, who undertook the
task of arranging a settlement of the difficulty.   Privately Rose maintained excellent
relations with both the Treasury and the Colonial Office during his years in London and,
to a unique degree, enjoyed the confidence of both departments.   Through his efforts
a compromise was eventually reached.   The Treasury in effect abandoned their intention to delimit the proportion of the funds used in each undertaking and accepted an
arrangement whereby the first issue of the guaranteed loan, ₤1,500,000, was divided
equally between the railway and the canals.   Canada, on her part, agreed to spend a
corresponding amount on these projects from unguaranteed funds.   It appears that Canada gained a credit towards this obligation from past expenditures on the railway. 98
The first moiety of the guaranteed loan for Canadian public works was thereby raised
in October, 1875, together with a smaller issue of securities not endorsed by the Imperial Government. 100

In spite of the compromise reached over the conditions governing the issue of the
first part of the Public Works loan, the Treasury still clung to their self-asserted right
to divide the loan funds.   Their insistence on this point caused perturbation in the
Mackenzie Ministry which did not approve either the Treasury's particular apportionment of the funds or their claim to control the apportionment.   They decided to con-
test the Treasury's division of the funds and thus force the matter to a decision well before it would become necessary to raise the second moiety of the loan.   Richard Cartwright, the Liberal Minister of Finance, was in London in the autumn of 1876 and
pressed his views strongly on the Colonial Office.   Privately the Office revealed that
it was in sympathy with the Canadian position.   "As the Treasury are unfortunately
wrong both in law and in policy I do not see how we can fail to support Canada," wrote
Herbert. 101

[The Treasury proposal] seems to me contrary to the spirit both of the Imperial and
Colonial acts, neither of which specify a fixed proportion to be spent on the Railway, and I moreover recollect that there was no intention on the part of H M Govt.

when the Imperial act was passed to interfere as to these proportions.

And it seems to me very inexpedient to meddle gratuitously in Canadian Finance irrespectively of the grievance felt by the Dominion Government at being thus interfered with. I therefore hope that as the Chancellor of the Exchequer, who understands our political relations with Canada, is giving the subject his attention, the condition imposed by the Treasury last year will be withdrawn. [102]

Carnarvon, who was untiring in his efforts at mediation between the quarrelling governments in Canada, also recognized the threatened danger to Anglo-Canadian relations contained in the Treasury attitude. He expressed himself as "content to abandon the use of the argt. which the Treasury proposal wd. put into my hands" because of the importance of respecting Canadian financial autonomy. [103] In writing privately to Sir Stafford Northcote, the Chancellor of the Exchequer, he was explicit on this point. "The question is more political than financial and I think you wd. only make difficulties without gaining any advantage by insisting, as the Treasury have a right to do, upon the particular appropriation of the money. I who have most to gain in any controversy on the Pacific Railway should hesitate to use the power which the Act gives me. I think the Treasury will do well to consider this. "[104] The Colonial Office approach to the Treasury was built around this strong and effective argument from the Secretary of State. It was true that the Treasury was technically entitled to give the guarantee under its own conditions, [105] and also true that the Act providing for the construction of the Canadian Pacific Railway stated that the Governor in Council could apply sums up to ₤2,500,000.for the railway, but these considerations were not material. The Canadian Act simply referred to the maximum amount that could be expended on the railway and could not be used as the basis for a division of the loan. [106] The railway question in Canada was a vexed one and the Secretary of State, although naturally anxious to see Canada spend as liberally as possible on the line, thought that insistence on the Treasury proposal would not necessarily bring about this desired end. The Treasury was therefore urged to withdraw their proposed apportionment of the loan. The Office concluded, "The question which is mixed up with many difficult and delicate matters appears to Lord Carnarvon to be one which should be determined by considerations of policy rather than by the technical and in his opinion somewhat strained construction of the Act of Parliament. "[107]

The Treasury response to this approach was promising, for the Lords Commissioners expressed themselves as anxious to support the Colonial Secretary's views as long as they could be sure they were carrying out the wishes of Parliament in granting the guarantee. It was clear that the Department had in mind the episode of the Intercolonial Railway loan, over which it had received such rough handling from parliamentary critics. Northcote put the Treasury's attitude succinctly when he discussed the case with Carnarvon. "The point to which I am anxious to look is this: Parliament guarantees a loan for certain purposes, and charges the Treasury with the duty of seeing that the money raised under that guarantee is applied to the purposes for which the guarantee was given. If it should, in whole or in part, be diverted to other purposes, Parliament would be justly

angry with the Treasury. "[108]   On the receipt of this reply Herbert at once became
more sanguine about the outcome of the question, although he still confessed himself
in doubt as to the tactics the Colonial Office should employ.

> This is most amicable in tone, and shows that it is only through inability to
> understand the case that the Treasury continues to give us and Canada so much
> trouble. . . .
> The Treasury defend their action by saying that if they did otherwise they
> might be called in question for ignoring the intention of Parliament. Nothing is
> clearer than that it is the will of Parliament as it was the intention in 1873, to
> avoid to the utmost such an interference in Canadian Finance as the Treasury now
> insist upon.
> But what are we to do? I have been several times with Mr. W. H. Smith
> [Joint Secretary of the Treasury], who is clearly overborne by the views of less in-
> telligent persons, and who is very anxious that we should not further press the re-
> quest of Canada.[109]

He and Carnarvon agreed that further pressure from Canada on the topic might be interpreted in England as a desire to avoid the Dominion's railway obligations.

But the Canadians were adamant in their insistence that the Treasury withdraw
their stipulations about dividing the loan. This meant that once again the Colonial Office had to marshal its arguments, familiar as they were, against the Treasury proposal.
"There wd. appear now to be no course open but again to press the Treasury to take the
reasonable view of their function, " wearily minuted Malcolm.[110] But on this occasion the Colonial Office received little satisfaction for its pains. The Treasury replied
with a curt note that they proposed to submit a draft case to the Law Officers concerning the apportionment of the Canadian Public Works loan. They asked the Office to
comment on the draft case and Herbert made a few minor changes in its wording.
"Even as so amended it is a miserable affair and shows clearly that the Treasury have
no decent excuse for persisting in the line they have taken up, " he wrote.[111]

Then followed an occurrence which Herbert, who on no score can be considered
naive in his understanding of the workings of the British public service, characterized
as "incredible. "[112] The Treasury submitted their case to the Law Officers,[113] who
modified their original opinion and upheld the Colonial Office point of view.   The
Treasury thereupon refrained from communicating the result of their reference to the
Colonial Office! This proceeding, which could not help but prejudice efficient relations between the departments, was brought to an end when the Colonial Office heard
privately that the opinion of the Law Officers had been given. Even so, it took an official letter from the Office to secure a copy of this opinion from the Treasury! Herbert exploded at this show of sulking from a sister department. "This is too bad of the
Treasury, but it is useless to point out to them their faults. "[114] Carnarvon agreed:
"It is very tempting to show them up but on the whole probably prudent to suppress
our opinion. "[115]

This neglect in fulfilling their responsibilities to another department was not the only example of the bad grace with which the Treasury received the legal rejection of their views on the apportionment of the Canadian loan. It was not until the Colonial Office had sent several letters, accompanied by urgent Canadian requests, that the Treasury consented to withdraw their condition. In October, 1877, Malcolm complained of their attitude: "The Treasury have acted badly in this matter.... When the case goes against them they simply refuse to do anything or answer any letters."[116] Throughout the winter of 1877 and the first half of 1878 the correspondence dragged on supplemented by numerous interviews between Rose, acting for the Canadian Government, and Treasury officials. In May, 1878, the Treasury partly capitulated by withdrawing their stipulation that Canada expend, pari passu with the guaranteed funds, an equal sum raised under her own surety. This was a decisive concession which Herbert greeted with relief. "... I hope the matter may be practically closed by this letter inasmuch as in their own perverse way the Treasury consent to give the relief required by the Dominion Government."[117] It was not until September, however, that the dispute over the apportionment of the guaranteed loan was settled. Then the solution was found to lie in the same arrangement which had been used in authorizing the first issue of the loan: that the funds raised under the Imperial guarantee would be divided equally between the railway and the canals. The Canadian Government offered this plan; the new Secretary of State, Hicks Beach, endorsed it as a principle of division; and the Colonial Office strongly pressed it on the Treasury. Now that the Law Officers had reported in favour of the Colonial Office contention, said Meade, there seemed no reason why "My Lords [could not]repose under the shadow of these functionaries' opinion in safety." He urged the Treasury to "be like Mrs. Dombey and make an effort."[118] To the Treasury the appearance of the case was changed by the new Canadian proposal for the division of the funds. The Department had always felt that it was acting in accordance with an apportionment made by Canada when it insisted that £2,500,000 be spent on the railway, and now that this apportionment had been modified, it was prepared to follow the Canadian lead and accept the new division. Welby wrote that "we should content ourselves with a defensible position" in order that the Department could appear before Parliament with having interpreted the guarantee Act in a reasonable manner.[119] He recommended that the Canadian proposal be accepted and Northcote followed his advice. After a few minor changes had been made, the Canadian arrangements for raising the second part of the Public Works loan were approved. Another issue of £1,500,000 in Canada Bonds was thereupon offered to English investors in December, 1878.[120]

Thus, over five years after The Canada (Public Works) Loan Act, 1873, had been given the Royal Assent, the Imperial guarantee authorized by the Act had been extended to the major part of the Canadian loan. The delay may be put down to several causes. Primarily there was the reluctance on the part of the Lords Commissioners of the Treasury to abandon a condition which made a certain expenditure on the railway necessary. My Lords were sensitive to parliamentary criticism after the experience of the Intercolonial Railway guarantee, and they felt that the Government must be careful not to lay itself open to the charge of neglecting the interests of the former Crown Colony of British Columbia. However the Treasury was hardly the department to consider this aspect of the question and particularly so after they had seen that both Lord Carnarvon and Sir Michael Hicks Beach felt no apprehension on this point. It is also true that wrong advice about their legal position, and an indiscreet political opinion, were furnished them by the Law Officers. The special and onerous responsibility of the Treasury as the guardian of the British Exchequer also influenced their conduct in the controversy. All these considerations caused misunderstanding between the two departments and between the Treasury and Canada. There remains, however, another factor in the Treasury outlook which was perhaps the weightiest of all in rendering difficult an accord with Canada over the question of Imperial guarantees. This factor was simply the failure of the Treasury to appreciate the nature of the connection which, after 1867, had grown up between Great Britain and Canada. It followed, as an inescapable corollary of this deficiency, that the Treasury did not always see the wisdom of entrusting the presentation of their policy towards Canada to the Department best able to express it. That this was the only satisfactory course of proceeding (and indeed the essential course when political considerations were involved in the relations) was aptly stated by Lord Carnarvon when, in 1877, he brought the dispute over the Canadian Public Works loan before the Beaconsfield Cabinet.

> It seems to me highly inexpedient, on political grounds, to assume any responsibility for, or to interfere in any way with, the financial arrangements of the Dominion; it is ... clear that there is no legal obligation on the Treasury in this matter ... and the only question at issue is one of policy. I do not hesitate on this ground, as responsible for and--as far as may be--acquainted with the political relations (which are as difficult and delicate as they are important) between this country and the Dominion, to urge that the condition should be withdrawn.[121]

REFERENCES

1. See the statement of loans granted or guaranteed to British colonies and foreign nations from 1820 to 1868 which is found in PP, 1870, XLI, no. 219. There are supplementary returns in PP, 1873, XLVIII, no. 36, and PP, 1877, XLIX, no. 274.

2. Minute by Kimberley, July 12, 1871, on Home Office to Colonial Office, July 7, 1871: CO 42/704. See also the caustic observation by E. Knatchbull-Hugessen, July 11, 1871, on Treasury to Colonial Office, July 8, 1871: CO 42/701.

3. Section 145 of the British North America Act (30 and 31 Vict., c. 3) made

mandatory the immediate construction of a railway to connect Halifax with the St. Lawrence River.

4. Hardinge, Life of Carnarvon, I, 340.

5. See Hansard, Third Series, CLXXXVI, 736-64 (March 28, 1867), for the debate on the resolution stage of the Bill. There was a short debate on second reading, April 2, 1867, 972-4. In the Lords there was a debate on third reading, April 11, 1867, 1453-65.

6. Ibid., 744 (March 28, 1867).

7. Ibid., 749.

8. Ibid., 762.

9. Ibid., CLXXXV, 1184 (Feb. 28, 1867).

10. Ibid., CLXXXVI, 753-4 (March 28, 1867).

11. Ibid., 764. The measure (30 and 31 Vict., c. 16) received the Royal Assent on April 12, 1867.

12. 31 Vict., c. 13, s. 27.

13. The correspondence containing the approval of the railway route by the British Government and the sanction of the Treasury for Rose's arrangements, is found in PP, 1867, XLVIII, no. 160; PP. 1868-9, XLIII, nos. 272 and 272-1; SP, 1869, no. 5; SP, 1870, no. 13; SP, 1880, no. 75, 2-10. See also CO 42/665, 674, 682.

14. Memo. by the Minister of Finance, Aug. 27, 1868; Report of Privy Council of Canada, Aug. 27, 1868: PP, 1868-9, XLIII, no. 272-1, 19-20, and in SP, 1869, no. 5, 22-4.

15. Speech on the Budget by the Honourable John Rose, Minister of Finance, Delivered in the House of Commons, Ottawa, May 7, 1869 (Ottawa, 1869), 18.

16. Ibid., 20.

17. Hansard, Third Series, CXCVI, 877-9 (May 28, 1869).

18. These papers were SP, 1869, no. 5. See Colonial Office memo., "Alleged Misapplication by Canadian Government of Proceeds of Guaranteed Railway Loan," June-July, 1869: CO 42/676.

19. Granville to Young, no. 97, June 1, 1869: CO 42/676. Printed in PP, 1870, XLIX, no. 244, 21, and in SP, 1870, no. 13, 5.

20. Memo. by the Minister of Finance, May 29, 1869, enclosed in Young to Granville, no. 56, May 30, 1869: CO 42/676. Printed in PP, 1870, XLIX, no. 244, 1-4, and in SP, 1870, no. 13, 10-14.

21. Minute by Rogers, June 14, 1869, on Young to Granville, no. 56, May 30, 1869: CO 42/676.

22. Report of Privy Council of Canada, June 18, 1869, enclosed in Young to Granville, no. 67, June 20, 1869: ibid. Printed in PP, 1870, XLIX, no. 244, 5-10, and in SP, 1870, no. 13, 18-23.

23. Young to Granville, confidential, June 24, 1869: CO 42/676. The depth of Canadian feeling on the subject is revealed in an exchange in the House of Commons on June 17, 1869: enclosure in ibid. Young defended the proceedings of his Privy Council in yet another dispatch--Young to Granville, no. 70, June 24, 1869: ibid. Printed in PP, 1870, XLIX, no. 244, 10-11, and in SP, 1870, no. 13, 6-7.

24. Confidential memo., "A Note on the Intercolonial Railway Loan Controversy," Dec., 1869, 3: T 1/6922A, no. 19904.

25. Treasury to Colonial Office, June 23, 1869: CO 42/682.

26. Minute by Rogers, June 23, 1869, on ibid.

27. Law Officers (Sir R. P. Collier and Sir J. D. Coleridge) to Colonial Office, June 28, 1869: CO 42/679. There was a supplementary opinion given on July 6, 1869. Printed in PP, 1870, XLIX, no. 244, 22-3 and in SP, 1870, no. 13, 8-9.

28. Granville to Young, no. 129, July 8, 1869: CO 42/676. Printed in PP, 1870, XLIX, no. 244, 21-2, and in SP, 1870, no. 13, 7.

29. Hansard, Third Series, CXCVII, 1445-56 (July 8, 1869).

30. It was hoped that this transfer would take place on December 1, 1869, but the outbreak of the Métis insurrection on the Red River delayed it until June 23, 1870.

31. 31 Vict., c. 41.

32. Memo. by Henry Jenkyns, Parliamentary Counsel, "Canada Defence Loan," June 29, 1869: T 1/6920 B, no. 19614. See also Treasury to Colonial Office, July 5, 1869: CO 42/682.

33. Minute by Rogers, July 6, 1869, on Treasury to Colonial Office, July 5, 1869: CO 42/682.

34. Minute by Monsell, July 7, 1869, on ibid.

35. Colonial Office to Treasury, July 12, 1869: CO 42/682.

36. Minute by Rogers, July 19, 1869, on Treasury to Colonial Office, July 16, 1869: ibid.

37. Ibid.

38. Colonial Office to Treasury, July 21, 1869: CO 42/682. The Colonial Office proposal in lieu of section 5 of the draft bill was adopted in the Rupert's Land Loan Guarantee Act, and used in the two subsequent Imperial guarantees of 1870 and 1873.

39. James Stansfeld (Third Lord of the Treasury) to Granville, private, July 30, 1869: ibid.

40. 32 and 33 Vict., c. 101, s.3, subs. 5. This arrangement was never actually utilized, for the Rupert's Land loan was not raised until three years after the money had been paid over to the Hudson's Bay Company. See below, 102 n. 66.

41. Hansard, Third Series, CXCVIII, 1330 (Aug. 5, 1869).

42. Ibid.

43. Ibid., 1334.

44. The proceedings by which the Rupert's Land loan was guaranteed are printed in PP, 1870, XLIX, no. 315. The Canadian acts authorizing the loan are 32 and 33 Vict., c. 1; 34 Vict., c. 3; 35 Vict., c. 5.

45. The delay was due to the tardy action of Sir John Young in approving a minute of his Privy Council. See Young to Granville, no. 163, Dec. 22, 1869: CO 42/678. Printed in PP, 1870, XLIX, no. 244, 17-18. It was not the only occasion in which Young proved himself dilatory in the conduct of official business.

46. Minute of the Treasury Board, Aug. 11, 1869, Report of Privy Council of Canada, Aug. 12, 1869, enclosed in Young to Granville, no. 112, Oct. 28, 1869: CO 42/677. Printed in PP, 1870, XLIX, no. 244, 12-15 and in SP, 1870, no. 13, 15-18.

47. Young to Granville, confidential, Oct. 30, 1869: CO 42/677. See also Report of Privy Council of Canada, Oct. 2, 1869, enclosed in Young to Granville, no. 117, Oct. 30, 1869: ibid. Printed in PP, 1870, XLIX, no. 244, 15-17.

48. Minute by William Dealtry, Nov. 11, 1869, on Young to Granville, no. 112, Oct. 28, 1869: CO 42/677.

49. Confidential memo., "A Note on the Intercolonial Railway Loan Controversy," Dec., 1869, 5: T 1/6922 A, no. 19904. Section 27 of the Canadian Act of 1867 provided that the guaranteed loan was to be used "for the purpose of constructing the said Railway."

50. Minute, Jan. 14, 1870, on Colonial Office to Treasury, Nov. 29, 1869: T 1/6922 A, no. 19904.

51. Debates of the House of Commons (Canada), 1870, I, 946 (April 7, 1870).

52. Ibid., 947.

53. Ibid., 949-50. This would appear to be a rather wanton example of "political licence" on Macdonald's part.

54. The facts of the case may be found in SP, 1870, no. 35.

55. Hansard, Third Series, CC, 1702-3 (April 12, 1870).

56. The correspondence is printed in PP, 1870, XLIX, no. 244.

57. Young to Granville, no. 79, April 21, 1870: CO 42/685.

58. Young to Granville, confidential, April 21, 1870: ibid.

59. Memo. by Sir John Rose on the Intercolonial Railway loan guarantee, May, 1870: CO 42/695.

60. Memo. by the Minister of Finance, April 20, 1870, enclosed in Young to Granville, no. 79, April 21, 1870: CO 42/685. There is a brief account of Hincks's role in the Intercolonial Railway loan controversy in R. S. Longley, Sir Francis Hincks (Toronto, 1943), 370-2. See also an article by the same author, "Sir Francis Hincks, Finance Minister of Canada, 1869-73," Annual Report of the Canadian Historical Association, 1939, 119-20.

61. Minute by Rogers, c. May 6, 1870, on Young to Granville, no. 79, April 21, 1870: CO 42/685.

62. Hansard, Third Series, CCI, 1844-50 (June 10, 1870).

63. Ibid., 1850-2.

64. Ibid., 1853.

65. Memo. by Sir John Rose on the Intercolonial Railway loan guarantee, May, 1870: CO 42/695. It was slightly revised for inclusion in the papers presented to Parliament: PP, 1870, XLIX, no. 244, 24-8.

66. Memo. by Sir John Rose on the Intercolonial Railway loan guarantee, May, 1870: CO 42/695.
The Intercolonial Railway loan guarantee was the subject of a further difficulty between the Treasury and Canada in 1872, when the Dominion proposed to raise the remaining moiety of the loan. For a time Rose, who was now in London permanently as a banker and official Canadian agent, feared that the Treasury conditions, would "open the old sore." (Rose to H. T. Holland, private, Aug. 7, 1872: CO 42/711.) However he was eventually able to arrange a settlement between the parties and the last part of the loan was successfully negotiated, together with the Rupert's Land loan, in September, 1873. SP, 1880, no. 75, 10-16. The dispute was over technical considerations and raised no questions of policy. The Colonial Office appears to have left the adjustment of the dispute almost entirely to Rose.

67. Hansard, Third Series, CCIII, 1257 (July 29, 1870).

68. See above, 67.

69. Hansard, Third Series, CCIII, 1259 (July 29, 1870).

70. Ibid., 1260.

71. 33 and 34 Vict., c. 82, s. 3, subs. 1.

72. The correspondence presenting the Canadian case is found in PP, 1872, XLIII, no. C-539. See especially Report of the Privy Council of Canada, July 28, 1871, enclosed in Lisgar to Kimberley, no. 149, Aug. 15, 1871: ibid., 9-11. Additional material is found in SP, 1872, no. 18.

73. Report of the Privy Council of Canada, Jan. 20, 1872, enclosed in Lisgar to Kimberley, no. 13, Jan. 22, 1872: CO 42/705. Printed in PP, 1872, XLIII, no. C-539, 13-14, and in SP, 1872, no. 18, 51-3.

74. Gladstone was in sympathy with the Canadian position over the Fenian claims although he apparently did not favour a guarantee as a form of compensation. His correspondence with Granville on this question is reproduced in P. Knaplund, Gladstone and Britain's Imperial Policy (London, 1927), 121-5. See also Joseph Pope, Memoirs of Sir John Macdonald (London, 1894), II, 113. Sir John Rose played an important part in securing the Pacific Railway guarantee for Canada. See M. H. Long, Sir John Rose and the Informal Beginnings of the Canadian High Commissionership, " Canadian Historical Review, XII (March, 1931), 34-6.

75 Kimberley to Lisgar, no. 58, March 18, 1872: CO 42/705. Printed in PP, 1872, XLIII, no. C-539, 14-15 and in SP, 1872, no. 18, 53-4. The British proposals were accepted by Canada in a Report of the Privy Council, April 15, enclosed in Lisgar to Kimberley, no. 95, April 15, 1872: CO 42/706. Printed in PP, 1872, XLIII, no. C-541, and in SP, 1872, no. 18, 55.

76. Hansard, Third Series, CCX, 1934-6 (April 29, 1872). There were further questions on May 6, CCXI, 284; May 10, 603-4; May 13, 652-3, and June 20, 1987-89. The correspondence which Gladstone tabled is found in PP, 1872, XLIII, no. C-541.

77. 35 and 36 Vict., c. 45.

78. Hansard, Third Series, CXII, 942-5 (July 11, 1872).

79. Ibid., 1514 (July 22, 1872).

80. Minute by Herbert, July 16, 1872, on notice of question by Sir Charles Dilke, July, 1872: CO 42/710.

81. Minute by Kimberley, July 18, 1872, on ibid.

82. Report of Privy Council of Canada, Sept. 17, 1872, enclosed in Dufferin to Kimberley, secret, Sept. 20, 1872: CO 42/708. Printed in PP, 1873, XLIX, no. C-702, 5-6.
It is apparent from the minutes made in the Colonial Office on this dispatch that Canada had wished the suggestion for the transfer of the guarantees to come from Great Britain but Lord Kimberley had been firm in his insistence that if Canada abandoned the Montreal fortifications, she must take the responsibility of proposing the new course of action. Minute by E. B. Pennell, Oct. 3, 1872, on Dufferin to Kimberley, secret, Sept. 20, 1872: CO 42/708.

83. Kimberley to Dufferin, secret, Dec. 5, 1872: CO 42/708. Printed in PP, 1873, XLIX, no. C-702, 6-7. The Canadian Government accepted the United Kingdom proposal in a Report of the Privy Council, Feb. 17, 1873, enclosed in Dufferin to

Kimberley, secret, Feb. 17, 1873: CO 42/715. Printed in PP, 1873, XLIX, no. C-702, 7-8. There is additional correspondence in PP, 1873, XLIX, no. C-750.

84. Hansard, Third Series, CCXVI, 1315 (June 24, 1873).

85. Ibid., 1320-4.
Dilke persisted in his opposition to the Canadian Public Works loan for months after the guarantee was granted. Thus when the charges of corruption were levelled against Macdonald's Government over the Canadian Pacific Railway contract, he demanded that the Treasury withhold the guarantee until the charges had been disproved. Gladstone's reply that the loan was raised in the name of the Dominion of Canada and not granted for any particular company or set of Ministers and that the United Kingdom would stand by its obligation, failed to satisfy him. Ibid., CXVII, 1430-2 (Aug. 1, 1873). Dilke returned to the attack a few days later and elicited the reply that the United Kingdom Act was permissive and that the guarantee could be withheld at the discretion of the executive. Ibid., 1527 (Aug. 4, 1873). In the following year, when the difficulties between the Dominion Government and British Columbia over the fulfilment of the railway clause in the Act of Union became apparent, he asked if this disagreement voided the Imperial guarantee. Ibid., CCXVIII, 1179-80 (April 27, 1874).

86. Ibid., CCXVI, 1327-8 (June 24, 1873).

87. Ibid., 1329. The debate in the Lords is found in ibid., CCXVII 4-8 (July 8, 1873).

88. 36 and 37 Vict., c. 45, s. 3, subs. 5.

89. 37 Vict., c. 2.

90. 37 Vict., c. 14.

91. Colonial Office to Treasury, June 25, 1874, in Confidential Print, "North America No. 74," April, 1875, 91-2: CO 807/5.

92. Law Officers (Sir Richard Baggallay and Sir John Holker) to Treasury, July 4, 1874, enclosed in Treasury to Colonial Office, July 8, 1874: CO 42/731.

93. Minute by Holland, July 9, 1874, on Treasury to Colonial Office, July 8, 1874: ibid.

94. Minute by Carnarvon, July 10, 1874, on ibid.

95. Minute by Herbert, July 9, 1874, on ibid.

96. Colonial Office to Treasury, July 15, 1874: CO 42/731.

97. Law Officers to Treasury, Oct. 14, 1874, in Treasury to Colonial Office, Nov. 2, 1874: ibid.

98. Treasury to Colonial Office, Nov. 2, 1874: ibid.

99. Treasury to Colonial Office, July 19, 1875: CO 42/738. Treasury to Colonial Office, Aug. 11, 1875: ibid. Treasury to Colonial Office, Oct. 19, 1875: ibid. See also Carnarvon to Officer Administering the Government of Canada, no. 209, Aug. 24, 1875: ibid.

100. SP, 1880, no. 75, 19-21.

101. Minute by Herbert, Feb. 21, 1877, on Dufferin to Carnarvon, telegram, Feb. 19, 1877: CO 42/748.

102. Minute by Herbert, Dec. 7, 1876, on Cartwright to Carnarvon, Nov. 21, 1876: CO 42/747.

103. Minute by Carnarvon, Dec. 18, 1876, on ibid.

104. Carnarvon to Northcote, private, Jan. 5, 1877: PRO 30/6/7.

105. Section 2 of 36 and 37 Vict., c. 45.

106. Herbert always maintained that clause 21 of the Canadian Pacific Railway Act did not prescribe a distinct apportionment of the loan between the two objects. The clause stated "not that ₤2,500,000 shall be spent on the Railway, but that not more than ₤2,500,000 shall be so spent. It is an entirely different thing for the Treasury to require that not less than ₤2,500,000 shall be so spent." (Minute by Herbert, Jan. 27, 1877, on Treasury to Colonial Office, Jan. 24, 1877: CO 42/752.)

107. Colonial Office to Treasury, Jan. 11, 1877: CO 42/747.

108. Northcote to Carnarvon, private, Jan. 8, 1877: PRO 30/6/7.

109. Minute by Herbert, Jan. 27, 1877, on Treasury to Colonial Office, Jan. 24, 1877: CO 42/752.

110. Minute by Malcolm, Feb. 20, 1877, on Dufferin to Carnarvon, telegraph, Feb. 19, 1877: CO 42/748.

111. Minute by Herbert, March 30, 1877, on Treasury to Colonial Office, March 28, 1877: CO 42/752.

112. Minute by Herbert, June 29, 1877, on Rose to Herbert, private, June 22, 1877: ibid.

113. Now Sir John Holker and Sir Hardinge S. Giffard.

114. Minute by Herbert, July 12, 1877, on Treasury to Colonial Office, July 2, 1877: CO 42/752.
On a later occasion, perhaps bearing in mind this episode in 1877, he was to write, "There is no hope of teaching the Treasury manners." Minute by Herbert, Jan. 13, 1880, quoted in Hall, The Colonial Office, 33.

115. Minute by Carnarvon, July 13, 1877, on Treasury to Colonial Office, July 2, 1877: CO 42/752.

116. Minute by Malcolm, Oct. 15, 1877, on Rose to Carnarvon, Oct. 13, 1877: ibid.

117. Minute by Herbert, May 30, 1878, on Treasury to Colonial Office, May 24, 1878: CO 42/754.

118. Meade to R. E. Welby (Treasury), private, Sept. 4, 1878: T 1/7720 A, no. 21033.

119. Minutes by Welby, Sept. 7, 11, on Colonial Office to Treasury, Sept. 4, 1878: ibid.

120. SP, 1880, no. 75, 23-8. The Treasury acceptance of the Canadian position is contained in Treasury to Colonial Office, Sept. 26, 1878: CO 42/754. See also Colonial Office to Treasury, Dec. 5, 1878; Colonial Office to Treasury, Dec. 21, 1878: T 1/7720 A, no. 21033.

121. Memo. by Carnarvon, "Canada Guaranteed Loan--(£3,600,000)," Dec. 5, 1877, Confidential Print, "North America No. 96": PRO 30/6/89.
The Canada (Public Works) Loan Act, 1873, embodied the last Imperial guarantee extended to a Canadian loan. In the summer of 1879, when the Conservatives returned to power, Macdonald and two of his colleagues visited England with the hope of obtaining a guarantee on a further loan for the Canadian Pacific Railway. Hicks Beach and Northcote refused to entertain the proposal, however. See E. M. Saunders, ed., Life and Letters of the Rt. Hon. Sir Charles Tupper (London, 1916), I, 275. See also Hansard, Third Series, CCXLVII, 173 (June 19, 1879) and CCXLIX, 820-1 (Aug. 12, 1879).

CHAPTER FOUR

THE GOVERNOR-GENERAL AND THE DISALLOWANCE OF PROVINCIAL ACTS

"If there is one respect in which I should have thought Canada especially fortunate it is in the existence of an external, impartial, and benevolent authority, to whom reference can be made with respect to disputes between the central and the local Legislatures." Lord Dufferin, 1874

THE STRUCTURE of Canadian federalism was planned in the closing months of the American Civil War. That momentous conflict, arising from the necessity of reaffirming the supremacy of the National Government in the American union, could not fail to impress the makers of the Canadian constitution as they sat in council at Quebec. Determined to profit from the tragic lessons of the American struggle, they projected a federal system which would assert, beyond all doubt, the hegemony of the central authority. Some of them, indeed, believed that the union of the British North American colonies should be a legislative one, and would have been happy to see the local assemblies of the various colonies merged into a general legislature. But years of separate existence had left their mark and the divisions of race and language were too pronounced for legislative union to be practicable. It was necessary to reconcile elements that were both diverse and stubbornly independent: a consummation which could only be achieved through federation. In the minds of Macdonald and his colleagues, however, federalism was to be of a type in which there would exist no opportunity for the appearance of centrifugal tendencies. The power of the Central Parliament was to be all-pervading throughout the union except in fields especially reserved for provincial control. This was the major principle governing the distribution of powers in the Canadian constitution. It was recognized and endorsed by Edward Cardwell when, in 1864, the confederation plan was first broached to the United Kingdom.

... it appears to her Majesty's Government that precautions have been taken, which are obviously intended to secure to the Central Government the means of effective action throughout the several Provinces; and to guard against those evils which must inevitably arise, if any doubts were permitted to exist as to the respective limits of Central and Local authority. They are glad to observe that, although large powers of legislation are intended to be vested in local bodies, yet the principle of Central control has been steadily kept in view. The importance of this principle cannot be over-rated. Its maintenance is essential to the practical efficiency of the system, --and to its harmonious operation, both in the general administration, and in the Governments of the several provinces.... [1]

---

1. For references to chapter IV see pages 127-32.

The supremacy of the Central Government in the Canadian federal structure was obtained primarily through the distribution of powers between the nation and the provinces. The provinces were allotted a modest list of local and private subjects of legislation; the Dominion was granted all the important functions of statehood, and, in addition, the remaining undefined powers, the residual powers of the British North America Act, were declared to lie with the National Government. Sir John Macdonald, with his confessed predilection for a unitary state, described in high satisfaction the consequences of this arrangement.

> We have strengthened the General Government. We have given the General Legislature all the great subjects of legislation. We have conferred on them, not only specifically and in detail, all the powers which are incident to sovereignty, but we have expressly declared that all subjects of general interest not distinctly and expressly conferred upon the local governments and local legislatures, shall be conferred upon the General Government and Legislature. We have thus avoided that great source of weakness which has been the cause of the disruption of the United States. We have avoided all conflict of jurisdiction and authority.... we have in fact ... all the advantages of a legislative union under one administration, with, at the same time the guarantees for local institutions and for local laws, which are insisted upon by so many in the provinces....[2]

The authority of the Dominion was still further increased through its constitutional authority to appoint and remove the Lieutenant-Governor in each province. This officer was to act as the agent of the Dominion in provincial affairs, just as he had represented the interests of the Imperial Government in the days when each province was a separate colony. The British North America Act gave him power to confer or refuse assent to provincial bills or reserve them for the consideration of the Federal Government. In addition, as if this supervision were not enough, the Act permitted the Dominion Government to disallow provincial laws in the same manner as the United Kingdom had previously been able to withhold assent from the legislation of the North American colonies. The principles on which federal disallowance was to be exercised were not defined in the British North America Act, but it appears evident that the framers of the constitution intended the power to be a further means of effecting the subordination of the provincial legislatures. Under the new federal system they were to be relegated, in effect, to the status of municipal councils. In practice provincial laws were disallowed at Ottawa on the grounds that they were beyond the competence of the local legislature to enact, or were prejudicial to the rights of citizens in other areas, or departed from sound principles of legislation. Assisted by the power of disallowance the Dominion Government was to be enabled to enforce its dominance in the Canadian federation; its legislation serving as a model for the emulation of the provinces, its restraining hand ready to discipline recalcitrant sections, and its policies to prevail in cases where divergence occurred with local statutes. Macdonald clearly conceived the role of the General Government in the federation as that of a mentor to the provinces, and during the two decades of his premiership he sought to fulfil that aim.[3]

This view of the purposes to be achieved from the use of the power of disallowance in Canada was not, at first, held by the Colonial Office. Apart entirely from the legal considerations involved, the Colonial Office attitude towards the question reveals a conception of the nature of Canadian federalism which differed remarkably from Macdonald's. The Department, although recognizing the supremacy of the Dominion Government over the provinces, was keenly aware of the importance of minority rights in British North America and of the dangers of legislation by powerful majorities. Bred in the confident laissez-faire tradition of mid-Victorian England, the administrators of Downing Street abhorred the possibility of interference by a strong authority in the affairs of a weaker. The federal power of disallowance was an obvious instrument by which oppressive and destructive influence could be exercised in the Canadian federation. In the hands of the Imperial Government disallowance had been for the North American colonies an example of impartial and disinterested supervision, and it must continue to retain that character under the new Canadian constitution. To that end the Office endeavoured to fix the ultimate responsibility for the disallowance of provincial acts, not upon the Canadian Privy Council representing the majority party in the Federal Parliament, but upon the Secretary of State himself. Forced to recede from this interpretation of the British North America Act the Department next sought to uphold the Governor-General as the final authority for the invalidation of provincial measures. Exercised on his personal responsibility the power of disallowance might become a stabilizing factor in the Canadian constitution, maintaining intact the defined fields of jurisdiction of the federal and provincial legislatures. The Mackenzie Government, however, opposed this attempt to provide the Governor-General with additional duties, raising against it the doctrines of colonial autonomy in domestic concerns and full ministerial responsibility. In the end, after a controversy in which the Office did not distinguish itself, the Canadian point of view was vindicated. The Department abandoned forever the hope that the Governor-General might act as a sort of balance wheel in the Canadian constitution and regretfully accepted the unchallenged right of the Central Executive to review provincial legislation.

The federal power to disallow provincial statutes was set down in a cumbersome fashion in the British North America Act. The Quebec Resolutions merely stated that any bill passed by a local legislature would be subject to disallowance by the Governor-General within one year after its passing.[4] In the Act itself a different form was used. After describing the procedure by which the Imperial Government might disallow Canadian measures or assent to reserved bills, the Act went on: these provisions "shall extend and apply to the Legislatures of the several Provinces as if those Provisions were here re-enacted and made applicable in Terms to the respective Provinces and the Legislatures thereof, with the Substitution of the Lieutenant-Governor of the Province for the Governor General, of the Governor General for the Queen and for a Secretary of State, of One Year for Two Years, and of the Province for Canada."[5] In other words the Dominion was to take the place of the United Kingdom Government in exercising the power of disallowance for acts of the Canadian provinces.

Macdonald, as first Minister of Justice in the Canadian Government, defined initially the procedure for the disallowance of local laws. In a memorandum, dated
June, 1868, which was circulated to all the provincial administrations, he drew attention to the fact that the power of disallowance was now in the hands of the Dominion.
As a consequence it was likely to be more frequently employed than when the Imperial
Government had exercised it over the separate autonomous colonies. Under the new
federal system some provincial laws would inevitably turn out to be unconstitutional,
or the different legislatures would clash in a field of concurrent activity. It would be
the duty of the Minister of Justice in the Federal Cabinet to examine all provincial legislation and to comment on measures that were objectionable from one cause or another. On his recommendation the legislation might be disallowed immediately by the
Canadian Privy Council, or referred back to the provinces for amendment or repeal;
failing which, disallowance would be finally signified. 6

Early in the following year, Macdonald, who had been thinking about the difficulties associated with the exercise of the power of disallowance, put some of his observations on paper for the Governor-General. There were several practical problems
involved in the question, he wrote. What was to be done, for instance, with provincial measures touching on reserved subjects which under the Governor-General's Instructions must be referred to London for approval or disallowance? For example, the
provinces possessed power to legislate in ways that might be contrary to British treaty
obligations, or might interfere with the royal prerogative, or infringe on the rights of
British subjects living outside the country. Ordinarily bills which emanated from the
Dominion Legislature affecting these subjects would be sent to London for the consideration of the Secretary of State and the signification of the Queen's pleasure. Was
the same procedure to be followed in the case of provincial acts, where the Governor-
General was empowered to represent the Queen? There was also a more fundamental
problem. What would become of the Dominion's supremacy in the Canadian constitution if its Privy Council became composed of "states rights" advocates, who might
refuse to advise the Governor-General to disallow measures that encroached on the federal powers? To Macdonald, this possibility, although too fearful to contemplate, was
none the less real during the first formative years of the Dominion's history. Every member of Parliament at Ottawa owed his position to the standing he possessed in a particular community and might conceivably look more to sectional than to general interests.
A strong central government was therefore essential until the new Confederation was
firmly established. "This is more especially the case now, when the General Government is new, and the Dominion has no associations, political or historical, connected
with it. We are all yet mere provincial politicians. By and bye it is to be hoped that
some of us may rise to the level of National Statesmen. "7

Sir John Young pondered quietly over these matters until circumstances provided
him with an opportunity to bring the subject before the notice of the Imperial Government. During its last session the Legislature of Ontario had passed certain acts which
Macdonald felt were ultra vires. He recommended their disallowance but asked the

Governor-General to refer the bills to the Crown Law Officers to see if they supported his view. Young complied, at the same time raising with the Colonial Office the more general problems which Macdonald had outlined. He requested advice on two specific points connected with the power of disallowance. What was to be done when a provincial act concerned a reserved subject? And what would be the duty of a Governor-General if he disagreed with his Privy Council over the validity of a provincial measure? The British North America Act was silent on both these questions. The Governor-General went on to say that he supposed that he should exercise the power of disallowance only on advice from his Privy Council, but he would appreciate definite instructions on this score. Young rather deprecated the idea of the Federal Executive disallowing provincial measures at all, for he proposed the establishment of a court of last resort in Canada, like the Supreme Court of the United States, which would constitute a tribunal of judicial review for the Dominion. Like Macdonald, the Governor-General recognized the difficulties that faced the young Dominion in defining the range of powers between the federal and provincial legislatures. The problem was at its most critical stage in the first years of Confederation, when the National Government possessed "no buttresses of prestige and tradition."[8] It was the same issue which had caused the Civil War in the United States, although the Governor-General added hastily that there was much more underlying amity between the provinces in Canada than there had ever been in the American union. By degrees, he felt, the provincialism that marked Canadian life would pass away and the country would become safe from the danger of sectional quarrels.[9]

Sir Frederic Rogers, when he received these dispatches, directed that the question of the constitutionality of the Ontario acts should immediately be placed before the Law Officers. "It is very unfortunate that these questions of jurisdiction should arise so soon and very desirable, that the Law Officers should give a clear and good opinion--to settle the question if possible.... It is most desirable that their opinions shd. be such as to carry weight, and, I shd. say, if their opinions are properly against the Provincial Legs. so much the better."[10] Young's request for instructions about the exercise of the power of disallowance, on the other hand, was a matter which the Colonial Office could answer without recourse to the Law Officers. The Permanent Under-Secretary thereupon gave the headings under which a dispatch to Canada should be prepared. Sir John Young must be told that the reserved subjects of clause 7 of his Instructions rested "on grounds of Imperial Policy" and that therefore he was not at liberty to assent to provincial acts touching them or to allow any Lieutenant-Governor to sanction such measures. Ordinarily the Governor-General would follow the advice of his Privy Council over disallowance; this would be the rule in all cases where the Privy Council advised him that an act was illegal or unconstitutional. If he were asked to sanction an act which he felt to be illegal, he was to refer home for advice. The same course would be followed if he felt an act to be unconstitutional, although it would be "impossible to relieve him from the duty of judging with respect to each particular case whether the objection to the act was sufficiently grave as, under all circumstances, to warrant a refusal to act at once on the advice tendered him," Rogers wrote.[11]   The

Permanent Under-Secretary went on to pour cold water on Young's proposal for a supreme court in Canada to decide constitutional questions. The true concern of the Colonial Office, he expressed privately, was to see that the rights of each element in the
Canadian federation were protected by the judicious exercise of Imperial influence.

[I see] no reason for the establishment of a Court of Law to pronounce on the
validity of laws passed by the Central or Provincial legrs. Any question of this kind
will of course be entertained and decided by Local Courts subject to an appeal to the
Judl. Committee of the P.C. and it does not appear in what respect this mode of
determination is inadequate or unsatisfactory.

With regard to Sir. J.A.M's apprehension of a "state rights" ministry I do not
think that the Home Govt. can undertake to protect Canada agn. such a possibility.
To do this wd. be to meddle in local politics. We ought only to see fair play and
shd. be very jealous of a step wh. wd. impair our reputation for fairness.

I think however that this is quite consistent with reading the Act of Parl. as intended to establish a strong central power. . . .

Only we must remember that the Provincial rights--the result of a careful com-
promise--are very real and within their limits cannot be shuffled aside without un-
fairness. [12]

The draft dispatch embodying these views was transmitted to the Law Officers for
their comments. They pronounced it "perfectly right and proper"[13] and it was then
sent out to Canada.[14] The tenor of the instructions, sufficiently vague as to allow an
easy adaptation to particular circumstances, met with approval from Macdonald and
his colleagues. The principles on which the Governor-General's action was to be based
were not questioned in any way. Indeed, the document was communicated to the Lieutenant-Governors of the provinces as a guide in the performance of their duties. Macdonald's favourable attitude may have been engendered by his hearing, at the same
time, that the Law Officers shared his opinion that the Ontario acts were beyond the
competence of the Legislature to enact. Fortified with this Imperial encouragement he
proceeded to disallow the measures with celerity, thus gaining an incidental pleasure
in frustrating the pretensions of his namesake, John Sandfield Macdonald. The important point is that in 1869 Sir John accepted the possibility of some Imperial supervision
in the exercise of the Dominion's power of disallowance. Six years later he was to repudiate this claim completely when it was reaffirmed by the Colonial Office.

Thus disposed of, the subject of the responsibility for the disallowance of provincial acts slumbered for some years. It was aroused through a controversy which disturbed Canada in the early seventies. The question of minority rights under a state educational system--the persistent casus belli in Canadian political history--came into
prominence in New Brunswick in the first decade of the Dominion's existence. In 1871
the Legislature of that Province, in approving a new method of rating taxpayers for the
payment of school fees, provided that the entire revenue from these exactions would
henceforth accrue to the state schools. Parochial schools, of which there existed many

in the Province, were denied a share of these funds. This meant that Catholic parents, if they wished to send their children to a religious institution, were forced to support, through taxes and contributions, two educational systems. The minority protested this change on the grounds that it destroyed privileges they had held in 1867, and appealed to the Dominion Cabinet to induce the New Brunswick Government to modify its policies. The whole subject was naturally brought up in the House of Commons, where the general sentiment was sufficiently critical of New Brunswick to pass a resolution asking for the opinions of the Crown Law Officers on the provincial legislation, with a view towards its disallowance. [15]

The Colonial Office referred the whole question, with its mass of accompanying memoranda and petitions, to the Law Officers late in 1872. The Attorney-General and Solicitor-General agreed with the Canadian Cabinet that the school laws were within the competence of the New Brunswick Legislature to enact and that the case was not one in which Imperial intervention or Dominion remedial legislation would be justified. [16] The Colonial Office, in the course of sounding legal opinion in England on the question, asked the Registrar of the Privy Council whether, under the circumstances, the Judicial Committee would consider granting the minority leave to appeal from a decision of the New Brunswick courts. The answer was supplied by Henry Reeve, the brilliant littérateur, leader writer for The Times and editor of the Edinburgh Review, who was for over forty years Registrar to the Judicial Committee of the Privy Council. Reeve, while admitting that the case could come before the Privy Council on appeal from Canada, stated emphatically that the Privy Council had no authority to intervene directly in the controversy. He went on to provide a rigid interpretation of the section on provincial disallowance in the British North America Act: "It appears ... that as the power of confirming or disallowing Provincial Acts is vested by the Statute in the Governor-General of the Dominion of Canada, acting under the advice of his constitutional advisers, there is nothing in this case which gives to Her Majesty in Council any jurisdiction over the question." [17]   The statement that the Governor-General could exercise the power of disallowance only on advice was obviously at variance with the views Rogers had laid down in 1869, but the discrepancy escaped the Office at this time. Reeve's letter was sent without comment to Canada in support of the assertion that the New Brunswick school case could not be submitted to the Privy Council for arbitration. This action was an error which was to plunge the Department into grave difficulties before two years had passed.

The New Brunswick Legislature, following the passing of the Act of 1871, gave further provocation to French and Catholic opinion throughout the Dominion by enacting several measures to legalize the assessments made under the original Act. Thereupon, in May, 1873, the Canadian House of Commons carried a resolution, against the wishes of the Government, asking the Governor-General to disallow these additional educational acts of the Province of New Brunswick. The original measure had been declared to be within the limits of provincial powers, but if the later acts could be pronounced invalid the machinery necessary for putting the new school system into operation would be destroyed. Lord Dufferin, when he transmitted this resolution to the Colonial Secretary, stated that he had followed his Ministers' advice in determining not to yield to the popular clamour to disallow the acts. He had authorized Sir John Macdonald to announce this decision to the House, at the same time telling the members that the question would again be submitted to the Imperial Government. [18]

It was not until the receipt of this dispatch that the Colonial Office began to consider thoroughly the importance and complexity of the problem of provincial disallowance. How far was the Governor-General bound to act on the advice of his responsible Ministers in cases of this kind? Could the Secretary of State decline to give instructions to a Governor who undertook to exercise the power of disallowance on his own initiative? Suppose the Cabinet had asked Dufferin to disallow the New Brunswick acts and he had refused? The British North America Act provided no illumination regarding these aspects of the question. Robert G. W. Herbert, who had succeeded Rogers as Permanent Under-Secretary in 1871, expressed his displeasure over the fact that the matter had been referred to the Office in such controversial circumstances. The manner in which the question had been submitted to the United Kingdom was not in accordance with the practice of responsible government and would make more difficult the elucidation of the principles underlying the use of the power of disallowance.

> I am inclined to think that the proceeding described ... in Lord Dufferin's despatch was not correct, and he should not have allowed Sir J. A. Macdonald to make that announcement to the House. If the Ministers were prepared to set at nought the Resolution of the House, and to decline (as they appear to have done) to advise the Governor as directed by the Resolution, that was a matter for them to settle with the House. And if they had advised Lord Dufferin to disallow the Acts he might then, I think, properly have requested advice from home as to whether it was right and constitutional for him to do so.
>
> I presume that he wished to help his Ministers out of a difficulty; but if (as would appear consistent with the general rules of Responsible Government, namely that Ministers shall be responsible for advising the Governor on all questions of importance and not of Imperial interests) it was their duty to tender advice to him on this case (although the Act does not say Governor-General in Council). I think the Secretary of State should not give an opinion, but tell Ld. Dufferin that he should have recourse to his Ministers. [19]

The Secretary of State, Lord Kimberley, approached the question of provincial disallowance from the standpoint of a firm belief in laissez-faire ideas. There must be no special intervention by the Colonial Secretary in Canadian domestic affairs; in this problem, as in others, the Governor-General must be advised by his Ministers in Canada. Kimberley went on to state that if the acts could be shown to be within the competence of the New Brunswick Legislature, then the Governor-General should be advised about them by the New Brunswick Cabinet--an ingenuous suggestion which revealed some confusion on his part about the principle of legislative review by the central authority in a federal state. He concluded with the uncompromising assertion that if British interference in the workings of the Canadian federation was fraught with danger, Dominion interference in provincial matters was an even greater evil: "If the Dominion Parliament and the Dominion Ministers are to advise the Govr. Genl. as to all Provincial Bills, it would follow that the Dominion Parliament would thus get the control of all matters of provincial Legislation, whereas the Confederation Act limited the powers of the Dominion Parliament expressly to certain subjects."[20] Here was a new view of the distribution of powers in the Canadian federal structure; a view which had implications for the problem of disallowance.

Herbert drew up a list of questions for the consideration of the Law Officers, for it had been determined to accept the Canadian suggestion and refer the New Brunswick school legislation to them a second time. On this occasion the Attorney-General and Solicitor-General were also asked what the action of the Governor-General should be if valid local acts were presented to him for disallowance. The Office pointed out that if the Governor-General was to be advised on all provincial acts by Ministers representing the majority group in the Dominion Parliament, it would follow that the General Legislature would become supreme even in fields of provincial jurisdiction. This would mean that the powers allotted to the provinces in section 91 of the British North America Act might be set aside. Would it therefore be proper for the Governor-General to refer to London for the opinion of the Colonial Secretary in a case where he disagreed with his Ministers?[21]

In the course of this reference the Department suggested that an important analogy to the Governor-General and the power of disallowance existed in the Queen's right to approve or reject colonial laws. In constitutional theory Her Majesty exercised this power at her own discretion. The Office clearly saw in this arrangement the most convenient solution of the Canadian dilemma, and although the conclusion was not drawn, it was certainly hinted for the benefit of the Law Officers. The wording of the reference suggested that a decision had already been reached and the Law Officers were simply asked to confirm it. This they did, in a thoroughly satisfactory manner. The New Brunswick acts were quite constitutional and the resolution of the House of Commons asking for their disallowance was an improper expression of opinion. "If such a resolution were allowed to have effect, it would amount to a virtual repeal of the section of the British North America Act, 1867, which gives the exclusive right of legislation in these matters to the Provincial Legislature." But most important of all was the statement that in cases of disallowance the Governor-General "must not pay regard to the advice of his responsible ministers of his Dominion but must act upon his own individual discretion."[22] This was the logical conclusion of the Colonial Office approach to the question, and it was speedily transmitted to Canada. Before sending the dispatch, Kimberley tactfully deleted the expression "must not pay regard" from the Law Officers' views on the responsibility for disallowance. A new version of the opinion was supplied. "... this is a matter on which you must act on your own individual discretion, and on which you cannot be guided by the advice of your responsible Ministers of the Dominion."[23] The revised opinion, however, proved hardly more palatable to Canada than the original would have been.

The subject of provincial disallowance now entered a second and more acute stage. In March, 1875, Edward Blake, one of the most determined advocates of Canadian autonomy in imperial affairs, took up the question by attacking the Colonial Office position on the disallowance of local legislation. Blake had shown no concern over the problem of the responsibility for disallowance in the earlier exchanges over the New Brunswick school acts in the House of Commons. After having been in the Cabinet for a brief period when the Liberals assumed office in November, 1873, he had broken with Mackenzie over the latter's promise to fulfil the "Carnarvon Terms" by constructing a section of the Pacific Railway. As a private member he had flirted with nationalist elements such as the "Canada First" group and had needled the Government with incisive criticism over its railway policy and for being what he considered "too subservient" to Imperial suggestion. He became interested in the subject of disallowance through reading the correspondence with the United Kingdom Government, printed for the Canadian Parliament in 1874.[24] These papers contained Kimberley's dispatch of June 30, 1873, with its categorical affirmation of the Governor-General's personal discretion to disallow local legislation. The implications of this statement, which infringed so obviously Blake's conception of the requirements of Canadian autonomy, aroused him to fierce action. His opposition to the British Government's stand on the question was made more bitter by the realization that it was based on an opinion of the Law Officers. Blake, for reasons which will become readily apparent, cherished at this time an implacable hostility to the Law Officers and their influence in the determination of Canadian constitutional questions. Some years before, in a speech on the disallowance by the Imperial Government of the Canadian Oaths Bill, he had talked, as Lord Dufferin expressed it, of "the impropriety of English lawyers 4000 miles away over-ruling the legal wisdom enshrined in the Canadian House of Commons...."[25] Dufferin might have added that the Law Officers had also overruled, on more than one occasion, the professional insight possessed by Edward Blake!

An examination of Blake's stand on the successive constitutional issues which came before the Canadian Parliament in the first years after Confederation reveals that his views were several times resisted by official English legal opinion. As a member of the Ontario Legislature Blake had supported the Anti-Confederation resolutions of the Nova Scotia House of Assembly; these resolutions had been declared invalid by the Law Officers. When Premier of Ontario in 1871-2 Blake had conferred the dignity of Queen's Counsel, only to learn, when the matter was referred to the Law Officers, that this right belonged exclusively to the Federal Government. He had espoused the Oaths Bill in the Dominion Parliament in 1873; it had been disallowed by the United Kingdom. He had denounced Lord Dufferin for consenting to prorogue the Canadian Parliament in the midst of the excitement over the Pacific Scandal; the Governor-General's actions had later been held to be strictly constitutional. Finally, he had supported the resolutions of 1873 which asked the Governor-General to disallow the New Brunswick school acts; this expression of opinion had been criticized by the Law Officers as beyond the powers of the Dominion Parliament. In extenuation it must be noted that Blake had only recently taken up the study of constitutional law and furthermore that his stand on some of these issues was dictated more by personal prejudice than by a sound analysis of the subject. Whatever the reasons behind his actions, there can be no doubt that the result of the encounters had piqued him and served to call forth the energy and dialectic which he was to devote to the disallowance question.

Early in March, 1875, Blake gave notice of a motion which he intended to move protesting against the Law Officers' opinion that the Governor-General was empowered to disallow provincial acts without the advice of his Privy Council. The motion was placed upon the order paper without any consultation with Mackenzie or the Liberal Cabinet. This was not surprising, for at this time Blake's estrangement from his leader was complete. Dufferin read the notice of motion with regret, and immediately wrote Mackenzie to urge that it be withdrawn. It was extremely undesirable that such delicate constitutional questions be discussed by the House of Commons, he said, since this only made more real the risk of a collision between Canada and the United Kingdom. The Governor-General undoubtedly had in mind, when he wrote these words, the controversy over the Oaths Bill, disallowed in 1873. Mackenzie replied that he would endeavour to persuade Blake to withdraw his motion because he felt the Government would be unable to resist it in the House.[26] Blake proved adamant, however, and Dufferin was obliged to add his considerable persuasive talents to the limited ones of the Prime Minister. He saw Blake in Mackenzie's presence and the three men discussed the meaning of Kimberley's dispatch of June 30. Blake considered that the personal power of disallowance granted the Governor-General resembled "an autocratic and extra constitutional exercise of the prerogative," and objected to it on those grounds. Dufferin countered by saying that he had never taken the instructions in that sense. The dispatch had been written soon after his arrival in Canada and he had felt that it was intended to remind him that he was the guardian of the legal rights of the provinces and responsible for preventing any infringement of the Imperial Act which united them. There had been nothing sinister in the British Government's instructions to its agent in Canada. "I concluded by reminding Blake that if there was one thing more apparent than another in all the correspondence which had recently taken place between the Imperial Government and Canadian Ministers, it was the extreme desire of the authorities at home to avoid everything approaching to an irritating control or interference with the domestic concerns of Canada, and to assist the Canadian Government in establishing their Parliamentary Institutions upon the freest and widest basis."[27] The outcome of the interview was that Blake consented to withdraw his motion on the condition that he be allowed to make a short preliminary statement on it in the House. The Government would then take up the subject with the Colonial Office through the medium of confidential correspondence. "By this means we shall have blunted the effects of Blake's wrong-headed procedure," commented Dufferin complacently.[28]

Blake's resolutions were moved in the Commons on March 31. In putting them forward Blake reviewed the history of the use of the power of disallowance in Canada and showed that disallowance had never been exercised but on the advice of responsible Ministers. It was a most delicate operation which must be conducted with extreme caution. This made it all the more necessary that ministerial responsibility be associated at all times with its use. He pointed out the discrepancy between the opinion of the Privy Council Office on the question of responsibility and that of the Colonial Office, which he characterized as fatal to Canadian autonomy: "It appears to me that it is impossible such a doctrine can be maintained consistent with the spirit and letter of the Constitution.... I maintain that the language which is contained in this instruction is of such a character that if it were acceded to by this Parliament, it would be destructive of the principle of responsible Government. That being the case, I conceive it to be the duty of this House, in some way or other, to re-affirm, as was often done in earlier days, the doctrine of responsible government...."[29] The substantive part of the motion was typical of Blake's forthright and aggressive manner. The Secretary of State's instructions of 1873 were not acceptable in the light of Canadian self-government. "... this House feels bound in assertion of the constitutional rights of the Canadian people, to record its protest against and dissent from the said instruction, and to declare its determination to hold His Excellency's Ministers responsible for his action in the exercise of the power so conferred by the said Statute."[30]

The disturbing feature, to the Colonial Office, of the proceedings in the Canadian Parliament was that Blake's motion was supported openly by both Mackenzie and Macdonald and several of their followers. Mackenzie stated that the principle behind the motion was "self-evident" and would not be challenged by anyone in the House.[31] Macdonald said that in England the Queen had lost the effective power to disallow colonial measures, the act being now performed by the Queen in Council. The same procedure should be followed in Canada. He had not objected to the instructions contained in Lord Kimberley's dispatch of 1873, simply because the pressure of business connected with the fall of his Ministry had prevented him from dealing with the matter. "I must say that when the despatch which has been commented upon by the hon. gentleman arrived here it rather surprised me; it went infinitely farther than I had idea [sic] it would go, and I say at once that I think the Minister who sent that despatch made a grave error in constitutional law."[32] Some of the Government's more radical supporters demanded that the motion be put to a vote to impress the Colonial Office with the determination of the Canadian Parliament on the issue, and Mackenzie had difficulty in restraining them. It was not until the Prime Minister stated that a Minute of Council protesting the instructions had been prepared and sent to Great Britain that the House agreed to let the motion be withdrawn.[33]

Lord Dufferin, after Blake's motion had been deflected, stated confidently to Carnarvon that "the matter is [now] left in as favourable a position as possible for the Colonial Office to deal with it."[34] The Office could hardly share his sentiments after pondering the combined effect of the Minute of the Privy Council and the unanimity of opinion expressed by the Canadian House. The Department was actually in an awkward position, for unconsciously it had issued the Governor-General with conflicting instructions regarding the exercise of provincial disallowance. The Privy Council view that the Governor-General must rely on the advice of his Ministers had not been formally approved by the Office, it is true, but it had been sent to Canada in an official communication and thus had had the result of cutting away some of the ground from under the feet of the Law Officers. There obviously existed a difference of opinion between high legal authorities in England over the question, and the Canadian Government recognized this fact. It was impossible to criticize Blake for seizing such a convenient opportunity to press home a statement of principle. Lord Dufferin made this point clear. "... I could plainly see that imagining that upon this special occasion he had caught the Law Officers [napping], he had determined to take his revenge."[35]   The Colonial Office was forced to turn, ruefully, to the task of repairing its damaged position. It was imperative that the claim of the Canadian Cabinet be combated, even if that meant repudiating the Privy Council Office's view of the question. Provincial autonomy would be jeopardized if the ideas of the Dominion Ministers were accepted. The true destiny of Canada, and the good faith of Great Britain in sanctioning the federal compact, alike required that the Governor-General, removed from all partisan influences by virtue of his office and background, exercise an independent discretionary power in the disallowance of provincial acts. To Herbert these broad considerations were fundamental to any discussion of the subject:

> ... unless we maintain as well as we can the protection carefully given to the independence of Provincial Legislation by the "British North America Act 1867" we shall not only be open to the charge of abetting the breaking of a solemn contract, but we shall effectually deter a (Roman Catholic) Colony like Newfoundland from entering the Dominion.[36]

And again:

> ... I am quite unable to see how the independence of Provincial Legislation on the subjects reserved to the Provincial legislatures can exist if the Dominion Ministers (being practically the Dominion Parliament) are to control that Legislation.
>
> I am surprised that none of the Provinces have protested against the summary way in which the House of Commons has disposed of their liberties; but I admit that if the Provinces are informed, and are content, we should not needlessly come to their rescue.[37]

It was decided that an answer to Canada should be delayed for a few months, to enable the Office to consult Lord Dufferin personally on the matter. The Governor-General was returning to England on vacation for the summer of 1875, and in view of his intimate association with Carnarvon, it was judged desirable to take him into the full confidence of the Secretary of State in the dilemma. Conversations were held between Carnarvon, Herbert, and Dufferin in June, and at the Permanent Under-Secretary's request, Dufferin drew up a short memorandum embodying his views on the subject. In this paper Dufferin stressed the twofold nature of the responsibility attaching to the office of Governor-General of Canada. Not only must the Governor act as a constitutional monarch in relation to his advisers in domestic matters, but he must also assert his responsibility, as an agent of the United Kingdom Government, to the Colonial Secretary. These two functions were not incompatible unless an extreme crisis arose, and even in an emergency negotiation between the parties could usually prevent an outright break. This idea was in keeping with a conviction which Dufferin had often expressed: that, in the event of a conflict between British and Canadian interests, it was better to confine the quarrel to the Governor-General and his Privy Council than to let it be waged directly between Canada and Great Britain. The Governor-General could always be recalled. In addition, "... I am quite convinced that the fewer the points of contact between our Governmental machinery here, and that at home, the less will be the friction and the chance of 'heated bearings' ...."38

Dufferin believed that in general it was advisable for the Imperial Government to maintain the right to review provincial legislation through the exercise of the discretionary power of the Governor. To support this assertion he cited the case of a Prince Edward Island land law, authorizing the purchase of estates on the Island belonging to absentee proprietors, which he had vetoed the year before. Admittedly the constitutional position of the Governor was extremely hazardous in operations of this kind, but the advantages to be gained from an impartial exercise of the power of disallowance outweighed the weaknesses of the procedure.

I was enabled to disallow [the Prince Edward Island Land Act] by dint of having persuaded my Ministers with some difficulty that it was iniquitous, but supposing that my Ministers had been more Radical or that they had a very great interest in acquiring the support of the Prince Edward Island Members, they might have refused to have acceded to my view of the case, in which event my position would have been very weak, for they would have been encouraged in their opposition to me by the consciousness that the Home Government would refuse to take any cognizance of the matter. On the other hand if I persevered in my determination, and a political crisis were to ensue, the Imperial Government would after all be required to pronounce upon the merits of the case, as they could scarcely abandon a Governor who had exercised the Prerogative of The Crown in a wise and laudable manner, and for the protection of the property of Her Majesty's British subjects.39

The Colonial Office deferred sending an answer to Canada for several more months in order to take the advice of the Law Officers. The Attorney-General and Solicitor-General reported on November 1, reversing the decision given by their Liberal predecessors two years previously. Sir Richard Baggallay and Sir John Holker announced that from their examination of the relevant clauses of the British North America Act, they felt that the Governor-General in Council alone possessed the power of assenting to or disallowing provincial acts.40 This opinion was a severe blow to the Office, which had counted on further support from the Law Officers in the controversy with Canada.

The consequence is that, as we are now advised, the Dominion Legislature, through the Dominion Ministers, may at any moment veto Provincial legislation on a subject expressly reserved to the Provincial legislature. The legislative privileges of the Provinces are thus reduced to a nullity.

This leaves the question in a most unsatisfactory position: and not improbably some Province may raise it hereafter when we shall have to take a fresh opinion. [41]

Carnarvon and Herbert again conferred with Dufferin, with the result that it was decided not to adopt the literal decision of the Law Officers, but to propose a middle course. This solution, put forward at Dufferin's suggestion, corresponded closely to his earlier-expressed conception of the function of a Governor in an autonomous colony. There was no attempt made to argue the Imperial Government's case from the technical construction of section 90 of the British North America Act. Instead the Colonial Office chose the safest course and confined themselves to generalities. As Malcolm wrote:

I am inclined to think Sir J. Pauncefote's recommendation [the suggestion that the technical points regarding the construction of section 90 be omitted from the dispatch] a politic one. We have to deal with a very able person in Mr. Blake and it would be well perhaps not to give him an opportunity of controverting the views of the S. of State especially as the argument of the despatch seems complete without the passage. But this is a matter of policy.... [42]

Lord Carnarvon's reply to the Canadian Privy Council took the form of a secret dispatch to the Governor-General. There was no need to press the problem of disallowance to a decision from the Judicial Committee of the Privy Council, the Colonial Secretary declared magnanimously, as the matter could be most satisfactorily settled without a fixed rule. Because of the dual character of his office, the Governor-General would normally be expected to consult his advisers on the subject of disallowance before reaching a final decision, which, however, would be based on his own judgment. There could be no question of ministerial responsibility being at stake, for by the British North America Act the Dominion did not possess the right to interfere in subjects that were within the limits of provincial jurisdiction. Thus Ministers would not feel it necessary to resign if they disagreed with the Governor-General on disallowance, and the Canadian Parliament could not properly hold them answerable for a failure to enforce their advice. Long before such a situation arose, the Colonial Secretary concluded, public feeling would have rendered an outright clash between the Governor and his Ministers highly improbable. [43]

Herbert possessed doubts about the efficacy of this dispatch in converting the Canadian Privy Council. It was a "soft answer" which, he felt, would "not turn away Mr. Blake's wrath." [44] Carnarvon added that although it was characterized by "a somewhat transparent reticence," he remained of the opinion that it was the most suitable answer which could be given Canada. [45] Within its limits the document attempted an ingenious solution to a difficult dilemma. The Office had been obliged to compose a statement which would reconcile the conflicting instructions it had issued the Dominion, and, at the same time, maintain Imperial control in an important aspect of Canadian domestic affairs. In view of these circumstances it is not surprising that the communication was intentionally vague and failed to give a distinct definition of the law. But there was a more serious criticism of the British reply. The instructions to the Governor-General, adroit as they were, did not really confront the practical difficulties involved in the disallowance of provincial legislation by an Imperial officer. Ultimate responsibility for this act would have to rest somewhere: either on the Canadian or on the British Cabinet. It was unlikely that the Canadian Privy Council would abdicate its declared function of tendering advice to the Governor, and also improbable that the Colonial Secretary's reasons for evading responsibility would commend themselves to the Canadian Ministers. Opinion in Canada could be easily consolidated against Imperial intervention in domestic subjects if the resignation of a Ministry were forced by the actions of a determined Governor. In this situation, then, the position and prospects of the Governor would be highly dubious. Could he be sustained from England by the support of the Colonial Secretary? Carnarvon, in another constitutional discussion of the same period, spoke of the Governor having "to account" to Her Majesty's Government if he compelled the resignation of his Ministers, [46] which would appear to indicate that support from Downing Street might not be forthcoming in the event that the Governor failed to form an alternative and viable Ministry. Even if support were to be extended, would it be tolerated in colonies that had, by the seventies, enjoyed responsible government for over twenty-five years?

At the time when this correspondence over disallowance was taking place with Canada, a similar difference of opinion between the Colonial Office and some of the Australian colonies was coming to a head. Its course parallels the Canadian controversy in important particulars, and influenced the Department in its treatment of the disallowance issue. The Australian case concerned the exercise of the prerogative of pardon, which although not a statutory function like the Canadian power of disallowance, nevertheless had several significant features in common with it. The Australian issue, like the Canadian, dated back to Lord Granville's period at the Colonial Office. In a manner not unlike his attitude towards the power of disallowance, Lord Granville (or Rogers) had shown a disposition to allow great weight to the advice of a Ministry in the pardoning of capital offences in the Australian colonies. [47] The concession had been partly withdrawn by Lord Kimberley when he assumed office, for in a circular dispatch of November, 1871, he asserted the Governor's exclusive right to dispense the Queen's prerogative of pardon, after a personal examination of each case. "Due regard" would have to be paid to the advice of Ministers, but this counsel must not be allowed to interfere with the Governor's authority to exercise an independent judgment, particularly in cases involving Imperial interests. [48] In New South Wales both the Colonial Secretary (Henry Parkes) and the Governor (Sir Hercules Robinson) objected to the divided responsibility for the prerogative of pardon which was outlined in Lord Kimberley's communication. Parkes drafted a cogent memorandum urging that there be either complete freedom on the part of the Governor to dispense the prerogative of mercy as he saw fit, or that he exercise it only under ministerial advice. Robinson also took this line, although he felt the second alternative would be much more practicable and would prove more favourable to the Governor's prestige.

After Kimberley left office in 1874 Lord Carnarvon carried on the discussions with New South Wales. He offered a new argument by claiming that since the prerogative of pardon was delegated personally by the Sovereign to her representative in a colony, it would not be fitting to have it used on other persons' recommendations. The power should only be exercised by the individual to whom it was granted. The analogy suggested between the Home Secretary advising the Queen about pardons, and colonial Ministers the Governor, was not really apposite, since colonial councillors were not appointed directly by the Queen, as were members of the British Cabinet. Actually it was the care of Imperial interests with which the Colonial Office was concerned in discussing the pardoning power in Australia; frequently in the Pacific area the ramifications of pardon extended to other colonies or foreign countries.[49] Eventually a satisfactory settlement of this constitutional problem was worked out in New South Wales and approved by both Governments. It embodied the principle that the Governor was bound to obtain the advice of his Ministers in exercising the prerogative of mercy, but that he might occasionally, and in a very narrow range of circumstances, disregard that advice and make a decision independently as an Imperial officer. The Colonial Office gave a little ground from its original position; the Australians did not ask for precise legal formulation; and in this slightly ambiguous state the question was put peacefully aside.[50]

The year 1876 opened with the controversy over disallowance nearing its climax. Edward Blake was now Minister of Justice in Canada. He had been furnished the papers relating to the pardoning issue in New South Wales and stimulated by the exchange, he took up the problem of the responsibility for disallowance with a new enthusiasm. In April, Dufferin transmitted to the Colonial Office a memorandum which Blake had written on the subject of provincial disallowance.[51] It was an answer to Carnarvon's dispatch of the previous November. The Governor-General remarked privately to the Colonial Secretary at the same time that he regretted that Blake had insisted upon reopening the discussion. Mackenzie and Blake had wished to communicate the contents of the memorandum to the Commons, Dufferin went on, but he had peremptorily refused to allow this to be done. It would have been an improper attempt on the part of the Ministry to extract credit from a confidential discussion of a delicate topic. "One has to be very sharp with these people, for they are always intent upon making a little political capital for themselves, no matter at whose expense," he complained.[52]

In this document, perhaps the ablest paper in the whole treatment of the disallowance topic, Blake described the complexities which surrounded any exercise of the function of disallowance: the difficulty of dealing with acts that are on the borderline between provincial and federal powers, or are only partly invalid, or are merely at variance with federal policy. He refused to accept the lessons of the Australian pardons controversy as having any significance for the Canadian question. There was a strict distinction between the prerogative of mercy and the power of disallowance. In the first case there was some justification, where a high prerogative and Imperial interests were involved, for the Governor's acting independently, but disallowance in

Canada was a purely statutory power which must be considered as similar to any other executive power exercised on advice. In contrast to the solution in the Australian issue, there must be a fixed rule about the procedure of disallowance, since the problem went to the heart of British constitutional government. The Canadian Parliament would not allow Ministers to escape responsibility for disallowance, Blake asserted. The Privy Council must account for action taken, even if it was not done by its own efforts or on its advice.

> The importance to the people of the advice given by Ministers is in precise proportion to its effectiveness. So long as the course pursued is dependent on the advice given, responsibility for the advice is responsibility for the action, and is therefore valuable: but it is the action which is really material; and to concede that there may be action contrary to advice would be to destroy the value of responsibility for the advice, --to deprive the people of their constitutional security for the administration, according to their wishes, of their own affairs--to yield up the substance, retaining only the shadow of responsible Government. 53

The Minister of Justice's determined opposition to leaving the question in a vague form forced the Colonial Office to fall back on its last line of defence--the construction of the disallowance provisions of the Act of Union of 1867. Herbert wondered in passing if it were profitable to pursue the discussion with Canada further, since Blake's view of the question resembled so closely the interpretation of section 90 which the Law Officers had given as legally correct. However there were good grounds for not following the Law Officers' opinion, but settling the question with a regard for the nice balance between federal and provincial powers that was embodied in the Canadian Confederation. There might be advantage, therefore, in arguing the matter from the strong position of the precise wording used in the disallowance clauses in the British North America Act:

> ... as an acquiescence in Mr. Blake's view involves the extremely serious consequence of admitting that all the provisions of the Act of Union intended to protect the right of the Provinces to legislate on special subjects are nugatory, I should be disposed to invite Lord Dufferin's consideration to [some further points]. ... Mr. Blake will like, and not dislike the further friendly discussion of the subject, which he will consider complimentary to himself; and being an honest man, will give fair consideration to any further point. 54

Thus the Colonial Office returned to Canada its views on the interpretation of section 90 of the Confederation Act. There was, in sections 10 to 13 of the Act, a careful distinction drawn between the "Governor General" and the "Governor General in Council" (the Canadian Cabinet). The Dominion Privy Council had claimed that the power of disallowance was vested in the "Governor General in Council," just as in sections 56 and 57 of the British North America Act the disallowance of Canadian acts was entrusted to the "Queen in Council. " The Colonial Secretary argued that if ministerial advice had been intended as an essential part of the exercise of disallowance, the proper term would have been used in clause 90. Instead, the vital section referred only to the "Governor General. "[55] And, as Herbert had said on one occasion, "In a compact of Union such as this Act is every word must be deemed to have special force. "[56] Carnarvon went on to state that the records kept at the Colonial Office of the drafting of the Act of Union furnished no evidence about the intentions of the Fathers of Confederation in regard to this section. His own memory was not helpful on the point, but he felt that the careful distribution of powers between the provinces and the Dominion suggested that the independent jurisdiction of each legislature should be safeguarded. Acceptance of the Canadian interpretation of clause 90 would mean a virtual repeal of the sections on provincial powers in the Act, and would allow a body dependent on a majority in the Canadian Parliament to be supreme throughout the country, even in fields of wholly provincial jurisdiction.

Dufferin replied in a rather fulsome fashion that this dispatch from the Colonial Office had been well received in Ottawa. "In fact the extraordinary kindness you have shown my Government, and the studied courtesy and delicacy of the language used in the public despatches you have addressed to them, have, I think, made them ashamed of their own coarse cantankerousness, and the certainty I always feel of receiving a communication from you, written in this spirit, strengthens my hands to a wonderful degree in all my intercourse with my Prime Minister. "[57] The hopes which Dufferin's words aroused that the matter would now be settled were, however, doomed to disappointment. Blake was anything but convinced by the Secretary of State's construction of section 90 of the British North America Act. He took up his pen again to justify the difference in terminology in the various sections simply on the grounds of brevity. Then he turned to the broader considerations behind the exercise of disallowance. He took exception to the charge that his view would mean a repeal of provincial rights by explaining that the Federal Parliament, containing representatives from all the provinces, would be unlikely to harm local interests. Similarly the Canadian Privy Council would not abuse its power of disallowance, because it would ultimately be held responsible, in both Parliament and the country, for its use. In fact the Dominion Cabinet would probably exercise disallowance in a more cautious and salutary fashion than the British Privy Council, which was removed from the Canadian scene. But, in the last resort, the difficulties in working out any solution to the problem of provincial disallowance other than the one involving the acceptance of advice were so insurmountable that they could not be countenanced. That the Governor should act on his own independent judgment in reviewing acts was unthinkable in a Colony of the political maturity of Canada. If he had a formal group of counsellors outside the Cabinet their existence would be clearly unconstitutional. He might act on instructions from the Colonial Office, but this would place disallowance in the hands of the Colonial Secretary, which was certainly not contemplated in the British North America Act. There was only one satisfactory alternative--disallowance on ministerial advice. [58]

To this reasoning, there was really no answer, although Herbert attempted to prolong the correspondence by further reference to the Colonial Office construction of section 90. The Permanent Under-Secretary also contended that under the Imperial Government's interpretation, the Governor-General would, in effect, be acting under advice, although perhaps not according to advice. He would be obliged to canvass the
members of his Privy Council for their opinions before considering how to treat a provincial bill. Then he might act against their advice, or according to their advice, de-
pending on his own judgment.[59] But by this time Herbert knew that the battle was lost
and the final exchanges on the question reveal a confident Blake controverting every
statement the Colonial Office put forward. Herbert minuted tactfully in these last days,
"I do not think we need continue the discussion. We shall not convert Mr. Blake, and
we need not draw out his anti-English feelings, which are at present in a quiet state."[60]

And thus the question was laid at rest, with a practical rule firmly established for
one of the more ambiguously worded sections of the British North America Act. The
Colonial Office had entered the discussion with the admirable intention of laying down
a mode of disallowance which would protect the rights of minorities in the Canadian
federation. But from the beginning its conduct of the controversy had been unsure. In
1873 it shifted its ground from a reliance on the United Kingdom Government as the
final determinant of disallowance to an insistence that the Governor-General exercise
an independent discretionary power. In its communications to the Dominion the Department tended to overlook a very important feature of the Canadian federal state: that
the same people who elected representatives to Parliament in Ottawa also elected the
members of the provincial assemblies. The Dominion Government was not an aloof
overriding authority but an administration which was dependent in the last analysis on
local support. Most significantly of all, the Office was influenced in its approach to
the problem of disallowance by the discussions with the Australian colonies over the pardoning power. In the end it attempted to apply the solution which had been reached in
Australia to the Canadian issue. The two problems were, however, very different in nature. Blake's debating advantage lay in the fact that he appreciated this difference
and instinctively recognized the only practicable solution possible for the disallowance
question. In the revision of the pardoning clauses of the Governor-General's Instructions
he was willing to see the essentials of the Australian modus operandi adopted, because he
accepted the existence of Imperial interests. The disallowance of provincial legislation
in Canada, on the other hand, was a subject which was completely domestic in almost
all its aspects.

In sharp contrast to the unfortunate manner in which the Office had approached the
issue was the attitude of Blake and the Mackenzie Government. They had fought the
battle throughout on sound constitutional lines, relying on the basic principle expounded
by Canadian political reformers ever since Baldwin's day. Blake said, at the conclusion
of the controversy, "... [my] main position ... has been that, under the letter and the
spirit of the Constitution, Ministers must be responsible for the Governor's action...."[61]
It was an assumption which the Office was forced, in the end, deliberately to admit. Ma
colm put the case for its acceptance rather neatly when he wrote: "... so long as the

Govr. Genl. has to act in the matter at all his advisers will be apt to maintain that he can do no act of a political complexion without their advice and that to admit any independent power of action in the Govr. Genl. wd. be to place him towards the provinces not in the relation wh. the Queen bears to the Colonial Legislatures but in that wh. the Secretary of State bears to them. "[62]   There is a comment by Herbert, written towards the close of his official career, which reveals how deeply this principle had impressed itself on his thinking by 1887. The Colonial Office, by its failure to rebut Blake's arguments over disallowance, had been "obliged to do away with a provision of the B.N.A. Act devised for the purpose of securing an impartial decision." This was regrettable, but probably inevitable. For, observed Herbert, "we must, I think, adhere to the decision that, on broad constitutional grounds, the Governor General must not do any important act of State except as his Ministers advise. "[63] Accepted in good faith and applied with moderation, Herbert's conviction possessed the dynamic power which has transformed the British Empire into the modern Commonwealth.[64]

REFERENCES

1. Cardwell to Monck, Dec. 3, 1864. Printed in Kennedy, ed., Documents of the Canadian Constitution, 548.

2. John A. Macdonald in the Confederation Debates in the Legislature of Canada, Feb. 6, 1865. Printed in Kennedy, ed., Documents of the Canadian Constitution, 558-9.

3. From 1867 to 1887, a period during which Macdonald was in power for fifteen years, the Dominion Government disallowed fifty-nine provincial acts. The power of disallowance was never exercised in later years with the same frequency. Dawson, Government of Canada, 253-8.

4. Section 51 of the Quebec Resolutions. Printed in Kennedy, ed., Documents of the Canadian Constitution, 545-6.

5. Section 90 of 30 and 31 Vict., c. 3.

6. Memo. by the Minister of Justice on disallowance, June 8, 1868: SP, 1869, no. 18, 1-2. The memo. was approved by the Privy Council on June 9, 1868.

7. Macdonald to Young, private and confidential, Jan. 18, 1869, enclosed in Young to Granville, confidential, March 11, 1869: CO 42/675. Printed in Pope, Memoirs of Sir John Macdonald, II, 297-8.

8. Young to Granville, no. 23, March 11, 1869: CO 42/675. Printed in SP, 1870, no. 35, 3-4.

9. Young to Granville, confidential, March 11, 1869: CO 42/675. A report by Macdonald on the Ontario acts, dated Feb. 20, 1869, is enclosed in Young toGranville, no. 22, March 11, 1869: ibid.

10. Minutes by Rogers, March 31 and April 8, 1869, on Young to Granville, nos. 22 and 23, March 11, 1869: ibid.

11. Minute by Rogers, April 8, 1869, on Young to Granville, no. 23, March 11, 1869: ibid.

12. Ibid.

13. Law Officers (Sir R. P. Collier and Sir J. D. Coleridge) to Colonial Office, April 30, 1869: CO 42/675.

14. Granville to Young, no. 85, May 8, 1869: ibid. Printed in SP, 1870, no. 35, 4-5.

15. Dufferin to Kimberley, no. 85, Nov. 6, 1872: CO 42/709.

16. There were opinions from the Law Officers on Nov. 29, 1872, Feb. 12, 1873, and April 7, 1873, since the Colonial Office had to reopen the question on several occasions when fresh documentary material was sent from Canada. The evidence bearing on the case is found in SP, 1872, no. 36; SP, 1873, no. 44; and SP, 1874, no. 25. See also Kimberley to Dufferin, no. 47, Feb. 18, 1873: CO 42/709, and Kimberley to Dufferin, no. 112, April 10, 1873: CO 42/722.

17. Henry Reeve (Registrar of the Privy Council) to Colonial Office, Dec. 13, 1872: CO 42/710. Printed in SP, 1873, no. 44, 64.

18. Dufferin to Kimberley, no. 137, May 27, 1873: CO 42/717. Printed in SP, 1874, no. 25, 8-9.

19. Minute by Herbert, June 12, 1873, on Dufferin to Kimberley, no. 137, May 27, 1873: CO 42/717.

20. Minute by Kimberley, June 13, 1873, on ibid.

21. Colonial Office to Law Officers, June 21, 1873: CO 42/717.

22. Law Officers (Sir J. D. Coleridge and Sir G. Jessel) to Colonial Office, June 24, 1873: CO 42/722.

23. Kimberley to Dufferin, no. 199, June 30, 1873: ibid. Printed in SP, 1874, no. 25, 13.

24. SP, 1874, no. 25.

25. Dufferin to Carnarvon, private, April 23, 1874: PRO 30/6/26.

26. Dufferin to Carnarvon, private, March 5, 1875: PRO 30/6/28.

27. Dufferin to Carnarvon, private, March 10, 1875: ibid.

28. Ibid. Blake's desire to reduce the independent powers of the Governor-General in the exercise of disallowance was probably inspired to some extent by his personal dislike of Dufferin. Temperamentally the two men were poles apart and while Blake was a Minister there existed continual friction between them, culminating in their quarrel over the Pacific Railway in 1876. Dufferin's obvious restlessness within the limits of a constitutional Governor's post could not fail to arouse Blake's suspicion and hostility.

29. Debates of the House of Commons (Canada), 1875, I, 1006 (March 31, 1875). The debate is found in ibid., 1003-10.

30. Ibid., 1004.

31. Ibid., 1007.

32. Ibid., 1008.

33. The Report of the Privy Council, to which Mackenzie referred, actually reached the Colonial Office before news of the debate in the Canadian Parliament. It contended that Lord Kimberley's instructions would subvert ministerial responsibility in Canada by compelling the Governor-General to rely for advice on an extra legal body, residing outside the constitution. Report of the Privy Council of Canada, March 8, 1875, received privately from Lord Dufferin about March 24, 1875, appended to Dufferin to Carnarvon, no. 67, March 11, 1875: CO 42/735. It was formally transmitted in Dufferin to Carnarvon, no. 91, April 8, 1875: CO 42/736. Printed in SP, 1876, no. 116, 84-5.

34. Dufferin to Carnarvon, private, April 9, 1875: PRO 30/6/28.

35. Dufferin to Carnarvon, private, March 10, 1875: PRO 30/6/28.

36. Minute by Herbert, March 27, 1875, on Dufferin to Carnarvon, no. 67, March 11, 1875: CO 42/735. Hall, The Colonial Office, 228, provides a completely misleading interpretation of this minute of Herbert's.

37. Minute by Herbert, April 29, 1875, on Dufferin to Carnarvon, no. 89, April 7, 1875: CO 42/736.

38. Dufferin to Carnarvon, private, June 1, 1876: PRO 30/6/29.

39. Confidential memo. by Lord Dufferin on disallowance, July 31, 1875, appended to Dufferin to Carnarvon, no. 89, April 7, 1875: CO 42/736.

40. Law Officers (Sir Richard Baggallay and Sir John Holker) to Colonial Office, Nov. 1, 1875: CO 42/738.

41. Minute by Herbert, Nov. 5, 1875, on ibid.

42. Minute by Malcolm, Oct. 16, 1875, on Lord Dufferin's memo. on disallowance, July 31, 1875: CO 42/736.

43. Carnarvon to Dufferin, secret, Nov. 5, 1875: ibid. Printed in SP, 1876, no. 116, 83-4.

44. Minute by Herbert, Oct. 16, 1875, on Lord Dufferin's memo. on disallowance, July 31, 1875: CO 42/736.

45. Minute by Carnarvon, Oct. 17, 1875, on ibid.

46. Carnarvon to Sir Hercules Robinson (Governor of New South Wales), May 4, 1875: SP, 1876, no. 116, 78.

47. Granville to Lord Belmore (Governor of New South Wales), Oct. 4, 1869: ibid., 5-6.

48. Kimberley to Officer Administering the Government of New South Wales, circular, Nov. 1, 1871: ibid., 6-7. See also Kimberley to Sir Hercules Robinson, Feb. 17, 1873: ibid., 10.

49. Carnarvon to Robinson, Oct. 7, 1874: ibid., 58-9. See also Carnarvon to Robinson, May 4, 1875: ibid., 77-9.

50. The Australian discussions over the exercise of the prerogative of mercy influenced Blake in his proposals for the revision of the Governor-General's Commission and Instructions in 1876. He insisted, however, that the independent action of the Governor-General in dispensing pardon should be contained within somewhat narrower limits than those allotted the Governors of the Australian colonies. See A. Todd, Parliamentary Government in the British Colonies (London, 2nd ed., 1894), 348-59, 361-6, and A. B. Keith, Responsible Government in the Dominions (Oxford, 1912), III, 1386-1404. The correspondence is printed in PP, 1875, LIII, nos. C-1202 and C-1248, from which the Canadian selection, SP, 1876, no. 116, is taken.

51. Dufferin to Carnarvon, no. 96, April 6, 1876: CO 42/742. Blake's memo. is dated Dec. 22, 1875, and was approved by a Minute of the Privy Council on Feb. 29, 1876. It is printed in SP, 1876, no. 116, 79-83.

52. Dufferin to Carnarvon, private, April 5, 1876: PRO 30/6/29.

53. Memo. by Edward Blake on disallowance, Dec. 22, 1875: CO 42/742.

54. Minute by Herbert, May 17, 1876, on Dufferin to Carnarvon, no. 96, April 6, 1876: ibid.

55. Carnarvon to Dufferin, no. 145, June 1, 1876: ibid. Printed in SP, 1877, no. 89, 453-4.

56. Minute by Herbert, March 27, 1875, on Dufferin to Carnarvon, no. 67, March 11, 1875: CO 42/735.

57. Dufferin to Carnarvon, private, June 28, 1876: PRO 30/6/29.

58. Memo. by Edward Blake on disallowance, Sept. 6, 1876, enclosed in W. B. Richards (Officer Administering the Government of Canada) to Carnarvon, no. 49, Sept. 20, 1876: CO 42/744. Printed in SP, 1877, no. 89, 455-6.

59. Minute by Herbert, Oct. 14, 1876, on Richards to Carnarvon, no. 49, Sept. 20, 1876: CO 42/744.
Herbert's views were embodied in the dispatch, Carnarvon to Dufferin, no. 318, Oct. 31, 1876: ibid. Printed in SP, 1877, no. 89, 456-7.

60. Minute by Herbert, Oct. 14, on Richards to Carnarvon, no. 49, Sept. 20, 1876: CO 42/744.
Blake's final arguments are contained in a Report of the Privy Council of Canada, Nov. 21, 1876, enclosed in Dufferin to Carnarvon, no. 258, Nov. 25, 1876: ibid. Printed in SP, 1877, no. 89, 458. The Colonial Office replied, closing the case, in

Carnarvon to Dufferin, no. 6, Jan. 4, 1877: CO 42/744. Printed in SP, 1877, no. 89, 458.

61. Report of the Privy Council of Canada, Nov. 21, 1876, enclosed in Dufferin to Carnarvon, no. 258, Nov. 25, 1876: CO 42/744.

62. Minute by Malcolm, Dec. 18, 1876, on Dufferin to Carnarvon, no. 263, Nov. 30, 1876: ibid.

63. Minute by Herbert, Dec. 15, 1887, on Lansdowne to Holland, confidential, Nov. 12, 1887: CO 42/791.

64. Although the Office suffered a defeat in these discussions, this outcome was not significant. A collision between the Governor-General and his Cabinet over disallowance has never occurred in Canadian history and there has never been a case in which disallowance has been exercised save on advice. Among the important constitutional developments in British imperial history the disallowance question in Canada is almost unique, for from first to last it existed purely as a subject of academic interest.

The controversy over the responsibility for the disallowance of provincial legislation is discussed in Todd, Parliamentary Government, 443-57, and in Keith, Responsible Government, II, 725-31. Todd supports Blake's view that the Governor-General must disallow only on advice, and Keith concludes that, practicably, it is a satisfactory rule of action.

CHAPTER FIVE

THE LORD CHANCELLOR AND THE QUESTION OF APPEALS
TO THE PRIVY COUNCIL

"I am inclined to think that we have not good ground, or at least that it is not ex-
pedient, to press for the maintenance of any further right on the part of a Canadian
British subject to appeal to the Privy Council [than] the Legislature and Courts of
Canada may assign to him." Sir Robert Herbert, 1875

UNDER THE STIMULUS of the nationalist movement in Canada in the seventies, the
Liberal Government of the Dominion called into question the historic function of the
Privy Council as the supreme appellate court for the overseas colonies of Great Britain.
The discussions which followed this assertion revealed once again the existence of dif-
fering shades of opinion within the Imperial Government towards the pressures of an expanding Canadian autonomy. The Colonial Office, conscious of its responsibility to
maintain harmonious political relations with the Dominion and understanding the motives behind the Canadian request, assumed a conciliatory position throughout the negotiations. It was the Lord Chancellor, the most important figure in the legal hierarchy
of the United Kingdom, who, on this occasion, set himself resolutely against the Canadian pretensions. The task was thus imposed upon the Colonial Office of moderating
the attitude of one of the parties concerned in the question and of reducing the substance of the demands made by the other. To this end the Office succeeded in arranging a compromise between the two protagonists which preserved the judicial unity of
the British Empire and at the same time granted Canada the unchallenged right to regulate appeals from her high courts to the Judicial Committee of the Privy Council. The
result was an empirical settlement of a complicated issue; a modus vivendi which determined the judicial relations between Great Britain and her self-governing colonies
for almost seventy-five years.

The subject of the appellate jurisdiction of the Privy Council came into prominence when, eight years after the achievement of Confederation, the Canadian Government decided to establish a high court of appeal for the Dominion. In a federal
state a strong judiciary is essential, for authority is inevitably divided between the
nation and the provinces. "There are," as Edward Blake expressed it, bound to be
"conflicting opinions as to the character of the Constitution, as to the absolute or relative range of Provincial and Federal powers, and as to the interpretation of the laws."[1]
A national judiciary, by adjudicating these complex problems, can render indispensable service to the harmonious working of a federal constitution. The central government without its own judiciary, as one of the architects of the American Constitution

1. For references to chapter V see pages 157-65.

observed, would be "a mere trunk of a body, without arms or legs to act and move." In British North America the need for a court having appellate jurisdiction over the whole country was even more pronounced than in other federations. For the great diversity in the elements that were brought together to form the Canadian nation, a diversity reflected in the many different legal codes used throughout the Dominion, required a supreme appeal court to provide a unifying influence in the development of both legal concepts and judicial institutions. The Fathers of Confederation noted the vital role of the Supreme Court in the exposition of the American Constitution and planned to establish a similar tribunal for the Canadian union. Section 31 of the Quebec Resolutions, drawn up in 1864, empowered the General Parliament to create courts for the execution of federal laws. This provision was incorporated into the British North America Act, and provided the statutory basis for the establishment of a supreme court of appeal in Canada: "The Parliament of Canada may, notwithstanding anything in this Act, from Time to Time, provide for the Constitution, Maintenance, and Organization of a General Court of Appeal for Canada, and for the Establishment of any additional Courts for the better Administration of the Laws of Canada."[2]

In the years immediately following 1867 there were several abortive attempts to establish a court of last resort for the new Dominion. On two occasions bills for this purpose were introduced into Parliament by the Macdonald Government, and the subject was mentioned in the Speech from the Throne. Both bills, however, were dropped by the Government after only cursory discussion. It became an open secret in Ottawa that this reluctance to proceed with the measures sprang from the Ministry's fear of offending its French-Canadian supporters. Quebec, with its separate traditions of race, language, and law, had the most reason to be anxious of the unifying effect of a court of appeal for the entire Dominion. In addition, Quebec, where wealth and litigiousness were often happily combined, had found that a reference to the Judicial Committee of the Privy Council from the provincial courts was in many cases a satisfactory culmination of the judicial process. In fact, the volume of litigation which was carried to the Privy Council from Quebec courts was far greater than that from all the other provinces of Canada combined. Thus the matter of an appeal court slumbered, while Macdonald's Government went down to defeat and the Liberals under Alexander Mackenzie took office. In 1874 another reference to the desirability of a supreme court was contained in the Speech from the Throne, but Mackenzie and his colleagues made no effort to prepare a bill. Could it be that the Liberals were to be frustrated by the same divisions of party composition that had forestalled Macdonald in this matter? The question was answered in the negative when, early in the session of 1875, another bill for the creation of a supreme court was introduced into Parliament.

Télesphore Fournier, Mackenzie's Minister of Justice, in sponsoring the Bill, noted that it contained no reference to the right of appeal to the Judicial Committee of the Privy Council. This was intentional, he said, although for his part he would like to see the practice discontinued. He was convinced that the right of appeal was abused by wealthy suitors and corporations in Quebec to prolong litigation beyond the means of ordinary individuals and thus obtain negotiated settlements which were favourable to their interests. He felt that on the whole there were more arguments against the preservation of appeals than for it and declared that he looked to the abolition of the practice at some future date.[3]   This pronouncement by the Minister of Justice seemed, to several members of the House, an obvious invitation to consider the question further when the Bill was being discussed in detail.   Sir John Macdonald, the leader of the Opposition, commended Fournier for bringing in a measure designed to achieve an object which he had long favoured.   (The Bill was almost a replica of one which Macdonald had introduced in 1870.)   He cautioned the House, however, against interfering with the right of appeal from Canada.   A link of empire would be severed if the appeal were prohibited.   In any event, the Canadian Parliament did not possess the power to cut off appeals, which could only be done by Imperial statute.[4]

On the second reading of the Bill, on March 16, Fournier's invitation to legislate on the question of appeals was taken up.   Aemilius Irving, a Liberal back-bencher from Hamilton, announced his intention of proposing an amendment to the Supreme Court Bill which would abolish ordinary appeals to the Privy Council.   Irving felt that it would be disparaging to the prestige of the new court if appeals were permitted to proceed directly from the provincial courts to the Privy Council. He proposed, therefore, that parties appealing from judgments in the local courts be compelled to appear before the Supreme Court.   Irving's main point, however, went much further than this.   He suggested that the House should consider prohibiting all appeals from Canada to statutory courts in Great Britain.   Even with this limitation it would still be possible to maintain the prerogative right of the Crown to hear appeals from any part of the Empire, "because he had found there was a distinction between an appeal to the Sovereign in Council and an appeal to the Appeal Court in the sense of the Judicial Committee of the Privy Council."[5]   The session had been a dreary one for the back-benchers, Irving complained, and the introduction of a controversial topic like the prohibition of appeals would ensure a lively debate.   The Supreme Court Bill itself was in no danger, for both sides of the House accepted its principle.   Thus, partly from capricious motives, partly from conviction, a new element in the doctrine of Canadian autonomy was advanced.

Irving's reference to a "statutory court" in Great Britain requires an explanation. It will be recalled that one of the measures associated with the reform legislation of Gladstone's first Administration was Lord Selborne's Judicature Act of 1873.   That enactment, which fused the systems of equity and common law, authorized the establishment of a final court of appeal for English cases.   To this court was to be transferred the appellate jurisdiction of the Privy Council and the House of Lords.   It was intended that the new court would come into operation in November, 1874, but the overthrow of the Liberal Government delayed its organization.   At the time the Supreme Court Bill was passing through the Canadian Parliament it was understood that Lord Cairns, Disraeli's Lord Chancellor, would confirm legislation to set up the new tribunal.   Thus when Irving introduced his amendment to the Supreme Court Bill in March, 1875, it was thought that there would soon be a new final appellate court for Great Britain, created by act of the Imperial Parliament.   Irving's amendment would have prohibited appeals to this statutory court, while retaining the subject's ancient right to seek

redress at the foot of the Throne. As it happened, Cairns withdrew his legislation authorizing the new appeal court shortly after the Canadian Supreme Court Bill was given
third reading, so that the old system of parallel appeals to the Privy Council and to the
House of Lords was continued. Thus, within Irving's meaning of the term, no "statutory court" with jurisdiction to hear colonial appeals existed in England at the end of
1875. In the larger sense the expression is misleading, however, for the appeal provisions of the Judicial Committee had been placed on a statutory basis in respect of the
colonies by United Kingdom acts of 1833 and 1844. [6]

It was not until the third reading of the Supreme Court Bill, when a lengthy discussion of the new court's composition and functions had been concluded, that Irving
found an opportunity to move his amendment. The substantive part of the amendment,
which became the much discussed clause 47 of the Supreme Court Act, stated that "The
judgment of the Supreme Court shall in all cases be final and conclusive, and no error
or appeal shall be brought from any judgment or order of the Supreme Court to any Court
of Appeal established by the Parliament of Great Britain and Ireland, to which appeals
or petitions to Her Majesty in Council may be ordered to be heard, saving any right
which Her Majesty may be graciously pleased to exercise as Her Royal Prerogative. "[7]
The amendment was accepted by Fournier and supported by several prominent legal
figures in the Liberal party, including T. A. R. Laflamme, [8] a future Minister of Justice. During the discussion which followed the presentation of the amendment, it became clear that members on both sides of the House believed that Irving's description
of the nature of appeals was correct, and that there did exist, in fact, two types of appeal to Great Britain. One, the ordinary reference to the Privy Council (which would
now fall within the jurisdiction of Cairns's statutory court) would be prohibited by the
amendment. The other type, the appeal "as a species of prerogative remedy in peculiar cases," as the Colonial Office later called it, would be retained and, indeed, was
expressly preserved by the saving clause at the end of Irving's amendment. This conception of the dual nature of appeals to the Privy Council undoubtedly enabled many
members of the House to vote for the amendment without injury to their faith in the
unity of the Empire. The Prime Minister, whom no one could accuse of possessing
feelings hostile to the imperial tie, stated that the amendment preserved the appeal to
England as a form of petition in "a final resort. "[9] Another Minister, J. E. Cauchon,
asserted that the special type of appeal continued by Irving's amendment was the "true
tie" between Canada and the mother country. [10] Qualified by these assurances and supported by the Government front bench, Irving's amendment was adopted on division by
a vote of 112 to 40. [11]

Macdonald's was almost the only voice raised in opposition to the amendment.
He declared that if passed it would ensure the Supreme Court Act's disallowance by the
Secretary of State within six months. When the amendment had been adopted he rose
again to complain of the "indecent haste" with which it had been forced on the House.[12]
The decision would undoubtedly be regarded in England as betraying a desire to break
the imperial connection.

Great as would be the benefit of a Supreme Court to the Dominion, it would not compensate for the injury that would be inflicted on the country in wounding the loyal sentiment of the people, and the feeling of uncertainty it would excite in England as to whether there was not an impatience in this country of even the semblance of Imperial authority. Those who disliked the colonial connection spoke of it as a chain, but it was a golden chain, and he, for one, was glad to wear the fetters.[13]

The Government chided him for perennially raising the loyalty issue, and Mackenzie remarked dryly that since appeals in civil proceedings were already limited by the law of Ontario to cases involving over $4,000, then loyalty in Ontario must be the exclusive prerogative of litigants whose suits exceeded that figure. It was improper of Macdonald to suggest that the Supreme Court Bill would be disallowed because of the insertion of the clause abolishing appeals; did he have secret knowledge of the intentions of the British Cabinet?

In the end the Bill became law,[14] although the Senate took strong objection to section 47, and an equal division had to be overcome by the casting vote of the Speaker.[15] Lord Dufferin gave his assent to it on April 8 (although he might have reserved it as touching the prerogatives of the Crown), and it was then transmitted to the Colonial Office. Privately the Governor-General informed Lord Carnarvon that any hesitation he might have felt in assenting to the Bill had been removed by the arguments of his Ministers, who had convinced him that the measure was within the competence of the Dominion Parliament.[16] A statement in favour of the Act, cast in the form of a memorandum by the Prime Minister, accompanied Dufferin's official letter to the Colonial Office. In this document Mackenzie developed the proposition that since the Canadian Parliament possessed the right to regulate appeals it might simply extend the principle and proceed to abolish them, as long as it preserved the special right of petition. Earlier colonial acts limiting the appeal had not been reserved by Great Britain, and there was no reason why this Act, the product of a legislature enjoying more extensive powers than any other in the colonial Empire, should excite objection.[17]

That the right of appeal to the Privy Council had been successfully limited in Canada before the passage of the British North America Act was unquestionable. In discussing this problem it is important to bear in mind the fact that historically appeals have come to the Judicial Committee in two ways: as of right, and as of grace (by special leave). The appeal as of right relates to the subject's ancient privilege of seeking a redress of grievances at the foot of the Throne and has normally existed only where it has been expressly created, by statute or otherwise. The appeal as of grace is founded on the inherent prerogative right of the Crown to exercise an appellate jurisdiction, and may be granted on purely legal grounds or for reasons of discretion. If a subject's ordinary appeal by right has been limited or refused, special leave to appeal may still be given by the Judicial Committee. The distinction between the two types of appeal corresponds roughly to Irving's interpretation of the process, except that he claimed that there were two bodies to which appeals could be directed, whereas in fact there was but one authority administering two classes of appeals. The dual nature of appeals is fundamental to a consideration of the appeal question in 1875-6 and indeed to the entire history of Privy Council appeals since that time.

The colonies of Upper and Lower Canada had limited appeals by virtue of the Constitutional Act of 1791, which stated that laws made by their legislatures would be binding within the provinces in which they were enacted.[18]   In 1794 the Judicature Act of Lower Canada prescribed that the judgments of the Colony's Court of Appeal would be final in all cases where the matter in dispute did not exceed the sum of Ł500.[19] A case arose over this measure in 1832 and was carried to the Privy Council. The Judicial Committee held that the Crown had lost the right to give leave to appeal by delegating the authority to limit appeals to the colonial Legislature. The King, acting as one branch of the Legislature and in company with the other branches, had the power to deprive any of his subjects, in any of his dominions, of their rights. Thus the right of appeal from Lower Canada could be taken away by the Crown with the assistance of the local Legislature.[20]   This decision of 1832, and the Lower Canada Act of 1794 which it upheld, concerned only the appeal as of right. The Crown's ability to grant special leave was not affected by the opinion of the Judicial Committee.

In 1833 the Judicial Committee of the Privy Council was formally constituted by statute, and in 1844 its colonial jurisdiction was defined, when it was given the power to admit appeals from any court in any colony of the Empire.[21]   Thus the appeal by special leave of the Crown was put on a statutory basis, with the result that this aspect of the Judicial Committee's jurisdiction could not be altered except by an act of the United Kingdom Parliament. The Canadian determination to regulate the appeal as of right was again shown in 1849, after the union of the Canadas, when a measure limiting appeals to actions involving more than Ł1,000 was passed by the Legislature and approved by Great Britain.[22]   The position by 1867 was, then, that the Crown's power to grant leave to appeal remained inviolate, while the right of the Canadian Parliament to regulate the appeal as of right seemed, for its part, to be equally unassailable. The passage of the British North America Act failed to make any change in this position.

The legal expert at the Colonial Office in 1875, Sir Julian Pauncefote, examined the Canadian Supreme Court Act, but did not express great concern over its provisions. It was possible that the prerogatives of the Crown were not sufficiently saved by section 47 of the Act and therefore a reference to the Law Officers was probably desirable. Sir Robert Herbert, in approving this recommendation, accepted without demur the Canadian contention that there were two types of appeal: "I do not think it was the intention of the 101st Section of the 'British North America Act 1867' to enable the Dominion Legislature to take away the right of appealing to the Privy Council. The Ministers also do not intend to do this--see Mr. Mackenzie's letter to Lord Dufferin annexed. Whether Clause 47 of the new act sufficiently saves this right is the legal question to be put to the Law Officers and the Privy Council."[23]   And thus the Act was forwarded to the Law Officers and to the Privy Council for consideration, although not before Herbert had received a note saying that the Lord President of the Council, the Duke of

Richmond, who had heard of the passage of the measure, was concerned over its effects on the judicial constitution of the Empire.[24]   The first signs of the approaching
storm were clearly visible on the horizon.

During the summer of 1875, Mackenzie, who was in England on public business,
had several conversations with Lord Carnarvon about the Supreme Court Act. Even at
this early stage Carnarvon had heard privately that the Law Officers entertained doubts
about the validity of clause 47. He therefore intimated to Mackenzie that the Colonial Office might be forced to recommend the disallowance of the whole measure. This
possibility, which so strikingly confirmed Macdonald's predictions, came as a shock to
the Prime Minister. It was made doubly unwelcome by the fact that the Conservative
leader, in campaigning during that summer, was continuing his criticism of the appeal
clause and confidently prophesying the Act's disallowance. To Mackenzie, therefore,
it became essential for the Government's prestige that the Act be not disallowed. He
was able to persuade Lord Carnarvon to accede to an informal arrangement regarding
it. The measure should be allowed to come into force unchanged, with the understanding that if the Law Officers finally objected to section 47, the Canadian Government
would be prepared to modify it in consultation with the Imperial authorities.   This
agreement was purely verbal, although its substance was confirmed in a minute of Herbert's, written just before a message was sent to Canada urging a delay in proclaiming
the Act.

> We cannot, I think, urge the Dominion Government to delay for any long time the
> bringing into operation [of] the new judicature system which is created by this Act
> (already assented to by Lord Dufferin) on account of the possible disallowance of the
> Act at a later stage in consequence of objections that may be held to be establish-
> ed against its appeal provisions. If these objections prevail we can probably ar-
> range with the Dominion Government for the amendment of the present Act, and so
> avoid its disallowance.[25]

Mackenzie had hardly reached Canada before he decided to put the Supreme
Court Act into force immediately. Literally he was acting within the letter of his agreement with the Colonial Office in instituting the new court at his own convenience,
although his precipitate haste and his failure to consult the Office were not in accord
with the spirit of the understanding. It is clear that the decision was dictated by the
strong will of Mackenzie's chief associate, Edward Blake. Up to this point Blake had
taken no part in the discussions over the Supreme Court Act. Indeed he had not even
been in the Government when the Act was passed. As a private member he had voted
for the amendment abolishing appeals but had refrained from speaking on the question.
His hostility to Mackenzie and the policies of his Administration explains his indifferent attitude towards the Supreme Court Act at this period. By the end of the session of
1875 the breach between Mackenzie and Blake had become so detrimental to the interests of the Liberal party that strong efforts were made to reconcile the two men. The
efforts were successful and Blake rejoined the Government as Minister of Justice in May.

At one stage in the negotiations he had been offered and had refused the post of Chief
Justice of the new Supreme Court.

By September, 1875, Blake had become passionately desirous of establishing the
Supreme Court of Canada. He regarded the new court as the keystone in the judicial
arch which had been erected since Confederation. Immersed in the details of the composition and jurisdiction of the new court, Blake had not yet come to examine the matter of appeals to the Privy Council. In his view it was essential, in the first place, to
bring the court into operation and this course he urged on the Prime Minister. Lord
Dufferin was absent from Canada on holiday, which meant that the Administrator of
the Government, the Lieutenant-General commanding the Imperial troops at Halifax,
was required to travel to Ottawa to proclaim the Act. Before issuing the proclamation
General O'Grady Haly telegraphed to the Colonial Office to ask if there was any probability of the measure being disallowed. The reply was not received from England for
a week, and during that time the Administrator consented to proclaim the Act. It came
into force on September 18, although appointments were not made and the court was
not constituted until the next month. [26]

Herbert made a characteristic observation on receiving the Administrator's telegram announcing that the Act had been proclaimed. He expressed his displeasure at
Mackenzie's haste in going ahead with the organization of the court but also acknowledged that allowance must be made for the special political conditions prevailing in
Canada. "We are accustomed to unsatisfactory proceedings on the part of the Dominion Government, which however it is only fair to remember is subject to political pressure which we cannot always fully appreciate. I agree in regretting that they should
have not complied with our request to delay action. "[27] And again, a week later, "I
feel satisfied that they were under the bonâ fide impression that the operation of the
Act was to commence at once and that we have no serious cause of complaint at their
proceedings. "[28]

It now appeared that the Mackenzie Cabinet, by proclaiming the Act, was embarked on a venture from which there could be no turning back. It objected to any delay whatsoever in creating the Court. The Prime Minister telegraphed the Secretary
of State to explain that he had interpreted the informal arrangement as applying only
to the appeal clause in the Act and that there would be no objection to establishing
the Court. He added significantly that the new Supreme Court judges had been drawn
from the provincial benches, and until their successors could be named the work of the
provincial judiciary was at a standstill. [29] Behind Mackenzie, urging him to decisive
action, was the figure of his brilliant but unstable colleague, the Minister of Justice.
"To pause now would be ruinous. If judges not appointed or if bill afterwards disallowed I must resign," he told Mackenzie on one occasion. [30] It was typical of Blake's
sensitive nature that he made every political issue in which he was engaged a matter
of personal honour.

The Colonial Office was itself divided in its attitude toward this Canadian pressure to institute the Supreme Court before the appeal question was settled. One school
of thought, represented by the younger officials like Malcolm, felt that the Act should

be disallowed immediately, or at least the threat of disallowance put clearly before
the Canadian Prime Minister to induce him to hold his hand.[31]   The other view-point,
the one which was eventually adopted, was expressed in the conciliatory words of the
Permanent Under-Secretary. "If the appeal clause of the Act proves to be ultra vires
I apprehend that the course to be taken will be to intimate to the Dominion Government that unless the clause is amended we must disallow the Act. We need not interfere with the establishment of the Court, etc. on account of possible or probable objections to its appeal jurisdiction."[32]   Eventually, after a hectic period of telegraphic exchanges, Haly was informed that the Imperial Government would not object to
the Supreme Court Act being brought into full operation, although it would have liked
to have had the appeal question decided first. Canada must be prepared to modify the
appeal provision of the Act if the opinion of the Law Officers was unfavourable to it."[33]

    With the Supreme Court at last constituted, Edward Blake turned his attention to
the question of appeals to the Privy Council. Assisted by a massive capacity for legal
research, analysis, and exposition, Blake succeeded in a few months in making the topic his own. He sent his first observations on the subject to Mackenzie on October 6, in
a memorandum which eventually found its way to the Colonial Office. Blake's arguments, inflexibly logical and direct, were illumined at all times by the ardour of his
faith in the progressive extension of Canadian autonomy. The problem of appeals to
the Privy Council was more than the subject of a lawyer's brief; it was an opportunity
to vindicate Canadian self-government. By various local acts, confirmed by the Privy
Council in 1832, the rule had been laid down that the right of appeal to the Sovereign
in Council was only to be allowed on terms prescribed by the colonial legislatures. Now
the question arose whether the authority to regulate appeals carried with it the authority to prohibit the appeal altogether. This was clearly the vital problem. To Blake
the extensive powers conveyed to the Canadian Parliament in the British North America Act permitted of only one answer.

    Now it is not pretended that any of the powers of self-government exercised
by the Provinces were under the British North America Act, 1867, taken away from
Canada or its Provinces to be re-vested in the Imperial Parliament; on the contrary,
while all the powers formerly belonging to the Provinces are retained, certain important additional powers ... are expressly conferred on the Dominion....
    It is thus obvious that in carrying out the general principle recited in the pre-
amble, the Imperial Parliament placed, or rather left, in the hands of the subjects
of Her Majesty resident in Canada, control as well over the judicial enforcement
of their laws as over the enactment and alteration of those laws.
    But if it was competent to Provincial authority, and is competent to Canada,
to make the judgment of Local Courts final in the vast majority of cases, it must
surely be, by the same process of reasoning, within its competence to make that
judgment final in all cases.... Unless therefore it should be intended to reverse
the settled current of Local Legislation, to assume a power which has never before
been used in like case, and to withdraw by the exercise of executive authority the

rights and liberties of Canada and the Provinces, conferred by the Imperial Parliament and established by the usage of so many years, it would seem to be impossible
to disallow the Act in question. 34

The Minister of Justice went on to reveal, in a final passage of the memorandum,
the fact that he shared the Canadian view that there existed two kinds of appeal to the
Privy Council. He proceeded further than most of his contemporaries in Parliament,
however, by asserting that the Privy Council's consideration of the second and extraordinary type of appeal--the application for special leave--must be governed by factors of policy rather than of law. It would, in most cases, be inexpedient for the Imperial Government to grant leave to appeal from a court of last resort in Canada, which
was both effective and competent.

[Clause 47] does not purport to do anything positively; no action can be taken by
anyone under colour of it. It simply purports to restrain an appeal. So that if but
for the clause there would be an appeal, there is still an appeal notwithstanding
the clause. And if we are to contemplate the occurrence of an event so unlikely
and so much to be deprecated, as that by Imperial Legislation such an appeal should
be given, that appeal can be taken, notwithstanding the clause in question, just as
it might, if so given, be taken in the cases in which appeals have been so long prohibited by the Provincial Statutes to which I have referred.
    The objection to such action by the Imperial Parliament would be political
--not legal; and would exist whether the clause in question were retained or repealed. 35

Herbert, who was to conduct most of the correspondence with Canada over the
Supreme Court Act, was impressed by the force of Blake's argument. "Mr. Blake's
memorandum is a very able one and he appears to me to have made a strong effort to
write temperately. "36 In large measure he became converted to the point of view
which Blake expressed, although he could never accept the proposition that it was desirable that appeals from Canada should be completely discontinued. He did believe,
however, that the Canadian Parliament indubitably possessed the fullest power to regulate appeals and that the Imperial Government should not insist on allowing appeals
against the wishes of the Legislature of Canada. This attitude he maintained even
when the Law Officers reported that the British North America Act did not envisage a
supreme court which would oust the Privy Council as the final court of appeal for Canada. They concluded, therefore, that appeals to the Privy Council from both national and provincial courts in the Dominion must be retained. 37 The Permanent Under-
Secretary refused to see in this legal opinion any contribution towards a solution of the
problem.

After considering this opinion with Mr. Blake's memorandum and attempting to give some weight to the proportionate [degree] in which our action in this

matter should be governed (1) by the statements made as to the law of the case and
(2) by considerations of policy, I am inclined to think that we have not good ground,
or at least that it is not expedient, to press for the maintenance of any further right
on the part of a Canadian British subject to appeal to the Privy Council [than] the
Legislature and Courts of Canada may assign to him. 38

Herbert's own basis for a possible settlement was contained in a letter which the
Department wrote to the Privy Council Office, transmitting a copy of the Law Officers'
opinion. In this communication it was stated categorically that the Office felt that the
prerogatives of the Crown were adequately saved by clause 47 and there was not, therefore, sufficient ground for disallowing the Supreme Court Act. The regulation of appeals was a responsibility of the Canadian Parliament which it would be inexpedient to
challenge. Regulation might be arranged in terms of the monetary amounts involved
in each case and might also take into consideration important questions of principle
whenever they arose. In any event the Crown should not be advised to grant leave to
appeal except in accordance with regulations mutually agreeable to Her Majesty's Government and Canada. 39

While the Office was endeavouring to work out a formula for the maintenance of
appeals which would be acceptable to other departments in Whitehall, it was being subjected to constant demands from Canada for a statement of its views. Blake, in particular, was intensely anxious to receive an answer to the points raised in his memorandum, and gave the Office little peace until a reply was furnished him. Herbert's
celebrated tact in managing the Ministers of self-governing colonies nowhere appears
to better advantage than in his dealings with the impatient Mackenzie Government at
this time. He told Carnarvon early in November:

When you see Mr. Cartwright you may like to suggest to him that he should
explain to Mr. Blake that the fullest consideration is being paid to his views--that
you are in no way opposed to them, nor do you at present gather that the Act need
be interfered with;--but that it is of course absolutely necessary for you to take
legal advice on so important a subject, and you feel confident the Canadian Government will not misunderstand the cause of the delay in disposing of a matter
which must necessarily be considered by the Privy Council as well as by the Law
Officers. 40

It was at this stage that the Supreme Court Act encountered the censure of the
highest legal authority in England, the Lord Chancellor. Lord Cairns, who held this
post as one of Disraeli's principal colleagues, is now remembered as perhaps the greatest equity judge in the history of English law. Blake himself was a leading equity lawyer, and in Cairns he found a formidable antagonist. Early in November the Lord Chancellor wrote to Carnarvon to express his strong distaste for the Canadian pretensions in
the matter of appeals to the Privy Council. Blake's memorandum excited no approval
from Lord Cairns.

I venture to hope you will not decide on the Canadian Appeal [question] without further consideration. What is desired appears to me to be equivalent to a complete severance of the strongest tie betw. our Colonies and the Mother Country. The Minister of Justice's Memo. is a mass of inaccuracy and bad reasoning. It may be summed up in one proposition:

Canada had a power given her to regulate appeals:

Ergo She may enact that there shall be no appeals whatever ... !41

The Lord Chancellor's attitude was clearly an additional complication in what was becoming a very difficult question. The news from Canada was also unpromising. Dufferin returned to the Dominion to find the Minister of Justice exhibiting one of his frequent displays of petulance. Always a difficult person with whom to conduct business, Blake became intolerably unstable when his emotions were aroused. Dufferin noted this temperamental manifestation in his Minister and warned the Colonial Office about it.

Blake is evidently very eager and excited about the matter, and although I purposely refrained from entering into any argument with him, he evinced a great capacity for ill temper on the subject, should he be thwarted in his present views. Amongst other things that he hinted at was the fact that there was a legal clique in England whose peculiar interest it was to promote a supply of Canadian Law suits in the English Courts of Justice.

I was so struck by the latent symptoms of his rancour, that I thought it as well to warn you by telegram of his state of mind. 42

Carnarvon, faced with these inauspicious circumstances, showed imagination and resourse. Correspondence between the Lord Chancellor, the Canadian Government, and the Colonial Office on the Supreme Court Act would certainly prove protracted and might only produce an inadequate settlement of the question. A better arrangement suggested itself in inviting Blake to England, where, in the moderating presence of the Colonial Secretary, he could discuss the whole matter with Cairns. Blake could be tractable and charming if he wished; Carnarvon was not vain in realizing his own powers of suasion; a personal conference with the Canadian Minister might easily adjust all the existing differences between the parties. A solution obtained in this way would be more likely to be accepted in Canada and would furnish a more permanent basis for the regulation of appeals than any reached through the medium of correspondence. 43 It was a fortunate inspiration which Mackenzie and Blake accepted with the best possible grace. Blake's duties in preparing for the 1876 session of parliament would make it impossible for him to visit England until the late spring of the following year. In the meantime the Canadian Government would leave the appeal jurisdiction of the new Court in suspense. Mackenzie also promised that if Blake could not convince the legal authorities in England of the soundness of clause 47, the Government would amend it at the next session of parliament. 44 The Governor-General thought that benefits additional to those contemplated by the Colonial Office would flow from Blake's journey to London.

It is a most happy thought your having Blake over. He is in very good humour and spirits, and I think that to find himself brought into contact with men superior to himself both intellectually and professionally, will be of great service to him. He lives here amongst toadies and flatters, which is bad for anyone, --while the civility and consideration with which I am sure you and your colleagues will be disposed to receive him, will send him back to us in a better temper with England. He is thoroughly high-minded and conscientious, very intelligent and well worth being educated into a more generous and genial frame of mind. [45]

The next step was to convince the Lord Chancellor that a personal consultation between himself and the Canadian Minister of Justice would be desirable. Cairns was, as Carnarvon told Dufferin, "dead against the Act"[46] and, indeed, looked upon the general tendency of colonial legislatures to interfere in the right of appeal with strong displeasure. Herbert, alarmed by this intransigent attitude, urged Carnarvon to go over the whole matter with Cairns in private discussion. The Lord Chancellor must be informed that there were important grounds of policy for going a certain way to meet the Canadian position. Canada must be conceded the right to control appeals if the Imperial Government was to deny her the authority to prohibit them. A recognition of this premise would afford a good opportunity of arranging a compromise on the issue. And, if an agreement were not reached with Canada, there might be grave consequences. "I would add to the Lord Chancellor in confidence that unless we can concede what the Canadians conceive to be their reasonable demand that some restriction shall be placed upon the vexatious carrying to England by wealthy suitors of cases which have been adequately considered on appeal in Canada, we shall find it impossible to resist their claim to independence in respect of judicial matters and this will involve serious political results."[47]

Conferences were held between the Colonial Secretary and the Lord Chancellor at the end of November, 1875.[48] The Duke of Richmond joined these discussions, from which emerged the fact that Cairns favoured drafting a new clause to be inserted in the Supreme Court Act in place of section 47. Cairns's substitute clause, which was approved by the Lord President, allowed appeals to the Privy Council from Canada only in cases involving the sum of $5,000 or more.[49] Monetary regulation, however, was to be accompanied by a saving clause preserving the Crown's right to grant leave to appeal in any case whatsoever.

Provided always that nothing in this Act contained shall extend or be construed to extend to take away or abridge the undoubted right and authority of Her Majesty Her Heirs and Successors upon the humble petition of any person or persons aggrieved by any Judgment Decree Order or Sentence of the said Supreme Court in Appeal to admit on consideration of the particular circumstances of the case his her or their appeal to Her Majesty in Council from any Rule Judgment Decree Order or Sentence upon such terms and securities limitations restrictions and regulations as Her Majesty in Council Her Heirs and Successors shall think fit.[50]

Carnarvon was not happy about the wording of the new clause. He was realistic enough to know, however, that it represented the maximum concession which could be obtained from Cairns. It had not been easy to arrange a satisfactory compromise with a Lord Chancellor "who though very learned in the Law is not equally appreciative of the distinction of large and small Colonies," he confessed to Dufferin.[51] To the same correspondent he expressed the sense of exasperation which he felt from the contact with a legal mind.

> I have had a great deal of trouble in inducing the Chancellor to take a political instead of a merely legal view of the question, and he considers his clause to be a considerable concession on his side. I have no respect for lawyers or the language with which they delight to darken common sense and according to the light of my poor intelligence I should have said that the conclusion of the clause nullified its commencement. But from a lawyer's point of view it is different and I am told that the sum and substance of the clause is really to give Canada what I understand she has desired and what I have thought reasonable.[52]

Cairns's substitute clause offered a possibility of settlement, in any case, and the Colonial Office lost no time in urging it upon Canada. If the clause were acceptable to the Dominion, there would be no necessity for Blake to come to England to discuss the Supreme Court Act with the Imperial legal authorities. Herbert wrote Dufferin to say that the Imperial Government could not possibly sanction a provision cutting off appeals altogether. (The existence of the Colonial Laws Validity Act, 1865, rendered this prospect impossible. The Colonial Laws Validity Act stated that any colonial law repugnant to the provisions of an Imperial act which through express wording was applied to the colonies, would be void to the extent of the repugnancy.[53] Since the Crown's right to grant leave to appeal from the colonies had been confirmed by British statute, any Canadian act purporting to limit it would be invalid.) The British Government would be prepared, though, to leave the mode and regulation of appeals to the Canadian Parliament, and Cairns himself had stated that he felt good cause would have to be shown before an appeal was allowed to go beyond the Supreme Court of Canada. The Governor-General was informed that many members of the English Parliament had been "pertinacious" in their concern over the effects of clause 47 and that there would almost certainly be questions when Parliament met in February.[54] Much unpleasant publicity would be avoided if the Government could announce that Canada had agreed to a modification of clause 47 which would maintain the appeal. A solution along these lines would help to forward plans for including Canadian securities in the approved list for the investment of British trust funds. Members of Parliament realized the relation between this subject and the matter of appeals, and a settlement of the Supreme Court issue would almost certainly be useful in promoting the other objective.[55]

It was now the turn of the Canadian Government to prove unhelpful. Early in the new year Dufferin telegraphed that his Ministers objected to the subordinate features of

Cairns's proposed clause and felt that it was impossible to settle the question by correspondence. "I conclude Mr. Blake likes the idea of coming home, " commented Herbert curtly. [56] Writing privately to Carnarvon, Dufferin provided the Mackenzie Government's reasons for rejecting the Lord Chancellor's substitute clause. Blake had once again proved the decisive factor in the Canadian attitude. His criticism of the amendment was twofold: first, that it imposed restrictions on Canada's judicial position by permitting the Privy Council to allow appeals even if they fell below the agreed monetary limit; and secondly, that it dealt with appeals to the Privy Council as if they were an aspect of the Queen's prerogative power, whereas actually they had been placed upon a statutory basis. [57] It was Blake's firm opinion, the Governor-General went on, that the subject of appeals could not be settled by correspondence; Lord Carnarvon had invited him to Great Britain to explain his views to the Imperial legal authorities and he had accepted the invitation. To abandon the plan of personal discussion would dishearten the Ministry's supporters and create confusion in the Dominion. There seemed to be one aspect of Blake's stand, continued Dufferin, through which agreement might be reached. The Minister of Justice's "hobby" was the assertion of Canada's autonomy in constitutional matters. If clause 47 were not criticized from this point of view, but from the vantage ground of policy and expediency, Blake might be persuaded to accept a compromise. There would be no reflection on his personal honour if the Canadian right to enact clause 47 was left unchallenged. "Blake's principal pre-occupation seemed to be to know whether the English Government would object to the abolition of appeal[s] as unconstitutional and ultra vires, or merely as contrary to public policy. If he is satisfied that the constitutional right of the Canadian Parliament to define the limits within which appeals are permissible will not be disputed, he would I think be ready to yield to considerations of utility.... "[58]

Blake's summary rejection of the Lord Chancellor's proposed amendment was partly caused by the fact that as yet he had not been furnished an answer to his memorandum of October 6. This had become a sore point with him, since he considered the failure to comment on his views as a personal slight. The Colonial Office explanation that the question was largely a political one demanding personal communication rather than correspondence failed to satisfy him. [59] Blake felt that as he had been frank in expressing his opinions to the British Government it was only right that he should receive similar consideration from London. He was soon to be engaged in argument, he claimed, with "powerful controversialists" in England and needed a knowledge of the counter-case to prepare himself for the struggle. Herbert had apparently once made the observation that Blake was entitled to a reply, and Dufferin had promised a document on the strength of this remark. [60] Consequently the Governor-General joined his Ministers in asking the Office to abandon its original decision and prepare an exposition of its views on the appeal topic. [61]

The Department, as a matter of fact, was not without guidance on the subject of appeals, for since August of the previous year it had possessed a document drawn up in the Privy Council Office defending the judicial unity of the British Empire. The decision was now reached to send this paper to Canada, accompanied by a memorandum composed by the legal staff of the Office and bearing the Lord Chancellor's mark of approval. In the dispatch transmitting these papers Carnarvon did not attempt to argue the question, but confined himself to pointing out the unsettling effect which any radical change in the procedure of appeals would have on public opinion on both sides of the Atlantic. Under present conditions the abolition of appeals would almost certainly be interpreted by many people as implying a weakening of the connection between Great Britain and the Dominion.

> At the present moment, and, indeed, as I firmly believe, in any consideration of so serious and delicate a constitutional question, the more statesmanlike course is to inquire, not whether the Dominion Legislature has or has not had vested in it the power of terminating appeals to this country from the local Courts, nor whether the Queen is able, or may be advised to give up, directly or indirectly, any part of her prerogative, but whether it is expedient for the Dominion Parliament, by its Legislation, to bring such questions to an issue. [62]

The memorandum prepared in the Privy Council Office was the work of Henry Reeve. [63] It provided a classic statement of the usefulness both to the colonies and to the mother country of the system of appeals to the Privy Council.

> It secures to every subject of Her Majesty throughout the Empire the right to claim redress from the Throne; it provides a remedy in certain cases not falling within the jurisdiction of ordinary Courts of Justice; it removes causes from the influence of local prepossessions; it affords the means of maintaining the uniformity of the law of England in those Colonies which derive the great body of their law from Great Britain; and it enables suitors, if they think fit, to obtain a decision, in the last resort, from the highest judicial authority and legal capacity existing in the Metropolis. [64]

In addition the memorandum enumerated the various special advantages which flowed from the operations of the Judicial Committee of the Privy Council. Their Lordships exercised a salutary influence on the standard of proceedings in colonial courts, for every judge was aware that his decisions might be carried to the Judicial Committee. In Canada the Privy Council played a useful role in arbitrating disputes between the Central Government and the provincial governments, between different races and religions; it protected the property of British subjects resident in the colonies; and it acted as a tribunal in conflicts between colonial and Imperial laws. All these points, here first expressed in a weighty manner, have appeared ad infinitum in the periodic discussions of the appeal question that have occurred from the seventies until the present day. Most of them were countered by Blake in 1876, but there was one feature of the appellate jurisdiction of the Privy Council which he could not hope to rebut. In the Empire of this period, in which Great Britain occupied a dominant position, both in law and in fact, the system of appeals to the Privy Council existed as a manifestation of that hegemony. The right to hear appeals was an attribute of an imperial power, which, in the last analysis, could only be divested by an act of pure self-abnegation. To renounce that right, to destroy the judicial unity of the Empire, would be truly, as Reeve said, "an abdication of Sovereignty itself."

> The Supreme Appellate authority of the Empire or the realm is unquestionably one of the highest functions and duties of sovereignty. The power of construing, determining, and enforcing the law in the last resort is, in truth, a power which overrides all other powers....
>
> This power has been exercised for centuries, as regards all the dependencies of the Empire, by the sovereigns of this Country in Council.... To abolish this controlling power, and to abandon each Colonial dependency to a separate Final Court of Appeal of its own, is obviously to destroy one of the most important ties which still connect all parts of the Empire in common obedience to the source of law, and to renounce the last and most essential mode of exercising the authority of the Crown over its possessions abroad.[65]

The more important of the two documents sent out to Canada at this time was the one drafted by W. R. Malcolm, the Assistant Under-Secretary at the Colonial Office supervising the work of the North American Department. Its significance lay in the fact that in its commentary on clause 47 the Canadian impression that there existed two authorities to which colonial appeals could be directed was abruptly upset. Cairns, in the only substantial change he made in the memorandum when it was submitted to him for his approval, pointed out that the "Court of Appeal established by ... Parliament," as envisaged by Irving, had never been created. Section 47 was therefore inoperative, because it preserved by its saving clause the right of appeal which it set out to deny.

> The promoters [of the Supreme Court Bill] appear, while admitting, of course, that no enactments of the Canadian Parliament could override Her Majesty's prerogative rights, to have drawn a distinction between an appeal to the Sovereignty in Council as a species of prerogative remedy in peculiar cases, and an appeal in the regular course leading to a reference to the Judicial Committee. This distinction, however, cannot be maintained. The appeal to the Sovereign in Council is one and indivisible. Every hearing of a case and every judgment delivered in the name of the Queen in Council is an exercise of the prerogative.... [66]

The Colonial Office memorandum concluded by remarking that the desirable object in these discussions was to effect a procedure which would restrain frivolous and vexatious appeals, while allowing appeals on important questions of law. Admittedly it was sometimes difficult to draw a distinction between these two classes of appeals. In the long run, however, the creation of a strong and respected Supreme Court in Canada, combined with an efficient code of regulation, would render the problem less burdensome. Eventually the right of appeal from Canada to the Privy Council, except in rare cases, would fall into disuse. Canadians would then not have been deprived of their rights, but would have renounced them.

Thus, regrettably late in the day and without ceremony, the correct status of the appeal in relation to the English judiciary was disclosed to Canada. Whether, if this information had been known to the Canadian Parliament at the time the Supreme Court Bill was being considered, it would have affected the support given to Irving's amendment, is a difficult matter to determine. What seems to be clear, however, is the fact that only a fraction of the members of the Canadian House would have voted for clause 47 if it had been described to them as prohibiting the appeal in all cases whatsoever. The Crown's right to allow appeals in exceptional circumstances was an aspect of the appeal procedure which most Canadians wished to retain in 1875. Blake and some of the Quebec Rouges were definitely not of this opinion but they were a minority in Canada then and for many years later. The fact that it was not until 1938 that the Parliament of Canada was next called upon to abolish all appeals to the Privy Council furnishes additional support for this statement.

The force of the Lord Chancellor's argument was not lost upon Blake when he came to study the memoranda sent from the Colonial Office. As he examined more closely the subject of Privy Council appeals he was forced to conclude that Cairns's reasoning was unanswerable. His doubts about the validity of the Canadian case were expressed in letters which he wrote at this time to a trusted friend, David Mills, one of the leading Liberal members from Ontario. There were two points on which he confessed uneasiness: whether the Canadian Parliament was the proper body to abolish appeals and, if so, whether it could be done by the ambiguous wording of clause 47 of the Supreme Court Act. On the first matter he wrote: "It cannot be denied that the prerogative to be interfered with is an ancient and important one and that legislation upon it, granting the constitutional power of Parliament to legislate, comes more fairly within the purview of the revision of the Imperial authorities than would mere domestic legislation."[67] His fears about the practical effect of section 47 were even stronger: "It does seem to me that if the first part of the 47th clause applies, as it fairly may, to all appeals, then the last part saves the prerogative of appeals to the Queen in Council. If so we are really fighting about nothing or less than nothing; since an unrestricted appeal is worse than a restricted one."[68]

The Minister of Justice went to England prepared to wage vigorous opposition with the Imperial Government over clause 47, but in his heart he must have known that the battle was already lost. Something of his uneasiness was transmitted to the Colonial Office when he wrote to request that the preliminary exchanges of opinion between Canada and Great Britain on the topic should be kept unofficial. Herbert shrewdly guessed the motives behind this suggestion. "I think he [Blake] may mean that they shall be considered unofficial and preliminary discussions--practically no doubt his object is not to have them published as he wishes to compromise or retreat. An unexpected pleasure."[69]

Blake's visit to London in the summer of 1876 was a not-altogether happy experience. He arrived to find the Beaconsfield Cabinet deeply immersed in the problem of Turkey, where a decision had to be taken as to whether Great Britain would join the continental powers in forcing the Turks to reform their government. For the first time since the death of Palmerston England seemed ready to play an active part in European affairs. Naturally the Near Eastern crisis had an unsettling effect on the minds of public men and the higher civil service. In addition Parliament was still sitting and Carnarvon, as one of the principal Government leaders in the Lords, was too occupied with the business of Westminster to spare much time for his colonial duties. Blake had a formidable list of topics, in addition to the Supreme Court Act, to discuss with various departments of the British Government. He had, for instance, to take up with the Foreign Office a proposed Canadian Extradition Act, with the Admiralty the establishment of Canadian maritime courts for the Great Lakes, with the Board of Trade the restrictions placed on Canada's shipping by the English merchant shipping laws, and with the Colonial Office the important matter of the revision of the Governor-General's Commission and Instructions. All these negotiations influenced the progress of the Supreme Court question and contributed to produce a situation which Blake, with his quick temper, often found almost intolerable. His private sense of exasperation was summed up in letters to his chief in Ottawa. "My bulletin will show you how frightfully slow the business is. I do everything possible to advance it, save being importunate for an interview; this I cannot undertake. But I have kept myself absolutely dis-engaged so as to be ready at any moment at which our Lords and Masters can find that they have half an hour to consider the affairs of their servants. "[70]

At the Colonial Office Blake had most of his dealings with the Permanent Under-Secretary, who, as it can be gauged from his earlier sentiments on the Supreme Court Act, was sympathetic to the general aims of the Canadian Government. But the Office had no final authority to decide the question of appeals and Blake soon discovered that in the Law Officers and the Lord Chancellor he had more formidable obstacles to surmount. He had several interviews with Herbert and Carnarvon and finally, on July 5, a meeting was arranged for him with the great Lord Cairns. Since coming to England Blake had learned that Cairns was adamant in the conviction that section 47 did not affect the continuance of the appeal. The Lord Chancellor favoured leaving the Act unchanged, therefore, but believed that the Canadian Government should at once legislate for the regulation of appeals. Herbert, of course, had long since come to the conclusion that in regulation lay a way out of the difficulty, although he envisaged a control of appeals by the Canadian courts and Executive that would virtually amount to a prohibition of references to the Privy Council. But could a compromise of this sort be negotiated with the unyielding Blake?

It is impossible not to sympathize with the Canadian dislike to the appeal to this Country. It ought to be practicable to devise some means of saving it for important questions of principle and preventing its vexatious use in ordinary litigation. If every petition for appeal to the Privy Council were reported upon first by the Courts whose judgment is appealed against and then sent to the Colonial Office

with the further report of the Dominion Cabinet, there could hardly be any question as to the Queen being adequately advised, so as to ensure the throwing out of
vexatious appeals. But will anything which preserves any appeal to England satisfy Mr. Blake?[71]

The truth was that Blake had shown a more inflexible attitude towards the abolition of
appeals than he knew was warranted on legal grounds. This piece of deception was occasioned by his desire to avoid any discussion of the principle of regulation. For regulation was, to the Mackenzie Government, politically inexpedient. It would mean, in
the first place, a withdrawal from the publicly understood effect of clause 47, with a
consequent loss of prestige, and it might make the total abolition of appeals much more
difficult for later generations to achieve. It would also be establishing no new principle,
for appeals were already limited from Canada by provincial enactments. "All or nothing" could be taken as Blake's motto in the appeal discussions with the Imperial Government, although in the end his inherent honesty made him consider thoughtfully the
basis on which regulation could be founded.

The interview with the Lord Chancellor, about which Carnarvon had felt some
apprehension, passed, in Cairns's own words, "in a satisfactory and friendly manner."[72]
Both men had been well prepared for the meeting! Cairns made at the outset his point
that clause 47 was inoperative and Blake was forced to agree that this interpretation of
the appeal provision was correct. There was, therefore, no necessity to disallow the
Supreme Court Act or seek its modification. When they passed on to discuss the subject of regulation, Blake seized the opportunity to argue for the abolition of appeals.
It was a forlorn hope. As he told Mackenzie in his report of the interview, not only
was the time insufficient for an exposition of the topic, but the Lord Chancellor was
clearly unresponsive.

> I said that while we did not and could not expect that the Government would of-
> ficially intimate their assent to such a policy, yet a consideration and discussion
> of it would be valuable.... I referred to our rights of legislation with which our
> rights of exposition and administration should be commensurate, and to the opin-
> ion that we should settle our own legal disputes among ourselves; to the unfamil-
> iarity of judges and counsel here with our laws and constitutional system, to the
> loss of power and prestige in the Supreme Court if not made final; to the danger
> that it might be passed over; to the [injustice] of so many intermediate appeals;
> to the great delay and frightful expenses.... [73]

Blake's remarks on this part of the interview ended: ".... no conclusion was reached
but I am not sanguine that he will assent to the abolition of the appeal."[74] After this
digression, Blake was forced to return to the question of the regulation of appeals. He
entered into a discussion on this subject with extreme hesitation, urging that the matter be given only a small place in the official correspondence arising from his visit to
England. His proposals for limiting appeals were severe. Regulation should be by Can-

adian act, not by an order in council from the United Kingdom; it should be based on a very high appealable value, with no discretion permitted anyone to allow appeals in cases below this value. There should be no right to appeal directly from provincial courts to the Privy Council. (In other words, Blake, in 1876, looked towards the day when the new Supreme Court would emerge as the court of judicial review for the Canadian federation.) In addition special provisions should be inserted in the code of regulation to guard against vexatious or frivolous appeals that might otherwise qualify for hearing as being above the specified monetary limit. Cairns approved these principles in general, and the Colonial Office also gave them its blessing, but to Blake they represented an imperfect alternative to abolition.

The interview, however, had not been completely unsatisfactory from Blake's point of view. It was true that Cairns had set his face against abolition but, on the other hand, he had conceded the fullest right, on the part of Canada, to control the flow of appeals to the mother country. Blake had gained this end armed only with an ineffective statutory provision. The experience had not been a pleasant one; it had been like fighting with one arm tied behind one's back, he told Mackenzie. [75]   There remained now only the question of tactics: the manner in which the Imperial Government's decision would be transmitted to Canada. This matter was vitally important to the Mackenzie Administration, which would be harmed politically if the news of the fate of the Supreme Court Act reached Canada inopportunely. To persuade the Disraeli Government to announce its verdict on the appeal question in a form compatible with Canadian self-respect was Blake's final task before returning to Ottawa.

He suggested to the Colonial Office, shortly after his meeting with Cairns, that a formal dispatch should be sent to Canada simply announcing that the Supreme Court Act had been approved and would be left to its operation. There should be no explanation of this decision. If it were judged necessary to add a word of comment on the effect of clause 47, the observations should be as brief as was consistent with clarity. Under no circumstances should the Imperial Government bring up the questions of abolition or regulation in communicating its views to Canada. These topics should be left completely open. Appeals might be safely left in an unregulated state for the time being; for this reason there was no necessity to precipitate a decision. [76]   In the meantime Lord Cairns had drawn up a draft dispatch announcing the British Government's decision on the subject of appeals. It contained a discussion of the regulation issue, which was urged upon the Canadian Ministry for consideration. [77]   Carnarvon generously sent this draft to Blake for his comments, noting that they had previously reviewed the whole question without reserve and might usefully continue the arrangement. [78] With most of what was contained in Cairns's dispatch Blake could find little objection. The only point at which his views differed from the Lord Chancellor's related to the desirability of mentioning the question of regulation. He was still firmly convinced that the most suitable course was to ignore this matter entirely in official communications. If the Lord Chancellor insisted upon referring to the topic it should be made the subject of a confidential dispatch to the Governor-General.

As your Lordship is aware, we are entirely uncommitted on that subject; I am quite clear that there must be either regulation or abolition at no distant day, but which is yet to be determined; and I am equally clear that the Government would have infinitely less difficulty in dealing with the question on the basis of regulation if there be no allusion to it; and their policy on the question should appear to be, as it in fact would be, quite spontaneous. [79]

Herbert recommended that the changes which Blake proposed in Cairns's draft should be accepted and the amended dispatch then went back to the Lord Chancellor. The Secretary of State accompanied it by no less than three personal letters written during the course of the next few days. Carnarvon felt that Blake's reasons for wanting the regulation question omitted from discussion were valid, and that if the matter was left to itself it might slumber for years. At any event it should not be raised in the rather heated atmosphere surrounding the Supreme Court Act. "There seems to me some force in this view: and I should be glad to avoid fresh controversies with Canada on these grave constitutional questions where it is practicable to do so. . . ."[80] When Cairns insisted on pressing the matter on Canada the Colonial Secretary wrote that Blake's suggestion of embodying it in a confidential dispatch to the Governor-General was a good one. "It is a course of proceeding to which on delicate subjects I have often had recourse."[81] He told the sceptical Cairns that he was convinced Blake was acting fairly with the Imperial Government in describing the parliamentary situation in Canada. Before agreeing to the suggested form of the dispatch Cairns nearly upset the course of the negotiation by proposing a declaratory act to affirm the United Kingdom's position in the light of clause 47. Carnarvon blanched at this idea, knowing the reception it would have from Blake and the Canadian Government. He wrote immediately to the Lord Chancellor explaining frankly that there was no excuse for courting trouble with Canada over the question of appeals.

[Blake's] own idea--clearly and confessedly--is to get rid of appeals. I think that here he is open to much abatement of terms and that he would be willing to retain the [appeal] provided that it could be made to weigh less heavily. It seems to me that there are several solutions of the question in this sense: but the whole matter is a very grave one: there are quite enough serious affairs pending between Canada and this country at this moment to make me at least desirous of not adding to them: and my wish and object wld. be to temporise and get rid of the more pressing embarassment of cl. 47 leaving the larger subject to the future.
Remember that whatever may be my own opinions or heresies as I fancy you consider them--I have as yet kept the position entirely in our hands. I have not led him to think that we could make a surrender of the right of appeal: and whilst I have told him that my own desire, and I felt sure, that of my colleagues would be to make any system of appeals as little burdensome or inconvenient as possible to Canadians, that great value was attached to the retention of the right in England. My own impression is that if the question were to be forced on for settlement--wh.

I hope we may avoid--we could only retain the right of appeal by making some modifications which would give a practical relief to those who now complain. [82]

Such plain speaking carried the day. Cairns dropped the suggestion of a declaratory act and accepted the plan of sending two dispatches to Canada. [83]

Before Blake left England in the late summer he drew up a memorandum[84] em-bodying his reply to the arguments of the Lord Chancellor and the Registrar of the Privy Council on the appeal topic. It is a state paper in the characteristic Blake vein, feat-uring strong dialectic charged with the faith of a devoted Canadian nationalist. Blake believed that the Parliament of Canada, in a subject in which it had been authorized to legislate, could abolish any prerogative of the Crown affecting the Canadian people. North American legislatures had modified royal prerogatives in the past, and they could do so again. The Canadian House possessed the power of establishing a judicial system for the Dominion and under this authority it might legislate to abolish appeals. The in-stalments of self-government which had been (and would be) conceded to Canada need not serve as precedents for other parts of the Empire, for Canada was more advanced politically than any other colony of the Crown. The Dominion must be allowed to de-cide for herself whether she wanted to retain appeals to the Privy Council if, as was so often stated, the right of appeal was of as much benefit to the colonies as to the mother country. "The jurisdiction existing for the benefit of the Colonies, and not for that of the Mother Country, Canada should be permitted, in this aspect of the case, to judge for herself, as there is no doubt she is the best judge; and to decline what she may con-ceive to be no longer an advantage."[85]   Blake claimed that Imperial interests would be safeguarded even if the appeal from Canada were cut off, for there would still remain the British Government's powers of reservation and disallowance over Cana-adian legislation. (This assurance wore a Jesuitical air, for during that very summer Blake had successfully persuaded the Colonial Office to alter the form of the Gov-ernor-General's Instructions to omit the sections detailing the subjects of reserved bills.)

Blake then turned to discuss several of the alleged advantages of the appeal sys-tem that had been put forward by its defenders. The suggestion that the legal attain-ments of English judges were higher than those of their Canadian counterparts he swept aside contemptuously. "The lives, liberty and property of the Canadian people are practically subject to their own laws; these laws they make, unmake and alter at pleas-ure. If they are fit to make, they should be fit to expound the law, its creation also should, by the same process of reasoning, be the work of the highest judicial authority and legal capacity existing in the metropolis."[86]   Similarly any fears that the prop-erty of British subjects held in Canada would not be protected by the Canadian courts were brusquely dismissed. That the appeal to the Privy Council was a link of empire Blake would not admit, for residents of Great Britain did not possess the privilege of referring to the Judicial Committee but took their appeals ultimately to the House of Lords. The Minister of Justice went on to develop a line of argument that was much in his thoughts at this time--that any advantage, in hearing Canadian cases, which

the Judicial Committee enjoyed from its impartiality was more than offset by its lack
of expert knowledge of the constitutional structure of the Dominion. This deficiency
was of particular moment when the Privy Council acted as a court of judicial review
for Canada. Then it became obvious that judges brought up under a unitary form of
government were often at a loss to interpret and expound a federal constitution.

> They may indeed learn from the argument in an isolated case the view of a partic-
> ular counsel upon a matter, but the daily learning and experience which Canadians
> living under the Canadian Constitution acquire is not theirs, nor can it be effective-
> ly instilled into them for the purpose of a particular appeal. I maintain that this
> training and learning, which can be given only by residence upon the spot, is of such
> vital consequence as to overbalance the advantages flowing from the probably sup-
> erior mental capacity of the Judges of the London Tribunal. [87]

He stated the same argument more forcefully four years later in the Canadian House.
"The British North America Act is a skeleton. The true form and proportions, the true
spirit of our Constitution, can be made manifest only to the men of the soil. I deny
that it can be well expounded by men whose whole lives have been passed, not merely
in another, but in an opposite sphere of practice; and these men must come to the consideration of these topics, at the greatest disadvantage and from the wrong point of
view." [88]

In making this point Blake had touched upon a major criticism of the system of
appeals to the Privy Council; a criticism which, however, he could not be expected to
foresee. This was the charge made frequently in later years, that the Privy Council, in
interpreting the British North America Act, diverged to a remarkable extent from the
intentions of the architects of the Canadian federation. Today this assessment of the
role of the Privy Council in the constitutional development of Canada is supported by
an impressive section of Canadian legal opinion.

Blake's memorandum was designed for the information of the Colonial Office and
English Government on the occasion when the question of appeals was next considered.
For there seems no doubt that Blake intended to reopen the subject at some convenient
opportunity, in spite of the unfavourable reception his proposals had obtained from Lord
Cairns. The whole drift of his final paper was directed towards justifying abolition and
in addition he apparently expressed his hopes verbally to several members of the Office
before he left London. Loose drafting of the clause prohibiting the right of appeal, caused by an imperfect knowledge of the English judicial system, had frustrated his efforts
in 1876, but with a more carefully phrased provision, the desired object might be achieved. It is unlikely, in view of the prevailing mood of the Canadian Parliament, that
Blake could have secured such a provision, and equally unlikely, because of the opposition of the legal elements in the Imperial Government, that a clause with this intent
could have obtained the necessary approval from the United Kingdom, even if it had
been a paragon of legislative draftsmanship. But it is possible that a compromise might
have been worked out, as on so many constitutional issues in the history of the British

Empire, which would have conceded the substance to Canadian assertiveness, while retaining the shadow in imperial dogma. At any event the problem of appeals, as it was regarded by English and Canadian administrators, had clearly not been disposed of in 1876. Malcolm, after reading Blake's memorandum, expressed the belief that the question had been given only a temporary and partial solution. Herbert, with the weariness of the senior official who has all the cares of the colonial empire for his province, concurred in this opinion. "I wish it were likely to remain long dormant."[89] As it happened, by 1878 the Liberals in Canada had fallen from power, and Macdonald and his party, safe in office for twenty years, refrained from opening the question of the abolition of appeals. The Colonial Office was never to encounter the subject again from a Canadian source.

And so Blake returned to Canada, with the Supreme Court Act unimpaired and approved by the British Government. The achievement was of considerable assistance to the political prestige of the Mackenzie Government, after Macdonald's dire prophecies of amendment or disallowance. But Sir John had gained his point as well, for his "golden chain" of empire, the right of appeal to the Privy Council, remained, for Canadian litigants, inherently strong. Blake acknowledged, in the terse report which he gave the Canadian Cabinet on the Supreme Court Act, that the consequences of his mission to London should not be too closely examined.

It was chiefly on this subject that a conference was desired by Lord Carnarvon, with whom, as also with the Lord Chancellor, the undersigned fully discussed the measure.

Eventually Lord Carnarvon informed the undersigned that Her Majesty's Government had decided that the Act should be left to its operation.[90]

Truly, only the essentials were being disclosed about the eventful history of clause 47 of the Supreme Court Act![91]

REFERENCES

1. Debates of the House of Commons (Canada), 1880, I, 253 (Feb. 26, 1880).

2. Section 101 of 30 and 31 Vict., c. 3.

3. Debates of the House of Commons (Canada), 1875, I, 284-8 (Feb. 23, 1875).

4. Ibid., 288-9.

5. Debates of the House of Commons (Canada), 1875, I, 746 (March 16, 1875).

6. See above, 138. Fournier had referred to this contemplated change in the appeal court structure of England in his remarks on introducing the Supreme Court Bill. He thought that it would have the effect of diminishing appeals from Canada since a court of law would not have the same attraction for Canadian litigants as a court of prerogative. Debates of the House of Commons (Canada), 1875, I, 286 (Feb. 23, 1875).

7. Ibid. , 976 (March 30, 1875).

8. Like Fournier, a prominent member of the parti Rouge. It is significant that most of the support for the amendment abolishing appeals came from this radical group in Quebec politics. See Dufferin to Carnarvon, private, Nov. 11, 1875: PRO 30/6/28.

9. Debates of the House of Commons (Canada), 1875, I, 979 (March 30, 1875).

10. Ibid. , 977.

11. Ibid. , 980.

12. Ibid.

13. Ibid. , 981.

14. 38 Vict. , c. 11.

15. Debates of the Senate (Canada), 1875, 724-38 (April 6, 1875).

16. Dufferin to Carnarvon, private, April 9, 1875: PRO 30/6/28.
Later Dufferin experienced some doubts as to whether a Supreme Court for Canada would be an unmixed blessing. He felt that the new Court's capacity to define the constitutional limits of the various legislatures in the Colony might allow the Dominion to withdraw legislation from Imperial review. In addition, in a dispute between the Governor-General and his Ministers, a decision in their favour by the Supreme Court would strengthen their hand. Dufferin felt that Blake's advocacy of a Supreme Court possessing final appellate jurisdiction was not altogether disinterested and that through his efforts Blake believed "he was forging an instrument for the further extension of Canadian independence. " (Dufferin to Carnarvon, private, June 1, 1876: PRO 30/6/29.) In general the Governor-General believed that the appeal was not important as a link of empire and might be abandoned except in the rare case of an important constitutional dispute. (Dufferin to Carnarvon, private, Nov. 11, 1875: PRO 30/6/28 and Dufferin to Carnarvon, private, Feb. 2, 1876: PRO 30/6/29.)

17. Memo. by Alexander Mackenzie on the Supreme Court Bill, 1875, enclosed in Dufferin to Carnarvon, no. 93, April 9, 1875: CO 42/736.

18. 31 George III, c. 31, s. 2.

19. 34 George III, c. 6, s. 30.

20. Cuvillier v. Aylwin, [1832] 2 Knapp, P.C. 72.
Keith claims that this decision was incorrect, for the Statute of 1794 expressly preserved the royal prerogative to hear appeals (Keith, Responsible Government, III, 1358). Surely the point at issue, however, related to the appeal as of right, which was the subject of the Lower Canada restriction confirmed by the Judicial Committee. This restriction of the right of appeal had been directly authorized by a Statute of the British Parliament--the Constitutional Act.

21. 3 and 4 William IV, c. 41; 7 and 8 Vict., c. 69.

22. 12 Vict., c. 63, s. 46.

23. Minute by Herbert, May 5, 1875, on Dufferin to Carnarvon, no. 93, April 9, 1875: CO 42/736.

24. Henry Reeve (Registrar of the Judicial Committee of the Privy Council) to Herbert, June 30, 1875: ibid.

25. Minute by Herbert, Sept. 17, 1875, on Officer Administering the Government of Canada to Carnarvon, telegram, Sept. 15, 1875: CO 42/737.
See also Carnarvon to Officer Administering the Government of Canada, no. 237, Oct. 5, 1875: CO 42/738.

26. Haly to Carnarvon, telegram, Sept. 22, 1875: CO 42/737. See also Officer Administering the Government of Canada to Carnarvon, no. 67, Sept. 28, 1875, Confidential Print, "North America No. 84," 76-7: CO 807/13.
The Supreme Court did not call its first cases until June, 1876. Frank MacKinnon, "The Establishment of the Supreme Court of Canada," Canadian Historical Review, XXVII (Sept., 1946), 269.

27. Minute by Herbert, Sept. 23, 1875, on Haly to Carnarvon, telegram, Sept. 22, 1875: CO 42/737.

28. Minute by Herbert, Sept. 30, 1875, on Haly to Carnarvon, telegram, Sept. 29, 1875: ibid.

29. Mackenzie to Carnarvon, telegram, Sept. 27, 1875: CO 42/740.

30. Blake to Mackenzie, telegram, Sept. 1875, quoted in F. H. Underhill, "Edward Blake, the Supreme Court Act, and the Appeal to the Privy Council, 1875-76," Canadian Historical Review, XIX (Sept., 1938), 250.

31. Minute by Malcolm, Sept. 25, 1875, on Haly to Carnarvon, telegram, Sept. 25, 1875: CO 42/737.

32. Minute by Herbert, Sept. 29, 1875, on ibid.

33. Carnarvon to Haly, telegram, Oct. 1, 1875: CO 42/737. Carnarvon to Officer Administering the Government of Canada, no. 237, Oct. 5, 1875: CO 42/738, provides a résumé of the telegraphic correspondence relating to the proclamation of the Supreme Court Act.

34. Memo. by Edward Blake on the Supreme Court Act, Oct. 6, 1875, enclosed in Mackenzie to Carnarvon, confidential, Oct. 6, 1875: CO 42/740.
Excerpts printed in L. A. Cannon, "Some Data Relating to the Appeal to the Privy Council," Canadian Bar Review, III (Oct., 1925), 457-8.

35 Memo. by Edward Blake on the Supreme Court Act, Oct. 6, 1875, enclosed in Mackenzie to Carnarvon, confidential, Oct. 6, 1875: CO 42/740.

36. Minute by Herbert, Oct. 25, 1875, on Mackenzie to Carnarvon, confidential, Oct. 6, 1875: ibid.

37. Law Officers (Sir Richard Baggallay and Sir John Holker) to Colonial Office, Oct. 15, 1875: CO 42/738.

38. Minute by Herbert, Oct. 25, 1875, on ibid.
From this moment on it can be said that the Colonial Office approach to the problem of Canadian appeals was based primarily on political considerations--i.e. the effect of the appeal on the relations between Great Britain and Canada. It is this fact which made for misunderstanding with the Lord Chancellor, who naturally took the contrary view and regarded the appeal from a purely legal standpoint.

39. Colonial Office to Privy Council Office, Nov. 1, 1875: CO 42/738.

40. Minute by Herbert, Nov. 3, 1875, on Dufferin to Carnarvon, telegram, Nov. 2, 1875: CO 42/737.

41. Cairns to Carnarvon, private, Nov. 2, 1875: PRO 30/6/6.

42. Dufferin to Carnarvon, private, Nov. 3, 1875: PRO 30/6/28. Dufferin's telegram was sent on Nov. 2, 1875: CO 42/737.

43. Carnarvon to Dufferin, private, Nov. 4, 1875: PRO 30/6/28.

44. Dufferin to Carnarvon, private, Nov. 11, 1875: ibid.

45. Dufferin to Carnarvon, private, Nov. 19, 1875: ibid.

46. Carnarvon to Dufferin, private, Nov. 4, 1875: ibid.

47. Minute by Herbert, Nov. 13, 1875, on Dufferin to Carnarvon, telegram, Nov. 12, 1875: CO 42/737.

48. Carnarvon to Cairns, private, Nov. 21, 1875: PRO 30/6/6.

49. Herbert had previously suggested a floor of $500 for appeal cases. Minute by Herbert, Nov. 13, 1875, on Dufferin to Carnarvon, telegram, Nov. 12, 1875: CO 42/737.

50. Clause proposed by the Lord Chancellor in lieu of section 47 of the Supreme Court Act, enclosed in Privy Council Office to Colonial Office, private, Dec. 2, 1875: CO 42/738.

51. Carnarvon to Dufferin, private, Jan. 20, 1876: PRO 30/6/29.

52. Carnarvon to Dufferin, private, Dec. 15, 1875: PRO 30/6/28.
See also Carnarvon to Dufferin, private, Feb. 18, 1876: PRO 30/6/29, for a similar outburst against the Lord Chancellor.

53. 28 and 29 Vict., c. 63, s. 2.

54. There is no evidence that the British Parliament was ever greatly concerned over the passing of the Canadian Supreme Court Act. There was a question asked about the Act in August, 1875, by a Liberal member for Coventry (Hansard, Third Series, CCXXVI, 616-17 [Aug. 6, 1875]) but there was no further discussion in 1876. As a matter of fact the debates on Cairns's Appellate Jurisdiction Bill in the summer of 1876 reveal that members took it for granted that the colonies were satisfied with the system of appeals to the Privy Council. Few members of the House, judging from those debates, were aware that the Minister of Justice of the senior colony of the Empire was in London at that very moment protesting against the right of appeal.

55. Herbert to Dufferin, private, Dec. 6, 1875: PRO 30/6/28.

56. Minute by Herbert, Jan. 11, 1876, on Dufferin to Carnarvon, telegram, Jan. 10, 1876: CO 42/741.

57. These observations applied with equal validity to clause 47 as well as to Cairns's substitute clause, as Blake discovered later. See above, 138.

58. Dufferin to Carnarvon, private, Jan. 7, 1876: PRO 30/6/29.
On another occasion the Governor-General declared: "... the chief ground which the Chancellor should take should be that of expediency, without challenging the right which we possess of limiting appeals...." Dufferin to Carnarvon, telegram, Feb. 1, 1876: CO 42/741.

59. Carnarvon to Dufferin, telegram, Feb. 2, 1876: CO 42/741.
The Colonial Office argument was not very convincing, in view of the Department's earlier wish that Canada should accept Cairns's proposed amendment without personal consultation.

60. Dufferin to Carnarvon, private, Feb. 9, 1876: PRO 30/6/29.

61. Dufferin also evinced a keen interest in the titles and dignities to be accorded the judges of the new Supreme Court of Canada. Devoted as he was to giving Canadian institutions an English rather than an American character and anxious to see the bench and bar in the Dominion elevated to fulfil some of the duties of a good aristocracy, he recommended that the usages of the Canadian Supreme Court be assimilated to those of the English high courts of appeal. (Dufferin to Carnarvon, private, Nov. 12, 1875: PRO 30/6/28.) To distinguish the judges of the new Court from the members of the provincial bench he urged that they be called "Lords Justices" and that their robes be modelled on the dress of the Lords Justices of Appeal in England. The Colonial Office opposed this suggestion but the Lord Chancellor somewhat unexpectedly endorsed it on the ground that everything should be conceded to the new Court that would add to its dignity. (Cairns to Carnarvon, private, Nov. 25, 1875: PRO 30/6/6.) The new designation had a favourable effect on Blake and Mackenzie who were very pleased with what they thought was an English compliment to the Canadian judiciary. (Dufferin to Carnarvon, private, Dec. 23, 1875: PRO 30/6/28.)

62. Carnarvon to Dufferin, no. 55, March 9, 1876: CO 42/745. Excerpts printed in Cannon, "Some Data Relating to the Appeal to the Privy Council," 458-9.

63. Lord Cairns was not impressed with Reeve's activities in the field of constitutional law. When Blake, in his interview with the Lord Chancellor, referred to Reeve's memorandum, Cairns put it aside "in such terms that I felt I could not properly spend time in debating it," Blake related. Blake to Mackenzie, July 6, 1876, quoted in F. H. Underhill, "Edward Blake's Interview with Lord Cairns on the Supreme Court Act, July 5, 1876," Canadian Historical Review, XIX (Sept., 1938), 293.

64. Confidential memo. by Henry Reeve (Registrar to the Judicial Committee of the Privy Council), "Memorandum upon the Supreme Court and Exchequer Court Act of Canada, and the right of Appeal from the Colonial Courts to Her Majesty in Council," 1875, enclosed in Privy Council Office to Colonial Office, Aug. 10, 1875: CO 42/738. Excerpts printed in Cannon, "Some Data Relating to the Appeal of the Privy Council," 459-63.

65. Ibid.

66. Colonial Office memo., "Supreme Court of Judicature," March, 1876, enclosed in Carnarvon to Dufferin, no. 55, March 9, 1876: CO 42/745. Excerpts printed in Cannon, "Some Data Relating to the Appeal to the Privy Council," 463-65.
This paragraph was based on one used by Reeve in his memo. The undivided nature of the appeal to the Privy Council was emphasized more strongly in the Colonial Office paper than in Reeve's memo. As a consequence Malcolm's paper had the greater influence in creating Blake's doubts as to the validity of clause 47.
Cairns and Malcolm were technically correct in their description of the appeal, although they clouded an already confused issue by not recognizing the effect of the acts of 1833 and 1844 upon the jurisdiction of the Judicial Committee. It is true that in both the case of the appeal as of right and the appeal by special leave the process can be traced back to the ancient role of the Sovereign as the fountain of justice to which every subject had a right to petition. Thus the Privy Council's jurisdiction rested ultimately on the royal prerogative as embraced in the sovereignty of the Crown. See the discussion of this point by Lord Jowitt in Attorney-General, Ontario and Others v. Attorney-General, Canada and Others, [1947] A.C. 127.

67. Blake to Mills, May 3, 1876, quoted in Underhill, "Edward Blake and the Supreme Court Act," 256.

68. Blake to Mills, May 29, 1876, quoted in ibid., 257.

69. Minute by Herbert, March 28, 1876, on Dufferin to Carnarvon, telegram, March 27, 1876: CO 42/741.

70. Blake to Mackenzie, July 13, 1876, quoted in Underhill, "Edward Blake and the Supreme Court Act," 258.

71. Minute by Herbert, July 1, 1876, on Blake to Carnarvon, June 29, 1876: CO 42/747.

72. Carnarvon to Dufferin, private and confidential, July 6, 1876: PRO 30/6/29.

73. Blake to Mackenzie, July 6, 1876, quoted in Underhill, "Edward Blake's Interview with Lord Cairns," 293.

74. Blake to Mackenzie, July 6, 1876, quoted in Underhill, "Edward Blake's Interview with Lord Cairns," 293.

75. Ibid., 294.

76. Blake to Carnarvon, private and confidential, July 12, 1876: CO 42/747.

77. Cairns to Carnarvon, private, July 13, 1876: PRO 30/6/6.

78. Carnarvon to Blake, private and confidential, July 17, 1876: PRO 30/6/42.

79. Blake to Carnarvon, confidential, July 18, 1876: CO 42/747.

80. Carnarvon to Cairns, private, July 17, 1876: PRO 30/6/6.

81. Carnarvon to Cairns, private, July 21, 1876: ibid.

82. Carnarvon to Cairns, private, July 21, 1876: ibid. (a second letter of July 21).

83. A public dispatch (Carnarvon to Dufferin, no. 240, Aug. 29, 1876: CO 42/745) advised the Governor-General that the Supreme Court Act would not be disallowed. The other communication (Carnarvon to Dufferin, secret, Aug. 29, 1876: ibid.) provided the reasons for the invalidity of clause 47. It suggested that the Canadian Parliament should consider the regulation of appeals, but deliberately refrained from entering into a detailed discussion of the matter. The hope was expressed that there would be few occasions in the future on which suitors would be permitted an appeal from the Supreme Court of Canada to the Privy Council. The secret dispatch is printed in Cannon, "Some Data Relating to the Appeal to the Privy Council," 471-3.

84. Private and confidential memo. by Edward Blake, "Observations on the confidential memoranda on the subject of the Supreme Court Act transmitted by Lord Carnarvon, 9th March, 1876," Aug., 1876, enclosed in Blake to Herbert, private, Aug. 15, 1876: CO 42/747. Excerpts printed in Cannon, "Some Data Relating to the Appeal to the Privy Council," 466-71.

85. Ibid.

86. Ibid.

87. Ibid.

88. Debates of the House of Commons (Canada), 1880, I, 253-4 (Feb. 26, 1880).

89. Minute by Herbert, Nov. 24, 1876, on Blake to Herbert, private, Aug. 15, 1876: CO 42/747.

90. SP, 1877, no. 13, 3.

91. See Appendix B, 322-3, for a brief discussion of the later history of appeals to the Privy Council from Canada.

The standard authorities on the Canadian constitution all state that a clause safe-guarding the right of appeal to the Privy Council was inserted in the Supreme Court Act in 1875 at the insistence of the Imperial Government. (See the interesting note on the references to the Supreme Court Act contained in certain books on the Canadian constitution, in Underhill, "Edward Blake and the Supreme Court Act," 262-3.) As Professor Underhill suggests, there can be no credence for this version of the events of 1875. A point which Professor Underhill has left open--whether the Mackenzie Minis-try was given any private intimation of the British Government's views on the appeal question before March 30, 1875--can also be settled. It appears certain from an ex-amination of the Colonial Office papers and the Carnarvon correspondence that the news of the passing of the Supreme Court Act took the Imperial Government complete-ly by surprise. There had been no preparation for a discussion of Canadian appeals in the Colonial Office or in other departments in 1875.

CHAPTER SIX

THE BOARD OF TRADE AND CANADIAN COMMERCIAL POLICY

"As we had given the ... colonies self-government, it was perhaps better that in matters of Customs' regulations we should assume that the colonies knew their own business better than we knew it. " Lord Kimberley, 1873

THE COMMERCIAL CONTROL of the British Empire did not end with the passage of mercantilism. When, in 1846, Parliament abandoned protection in Great Britain and went on to sweep away the restrictions on economic activity contained in the Old Colonial System, it did not abdicate the function of supervising the commercial life of the British Empire. For one set of guiding principles it substituted another; yet its claim to regulate commercial policy, both in Great Britain and in the colonies, remained asserted and, for a time, unchallenged. Peel and Russell, by bringing about the demolition of the mercantilist order, ensured that the doctrines of free trade and laissez-faire were from this time forward to underlie the economic organization of Great Britain. Free trade was, however, an economic principle which was never so advantageous as when it was operating on a universal scale, making world-wide the benefits of an unrestricted division of labour. Earl Grey, than whom no more uncompromising advocate of the free trade system could be found, realized this truth and saw clearly the means by which it could be attained. Imbued with the ardour of a doctrinaire, Grey believed that those outside the free trade circle should be compelled to come in. And what better way to begin the crusade than to create in the British Empire the model for a free trade world? "It has always been held to be one of the principal functions of the Imperial Legislature and Government to determine what is to be the commercial policy of the Empire at large, and to prescribe to the various Colonial Legislatures such rules as are necessary for carrying that policy into effect, " he declared. [1]

In the attempt, lasting from 1846 until almost the end of the century, to convert the colonies of Great Britain to the commercial policy of the mother country, the Colonial Office played a changing role. Under Grey, Colonial Secretary from 1846 to 1852, the Department was active in endeavouring to force the colonies to conform to free trade principles. During these years several colonial acts encouraging economic life by bounties and subventions were disallowed. The section in the Royal Instructions which forbade a Governor to give his assent to legislation imposing differential duties or conflicting with the treaty obligations of Great Britain was pointedly upheld. The Australian colonies were denied, by the Government Act of 1850, the right to grant preferential tariff treatment to each other or to foreign countries. Then, with Grey's departure, the Office became less eager to press its commercial views upon the larger settlement

---

1. For references to Chapter VI see pages 201-13.

colonies. Conformity as a rule of action was given up, to be replaced by the more limited aim of ensuring that the colonies did not enact objectionable tariff legislation. Eventually this desideratum as well was renounced and the Colonial Office acquiesced in the freedom of the larger colonies to frame their own commercial policies irrespective of the interests of the mother country. The process by which the transformation of the Department's attitude occurred was inspired almost exclusively by developments in British North America. This fact provides the clue to its explanation. It was from the North American provinces, particularly the great Colony of Canada, that local autonomy was most strongly urged upon the Imperial Government. And conversely, it was Canada which over the years gained the most extensive concessions of self-government from the mother country. The formation of the federal union in North America promoted this devolution of authority and hastened the achievement of fiscal independence in the British Dominions. In the end the reasoning which lay behind the Colonial Office's dealings with the colonies on commercial questions was amply vindicated. That assumption was apopthegmatically expressed by Lord Kimberley in 1873, after it had been used as the basis of action for many years: ". . . the principle of self-government was even more important than the principle of free trade. "[2]

The moderation, and later, abstinence, with which the Colonial Office indulged in the sponsorship of laissez-faire doctrines was not shared by other departments in Whitehall. The Board of Trade, and to a lesser extent the Treasury, continued to represent the orthodox economic thought of the age. The Board's relations with the Colonial Office remained significant throughout the period after 1867. Originally, as a Committee of the Privy Council for Trade and Plantations, the Board of Trade had been the agent by which the sanction of the Crown was extended to colonial legislation. This function had long ago been transferred to the Secretary of State for the Colonies, but the procedure of referring colonial acts of a commercial nature to the Board continued in existence throughout the nineteenth century. As far as Canadian legislation was concerned, of course, the necessity of gaining the approval of the Board had lapsed by 1867, although its power to advise the Office on a desirable commercial policy for the Empire remained unimpaired. The many protests which the Board addressed to the Department over Canadian tariff measures were sometimes transmitted to the Colony in a modified form calculated not to pique North American sensibilities. More often, however, the Office judged it best to ignore or suppress these representations. For during these years the Department was pursuing towards Canada a conscious policy on commercial questions; a policy from which it was not to be deflected by the views of other offices in Whitehall. Elliot, the veteran Assistant Under-Secretary in charge of North American affairs, described this role clearly when he wrote, "The Colonial Office does not exist to be a vehicle of other people's opinions and feelings, but in order to be the organ of the Government for maintaining proper relations with the Colonies. "[3] It was a conception of its function which the Office realized with a competence born of long experience.

I

The original statutory basis of the claim for fiscal autonomy in the British colonies has been identified in a declaratory Act[4] of 1778, passed in the midst of the American Revolution as a belated concession to colonial grievances. The renunciation by the Imperial Parliament of its right to tax the North American colonies for any purpose except that of the regulation of trade became the point of departure for the colonial movement for financial independence. In the period of renewed mercantilism which followed 1784 the mother country made full use of its unassigned legislative authority by passing act after act to shape colonial tariffs in conformity with the requirements of the imperial commercial structure. Yet in 1846 the concept, tentatively stated in 1778, received substantial and triumphant confirmation. For in that year, the Government of Lord John Russell complemented the ending of protection in Great Britain by passing a statute which freed certain of the British colonies from the restrictive practices of the Old Colonial System. The repeal of the Corn Laws and other measures had begun to sweep away the colonial preference in the British market. It was therefore merely equitable that the British preference in the colonial tariffs should be terminated as well. The Enabling Act[5] of 1846 allowed the British colonies in North America and Mauritius to repeal or reduce, with the same effect as a measure of the United Kingdom Parliament, the duties imposed by Great Britain on their imports. Bolstered by this authority the legislatures of the North American colonies proceeded to repeal the Imperial tariffs and to create their own modest substitutes.

The earliest indigenous customs tariffs in Canada were enacted principally for revenue purposes but from the beginning they embodied features which went beyond considerations of a strictly fiscal nature. For instance the Canadian tariff of 1850[6] provided that any article, "the growth, produce or manufacture" of the other colonies in British North America, might be admitted into the Province of Canada without payment of duty. In succeeding years the other North American colonies enacted similar provisions in their tariffs, Newfoundland embarking on an interesting precursor of imperial preference by including the United Kingdom within this arrangement. By these measures complete free trade within the Empire, the aim of the statesmen of 1846, was rendered impossible almost upon its inception. Grey, with his doctrinaire abhorrence of differential duties, protested the Canadian action, but could not bring himself to disallow the legislation of 1850. It is possible that he felt the venture would lead to a commercial union of British North America, which he favoured, and might contribute, ultimately, to political union. Nevertheless his acceptance of intercolonial free trade in North America was a significant decision since it failed to resist the first detraction from the ideal of free trade within the British Empire and resulted in a serious weakening of the Imperial Government's prohibition of differential duties.

Four years later a commercial project, beside which the arrangement of 1850 was but a pale alternative, was effected in the form of the celebrated Reciprocity Treaty.[7] This convention allowed natural products from the United States to enter the North American colonies duty free in return for reciprocal concessions at the American border.

F or the first time in British colonial history a group of colonies imposed differential duties in favour of a foreign state and against imports from the mother country and the rest of the Empire. The Colonial Office, which had endorsed the project from the be-ginning, was, however, unconcerned. Even Grey, converted by Elgin's advocacy, gave the plan his support on the grounds that it would forestall annexation with the United States and enable the colonies to assume more of the burden of their defence. It was left to the Board of Trade to point out the fundamental principle which the Treaty of 1854 violated. In the end Grey experienced similar qualms, but the dictates of ex-pediency carried the day. For future generations in Whitehall the Reciprocity Treaty marked the beginning of evil; the descent into Avernus. For, as Morrell states dis-tinctly, the Reciprocity Treaty was "attained by means which in reality, though not in appearance, were inconsistent with Grey's aim of a free trade Empire, ... by conced-ing the claim to special treatment he took a long step towards the concession of the coming claim for full fiscal autonomy."[8]

The Colony of Canada went on, in the same momentous decade, to shape her ec-onomic policy even farther from the wishes of the Imperial Government. In 1858 the Cayley Tariff,[9] by a substantial increase in duties over those prevailing since 1850, showed that Canada had come to depend on customs receipts for most of her revenue. It ended the period of virtual free trade which had characterized the Empire's com-mercial intercourse (with the exception of the Reciprocity arrangement) since 1846. A. T. Galt, the Minister of Finance in the Cartier-Macdonald Administration, pro-posed in the following year a tariff[10] which exceeded the Cayley measure in the duties it levied on foreign and British imports. This tariff, like its predecessor, was not dis-allowed by the Colonial Secretary. A remonstrance against it by English manufactur-ers called forth Galt's classic vindication of colonial fiscal autonomy.

> Self-government would be utterly annihilated if the views of the Imperial Govern-ment were to be preferred to those of the people of Canada. It is, therefore, the duty of the present Government distinctly to affirm the right of the Canadian Legis-lature to adjust the taxation of the people in the way they deem best, even if it should unfortunately happen to meet the disapproval of the Imperial Ministry. Her Majesty cannot be advised to disallow such acts, unless her advisers are prepared to assume the administration of the affairs of the Colony irrespective of the views of its inhabitants.[11]

This justly famous affirmation has, however, been assigned an importance in British imperial history which it lacked at the time. Although it ended the practice of the British Government supporting private representations against the Canadian tariff it did not mean that the Canadian right to frame an independent commercial policy had been endorsed by Whitehall. The Board of Trade remained singularly unconvinced by Galt's explanations, and in 1859 the Board of Trade was still a principal arbiter of the economic life of the Empire. In the eyes of the Board, the justification for the Galt Tariff was to be found in "the financial exigencies of Canada, and the difficulty, if

not impossibility under the peculiar circumstances of the Province of raising the necessary amount of revenue from any other source than the Import duties upon manufactures...." Yet the fiscal policy of the "most important Colony" of the Crown was nevertheless to be regretted, as tending to the "mischievous purpose of protection."[12] The
Colonial Office, in the same year as the passage of the Galt Tariff, vetoed a Canadian
Act providing retaliatory measures in the coasting trade of the province. Canadian
autonomy was hardly securely established in 1859; in fact Galt's words represented a
hope for the future rather than a description of the current position.

Galt is partly responsible for the acceptance by the British Government of the right
of Canada and the other North American colonies to arrange a thoroughgoing system of
differential duties among themselves. This latter achievement has been overshadowed
by his dramatic encounter with the Sheffield memorialists over protection, but it was
probably of more permanent significance. For differential duties could not be excused on the basis of fiscal necessity; they were an aspect of commercial policy utterly at
variance with all the tenets of free trade. The tariff of New Brunswick, as drawn up in
1859, provided for the admission of certain goods from British North America, the
United States, and the West Indies without payment of duty. In the same year Galt
drafted a memorandum advocating complete intercolonial free trade in British North
America and an assimilation of the tariffs of the respective colonies. Of course both
these plans embodied differential duties, and it was this aspect of them which excited
opposition from the English Government. In a letter to the Colonial Office of March,
1860, the Board of Trade provided an exhaustive free trade critique of the principle of
differential duties. The Board's objections are worthy of brief notice at this point, for
they remained remarkably constant over the years that followed. At the outset it was
recognized that the assimilation of the separate tariff structures in the British Empire
was an impossible objective, since the various colonial regions were so diversified in
their economic life. Particular areas, such as British North America, might be allowed to form trading units, but if such schemes were sanctioned it would be difficult to
resist similar plans in the future. Thus the Empire might be split into competing and
exclusive commercial systems. Additionally, it would be clearly intolerable if region-
al groups were permitted to discriminate against imports from Great Britain or imports
from foreign countries with whom the United Kingdom had "most-favoured-nation"
treaties. Yet exactly these conditions seemed to be implied in many of the schemes
proposed for intercolonial reciprocity. If the colonies were to give exemption from
tariff charges to colonial goods they must give the same exemption to similar products from all countries, or the plan would simply be a means of affording protection.
The Board had noticed that in British North America tariffs which were imposed for
revenue served a protective function as well; a conclusion which was underlined by
the failure of the North American colonies to levy excise duties on protected goods
which were produced at home. In Great Britain customs charges were only placed on
goods of which the country's entire supply was imported from abroad. The assimilation of tariffs was in theory a desirable goal, but if North American tariffs were made
to conform to the high Canadian level there would be further difficulties for the English exporter to the New World.[13]

To these arguments Galt made strong reply, characterizing them as peculiarly suited to the interests of a mature industrial community committed to free trade doctrines. He stated that Canada could not place foreign countries on the same footing as the other British colonies in North America unless those countries were prepared to offer the province countervailing advantages. [14] The Colonial Office accepted Galt's defence of intercolonial free trade and came to the conclusion that it would be injudicious to urge further the Board's views on Canada. Elliot pronounced that the time had arrived when it was no longer feasible for English officials to dictate the terms of the Canadian budget. [15] Rogers and Newcastle showed themselves favourable to the Canadian point of view and the Board was informed that from aspects both of justice and policy Her Majesty's Government should not oppose the establishment of free commercial intercourse in North America. "Seeing they are either contiguous or closely neighbouring portions of British Territory, the circulation of their productions amongst each other free of customs duties could afford no more just ground of complaint to foreign nations than a similar free traffic between one county and another in Great Britain." [16] This decision was communicated to Canada and the other North American colonies, [17] and, confronted with a fait accompli, the Board of Trade had to concede the point.

The extension, before 1867, of the existing reciprocal arrangements among the British North American provinces was hampered by the reluctance of the Maritime colonies to sacrifice an important source of revenue. [18] With the union of the three colonies, however, the plan became a reality. The British North America Act provided that all "articles of the Growth, Produce, or Manufacture of any one of the Provinces shall, from and after the Union, be admitted free into each of the other Provinces." [19] Thus the entry of the British North American colonies into a wider national life saw them well equipped to undertake a commercial policy suited to the new country's requirements. The provinces had behind them a series of significant precedents which could be invoked to justify measures inconsistent with the free trade point of view. The establishment of differential duties and legislation of a protective character remained, after 1867 as before, the features of the Dominion's tariff arrangements which occasioned the greatest uneasiness in London.

II

The Board of Trade's distaste for preferential tariff arrangements among the North American colonies found expression within a year after the passing of the Act of Union. The first tariff of the Dominion of Canada extended to Prince Edward Island and Newfoundland (who had remained outside the federation) the provisions of the former intercolonial exemption on food-stuffs and raw materials. [20] Prince Edward Island reciprocated by granting a similar privilege to Canada. The Island Legislature went a step farther, however, by enacting that Canadian food-stuffs should be admitted into the Colony duty free, notwithstanding the fact that they might have passed through the United States to reach their destination. [21] Lieutenant-Governor Dundas gave his assent to the measure and confidently transmitted it to the Colonial Office, stating that it simply expanded an earlier Act allowing an exemption on flour brought directly from Canada. [22]   The Duke of Buckingham, the Colonial Secretary, balked at the Act, not because it imposed differential duties, but because he foresaw an opportunity for fraud and a consequent train of disputes with the United States. [23]   The Board of Trade, to whom the Act was referred, added to his observations the fear that the legislation might stimulate the republic to retaliatory tariffs. They were not prepared to recommend disallowance, but they felt that the Island Government should be distinctly informed of the strong objections to the Act. [24]   With these views before it the Office again considered the Act. Rogers felt that it should be sanctioned, although he pointed out that it would constitute an awkward precedent in other areas of the Empire such as Australasia. Buckingham continued to be disposed towards disallowance, although Rogers urged him to avoid this course. Rejection of the Act would, he said, only provoke bitterness between the Home Government and the Colony and there was no "Imperial reason for incurring this evil." [25]   In the end Buckingham agreed to the sending of a dispatch to Charlottetown, asking for more information before advice was tendered to the Queen about the measure. [26]   When, later in the year, this information was received, the Act was allowed. [27]

During the course of this discussion on the Prince Edward Island legislation the Board of Trade pointed out that a similar system of differential duties had been set up in Canada, and that the same objections applied to it. They suggested that the attention of the Dominion Government be called to this fact. [28]   Somewhat reluctantly the Colonial Office forwarded the correspondence to Canada and asked for the observations of the Government upon the Canadian statutes. [29]   The Macdonald Government replied to this Imperial disapproval of their tariff policy in a memorandum which was to become a classic defence of the principle of preferential duties for special regions within the Empire. The document was the work of John Rose, the Minister of Finance, and was the first of two papers in which Rose justified, in the light of the state of the North American economy in the late sixties, the differential duties established by Canada. Later, the two memoranda were to play a significant role in the related controversy over differential tariffs in the Australasian colonies.

Rose devoted the early section of his remarks to a history of differential duties in British North America, pointing out that they had come into existence during the period when Earl Grey headed the Colonial Office. The principle had been formally conceded in 1861, Rose stated, and from that time until the present there had been no remonstrances from London against differential duties in the Canadian tariff. The Minister of Finance went on to defend preferential duties as a useful step towards the establishment of political union. It had been the Imperial Government's attitude for several years that the federation of British North America was desirable and in the best interests of the Empire and the colonies concerned. It had been hoped that Prince Edward Island would enter the new Dominion, but as yet she had not seen fit to do so. The establishment of differential duties, "the reciprocal free exchange of natural products," was a measure designed to bring about closer union with the Colony. If Prince Edward

Island were a province of Canada there would be no objection on Great Britain's part to her maintaining intimate tariff arrangements with the Dominion; thus, at a time when forces were working for this political connection it was difficult to see how opposition to closer commercial association could be sustained. It would be decidedly wrong to rebuff the Island for offering favourable trade concessions to Canada, and Rose therefore asked that the Dominion's legislation be confirmed by the British Government.[30]

The Colonial Office accepted this explanation with celerity, Elliot modifying the covering dispatch which was sent with the Rose memorandum to the Board of Trade, "with the view of leading the Board ... in [our] direction--or at all events not in the contrary direction."[31] The Board of Trade acceded to the Colonial Office suggestion and pronounced that they would not advise the disallowance of the Acts.[32] No immediate action was taken with regard to the Canadian measures, however, because they were found to incorporate further objectionable features.

The Dominion's first tariff, beside providing for reciprocal free trade with the other British colonies in North America, offered reciprocity in natural products to the United States.[33] The Reciprocity Treaty had been abrogated in 1866, and this new arrangement, which was made contingent upon the United States granting the same facilities to Canada, was designed to achieve the objects of the Treaty by means of concurrent legislation.[34] After a delay of almost six months the Board wrote to the Colonial Office to point out this further unorthodoxy which remained uncombated in the Canadian tariff. The letter, which was signed by T. H. Farrer, the Permanent Secretary to the Board, showed strong evidence of having been composed by that most ardent of free trade advocates. During the twenty-one years in which he headed the staff of the Board of Trade, Farrer addressed many letters to the Office on the tariff heresies of the colonial Empire. All were masterful expositions of the doctrines of free trade, written from the standpoint of the classical principles of political economy. They revealed the accuracy of the following estimate of Farrer: he was "dogmatic in his views, and of a controversial temperament in economic matters, especially distrustful of the extension of state interference, and a free trader of unyielding temper...."[35] The communication of June, 1868, was a not uncharacteristic product of Farrer's abilities and prejudices.

The Board concentrated their criticism of the Canadian tariff on the offer to allow specified American imports into the Colony without payment of duty, in the event the United States offered similar concessions to Canada. This proceeding Farrer described as tending to lead to momentous results. Great Britain was under obligation, by virtue of "most-favoured-nation" clauses in trade treaties, to extend to many foreign countries as favourable an entry into her colonial possessions as was enjoyed by any foreign country. If Canada conceded a measure of trade preference to the United States, therefore, many European nations would be entitled, under treaties with Great Britain, to demand the same terms of admittance into the Canadian market. Eventually, if the admirable practice of "most-favoured-nation" clauses were extended to all commercial agreements, as the Board of Trade hoped would take place, the situation might conceivably be reached in which the only countries paying duties to Canada would be the United Kingdom and the British colonies outside North America! Then, said Farrer, with dramatic effect, "the old Colonial system, by which the trade of the Colonies was contracted and crippled in order to protect the manufacturers and traders of the mother country will be reversed, and the Colony will protect its own trade and manufactures at the cost of the mother country, whilst the mother country is, at the same time, submitting to heavy burdens of another kind for the defence and protection of the colony."[36] It was for the Secretary of State to determine whether such a consequence should be tacitly sanctioned by the Imperial Government through an approval of this Canadian tariff.

The Colonial Office staff questioned Farrer's estimate of the catastrophic effect of the Canadian offer to the United States. H. T. Holland, the legal adviser, felt that the grounds on which the Canadian Act could have been disallowed had been abandoned long ago. By sanctioning the Reciprocity Treaty Her Majesty's Government "deviated from the rule which forms the fundamental principle of their Commercial policy, but the political motives outweighed considerations of purely Commercial expediency."[37] It must now be determined whether there existed at the present moment political motives similar to those which had condoned the Treaty of 1854. Without entering into a discussion of the question Holland submitted that there did, and recommended that the legislation be allowed. He felt, however, that Canada must be prepared to admit similar goods from other countries on the same terms as she accorded the United States. He observed that the Governor-General had been remiss in approving the Act without qualification, for, under his Instructions, it should have been reserved because it imposed differential duties. Elliot supported Holland's general recommendation, but disagreed with him on the question of a reproof for Lord Monck. Reciprocity with the United States had been promoted by Great Britain, its abrogation had been much regretted by the British Government, and there had been several official attempts to create a new arrangement. In the face of these circumstances it was scarcely fair to expect that the Governor-General should assume that reciprocal free trade in North America was at variance with the policy of the United Kingdom.[38] Sir Charles Adderley, the Conservative Parliamentary Under-Secretary, with his well-known support of colonial autonomy, took a different line. Commercial treaties concluded between England and foreign countries could not and should not be made to apply, automatically, to the larger settlement colonies. "Such treaties ... affecting Canada are certainly in practice, whatever the theory, subject to the consent of their Parliament," he stated.[39] The important aim for Canada was to improve the Dominion's commerce with the United States by developing the principle of reciprocity.

The Department, in transmitting the Board of Trade letter to Canada, followed Farrer's example by emphasizing the American offer in the Dominion's tariff arrangements. The concessions to the United States might have to be extended to other countries which enjoyed treaty relations with Great Britain, the Canadian Government was warned. Would there exist any serious inconvenience in such an enlargement, the dispatch asked? For, the Secretary of State concluded, "I fear that no distinction could be agreed to."[40]

The Canadian answer to these animadversions was again cast in the form of a memorandum by the Minister of Finance. Rose, following the trend of the discussion, devoted himself to a justification of differential duties in favour of imports from the United States. These concessions opened up serious and controversial aspects of the colonial power to levy tariffs, he admitted. In approaching the current question one must assume that it was in the best interests of both countries that goods be exchanged between them on a reciprocal basis. This principle had been a desideratum in Canadian economic policy since the abolition of the Corn Laws, when the first attempts had been made to gain a special entry into the United States market. Great Britain had cordially approved this tendency and had provided practical assistance, through the services of the British Minister in Washington, in negotiations with the American Government. When the Reciprocity Treaty was faced with termination by the United States the British Government had worked for its extension and, later, for a renewal of the instrument. There had always been doubts as to the correct means of achieving reciprocity between the two countries, as it had been contended that the conclusion of a treaty effecting the scheme interfered with the power of the House of Representatives to initiate money bills. The critics of the treaty procedure claimed that under the Constitution the object could more properly be obtained by concurrent legislation in the United States and Canada. This had been attempted in 1848, but the Bill which was prepared in the United States had been defeated in the American Congress. A Canadian Bill, containing a clause almost exactly similar to the one which the Board of Trade now noted, had been passed by the Province and approved by the Imperial Government. The Board of Trade had offered no objection, as the matter was one which, in their own words, could be left entirely to the "decision of the Provincial Legislature."

The provision in the Dominion tariff now under review was designed to achieve the same purpose: to provide for reciprocal trade between the two countries by concurrent legislation, if the United States wished to adopt that procedure. There could, therefore, be no reasonable disagreement on the part of the British Government to a proceeding which they had endorsed, in spirit and in letter, for two decades. The clause, if put into effect, would not reduce imports from Great Britain, for most of the articles which Canada obtained from the United States were products that were not normally available from other countries. The "important national considerations" which had dictated the negotiation of the Treaty of 1854 existed in even greater force at the present time, and demanded that Great Britain continue to support the project with the same energy that she had shown in the past. On her part Canada would refrain from violating the treaty engagements of the mother country and would pay respectful attention to the rules of political economy expounded by the Board of Trade.[41]

Put on this special and exceptional basis, the establishment of differential duties in the Canadian tariff could not fail to be sanctioned by the Imperial Government. The Board of Trade insisted, however, that Canada be told that if customs privileges were accorded the United States, a similar immunity must be given the products of the United Kingdom and foreign countries. This stipulation was absolutely essential in the case of countries which had "most-favoured-nation" treaties with Great Britain.[42] As this

was the point to which Holland had drawn attention, it was stressed in the dispatch ultimately sent Canada, approving the American offer in the Dominion's tariff.[43]   The
United States failed to respond to this liberal commercial gesture by the Dominion and
the Imperial Government's specification was, therefore, never acted upon. In the light
of the fact that more unorthodox features in the Canadian tariff were later accepted
without reservation by Great Britain, it is doubtful whether it would ever have been
pressed upon the Colony.

Rose journeyed to Washington in the summer of 1869 where, in company with Edward Thornton, the British Minister, he discussed with the Grant Administration the subject of a reciprocity arrangement. The Minister of Finance had in mind a comprehensive adjustment of existing differences between the two countries, and was prepared to
negotiate a settlement covering the fisheries, the coasting trade, and copyright and extradition matters in addition to commercial topics. He offered free trade in raw materials and, as his most important bargaining point, the free exchange of certain manufactured articles. This was a concession which had not formed part of the Reciprocity
Treaty, but it was unavailing. The Secretary of State, Hamilton Fish, showed little
enthusiasm for the Canadian offer and complained that the Executive had no power to
reduce import duties without congressional sanction. The atmosphere in Washington
was obviously so unpropitious to the idea of freer trade with Canada that Rose returned
to Ottawa after only a brief visit.[44]   Faced with this indifference to their proposals,
the Macdonald Government tried a new form of commercial bargaining. It was destined to land them in difficulties with the Imperial Government, just as their reciprocity offer had done.

In the spring of 1870 Canada embarked on the new policy by introducing retaliatory duties into her tariff structure.[45]   Certain goods such as coal, salt, wheat, and
meal, which had formerly been on the free list, were now made dutiable. The levies
on coal and salt were frankly discriminatory in character. The one on coal was imposed in an effort to compel the United States to repeal its duty on Nova Scotia coal,
applied after the abrogation of the Reciprocity Treaty. The salt duty was directly aimed at imports from the large American salt industry in New York State. It was charged
on all foreign salt, but the Act provided that salt from Great Britain could be admitted
free--the only instance of a direct preference to the mother country in the Canadian
tariff between 1846 and the Fielding Tariff of 1897.[46]   It was not long before the new
duties attracted the critical attention of foreign governments and the Board of Trade.
The Ambassador of the North German Confederation protested that the Canadian tariff
violated the commercial treaty of 1865 between Great Britain and the Zollverein. This
treaty was a rather special example of the "most-favoured-nation" type, for it provided that Germany should enjoy the same conditions of trade with the British colonies as
the mother country herself. The German note was referred to Canada where the Privy
Council explained that the duty on German salt had been an oversight. There was, however, no necessity for modifying the tariff as German salt was admitted free in any case
because of its requirement in the fishing industry.[47]   The Colonial Office accepted
this assurance, although both Rogers and Kimberley felt that the salt duty was objec-

tionable because "it gives ground of complaint to any nation having a favoured nation clause."[48]   Kimberley's reply to the Canadian explanation stated that an early opportunity should be taken to bring the tariff system of Canada into accordance with Great Britain's treaty obligations.[49]   This would require either that the duties be repealed or that they be made to bear equally upon all foreign imports.

The disapproval of the Office was mild compared to that voiced by the Board of Trade. Sir Louis Mallet,[50] one of the secretaries to the Board, followed Farrer's example by writing a long and heated dispatch to the Office, in which adequate expression was given to the salutary principles of free trade. Mallet was opposed to the salt duty for two reasons. In the first place it created a particularly glaring case of differential duties in an Empire which was being led away from those practices, and secondly, it attempted to use duties as a means of retaliation against a foreign country. Of all the functions of differential duties, this was the most reprehensible.

Her Majesty's Government while abstaining from all attempts to impose upon the Colonies the sounder and more advanced policy of the mother country--partly in deference to the principle of local self-Government and partly from a recognition of the difficulty in young communities, with a scattered population, of always dispensing with taxes which incidentally involve protection, --has hitherto steadily and uniformly resisted the proposals which have been occasionally made by Colonial Governments to resort to that form of protection which consists in discriminating duties.

Irrespective of all questions as to the due limits of Imperial control over the commercial policy of the Colonies, a sufficient reason exists for such a course, in the fact that nothing tends so directly to international irritation and hostility as a policy of discrimination, and that the relations of the Home Government with foreign countries may be thus embarassed and compromised.

It is on this account no less than in deference to economic principle, that while on the one hand, Parliament has carefully removed all trace of protection to the products of the British Colonies in the United Kingdom--on the other, Her Majesty has been advised, in the exercise of the powers vested in the Crown, to insist on the equal treatment of British and Foreign Products, in the Tariffs of the British Colonies.

But the Act of the Canadian Legislature now in question, not only infringes this important rule of Imperial policy, by imposing a tax upon foreign Salt, from which British Salt is exempt--but would moreover have the still more mischievous effect, (in consequence of the Treaty rights possessed by most foreign Countries) of creating an invidious distinction between the Salt of the United States, and that of other foreign countries, which would be directly calculated to provoke unfriendly feeling, and retaliatory measures, on the part of the former.[51]

It was to be regretted that with the end of the Reciprocity Treaty Canada had not continued to extend its provisions to the United States, irrespective of the fact that the

Dominion received no concessions in return. It now appeared that the United States was moving towards lower tariffs (since the Tariff of 1870) so that this Canadian Act would inevitably create bad feeling and suspicion. The Board recommended that Canada be asked to amend the Act before it was allowed.

The Office had already remonstrated mildly with Canada over the effect of the salt duty of 1870 and it was decided that this was a sufficient action to take for the moment. For, by 1871, the larger question of the right of the autonomous colonies to levy differential duties was coming to a head through the interminable discussions which, ever since 1866, had been taking place with the Australian colonies. Now it might be possible to arrive through this correspondence at a modus operandi which could be applied to all the self-governing dependencies. [52] Transmitted to the Board, the announcement that a protest had been sent to Canada against the tariff of 1870 was welcomed heartily. The Board went on, however, to make a shrewd criticism of the Colonial Office tactics in the matter. It was an objection of which the Office was not unaware: that to approve a Canadian tariff containing these irregular features might be to concede the point entirely in later discussions.

> If [differential duties] were sanctioned, it appears to My Lords that it would be very difficult, if not impossible, to resist the application of a similar principle to other branches of the Canadian tariff--and if sanctioned in Canada, equally difficult to disallow similar measures in other British Possessions--and thus it might well be that Her Majesty's Government might find itself involved in a chain of inconvenient precedents which might place it beyond their power to restrain a course of Colonial Legislation tending to undermine and subvert the international commercial policy, which this Country has for so many years pursued with such beneficient results. [53]

The Canadian action might also stimulate the United States to a retaliatory policy directed against Great Britain, which would injure the most important branch of the export trade of the mother country. In spite of its protectionist tendencies, the United States had not as yet adopted discriminatory tariffs, and it was to be hoped that it would never embark on such a course of action.

Before the Colonial Office was forced to argue the question further with Canada, the Dominion abruptly brought the episode to an end by repealing the duties on salt and coal. [54] This was done by the Cabinet while Sir John Macdonald was in Washington as one of the British plenipotentiaries on the Joint High Commission, and revealed the partial failure of the policy of retaliation. [55] Thereafter Macdonald and his colleagues became increasingly convinced that in protection lay a more desirable tariff principle for Canada than mere retaliation against the United States. The Colonial Office first learned the news of the repeal from a note in The Times and had to request official confirmation from Canada. "I would not refer to the telegram in the Times as it would not look very well if the correspondence is ever published," directed Kimberley in authorizing the reference. [56] It turned out later that the statute repealing

the duties had been in the possession of the Office for some months;[57] a fact which induced the Department to drop the subject rather peremptorily. Kimberley had never
shown any enthusiasm in raising the question of the salt duty with Canada and once it
became apparent that the basis of the controversy might be removed he prevented the
Board of Trade correspondence from being sent to Ottawa.[58]

The retaliatory duties of 1870 were not the last which Canada imposed before the
Colony plunged into the full current of protective legislation. In 1872 there was another, and highly significant, example in the Dominion tariff of discrimination against
American imports. Again it was the action of the United States Congress which inspired the Macdonald Ministry to take this step. In the early months of 1872 Congress
placed a tariff of ten per cent on tea and coffee imported into the United States through
Canada. This action prejudiced the interests of a section of the Canadian exporting
business, and the Dominion Government hastily retaliated by imposing countervailing
duties on tea and coffee imported from the United States.[59] At the same time Canada promised to repeal the duties if the United States would repeal hers. The Canadian action did not influence any commercial treaty entered into by Great Britain,
and thus could not be resisted on the grounds of international obligations. But it so
boldly set up a differential tariff and was so obviously pointed at the trade of one nation that the British Government was obliged to take notice of it. Here was no promise of commercial concessions that might never be implemented, or immunity for the
trade of a few small colonies within the economic orbit of Canada, but a tariff differential adversely applied to the trade of Great Britain's largest customer.

It was the practice at this time for certified copies of the acts of the Parliament
of Canada to be sent to the Colonial Office after the measures had received the Royal
Assent. This meant that it was usually some time after the end of the session before
Canadian legislation reached London for the approval of the Secretary of State. Only
in special cases was a copy of a bill sent to the Colonial Office before it was discussed in Parliament or before it received the sanction of the Governor-General. The legislation imposing duties on tea and coffee came at the end of the governorship of Lord
Lisgar and was assented to by him in the usual manner. The first news the Colonial
Office had of the new duties was a report in The Times (it seemed to be the fate of the
Office to hear of the changes in the Canadian tariff through the columns of The Times)
on June 12, 1872. Mallet of the Board of Trade wrote immediately to Herbert to ask
whether the information about the discriminatory duties was correct. "I trust that you
will not sanction such an outrage. It will make our present language to France [the
negotiations leading to the Anglo-French commercial treaty of 1873] not only undig-
nified and illogical which it is [already]--but ... ridiculous and pharisaical into the
bargain."[60] The Office delayed almost two months before sending to Canada for information,[61] probably in the hope that some official explanation would be vouchasfed
in the meantime. But nothing arrived until a reply to Kimberley's request came from
Lord Dufferin, who had succeeded Lisgar as Governor-General in June, 1872. It consisted of a memorandum by Sir Francis Hincks, the Minister of Finance, detailing the
circumstances which had given rise to the duties on tea and coffee but offering no justification for them.[62]

The Colonial Office was thus faced with a differential duty which was a fait accompli.   Unless Canada could be induced to modify the measure, disallowance would
provide the only means of enforcing the Imperial Government's free trade ideas. The
chagrin which the Office felt in this difficulty was enhanced by the realization that the
well-established procedure for dealing with colonial legislation had been responsible for
the question reaching such an aggravated form. The fact that the Department knew little about the tendency of Canadian legislation until it had received a bound volume of
the statutes was undoubtedly productive of much inconvenience. An improvement
might be effected here by requiring the Governor-General to send home a list of acts
that had been given the Royal Assent. But in this episode a second safeguard against
objectionable legislation had also failed. The Governor-General, an Imperial Officer,
had been remiss in the performance of his duties. His Instructions required that he reserve his assent from bills creating a differential tariff. This Lord Lisgar had not done,
and to Herbert in this violation of the Royal Instructions lay "the beginning of evil" in
"an awkward case."[63]

Be that as it may, the Act was now on the statute books, and the vital question of
the principle which had inspired it remained to be decided. Herbert felt that the prohibition of differential duties in the Empire must be maintained, although he recognized the inconvenience that would be caused if the Act were suspended, and confessed
that he did not relish the prospect of a "collision" with the Dominion Government on a
fiscal topic. But it was essential that the Empire preserve at all costs a tariff policy that
was not mutually exclusive, or the very basis of unity would be shattered. "...I would
hope that I am attaching more importance than I need to this case; but I do not at present see how to pass it over, nor indeed how ultimately to deal with this class of questions except by erasing the injunction against Differential legislation from the Instructions and leaving the Colonies free to legislate for fiscal purposes exactly as they choose:
when they will hardly be Colonies."[64] With shrewd caution the Permanent Under-Secretary recommended a further delay before taking definite action. He also suggested
to Kimberley that the Board of Trade should not be invited to comment on the Canadian
Act until the matter had been discussed further with Canada and in the Cabinet. "It
may be more convenient not to have on record one of their strong Free trade manifes-
tos, however deserved," he remarked.[65] Knatchbull-Hugessen, the Parliamentary
Under-Secretary, agreed with Herbert that colonial self-interest in commercial affairs,
if left unchecked, would weaken the imperial structure. In a comment filled with fore-
boding he noted sadly that in these consequences only "sentiment" would remain of the
colonial tie.

I think the question is one of a serious character, but it is one which must be
faced, and that with the knowledge that it must affect our dealings with the Colonies.... The first idea which rises to my mind is that in the case of great and
growing communities like Canada and the Australian colonies, the power of Great
Britain to impose upon them her fiscal policy and arrangements can be but temporary, and that, in fact, if they do not cheerfully and willingly acquiesce, the sooner,

and with the better grace, we give way to them, the better for both. But neither they nor we must lose sight of the fact that as soon as this is the case, a violent wrench is given to the tie which binds us together. How can we any longer speak of Colonies as "an integral part of the empire" if their fiscal policy is to be founded on entirely different and antagonistic principles to our own? Very soon, the only tie left between us will be the Governor--backed by whatever strength may still be left in the "sentiment" towards the mother country which our Policy has not of late years done much to encourage. I think the present question is one for the Cabinet, for it involves the whole of the larger question of our dealing with these large Colonies in relation to fiscal matters. [66]

An escape from the difficulty fortunately presented itself to the Office in a proposal of Sir George Cartier, Macdonald's veteran colleague, who was in London on public business in the winter of 1872-3. Cartier suggested that the Tea and Coffee Act should not be disallowed, but its operation be delayed until the Colonial Office felt able to consent to the issue of an order in council bringing the Act into force. Kimberley accepted this plan with misgivings, fearing its effect on the Australian movement to gain the same commercial freedom which Canada possessed. [67] Cartier's plan could lead to only one result and it is very probable that the Colonial Secretary understood this when he acquiesced in it. Within a short time it was seen to be impossible to withhold the order in council implementing the Act, simply because Canadian merchants had already committed themselves to the importation of tea and coffee under the new arrangement. For these reasons before the end of the year Kimberley felt himself obliged to sanction the measure. In doing so he noted that it did not infringe any treaty stipulation between Great Britain and the United States and that it established virtual free trade in tea and coffee, except for discrimination against the United States. The dispatch concluded with a saving clause which preserved nothing. "I have to request that it may be clearly understood that [Her Majesty's Government's] acquiescence on this occasion is not to be taken as implying any countenance on [its] part to the system of retaliatory or discriminating duties. "[68]

The allowance of the Canadian Tea and Coffee Act of 1872 administered the coup de grâce to the Colonial Office's prohibition of the levying of differential duties by the Australasian colonies. The controversy over this question with the colonies in Australia had smouldered, with increasing heat, ever since 1866. [69] The Office's position in the exchange had been made more difficult by the existence of irregular tariff legislation in British North America, and in the last resort Canadian precedents in the field of preferential duties were to prove decisive for Australia. The statutory basis of the tariff disability of the Australian colonies lay in the Government Act of 1850, which contained a section stipulating that no new duty could be applied on goods from "any Country or Place" which was not also levied on similar goods from all countries. The Act contained as well a clause prohibiting duties which might be at variance with British commercial treaties. [70] The latter clause was repeated in the Act granting representative government to New Zealand. [71] This Imperial legislation effectually prevented the Australasian colonies from setting up differential tariffs among themselves or in favour of foreign countries. By the mid-sixties the Pacific colonies had become restless under this limitation of their fiscal autonomy, and in 1866 New South Wales pressed the British Government for the repeal of the restrictive legislation. In the following year Tasmania passed a bill embodying the principle of differential duties, only to have it vetoed by the British Government. New Zealand undertook unauthorized and futile negotiations with the United States for a commercial treaty in 1869-70, and in the latter year the Melbourne conference brought together most of the Australian colonies in a joint demand for greater freedom in tariff legislation. As a group, the Antipodean colonies were obviously moving towards protection, Julius Vogel's terms of public office in New Zealand from 1869 to 1876 typifying this general trend. Additional tariffs with preferential features followed from New Zealand and the other colonies, and the problem steadily grew in scope and intensity of feeling during these years.

Throughout the discussions the Australian governments contended that they could not fairly be denied what British North America already possessed. C. Gavan Duffy, Premier of Victoria, in a memorandum written in 1871, said, "we are unable to comprehend any peculiar claim the North American Colonies have to exercise powers which cannot be safely entrusted or indeed can be legitimately denied, to the Colonies of Australia."[72] Vogel, towards the end of the controversy, demanded categorically that Australasia should be put on an equality with Canada in respect to tariff legislation: "The Australasian Colonies ask for nothing new. They desire nothing which is not sanctioned by precedent;.... All that has been asked has been granted to Canada: why should a different result follow the application of the Australasian Colonies?"[73] The Colonial Office could not hope to satisfy these representations by emphasizing the "peculiar and exceptionable" circumstances arising out of the desire to promote political union, which had justified intercolonial free trade in North America. Nor was the statement, that reciprocity between Canada and the United States was not a principle of commercial relations applicable to Australia since it was based on "the contiguity of their respective territories along a frontier line now extending across the entire continent," well received in the Australian capitals. Both these explanations were obviously as valid for Australia as for Canada.

The three Secretaries of State of this period, Buckingham, Granville, and Kimberley, agreed that a customs union (the abolition of all duties between the colonies) would be desirable for Australia, but concurred in the opinion that differential tariffs would prove unsound and dangerous. Rogers, on the other hand, favoured an acquiescence in the Australian demands. He did not feel that the colonies should be asked to forbear from imposing preferential duties simply because large commercial principles were at stake.[74] Herbert, his successor, concurred in this estimate; there was a good deal "to be said against a restriction which prohibits two members of the same Empire from entering into reciprocal fiscal agreements."[75] Kimberley eventually came round to this attitude himself, after receiving strong advice to yield from several ex-governors of the Australian colonies. It was the other members of the British Cabinet, particularly Gladstone, who proved adamant in the matter. Gladstone, with his strongly-expressed sympathy for colonial autonomy, would seem to be inconsistent in taking up an attitude against the Australian aspirations. It is plain that he believed in the commercial unity of the British Empire as being fundamental to its continued existence; differential tariffs would mean, as he expressed it, "the reductio ad absurdum of colonial connection."[76]   In addition Gladstone was much concerned over England's ability to fulfil her treaty engagements with foreign powers, and saw this capacity prejudiced if the Australian colonies were to be allowed freedom to impose varying tariff rates. The controversy might have been ended by 1872, for Gladstone would have been compelled to give way ultimately, but was prolonged by a demand made by Vogel for independent colonial authority to negotiate commercial treaties. This new claim gave the Colonial Office a chance to argue the question of fiscal autonomy from another aspect; however, the Australian colonies, after disclaiming Vogel's request, returned to their original insistence for the right to make differential tariff arrangements. The matter rested in this state until the allowance of the Tea and Coffee Act at the end of 1872 created a further Canadian precedent to undermine the British stand. In February, 1873, Kimberley again urged the Prime Minister that the Australian colonies must be granted the power to make preferential agreements among themselves and Gladstone reluctantly concurred: "I perceive you will give the Australian colonies what they want. Some time hence they will probably ask for like favour with reference to their Commercial Intercourse with Foreign Powers & these also will be given. It is well however that they should bear in mind that we cannot exempt them from the obligations of any existing Treaty."[77]

A Bill[78] was accordingly prepared which conceded this right, although it denied the Australian colonies the authority to levy differential tariffs on imports from foreign countries. The measure passed through the Commons in 1873 without a debate but in the Lords it was the recipient of bitter criticism from that uncompromising free trader, Lord Grey. Grey went further than Gladstone in expounding the belief that the Empire must possess a common commercial policy or it would cease to exist. Where the interests of all are concerned, he declared, there must be a single authority. If the present trend in colonial tariffs were continued, all that would be left of the imperial connection would be the mother country's responsibility to defend the Empire, which might become an onerous burden in time of danger.[79]   In Committee Grey renewed his opposition to the Bill by denying that in tariff matters the Australian colonies knew their own interests best. How could people ignorant of the writings of Smith and Ricardo appreciate the wisdom of a free trade policy, he asked petulantly? Australia must either conform to the commercial policy of Great Britain or leave the Empire.[80] To this protest Kimberley made the very effective rejoinder that it had been Grey who had sanctioned the first example of differential duties in the free trade Empire twenty-three years before, so that on the former Colonial Secretary's shoulders should rest much of the responsibility for the commercial tendencies which Great Britain had allowed since that time.[81] It was a conclusive and incontrovertible accusation.

The passage of the Act relieving the Australian colonies from the British Parliament's prohibition of differential duties marked a decisive concession of principle. It set the seal of Imperial recognition (for it could hardly be described as favour) on the right of the self-governing colonies to frame a tariff policy embodying differential features. The Canadian experience had been fundamental in securing the admission of this claim and the Dominion was to continue to lead the Empire in the assertion of fiscal autonomy. Although Canada failed to legislate in the direction of differential tariffs to the same extent after 1873 as before, the right to enact such duties was occasionally affirmed during the latter period.

In 1876 Edward Blake, as part of his plan to bring the prerogative instruments appointing the Governor-General more distinctly into accord with the position of that officer in relation to his responsible advisers, secured the omission from the Royal Instructions of the section requiring the reservation of certain classes of bills. The Governor-General retained his general power of reservation and the Imperial Government continued to exercise the right of disallowance, but from henceforth the injunction to suspend automatically tariff legislation imposing differential duties or clashing with the treaty obligations of Great Britain disappeared from the Instructions. Over the years this change tended to enhance the freedom of action of the Canadian Parliament in these subjects. The Imperial Government, in consenting to the removal from the Instructions of the sections dealing with reserved subjects, insisted, however, that it was not giving up the power to invalidate discriminatory tariff measures in the autonomous colonies. In 1878, when Lord Lorne succeeded Dufferin as Governor-General, the revised Instructions came into use for the first time. The publication of the new Instructions thus coincided in Canada with the advent of the Macdonald protectionist tariff; a fact which created a widespread impression that the two circumstances were linked. It was in order to combat this view that the Office acquiesced readily when Lorne later asked if the correspondence concerning the modification of the Instructions could be published for the Canadian Parliament. Herbert wrote on the Governor-General's telegram: "... I think there is no objection to its production. On the contrary it will serve (as no doubt is desired) to dispel the belief, apparently fostered by Sir John A. Macdonald, that there has been some change of policy here with regard to differential duties."[82] It was true that in 1879 the Imperial Government had not formally modified its disapproval of the principle of differential duties but by this time its attitude towards this manifestation of colonial autonomy was hardly of consequence in dealings with the senior Colony of the Empire.

Having been granted the power to impose preferential duties in favour of the other North American colonies, the Canadian Government went on to insist that this authority gave it the right to extend the same treatment to other colonies of the British Empire and to Great Britain herself. This declaration was stated in 1882, at a time when unofficial enquiries were being made from Canada to Jamaica regarding the possibility of a trade agreement between the two regions. The proposal had been advanced that the Dominion would reduce her duties on rum, sugar, and fruit from Jamaica, if that Colony would grant similar concessions to Canadian flour, fish, and lumber. The Colonial Office learned of these "feelers" from the Governor of Jamaica, who suggested that he pay a visit to Ottawa to discuss the matter with the Dominion authorities.[83] Kimberley balked at this proposal. There was a good possibility that a protectionist Canada

would insist upon major concessions from Jamaica, added to which Sir Anthony Musgrave, the Governor, was "notoriously unsound in his opinion on these subjects" and
could not be trusted to enter into negotiations with Canada.[84]   Musgrave was therefore forbidden to explore the topic. At the same time a dispatch was sent to Ottawa,
stating that Her Majesty's Government would not sanction any arrangement for reciprocal trade with Jamaica which necessitated the creation of differential duties in favour of Canada.[85]   The Canadian reply, a Report of the Privy Council dated October
26, 1882, declared that the negotiations had been private and unofficial and that there
seemed no prospect of any convention arising from them. The Cabinet went on to record its emphatic dissent from the rule that there could be no discriminatory duties
between various parts of the British Empire. Differential tariffs among the North American colonies, and even the prospect of reciprocal free trade in British North America, had been allowed by the British Government on various occasions, and these precedents served to sanction any wider arrangements that might be desired.

> ... the Canadian Government claim that it is competent for any of the Colonies
> possessing representative and responsible Governments to enter into mutual agree-
> ments for either partial or absolute free trade with the Mother Country or with each
> other or with both--discriminating against other countries.
>
> The same principle should also apply in the Crown Colonies, but as their ac-
> tion must be through Her Majesty's Government it is evident that their wishes can-
> not be carried into effect without the sanction of the Imperial Executive--negotia-
> tion with such Colonies does not seem to promise any beneficial results--until this
> principle be conceded--that trade should be rendered as free as practicable be-
> tween the various portions of the Empire having regard solely to their own interests,
> and unfettered by any obligation to treat others with equal favour.[86]

The Colonial Office response to the expression of this claim, with its implied re-
buke to the Imperial Government for not recognizing the desirability of tariff concessions made within the Empire, was that "the vexed question of inter-colonial reciprocity" should not be discussed further. Herbert wrote: "... I agree that it is undesirable to discuss with Canada, until we are forced to do so, the doctrine laid down in
the minute. When Colonies are geographically capable of being formed into a working "group" we have admitted the principle of special reciprocity arrangements."[87]
Kimberley added, with his well-known caution, that the Department need not pursue
this exchange, in which the Canadian Government had found an opportunity "to air
their peculiar theories. " "The Canadian Govt. have twisted into a general declaration of policy a statement which of course applied only to the particular case under
discussion, namely Jamaica: but it would not be convenient to correct this mistake,
as to do so might imply a declaration that we would sanction differential duties in
certain cases, to which it would be very unadvisable to commit ourselves."[88]   The
Canadian challenge was therefore not taken up, so that in the eyes of the Macdonald
Government another commercial principle was thought to have been conceded by default![89]

The desirability of enlarging Canadian trade with the British colonies in the West Indies was a theme which was constantly expressed in the Dominion during the latter decades of the nineteenth century. The support which the project attracted, both in Canada and in the Caribbean colonies, inspired many attempts at the establishment of commercial agreements and excited a few proposals for the political union of the two areas. These efforts invariably raised the question of the Imperial Government's attitude to the creation of differential tariff arrangements within the Empire. In 1882 the Colonial Office had refrained from controverting the views of Canada on this subject because it seemed unlikely that the issue would be raised in a tangible form. Throughout succeeding years the Department maintained the same general position: in private expressing its uneasiness over the progress of the discussions but failing to lay down a specific prohibition of the principle at stake. In the end the efforts to arrange preferential trade agreements between the West Indies and the mainland of North America, either with Canada or the United States, came to nothing. Thus the Office was spared the necessity of ever taking a definite stand on the question. It is doubtful, however, that even if circumstances had impelled official action, the Canadian freedom to enact differential tariffs in favour of other parts of the Empire would have been limited. By the year 1887, it is clear that the Dominion's claims in this direction had made a strong impression upon the Office and had even gained a few converts among the Department's permanent heads.

Two years after the Canadian position on this subject had been defined, the Dominion's High Commissioner was instructed to inform the Imperial Government that Canada was prepared to make the same concessions to the trade of the British West Indies as she had offered the Spanish islands. Herbert welcomed this proposal, reiterating his conviction that reciprocity was justified in the case of groups of colonies which were geographically contiguous and possessed complementary economies. The concessions afforded the Australian colonies in 1873 had settled this point, he declared: "It is of great importance to the West Indies that this overture from Canada should be assisted and not checked. There is a precedent in "The Australian Colonies Duties Act 1873" ... and the cases are similar as Queensland, the sugar producing Colony, stands in the same relation to Victoria or South Australia (the wheat colonies) as the West Indian Islands stand in towards Canada."[90]

In 1885 a trade delegation from Jamaica visited Canada to discuss, with the Macdonald Government and with business groups, the question of increased commercial intercourse between the two colonies.[91] The Governor-General reported this visit to London and pointed out that a serious obstacle to the realization of the project lay in the fact that the Colonial Office had insisted that any concessions granted Jamaica must be extended to the other West Indian colonies.[92] If this condition were required it would mean that Jamaica would lose all competitive advantage over colonies like Barbados and Trinidad in supplying sugar to the Dominion. It would also ensure the failure of the arrangement for it was unlikely that Canada could afford the loss of revenue consequent upon so much of her sugar entering the country free of duty. Herbert regarded this aspect of the case sympathetically.

It is perhaps questionable whether H. M. Govt. ought to insist on the inclusion
of all the West Indian Colonies in any such arrangement as that under discussion, especially as, knowing that the negotiations are going on they have not expressed any
desire to be parties to the arrangement.

If the Canadian market is not large enough to take in more than Jamaica, ought
the arrangement to be broken down because it does not take in more? [93]

Lord Dunraven, the Parliamentary Under-Secretary, was more hesitant in his attitude
to Canadian requirements. It would be, he remarked, a serious step to sanction an arrangement which would result in differential duties being set up against the other West
Indian islands. [94]   By the end of the year it was apparent that the Macdonald Government was not prepared to consider the Jamaica proposals, and the plan fell to the ground.

The final years of the period under review also witnessed various suggestions in
Canada regarding the imposition of differential duties for (and against) foreign countries.
Here again no success was attained in the Dominion's efforts to conclude commercial
arrangements, either with the United States or with European nations. But the projects
gave the Colonial Office an opportunity of noting the direction in which Canadian commercial policy was tending and prepared them for the inevitable concessions of the future. In comments on the many proposals which constitute Canada's early experience
in international negotiations the Colonial Office revealed a growing readiness to accept
the principle of reciprocal trade agreements between a colony and a foreign power.
There were moments of doubt and hesitation, it is true, but in general the freedom of
the Dominion to work for arrangements of this nature was increasingly recognized.

The commercial relations between Canada with the United States inspired, of course,
the largest share of the Colonial Office's reflections on the principle of differential
duties applied to areas outside the Empire. In the reciprocity negotiations which the
Mackenzie Government conducted with the Grant Administration in 1874, the Office
seemed prepared to follow the lead of the Board of Trade in insisting that the Dominion grant equal concessions to Great Britain. The Board at that time strongly recommended that the same exemptions be given to countries possessing "most-favoured-
nation" arrangements with the United Kingdom. [95]   Herbert, while recognizing that
this was "the English commercial point of view," felt that it was a reasonable requirement to ask of Canada. [96]   There would have been little objection from Canada to this
stipulation, for it appears that Mackenzie, who was at heart a free trader of the Cobden variety, was prepared to grant British exporters the advantages of any reductions in
duties afforded to the United States. [97]   It may be questioned whether the republic
would ever have accepted a treaty accompanied by these conditions, but the assurance
was at least made by Mackenzie. George Brown's reciprocity convention died in the
American Senate in 1875, so that the dilemma never obtruded itself on the Canadian
Government.

The legal difficulties which were caused by the relation between Canadian-American reciprocity and England's "most-favoured-nation" treaties were as nothing compared to this question of the project's effects upon British exports to Canada. In 1876,

when a resolution favouring free trade with Canada was introduced in the American Congress, the Office pointed out that tariff reductions between the United States and Canada would almost certainly hurt English trade with the Dominion. A member of the staff observed that once Canada and the United States discovered "how many interests they have in common" through freer trading practices, political union would result. "I cannot think therefore," he went on, "that it is to the interests of this country to promote Reciprocity between the U.S. and Canada...."[98] The following year the topic of reciprocity arose again, when the British Legation in Washington reported that it had been approached by the State Department on the subject. Malcolm remarked that such overtures posed "an extremely awkward question for us." If the Canadian people wholeheartedly endorsed reciprocity, he confessed that he did not see "how we could ultimately refuse it."[99] Herbert added that the American interest in reciprocity should be encouraged. He felt that if the United States was prepared to alter its tariff considerably, then reciprocity would be desirable. Malcolm's "extremely awkward question" could only be answered, in his opinion, "by allowing Canada to admit U.S. goods at lower rates than others, including English, if the treaty so requires."[100] Carnarvon agreed with Herbert's conclusions, although he noted the problems which a Canadian differential tariff would produce. "... I also see that we may find ourselves before long in a difficult region of diplomacy...."[101] The enactment of the "National Policy" in 1879 did not change the essential elements in the situation as the Department saw them. The Canadian protective tariff of that year had had the effect of reducing imports from both Great Britain and the United States, but the latter country had suffered the greater impairment of its trade. A reciprocity arrangement would simply reverse this advantage, which would mean a further fall in English exports to the Dominion. However, reciprocity could hardly be opposed on those grounds alone, and Herbert summed up the feeling of the Office in 1881 when he wrote, "We cannot prevent this reciprocity if it is seriously desired on both sides."[102]

The movement for Commercial Union between the United States and Canada, which came to a head in 1887, provided an admirable opportunity for the Colonial Office to consider the manifold implications of Canada's commercial policy. Commercial Union, or a North American Zollverein, as it was sometimes called, envisaged the removal of all customs barriers between Canada and the United States and the establishment of a common tariff against foreign countries. The demand for it was largely created by the widespread decline in business activity which took place in Canada after about 1882. The "National Policy" had not resulted in a home market adequate for Canadian manufacturers, while the high American tariffs prevented farmers and primary producers from disposing of their goods across the border. Thus the scheme of Commercial Union, which had been promoted spasmodically ever since the abrogation of the Reciprocity Treaty, was revived. Goldwin Smith, always the advocate of a "Continental policy" for Canadian economic development, became the leader of the new campaign, which rapidly attracted large popular support. The Liberal party, in 1888, adopted a platform, euphemistically labelled "unrestricted reciprocity," which embodied many of the features of Commercial Union, except that it was proposed that each country would maintain a separate tariff structure against the outside world. The Conservatives almost automatically declared against such close economic association with the United States, branding the proposal "veiled treason." It would eventually destroy the imperial connection, Macdonald stated, because it would inevitably be followed by the Dominion's political absorption into the United States. The conflicting viewpoints on Canadian economic development were put to the test of public opinion in 1891, when Macdonald fought his last election. "The old man, the old flag, and the old policy" were sustained, but the victory failed to suppress reciprocity sentiments in Canada. The Conservatives were returned to power for five more years, but the settlement of the pressing economic questions of the time was merely postponed into the future.

The origins and progress of the Commercial Union movement were fully explained to the Colonial Office in the autumn of 1887 by Lord Lansdowne.[103] The Governor-General's dispatch excited a flow of comment from the Office which provides an excellent illustration of the British official attitude towards Canadian commercial policy in the eighties. Bramston, an Assistant Under-Secretary, made the point that he did not feel Commercial Union would reduce British exports to the United States, for the existence of a high American tariff (which would be unchanged under Commercial Union) had not seriously interrupted that trade. The purchase of British goods by Canada would also be unaffected, he thought. His sanguine outlook about the consequences of Commercial Union led him decry the idea that annexation would be promoted by closer economic intercourse. He did not feel that Canadians would give up their own form of government for "the mischiefs involved in the recurring Presidential Elections." However, if Canada really desired annexation, "England will not be able to prevent such a consummation."[104]

Herbert regarded Commercial Union as a policy which was not likely to be adopted by Canada, although a moderate form of reciprocity might be attempted successfully. The Maritime provinces and British Columbia were dissatisfied under the present protective system of the Dominion, and would have to be given concessions in the Canadian tariff. Otherwise the disruption of the federation might occur.[105] Thus the question of a comprehensive preferential agreement between Canada and the United States was a momentous one, to be considered carefully by Her Majesty's Government. Nothing would have to be done until circumstances were further advanced, but the prospect obviously possessed important bearings on Great Britain's treaty obligations and on the imperial tie itself.

As to the "most favoured nation point" if Canada should insist on Commercial Union with the United States we should have to tell the countries having m.f.n. rights in Canada under our Treaties that so much of those Treaties must perish; at the risk of having the whole of those Treaties denounced.

The Government and the House of Commons would probably attempt to resist the demand of Canada in this matter, ... and in doing so would seriously imperil the union of the Australian Colonies, as well as Canada, with this country.

The Colonies will not endure serious interference with their fiscal policy: and if we interfere with it, we shall assume direct responsibility for the soundness and solvency of their finance.

On the other hand, after having been obliged, as I anticipate that it would be, to yield a sulky consent to this Commercial Union, Great Britain would no doubt intimate pretty clearly that a Dominion which had so differentially treated it must not look for the same amount of defence against foreigners as it now claims: must, in fact, look to the United States for everything. [106]

Holland, the Secretary of State, with the concern of a participant in the English political scene, noted that a Commercial Union between Canada and the United States would have some effect on the tariff debate in England. The consequences of such an arrangement would be real, although they would be hard to measure and might operate in favour of either camp. As for the larger question of Canada's annexation into the United States, he agreed with Bramston that it was not at all inevitable. "Speaking generally, I should be disposed to think that we should reluctantly and under protest assent to the Commercial Union, and then let the question of political Union settle itself. I do not feel at all sure that the Dominion would desire to have political as well as Commercial Union with the U. States, unless we forced it on; and such a course I should think we should hardly be prepared to take."[107]

The Colonial Office displayed a sterner attitude towards Canadian desires to give preferential treatment to foreign countries that were not as intimately connected with the Dominion as was the United States. The conversations which Sir Alexander Galt, the first Canadian High Commissioner, held with Spanish authorities in 1881, looking to a commercial convention between the Dominion and the Spanish West Indies, excited some concern in the Office. Leonard Courtney, the Parliamentary Under-Secretary, thought that there were serious objections to the terms which Galt was authorized to offer the Spanish Government. If Canada reduced import duties on sugar from Cuba there would be an outcry from the British sugar islands--and subsequent embarrassment to the Colonial Office. For the Department would then have been put in the position of approving the action of one colony even though it resulted in hardship to other colonies: colonies where its responsibilities were more pronounced than in the case of Canada. Similarly if Cuba offered a reduction to Canadian coal the mining interests of England would demand comparable treatment, yet Great Britain had no tariff advantages which it could give in return. There would have to be a clear understanding with Canada on these points, Courtney declared, and suggested that it might best be obtained by the Colonial Secretary engaging in a serious talk with Galt.[108] Kimberley agreed to see Galt and discuss the question with him, although he remarked that there was little the Colonial Office could do if Canada proved determined to reach an agreement with the Spanish colonies in North America. "I apprehend that having conceded to Canada the full right to frame her Tariff as she pleases and having further conceded to her exemption from any of our Commercial Treaties to which she does not wish to be a party and to negotiate Commercial Treaties for herself, we shall not be able to object to her making such stipulations as she may think [best] for her own interest. But the question is one of very serious importance...."[109] He saw the High Commissioner in March, 1882, and received the assurance that Canada would not give any advantage to Spain over trade from Great Britain or the other parts of the Empire. This was a useful beginning, observed Kimberley, for Galt had admitted the principle of equal treatment. There was now no need to press the matter further until the negotiations seemed to promise success.[110]

A treaty regulating trade between the United States and the British West Indies, drawn up in 1884-5, raised the same point in another form. Canada demanded that any concessions which the West Indies granted to imports from the United States should be extended to her trade as well.[111] The Colonial Office supported this claim, since in the discussions over the treaty the West Indies had promised not to discriminate against imports from Great Britain. There was hardly a reason for refusing this concession to Canada, the Office observed, provided the Dominion was ready to offer the same terms as the United States.[112] Reciprocity between the United States and the British West Indies was not achieved by this treaty, however, for the instrument was never approved by the British Government. It was dropped when it was found to impose limitations upon "most-favoured-nation" clauses in British commercial agreements.[113]

In November, 1882, Galt endeavoured to promote his negotiations with the Spanish Minister in London by threatening the imposition of additional duties on Spanish goods if that country did not enter into satisfactory commercial relations with Canada.[114] This was little more than personal coercion, for Galt had no authority to make such a declaration. It constituted an anticipation of discriminatory duties of the most severe kind, however, and Herbert at first felt that Great Britain could hardly overlook it. He talked, in a quite untypical manner, of the possibility of having to disallow a Canadian act imposing such duties.[115] Bramston pointed out that the principle of using differential duties as an aid in commercial bargaining had already been recognized by the sanctioning of the Canadian tariff Act of 1879, which allowed the Governor in Council to remit duties on French and Spanish wines if those countries came to terms with the Dominion. He added that as a result of the large powers of legislation granted Canada by the British North America Act he doubted whether the Imperial Government could or should interfere.[116] This advice calmed Herbert, who wrote in a more characteristic vein, "It is most desirable to avoid interference if possible; and I think we can avoid it." He suggested that the Foreign Office be informed that the Department did not feel the legislation contemplated by Galt should be contravened unless very strong reasons presented themselves against it.[117] Derby agreed and the Foreign Office subsequently endorsed the proposal. It registered a protest against Galt's threats, however, and asked that Canada be told that she acted on her sole responsibility in adopting this course of action.[118] Galt's threat was not implemented in the Canadian tariff of 1883, nor was it successful in inducing Spain to grant commercial concessions to the Dominion.

III

Among the aspects of the commercial policy of the larger settlement colonies which aroused sentiments of misgiving in Whitehall, differential duties was but the greatest in a catalogue of sins. Protection, which emerged in the period under review as a guiding principle in the framing of the Canadian tariff, represented another regrettable tendency running counter to free trade doctrines. In its response to the appearance of protective legislation in the Dominion the Colonial Office adopted a remarkably tolerant and laissez-faire attitude. This outlook resulted partly from a knowledge of the elements in the Canadian scene which gave rise to protection, and partly from a lessening faith, among the senior officials, in the efficacy of free trade principles. These factors are particularly noticeable in the attitude of Carnarvon and Herbert; they are less visible in the mind of Kimberley, who resembled Grey in the intensity of his commercial convictions. From a stand of combative hostility to unorthodox commercial legislation assumed in the period 1846-52, the Office withdrew to a position in which Canadian tariffs were sanctioned without question, regardless of the pressures brought to bear on the Department from English manufacturing interests. The Board of Trade remained stubbornly wedded to the promotion of the gospel of free trade, but its influence on the Colonial Office waned perceptibly during these years. To the Board was still sent Canadian tariff legislation for comment, but little attention was paid by the Office to representations which the Board might make on these measures. The Department revealed throughout these years a deliberate reluctance to exercise any power that might be interpreted as infringing upon the domestic autonomy of Canada, and tariff legislation came to be seen increasingly as lying within this hallowed province. The Imperial responsibility for the control of trade, which limited Durham's concept of colonial self-government, was almost completely renounced in British policy towards Canada during the two decades following 1867.

The acceptance of a rigorous protective tariff in Canada was made easier for the Office by its having to witness the growth of a strong spirit favouring protection in the Dominion. Thus, when the blow finally fell in 1879, the Department was prepared for it. The tariffs of the first Macdonald Government, although embodying objectionable features, were designed mainly for revenue; a characteristic which was continued in the legislation passed by the Liberal Administration of Alexander Mackenzie. The serious commercial depression of the seventies retarded Canadian economic development and fostered the conviction, primarily among manufacturing groups in central Canada, that in protection the country would find a policy leading to national prosperity. As early as 1875 a meeting of Canadian industrialists, held in Toronto, passed resolutions advocating a tariff with a general rate of twenty per cent upon foreign manufactured products. These resolutions were transmitted to the Colonial Office by the Governor-General, so that the Office was able to observe, as one member put it, that "the Canadian manufacturers are certainly out and out protectionists."[119] The impression that the growth of such a sentiment could be resisted by Great Britain was deprecated by Herbert. "Protection is a strong growing weed, and it is quite possible that before long we may have to accept the Commercial independence of some of the great Colonies. We cannot indeed prevent the Colonial Legislatures from imposing such duties as they may for any reason think advantageous to the interests of the countries for the good government of which they are responsible...."[120] In the following year Herbert remarked that the Office should not endorse criticisms of the Canadian tariff made by British manufacturing interests. "... I am satisfied," he wrote, "that we shall have to give up all pretension to dictate, to such a country as Canada now is, the fiscal policy which is most acceptable to British manufacturers."[121] The Permanent Under-Secretary was thus reducing still further the several objections which the Imperial Government had conventionally presented against a Canadian protective tariff. A tariff was no longer to be considered unacceptable because it injured British exports, or even because it impaired the commercial unity of the Empire.

It was fortunate that the heads of the Office were coming to be of this opinion, for they were soon faced with a radical adjustment of the Dominion's tariff structure. In 1878, after a five-year Liberal interregnum, Sir John Macdonald was returned to power, winning a majority in every province in the Dominion except New Brunswick. The election had been fought by the Conservatives on the issue of protection versus a moderate revenue tariff and once in office Macdonald showed that he intended to pursue a policy of economic nationalism. In March, 1879, Sir Leonard Tilley, the Minister of Finance, introduced a new tariff measure,[122] the "National Policy," into the Dominion Parliament. The Tilley Budget provided for a rise in the duties on manufactured goods from the seventeen and one-half per cent rate laid down in 1874 to a level as high as thirty or forty per cent. It also substituted, in many cases, specific duties for an ad valorem levy, and gave special protection to the iron and steel industry of Nova Scotia, the textile manufacturing of Ontario and Quebec, and the coal mines of Nova Scotia. The new tariff was designed to have several uses. "The National Policy promised not only to preserve the home market by protection and to open the United States market by retaliation, but to provide a revenue adequate for the country's needs.... It promised national self-sufficiency."[123] In addition the Tilley duties provided a small measure of preference for British goods; a circumstance which the Government hoped would soften the critical reception which the new tariff was bound to receive in Great Britain. Macdonald, Tupper, and Tilley, in England in the summer of 1879 on public business, explained to the Colonial Office the nature of this British preference.

> The Government of Canada are prepared, under arrangements with the Imperial Government, and with the assent of the Canadian Parliament, to give distinct trade advantages to Great Britain, as against foreign countries, and they sought to do so in their arrangement of the present tariff, to a limited extent; but, believing that the Imperial Government were not favourable to direct discriminating duties, the object in view was sought and obtained through a somewhat complex classification of imports.

> The policy of Canada towards British manufacturers is not, therefore, such as to exclude them from our markets, but points to an arrangement that, if adopted,

might give us sufficient for revenue purposes, and at the same time be of infinite advantage to the Empire. [124]

The Colonial Office first heard of the new tariff when it was introduced into the Canadian House of Commons. [125]   Then Lord Lorne's telegram announcing the significant departure occasioned regret but no desire to obstruct the new policy.   Herbert stated:

> This is a stiffish protective tariff. It is not in the province of H. M. Govt. to comment upon--still less to interfere with, its policy.
> The answer will, I suppose, be that H M Government does not desire to ask for any differential provisions in favour of British Goods, more especially as if such provisions were made it would be inferred that this Government is a party to the fiscal policy of the Dominion; which of course is a matter for the decision of the Canadian Legislature. [126]

He drafted the reply, which was the only official comment made by the United Kingdom on the longest step yet taken towards protection in the British Empire. "... [the] general effect appears to be, as Her Majesty's Government regret to observe, an increase of duties already high. They deem however the fiscal policy of Canada to be a matter the decision of which, subject to treaty obligations, rests with the Dominion Legislature. "[127]

Outside the Department the news of the "National Policy" was not received so placidly. The British industrial community rose up in arms against the new duties and a flood of protests poured into the Office from chambers of commerce, manufacturer's associations, and other interested groups. The Office duly forwarded these representations to Canada, occasionally omitting passages that might cause offence to the Canadian Government. For, as a clerk minuted, "the Canadians are very jealous of their rights, and are inclined to be indignant at any indication of what they call the "selfish" policy of this country in trade matters. "[128]   In the public discussion John Bright vented his spleen against Canada for adopting a tariff injurious to British interests while at the same time expecting to receive financial favours from the mother country. It was the same protest he had made in 1867, but this time it was more than slightly heightened by the imposition of the new duties. "The policy of the Canadian Government [the adoption of the "National Policy"] seems to me injurious to the inhabitants of the Dominion, and, if persisted in, will be fatal to its connexion with the mother country. To shut out the manufacturer of England is bad enough; but at the same time to seek to borrow money from her, or seek a guarantee for a loan, is a scheme and a policy so impudent that it cannot succeed. "[129]   In the House Bright warned of the prospect of a tariff war within the Empire being brought materially closer by the new Canadian duties. His request for papers bearing on the question elicited the reply from Hicks Beach that the changes had been announced without communication with Her Majesty's Government. The Colonial Secretary then gave the House the text of the telegram which had been sent to Canada, characterizing it a perfect expression of the views of the Government on the subject. It could be fairly stated, he went on, that there was no feature of the new Canadian customs structure which had not already been sanctioned by Great Britain.[130]

The Board of Trade also expressed a strong censure of the tariff of 1879. The Board's views were contained in several letters, written in reply to a number of memoranda issued by the Canadian Government defending the new tariff.[131] T. H. Farrer was responsible for the communications from the Board on this occasion, which as always provided a good statement of free trade principles, expounded against the background of the changing international scene at the end of the seventies. The arguments were at first purely selfish. The depression which the United Kingdom was experiencing at that time would undoubtedly be magnified by the Canadian action in diminishing imports from the mother country. Canada in the past had been an exporter of primary products and it was now unnatural for her to change her economy by encouraging the growth of manufacturing. She should buy from England, which could produce secondary goods more cheaply than herself, and not divert men and money to new occupations. If the Dominion had been primarily interested in revenue from her tariff structure it could have been obtained more efficiently from low customs duties and from excise taxes on a few articles of general consumption. In reality the new tariff was drawn up to achieve protection and any Canadian attempts to describe it in any other sense were hypocritical.

Turning to the Canadian offer of a preferential rate for British imports, Farrer rejected it with scorn. Great Britain had no desire for such privileged treatment. It was better for her to trade with the whole world than to concentrate on a small colonial market. The proposal had been advanced that Great Britain should give Canada a quid pro quo in the form of a loan or a guarantee in exchange for differential tariff rates. Farrer expressed genuine horror at this idea--to "purchase" a tariff reduction would be contrary to the fundamental rules of free trade.[132] He went on to discount the project of an imperial Customs Union, which was beginning to be aired at this time. The suggestion that the colonies offer British products preferential rates, in return for a privileged entrance into the English market, he characterized as "the idlest of idle dreams."[133] There was quite frankly not enough British trade with the whole colonial Empire to make the scheme attractive to English manufacturers. These interests would not submit to any impediment in their trade with the United States and the rest of the world, and it was unreasonable that they should be asked to do so. The fact that there existed as well a number of "most-favoured-nation" treaties between Great Britain and foreign countries furnished an additional argument against discriminatory tariffs within the Empire. The only way in which Canada could assist the growth of British trade was through the abolition of her protective tariff and the creation of exclusively revenue duties. The present course of the Dominion's commercial policy was bound to prove injurious to the trade of the two countries, and would eventually undermine the basis of political relations. For the existence of a flourishing economic intercourse between the mother country and her largest Colony was the most effective weapon against the spread of dangerous anti-imperial sentiments both at home and abroad.

It is not within the province of the Board of Trade to enter at any length on this part of the subject, but they will scarcely be exceeding their functions in remarking how largely relations of a political and international kind depend upon commercial inter-course. The past history of Great Britain and her dependencies illustrates in the strongest way the effect which a liberal or illiberal policy in the matter of commerce may have upon the connexion between the different parts of the empire. Nor should it be forgotten that, when suggestions have been made to the effect that the colonies may become a burden and embarassment to the mother country, one of the most forcible reasons which has been given in answer to these suggestions has been that there is a commercial [interchange] between the mother country and her colonies such as does not exist between the United Kingdom and any foreign country.134

The majority of the Colonial Office staff who read the correspondence from the Board of Trade on the tariff of 1879 were of the opinion that Farrer had stated the case for free trade with incontrovertible cogency. "I confess I think Mr. Farrer's letter is un-answerable," wrote Earl Cadogan, the Parliamentary Under-Secretary.135 Herbert, however, revealed that he possessed reservations about the general validity of Farrer's opinions. In his comments on the Board of Trade letter he betrayed a mild sympathy for the idea of preferential trading arrangements within the Empire by proclaiming views which were later to make him a supporter of Joseph Chamberlain and the "Tariff Re-form" movement:

> This is an able letter, as anything of Mr. Farrers would be.... But he seems to me to go rather too far in his opposition to any arrangement between this coun-try and a colony or colonies for reciprocal differential tariffs. If the parties to such an arrangement can supply each other's ordinary requirements; and if the higher duties payable by outsiders are as inconsiderable as not to exclude their products from the market requiring them; there would seem to be some real virtue in a tar-iff arrangement which, without injuriously affecting consumers, would collect from outsiders a reasonable payment for the privilege of using the markets of the contract-ing parties.136

To Herbert Canada's determination to construct the Pacific Railway without further Im-perial assistance meant that the Dominion was entitled to special consideration in the framing of any tariff programme she thought desirable. He recommended that the Board of Trade's views be withheld from Canada and that the topic be laid at rest. Hicks Beach agreed with the Permanent Under-Secretary that Farrer had overstated the free trade case. "There is something to be said on the other side," he commented.137 He concurred in Herbert's direction to take the subject out of official discussion with Can-ada. Thus the Macdonald Tariff of 1879, the basis of all succeeding protective legisla-tion in the Dominion's history, was sanctioned by the Colonial Office without the hint of a remonstrance from Downing Street. The twenty years that had elapsed since 1859 had indeed been a lifetime in the conduct of intra-imperial commercial relations!

The divergence between the Colonial Office and the Board of Trade over the general applicability of free trade principles became wider as the decade progressed. In 1880, for instance, Canada proposed to subsidize a line of steamers running to Brazil in order to open up trade with that country. The Board criticized this project as an artificial diversion of economic life; an undesirable example of government interference into commercial activity. An Office clerk described Farrer's arguments on this occasion as "text-book dicta," and Pennell questioned the expediency "of continually lecturing the Canadian Govt. on the subject of free trade."[138] Herbert added that laissez-faire dogma might, in fact, be losing a good deal of its validity in the changed international atmosphere of the later nineteenth century.

> Mr. Farrer's views would not, I fear, be accepted in Canada of in many other Colonies and I would not send them to the Dominion Government. They are no doubt based on the doctrines of Political Economy, but those doctrines were formulated so as to suit the requirements of the trade and commerce of these Islands, and the English formula of Free Trade would be [destructive] to trade in many other countries. The struggle for commercial existence is now very keen all over the world and it is quite useless to suggest that special commercial conventions, and subsidies to lines of steamers, for the purpose of getting hold of particular markets, are unsound in principle....[139]

Another time Herbert directed that a copy of an address in which Sir Leonard Tilley had praised the "National Policy" for bringing back prosperity to Canada should not be sent to the Board of Trade.

> It is unfortunately the case that those free trade principles which are generally accepted in England, as axioms of unquestionable application to all countries alike, coincide with the peculiar commercial interests of these Islands; so that when a Free Trader is giving a Colonist what he honestly believes to be the best advice for the latter he is thought to be keeping his own interests too much in view.
>
> If we send these papers to the Board of Trade we shall probably elicit an able rejoinder from the Free Trade point of view, but as it is useless and probably inexpedient to lecture Canada on the subject, we may as well not "draw" the Board of Trade.[140]

Kimberley agreed that the speech should not be referred to the Board. Although not sharing Herbert's doubts about the efficacy of free trade principles he felt that the Board of Trade could hardly convert Canada at this late date. There were plenty of books available on political economy which gave the free trade point of view and the Board was unlikely to add very much to the arguments that had been stated in them.[141] Two years later, when the Admiralty complained about customs duties being charged on stationery imported for the use of naval establishments in Canada, Herbert expressed the opinion that only "official" stationery could properly enjoy the exemption. Canada required revenue for her public services and it was not reasonable that a variety of imports destined for military stations in the Dominion should be relieved from the application of the Canadian tariff. He went on to give a cautious commendation of the "National Policy" as it appeared to him to be operating at that time: "The Dominion Tariff is defensible, and is working well, from a revenue point of view.... Canada is engaged in a very heavy undertaking and requires every dollar she can raise; and in a new country not much can be raised otherwise than through the Customs. If its protectionist aspect is objectionable we must wait till circumstances admit of a change."[142]

An alteration was made in these years in the Colonial Office's procedure for the handling of protests from English manufacturers over the Canadian tariff. The Office had failed to support these representations for many years, and Herbert, in 1881, felt that it was no longer desirable for the Department to transmit them to the Canadian Government. The practice tended to identify the Office with the protest and might conceivably become a source of irritation to the Dominion. He recommended that in future English manufacturers be told to address their representations directly to the Canadian Minister of Finance.[143] Kimberley concurred in this suggestion, which thus became the normal practice of the Office.[144] Herbert would have extended this policy to the point where the Imperial Government would have given up all right of remonstrance against changes in the Canadian tariff. Kimberley drew the line at this proposal, however. The United Kingdom had abandoned the right to control the tariffs of colonies with responsible government, he admitted, but this did not mean that the Imperial Government should also renounce its prerogative to protest undesirable features in the commercial legislation of the overseas territories. Great Britain performed this operation constantly when foreign nations imposed duties prejudicial to English trade and he felt the same practice should be followed with regard to the autonomous colonies. To do otherwise would be to place Great Britain in a less favourable position towards her colonies than she was towards foreign countries.[145] Consequently the Secretary of State directed that observations made by the Treasury and the Commissioners of Inland Revenue on the Canadian tariff of 1880 should be sent to Ottawa for the information of the Canadian Cabinet.

The last major protest by British manufacturers against a Canadian tariff came in 1887, when the Macdonald Government imposed increased duties on iron and steel imports into the Dominion. The Tariff Bill[146] was introduced into the Dominion Parliament on May 12, 1887, and as soon as the news of its provisions reached England there was a spate of protests from the iron industry of the mother country. The British Iron Trade Association asked to be allowed to send a deputation to wait upon the Colonial Secretary to present the industry's representations. At first Sir Henry Holland, the Secretary of State, refused to receive such a body. The advice on which he acted was that of Herbert's, who stated, "I think we could not justify such an interference into Canadian self Government as would be involved in hearing an ex parte statement on behalf of the Iron Trade before we have heard what is the nature, extent and object of the Canadian tariff alterations...." In spite of the increases, the Canadian duties on iron imports would still be lower than the American rate on similar products, he pointed out.[147]

Eventually, after the Office had been subjected to considerable unofficial pressure, Holland agreed to hear the iron industry's point of view in a private meeting in the House of Commons on May 23. He was non-committal in his reply to the delegation, giving it the same answer as the First Lord of the Treasury (W. H. Smith) had supplied to a questioner in the House: that any representations on the new tariff should be addressed directly to Canada. 148   Later the Government relented a little by transmitting to the Canadian Cabinet in an official dispatch from the Secretary of State the various memorials against the tariff. The attitude of the Colonial Office to these protests was exceedingly ambiguous, however, the dispatch merely pointing out the dissatisfaction which existed in Great Britain over the new tariff.

> Your Government are aware from previous communications which I have already forwarded to you, that great dissatisfaction is felt in this country amongst mercantile firms interested in the iron trade, in consequence of the action of the Government of the Dominion in proposing the imposition of these duties, and the matter has also formed the subject of discussion in both Houses of Parliament, where much adverse opinion has been expressed.
> I think it right to call your attention to the feeling which exists in this country, and have no doubt that your Government will give consideration to the various representations which have been made on the subject. 149

Long before this communication reached Ottawa, the Canadian Act had been given the Royal Assent. The Macdonald Government made a partial concession to the outburst in England by reducing slightly the duties on certain types of imported iron. But the Cabinet clung fast to the main elements in the new tariff; the Minister of Finance, in a memorandum written in defence of the measure, asserting that it would result in a strengthening of the economic life of the Empire. Canada imported more iron products from the United States than from Great Britain, and by ceasing to be dependent on foreign sources for iron would gradually build up a more self-sufficient economy. This, in turn, would make the Dominion of greater value to the Empire if war threatened. 150   The Colonial Office was unimpressed by Sir Charles Tupper's arguments on this occasion, although Herbert, for one, found reasons to condone the Canadian stand.

> It is also very much a question of satisfying the Eastern Provinces which it is difficult to keep in the Dominion.
> The difficulties of the Canadian Government are great, and I am disposed to think that the alternatives to this regrettable fiscal policy would be a far greater evil.
> But we cannot interfere. 151

In the Imperial Parliament the new Canadian tariff was discussed heatedly and extensively, particularly in the Lords. Lord Lamington (the former Alexander Baillie

Cochrane) was persistent in his criticism of the duties and in his demands for the publication of the correspondence on the subject. The Earl of Onslow, the Parliamentary Under-Secretary, insisted that the correspondence with Canada on the measure was not significant (which was true) and that there would be no point in presenting it to the House. When it became apparent that Lamington's views were supported by most of the members of the Chamber, the Government gave in and consented to bring down the correspondence. In fact, the Salisbury Ministry showed itself extremely sensitive to public opinion on this issue, on at least two occasions withdrawing from decisions which it had made because of the pressure of feeling at home. Granville was a strong supporter of Lamington in his condemnation of the Canadian tariff. He felt that it was quite proper that the Government had refused to interfere in the matter, but urged that strong representations be made to the Dominion about the injurious effect which the duties would have on the British iron trade. He remarked that the consequences of the Canadian action should be remembered when the Dominion next approached Great Britain for special favours or assistance. A Canadian proposal for a subsidy to maintain a line of steamers across the Pacific had recently been made and Granville implied that a cool reception to this scheme might have the effect of rendering Canada more amenable in her tariff arrangements.[152] Salisbury, speaking for the Government, agreed that the imposition of the new tariff would undoubtedly effect the consideration of the plan for a steamship service to the Orient, and Goschen, the Chancellor of the Exchequer, provided a similar assurance in the House sometime later.[153] Against this type of thinking people like Carnarvon and the Earl of Dunraven opposed themselves, arguing that the Pacific route was too vital for the security of the Empire to be jeopardized by any petty bitterness with Canada. It was hardly just to expect Canada to grant England concessions in her trade when the mother country had nothing left to give the Dominion in return.[154] Dunraven, in making these observations, was clearly thinking of a scheme of imperial preference and went on to praise the tariff of 1879 for marking a new departure in commercial policy. That principle should be continued, he said, for it would eventually lead to the consolidation of the Empire as a gigantic trading unit.[155]

The last word on the Canadian duties of 1887 (and indeed on the whole subject of Imperial remonstrances against colonial tariffs) was uttered in these debates by the Prime Minister. Salisbury gravely informed the House that the Government's sympathy with the British iron industry would have to be "platonic." It would be futile for Great Britain to protest strongly to Canada; the tariff of 1887 was an accomplished fact, and protection was an established policy in North America. In fact the protective principle was more than a rule of action adopted in an isolated colony; it was now a world-wide movement, making conquests in many areas in all stages of economic development.

Of course, so far as any exhortations on our side are likely to affect the policy of Canada, they will not be spared; and any facts with which the iron trade may arm us, and which will enable us in any degree to modify the opinions of the statesmen of Canada, shall be put forward with all the authority we possess. But I will not conceal my belief that we are dealing with a stronger stream of opinion than any exhortations of statesmen in Downing Street are likely to affect, and that we must look for relief rather to the inevitable failure which the teachers of Free Trade have told us with great confidence has attended all the experiments of Protection in the past, and which, no doubt, will ultimately bring home to the Canadians the error they are committing.[156]

Salisbury's words, coming in the year of the first Colonial Conference, represented the swan song of the confident era in which free trade and laissez-faire ideas dominated economic activity. That era was soon to be succeeded by a grimmer and more competitive age. In the latter part of the century it was Great Britain who found herself isolated in an adherence to free trade, and the colonies who came to belong to the main current of thought on commercial regulation. By 1887 the long movement for the achievement of a free trade empire had failed, and the Colonial Office, once in the vanguard of the campaign, had resigned itself to the task of presiding over the last rites for a dead principle. The fiscal autonomy of the larger British colonies had been ultimately disclosed as incompatible with the economic unity of the Empire; but yet was it not to the credit of the Office that it had seen in the former consideration the more constructive of the two goals of endeavour?[157]

REFERENCES

1. Earl Grey, The Colonial Policy of Lord John Russell's Administration (London, 1853), I, 280.

2. Hansard, Third Series, CCXVI, 156 (May 20, 1873).

3. Minute by Elliot, March 9, 1861, on Officer Administering the Government of Canada to Newcastle, no. 2, Jan. 2, 1861: CO 42/626.

4. 18 Geo. III, c. 12.

5. 9 and 10 Vict., c. 94.

6. 13 and 14 Vict., c. 3.

7. The standard work on the achievement of the Reciprocity Treaty is D. C. Masters, The Reciprocity Treaty of 1854 (London, 1936). See also the same author's "Reciprocity and the Genesis of a Canadian Commercial Policy," Canadian Historical Review, XIII (Dec., 1932), 418-28.

8. Morrell, British Colonial Policy. 230.

9. 22 Vict., c. 76.

10. 22 Vict., c. 2.

11. Report by the Minister of Finance, Oct. 25, 1859, enclosed in Head to Newcastle, no. 118, Nov. 11, 1859: CO 42/619. The correspondence relating to the Canadian tariff of 1859 is printed in PP, 1864, XLI, no. 400.

12. Board of Trade to Colonial Office, Jan. 17, 1860: CO 42/624.

13. Board of Trade to Colonial Office, March 14, 1860: ibid. There are similar statements containing the theoretical objections to differential duties which date from the period when the Colonial Office felt strongly on this point. See the circular dispatch of Lord John Russell, July 12, 1855, and Molesworth to the Governors of the West Indian Colonies, circular, Aug. 11, 1855: PP, 1856, XLIV, no. 431, 1-4.

14. Memo. by the Minister of Finance, Aug. 20, 1860, enclosed in Officer Administering the Government of Canada to Newcastle, no. 2, Jan. 2, 1861: CO 42/626.
Galt's promotion of Canadian fiscal autonomy in the years 1859-60 is described in D. C. Masters, "A. T. Galt and Canadian Fiscal Autonomy," Canadian Historical Review, XV (Sept., 1934), 276-82.

15. Minute by Elliot, March 9, 1861, on Officer Administering the Government of Canada to Newcastle, no. 2, Jan. 2, 1861: CO 42/626.

16. Colonial Office to Board of Trade, March 23, 1861: ibid.

17. Newcastle to Monck, no. 2, Nov. 5, 1861: ibid.

18. There were additional and unsuccessful proposals in 1862. See SP, 1863, no. 14.

19. 29 and 30 Vict., c. 3, s. 121.

20. 31 Vict., c. 6, s. 123, subs. 10, and c. 7, ss. 2 and 3.

21. 30 Vict., c. 2.
This provision was apparently designed to encourage a line of American steamers to continue a freight service from Portland, Maine, to Charlottetown. During the winter Canadian goods were often shipped by rail from Montreal to the Atlantic seaboard at Portland, so that the Government of the Colony could fairly claim that it was help-

ing to provide a market for Canadian products through the tariff concession. See Report of the Executive Council of Prince Edward Island, Sept. 4, 1867, enclosed in Dundas to Buckingham, no. 77, Sept. 10, 1867: CO 226/103. Printed in SP, 1869, no. 47, 16-18.

22. Dundas to Buckingham, no. 58, June 5, 1867: CO 226/103.

23. Minute by Buckingham, July 13, 1867, on ibid.

24. Board of Trade to Colonial Office, July 8, 1867: CO 226/103. Printed in SP, 1869, no. 47, 16.

25. Minute by Rogers, July 12, 1867, on Board of Trade to Colonial Office, July 8, 1867: CO 226/103.

26. Buckingham to Dundas, no. 21, July 26, 1867: ibid. Printed in SP, 1869, no. 47, 16.

27. Buckingham to Dundas, no. 28, Nov. 14, 1867: CO 226/103. Printed in SP, 1869, no. 47, 18.

28. Board of Trade to Colonial Office, Oct. 31, 1867: CO 226/103.

29. Buckingham to Monck, no. 113, Nov. 14, 1867: ibid. Printed in SP, 1869, no. 47, 15.

30. Memo. by the Minister of Finance, Jan. 13, 1868, enclosed in Monck to Buckingham, no. 19, Jan. 25, 1868: CO 42/667. Printed in SP, 1869, no. 47, 1-3.

31. Minute by Elliot, Feb. 20, 1868, on Monck to Buckingham, no. 19, Jan. 25, 1868: CO 42/667.

32. Board of Trade to Colonial Office, March 12, 1868: CO 42/673.

33. 31 Vict., c. 7, s. 4.

34. The offer remained a feature of all Canadian tariffs until the year 1894. See Keith, Responsible Government, III, 1144.

35. Dictionary of National Biography, Supplement, XXII, 627.

36. Board of Trade to Colonial Office, June 25, 1868: CO 42/673. Printed in SP, 1869, no. 47, 13-14.

37. Minute by Holland, July 1, 1868, on Board of Trade to Colonial Office, June 25, 1868: CO 42/673.

38. Minutes by Elliot, July 10, 1868, on ibid. , and July 20, 1868, on Buckingham to Monck, no. 163, July 24, 1868: CO 42/673.

The Governor-General's Instructions bade him reserve any bill imposing differential duties, or interfering with the treaty engagements of Great Britain. If the Canadian Act did not affect the second of these prohibitions, it obviously concerned the first.

39. Minute by Adderley, July 11, 1868, on Board of Trade to Colonial Office, June 25, 1868: ibid.

40. Buckingham to Monck, no. 163, July 24, 1868: ibid. Printed in SP, 1869, no. 47, 12-13.

Elliot added the last sentence, "lest the Canadian Govt. should think they have it quite at their own [discretion]." Minute by Elliot, July 20, 1868, on Buckingham to Monck, no. 163, July 24, 1868: CO 42/673.

41. Memo. by the Minister of Finance, Sept. 3, 1868, enclosed in Monck to Buckingham, no. 171, Sept. 15, 1868: CO 42/670. Printed in PP, 1873, XLIX, no. C-703, 14-17, and SP, 1869, no. 47, 6-9. A. H. U. Colquhoun reproduced Rose's memo. , with rather misleading notes, and calling it "An Unpublished State Paper, " in Canadian Historical Review, I (March, 1920), 54-60.

42. Board of Trade to Colonial Office, Nov. 20, 1868: CO 42/673.

43. Granville to Officer Administering the Government of Canada, no. 3, Dec. 29, 1868: ibid. Printed in SP, 1869, no. 47, 3.

The tariffs of 1867 and 1868 each contained a provision for reciprocal trade with the United States and were thus approved simultaneously in Granville's dispatch.

The delay in sanctioning the Act was due to the necessity of asking the Treasury's approval of the Canadian legislation, which was not obtained until December. Treasury to Colonial Office, Dec. 12, 1868: CO 42/673.

44. See A. H. U. Colquhoun, "The Reciprocity Negotiations with the United States in 1869, " Canadian Historical Review, VIII (Sept. , 1927), 233-42.

45. 33 Vict. , c. 9.

46. E. Porritt, Sixty Years of Protection in Canada, 1846-1907 (London, 1908), 270.

47. Report of the Privy Council of Canada, Sept. 28, 1870, enclosed in Young to Kimberley, no. 224, Sept. 28, 1870: CO 42/688.

48. Minute by Rogers, Oct. 12, 1870, on Young to Kimberley, no. 224, Sept. 28, 1870: CO 42/688.

49. Kimberley to Young, no. 274, Oct. 19, 1870: ibid.

50. Mallet, who later became Permanent Under-Secretary at the India Office, was associated with Cobden in the negotiation of the commercial treaty with France in 1860. He was a leading exponent of Cobdenite economic thought, and, after Cobden's death, "the chief official representative of free trade opinion" (Dictionary of National Biography, XXXV, 428).

51. Board of Trade to Colonial Office, Feb. 13, 1871: CO 42/701.

52. Minutes by Holland and Knatchbull-Hugessen, Feb. 15, 1871, on ibid.

53. Board of Trade to Colonial Office, March 21, 1871: CO 42/701.

54. 34 Vict., c. 10.

55. In the autumn of 1870, the Canadian Government had been in high hopes over the effects of its new tariff. A motion to repeal the import duties on Canadian coal was lost by a narrow margin in the United States Senate, and the policy of retaliation seemed to promise eventual success. See Young to Kimberley, no. 223, Sept. 28, 1870: CO 42/688.

56. Minute by Kimberley, July 26, 1871, on Board of Trade to Colonial Office, March 21, 1871: CO 42/701.

57. Lisgar to Kimberley, no. 217, Dec. 29, 1871: CO 42/700.

58. Minute by Kimberley, July 26, 1871, on Board of Trade to Colonial Office, March 21, 1871: CO 42/701. See also Board of Trade to Colonial Office, Sept. 26, 1871: ibid.

59. 35 Vict., c. 11 and 12.

60. Mallet to Herbert, private, June 17, 1872: CO 42/708.

61. Kimberley to Dufferin, secret, Aug. 12, 1872: ibid.

62. Report of the Minister of Finance, Sept. 7, 1872, enclosed in Dufferin to Kimberley, secret, Sept. 13, 1872: ibid.

63. Minute by Herbert, Sept. 27, 1872, on Dufferin to Kimberley, secret, Sept. 13, 1872: CO 42/708.

64. Ibid.

65. Herbert to Kimberley, private, Oct. 5, 1872: CO 42/708.

66. Minute by Knatchbull-Hugessen, Sept. 30, 1872, on Dufferin to Kimberley, secret, Sept. 13, 1872: ibid. This minute is incorrectly attributed to Kimberley in Neuendorff, Evolution of Dominion Status, 48.

67. Kimberley to Gladstone, Oct. 14, and Oct. 30, 1872, cited in Knaplund, Gladstone and Imperial Policy, 118-9.

68. Kimberley to Dufferin, secret, Dec. 5, 1872: CO 42/708.
Macdonald congratulated Cartier for having "converted" Kimberley to an acceptance of the Tea and Coffee Act. See J. Boyd, Sir George Etienne Cartier, Bart. (Toronto, 1914), 327.
The Act came into force Jan. 1, 1873.

69. The correspondence on the Australasian differential duties controversy is printed in PP, 1872, XLII, no. C-576, and 1873, XLIX, no. C-703. See also Keith, Responsible Government, III, 1164-83, for a discussion of the question.

70. 13 and 14 Vict., c. 59, ss. 27 and 31.

71. 15 and 16 Vict., c. 72, s. 61.

72. PP, 1872, XLII, no. C-576, 19.

73. PP, 1873, XLIX, no. C-703, 8-9.

74. Rogers's attitude to the question is illustrated in Knaplund, Gladstone and Imperial Policy, 106, and Hall, The Colonial Office, 234.

75. Knaplund, Gladstone and Imperial Policy, 106.

76. Ibid., 108.

77. Ibid., 120.

78. 36 and 37 Vict., c. 22.

79. Hansard, Third Series, CCXV, 2000-6 (May 15, 1873).

80. Ibid., CCXVI, 153-54 (May 20, 1873).

81. Ibid., 156-8.

82. Minute by Herbert, March 19, 1879, on Lorne to Hicks Beach, telegram, March 18, 1879: CO 42/756.

83. Musgrave to Kimberley, confidential, June 7, 1882: CO 137/505.

84. Minute by Kimberley, July 8, 1882, on ibid.

85. Kimberley to Lorne, confidential, July 29, 1882: CO 137/505. Printed in SP, 1883, no. 89, 38.

86. Report of the Privy Council of Canada, Oct. 26, 1882, enclosed in Officer Administering the Government of Canada to Kimberley, confidential, Oct. 28, 1882: CO 42/772. Printed in SP, 1883, no. 89, 38-39.
This episode was partly responsible for Macdonald's cordial dislike of Lord Kimberley. On an earlier occasion he had called him "a Free trade doctrinaire of the most restricted and illiberal kind." (Debates of the House of Commons [Canada], 1882, I, 1076 [April 21, 1882].) Kimberley's communication over the Jamaica proposals he later characterized as an "imperious dispatch" containing "an exploded doctrine." "Lord Kimberley [was] rather behind the age in regard to colonial matters," he stated. (Ibid., 1890, II, 3684 [April 21, 1890].)

87. Minute by Herbert, Nov. 23, 1882, on Deputy-Governor to Kimberley, confidential, Oct. 28, 1882: CO 42/772.
Two years later, in 1884, Herbert's views were powerfully confirmed by a similar expression of sentiment from the Board of Trade. This remarkable, if isolated, utterance was inspired by the commercial discussions of that year between the British West Indies and the United States. The Board felt that even if the proposals agreed on meant the establishment of differential duties they should be sanctioned, for, like Great Britain, the Colonies must be allowed "to do what they find good for their own interests." The unity of the Empire would not be promoted by denying to the colonies the freedom to enter into commercial engagements which they considered advantageous. "Freedom and self-government are even more important than freedom and equality in trade; the acceptance of these in the Colonies seems, as the Colonies advance, to involve their right to make their own commercial arrangements." (Board of Trade to Foreign Office, Oct. 23, 1884, enclosed in Foreign Office to Colonial Office, Oct. 25, 1884: CO 318/275.)

88. Minute by Kimberley, Nov. 30, 1882, on Deputy-Governor to Kimberley, confidential, Oct. 28, 1882: CO 42/772.

89. The Colonial Office reply to the Canadian claim, Kimberley to Deputy-Governor of Canada, confidential, Dec. 7, 1882: CO 42/772, simply acknowledged receipt of the Minute of Council. It is printed in SP, 1883, no. 89, 39.

90. Minute by Herbert, July 25, 1884, on Lansdowne to Derby, no. 135, June 19, 1884: CO 42/777.

91. The episode is described in A. R. Stewart, "Canadian-West Indian Union, 1884-1885," Canadian Historical Review, XXXI (Dec., 1950), 369-89.

92. Lansdowne to Stanley, confidential, July 17, 1885: CO 42/781. The Colonial Office injunction was made in Derby to Governor of Jamaica, May 1, 1885.

93. Minute by Herbert, Aug. 10, 1885, on Lansdowne to Stanley, confidential, July 17, 1885: ibid.

94. Minute by Dunraven, Aug. 11, 1885, on ibid.

95. Board of Trade to Colonial Office, immediate and confidential, June 9, 1874: CO 42/731.

96. Minute by Herbert, June 9, 1874, on ibid.

97. G. P. de T. Glazebrook, Canadian External Relations: An Historical Study to 1914 (Toronto, 1942), 146.

98. Minute by E. Blake (Colonial Office), Jan. 10, 1876, on Foreign Office to Colonial Office, Jan. 6, 1876: CO 42/746.

99. Minute by Malcolm, Sept. 14, 1877, on Foreign Office to Colonial Office, Sept. 13, 1877: CO 42/750.

100. Minute by Herbert, Sept. 18, 1877, on ibid.

101. Minute by Carnarvon, Sept. 19, 1877, on ibid.

102. Minute by Herbert, Feb. 12, 1881, on Foreign Office to Colonial Office, Feb. 8, 1881: CO 42/769.

103. Lansdowne to Holland, confidential, Oct. 31, 1887: CO 42/791.

104. Minute by Bramston, Nov. 17, 1887, on ibid.

105. Herbert felt that the United Kingdom could not coerce Nova Scotia to remain in the union if she desired to withdraw from it. On the other hand Nova Scotia
should not be allowed to revert to the status of a separate Colony if she left the Confederation. "Probably it would be best in all ways for a Province seceding from the
Union to enter the United States," he concluded. (Minute by Herbert, Nov. 20, 1887,
on Lansdowne to Holland, confidential, Oct. 31, 1887: CO 42/791.)

106. Minute by Herbert, Nov. 20, 1887, on ibid.

107. Minute by Holland, Nov. 23, 1887, on ibid.
The Board of Trade subsequently reported that Commercial Union in North America would conflict with Great Britain's treaty with the German Zollverein of 1865 which
stipulated that produce from the Zollverein must not be subjected to a higher rate of
duty in entering British colonies than imports from any other country. Board of Trade
to Colonial Office, confidential, Dec. 13, 1887: CO 42/792.

108. Minute by Courtney, Dec. 30, 1881, on Foreign Office to Colonial Office,
Dec. 26, 1881: CO 42/769.

109. Minute by Kimberley, Jan. 2, 1882, on ibid.

110. Minute by Kimberley, March 22, 1882, on ibid. See also Foreign Office
to Colonial Office, March 4, 1882: CO 323/352.
The same promise was made by Sir Charles Tupper in 1884 when he requested
permission to enter into commercial negotiations with Spain. (Tupper to Colonial Office, Oct. 1, 1884: CO 42/778.) It was upon this understanding that the negotiations
were authorized by the British Government. See Foreign Office to Colonial Office, July
26, 1884; and Foreign Office to Colonial Office, Oct. 20, 1884: CO 42/779.

111. Tupper to Colonial Office, Dec. 29, 1884: CO 42/778.

112. Minute by Edward Wingfield, Jan. 3, 1885, on ibid.

113. See PP, 1884-5, LXXI, no. C-4340, for the correspondence relating to this
agreement. See also Todd, Parliamentary Government, 272-3.
The principle that a colony should not give a tariff concession to a foreign country that was not granted to the United Kingdom or the other parts of the Empire as well
was invoked by Canada on several occasions in succeeding years. In 1890, for instance,
the Dominion protested against the convention which Sir Robert Bond of Newfoundland
negotiated with the United States providing preferential treatment for American imports
into the Colony. Great Britain thereupon forbade Newfoundland to pass the legislation
necessary to bring the treaty into effect. Two years later Canada broke off commercial

negotiations with the United States because it was considered impossible to discriminate against the mother country, as the American proposals required.

114. Copy of Galt to Spanish Minister in London, unofficial and confidential, Nov. 17, 1882, enclosed in Galt to Colonial Office, Jan. 19, 1883: CO 42/775.

115. Minute by Herbert, Jan. 25, 1883, on Galt to Colonial Office, Jan. 19, 1883: ibid.

116. Minute by Bramston, Jan. 26, 1883, on ibid.
The legislation cited by Bramston was 42 Vict., c. 15, s. 12.

117. Minute by Herbert, Jan. 26, 1883, on Galt to Colonial Office, Jan. 19, 1883: CO 42/775.

118. Foreign Office to Colonial Office, Jan. 31, 1883: CO 42/776. The Colonial Office sent the substance of this reply to Canada, in Derby to Lorne, secret, Feb. 1, 1883: CO 42/775.

119. Minute by Malcolm, Dec. 15, 1875, on Dufferin to Carnarvon, no. 168, Dec. 1, 1875: CO 42/737.

120. Minute by Herbert, Dec. 15, 1875, on ibid.

121. Minute by Herbert, March 10, 1876, on Foreign Office to Colonial Office, Feb. 24, 1876: CO 42/746.

122. 42 Vict., c. 15.

123. O. D. Skelton, "General Economic History, 1867-1912," Canada and Its Provinces (Toronto, 1914), IX, 144-5.

124. Saunders, ed., Life of Sir Charles Tupper, I, 275.

125. The Office had been promised the details of the impending changes in the previous autumn, before the measure was submitted to the Canadian Parliament, but the information was never sent. (Hicks Beach to Lorne, telegram, Feb. 8, 1879: CO 42/756.)

126. Minute by Herbert, March 10, 1879, on Lorne to Hicks Beach, telegram, March 10, 1879: ibid.

127. Hicks Beach to Lorne, telegram, March 12, 1879: ibid.

128. Minute by Pennell, April 18, 1879, on Secretary, Huddersfield Chamber of Commerce to Colonial Office, April 17, 1879: CO 42/759.

129. H. J. Leech, The Public Letters of John Bright, quoted in Porritt, The Diplomatic Freedom of the British Dominions, 375.
Earl Grey's denunciation of the "manifest absurdities" of the "National Policy" took the form of a long article in the Nineteenth Century. See Earl Grey, "How Shall We Retain the Colonies?" Nineteenth Century, XXVIII (June, 1879), 935-54.

130. Hansard, Third Series, CCXLIV, 1311-13 (March 20, 1879). The papers presented to the House are PP, 1878-9, LI, nos. C-2305 and C-2369. Some of the dispatches are also available in SP, 1879, no. 155.

131. Board of Trade to Colonial Office, confidential, Aug. 14, 1879: CO 42/759, and Board of Trade to Colonial Office, confidential, Dec. 4, 1879: ibid.

132. Board of Trade to Colonial Office, confidential, Dec. 4, 1879: ibid.

133. Ibid.

134. Board of Trade to Colonial Office, confidential, Aug. 14, 1879: CO 42/759.

135. Minute by Cadogan, Dec. 16, 1879, on Board of Trade to Colonial Office, confidential, Dec. 4, 1879: ibid.

136. Minute by Herbert, Dec. 16, 1879, on ibid.

137. Minute by Hicks Beach, Dec. 19, 1879 on ibid.

138. Minutes by W. H. Mercer and Pennell, Feb. 20, 1880, on Board of Trade to Colonial Office, Feb. 19, 1880: CO 42/764.

139. Minute by Herbert, Feb. 27, 1880, on ibid.

140. Minute by Herbert, Sept. 13, 1880, on Lorne to Kimberley, no. 256, Aug. 27, 1880: CO 42/762.

141. Minute by Kimberley, Sept. 15, 1880, on ibid.

142. Minute by Herbert, Oct. 7, 1882, on Admiralty to Colonial Office, Sept. 23, 1882: CO 42/773.

143. Minute by Herbert, Jan. 18, 1881, on Secretary, Incorporated Chamber of Commerce of Liverpool to Colonial Office, Jan. 13, 1881: CO 42/770.

144. This rule was followed except on special occasions, as when in the case of the tariff of 1887 the English protests were so concerted that the Department was forced to take notice of them.

145. Minute by Kimberley, Oct. 26, 1880, on Treasury to Colonial Office, Oct. 8, 1880: CO 42/764.

146. 50 and 51 Vict., c. 39.

147. Minute by Herbert, May 23, 1887, on Secretary, Liverpool Chamber of Commerce to Colonial Office, May 19, 1887: CO 42/792.
The memorials from the English iron industry and other correspondence relating to the Canadian tariff of 1887 are printed in PP, 1887, LVIII, no. C-5179.

148. Minute by Holland, May 23, 1887, on Secretary, Liverpool Chamber of Commerce to Colonial Office, May 19, 1887: CO 42/792.
The Canadian duties were brought up in the House of Commons on several occasions. See Hansard, Third Series, CCCXV, 521-2 (May 19, 1887) and ibid., 1743, (June 13, 1887).

149. Holland to Lansdowne, no. 186, July 7, 1887: CO 42/792. Printed in PP, 1887, LVIII, no. C-5179, 33-4, which brings together most of the correspondence with Canada relating to the new duties.
This statement of the critical feeling existing in England in 1887 against the Canadian tariff was intended, not so much for the information of the Macdonald Administration, as for the Government's questioners in Parliament. See Minute by Onslow, July 7, 1887, on Secretary, Barrow-on-Furness Chamber of Commerce to Colonial Office, June 25, 1887: CO 42/792.

150. Memo. by Minister of Finance, endorsed by a Report of the Privy Council of Canada, June 30, 1887, enclosed in Lansdowne to Holland, no. 293, July 21, 1887: CO 42/791. Printed in PP, 1887, LVIII, no. C-5179, 38-40.

151. Minute by Herbert, Aug. 12, 1887, on Lansdowne to Holland, no. 293, July 21, 1887: CO 42/791.

152. Hansard, Third Series, CCCXVI, 375-8 (June 17, 1887).

153. Ibid., 385-7, and CCCXVIII, 913, (Aug. 2, 1887).

154. Ibid., CCCXVI, 378-81, 381-3 (June 17, 1887), and 1554-61 (July 4, 1887).

155. Ibid., 1554-61 (July 4, 1887).

156. <u>Hansard</u>, Third Series, CCCXVI, 386 (June 17, 1887).

157. See Appendix C, "A Note on the Later Development of Canadian Fiscal Autonomy, " 324 -5, for a brief recital of the progress of this trend after 1887.

CHAPTER SEVEN

THE FOREIGN OFFICE AND THE NEGOTIATION OF COMMERCIAL TREATIES

"It is inevitable that there should be an increasing number of cases in which the greater Colonies will require H.M. Govt. to negotiate on their special behalf treaties which do not concern Great Britain or other parts of the Empire. There is no objection in principle, I think, but the contrary; and no great difficulty in conducting these separate colonial negotiations. " Sir Robert Herbert, 1881

RESPONSIBLE GOVERNMENT carried with it as an inescapable corollary the duty to regulate commercial policy. The larger settlement colonies, led by Canada, asserted the claim that they possessed this function within a few short years after the concession of local autonomy had been made. Their decision to embark on protective tariff policies, and their readiness to grant preferential treatment to each other and to foreign countries encountered the censure, but not the prohibition, of the mother country. In the end the principle that the colonies should be allowed to pursue their own fiscal policies regardless of the views held on the subject in England was given reluctant acquiescence in Whitehall. Granted this freedom, it was inevitable that the more important colonies should sooner or later demand a voice in the negotiation of commercial treaties affecting the Empire. In the first instance, the colonies requested that their representatives be associated with the Imperial Government in treaty discussions, but when this point was achieved they moved on to claim the power to negotiate trade arrangements themselves. Similarly, it was inevitable that the autonomous colonies would become restless under a treaty system by which they were automatically bound by the operation of Imperial engagements. They demanded, therefore, to be released from existing treaties which they considered prejudicial to their interests and sought the right to adhere at their own volition to new commercial instruments concluded by the mother country. It was in the achievement of these objectives, a lengthy process which extended well into the twentieth century, that the treaty-making power of the British Dominions was realized.

In every sense of the phrase, the Colony of Canada "set the pace" in the evolution of the settlement colonies to complete fiscal autonomy. Her geographical position brought her naturally into intimate relations with neighbouring British colonies and with foreign countries; the nature of her economic activity dictated an independent and vigorous commercial policy; and her familiarity with constitutional experiment produced among her leaders a group of forceful advocates of colonial self-government. Just as the Colony had initiated significant departures in the framing of her domestic tariff, so she led the way towards the attainment of the treaty-making power in the overseas Empire. Dependent as she was on external trade Canada found it increasingly necessary to develop commercial relations with regions on both sides of the Atlantic. In this process of widening the trade interests of one Colony the diplomatic mechanism of the Empire had to be utilized for the achievement of purely Canadian ends. It was but natural that the Dominion Government would wish to influence the course of negotiations carried on in her behalf, and to approve agreements which might be reached. Canadian participation in efforts to achieve commercial undertakings, at first limited to a humble advisory position, became steadily more pronounced during the period under review. By 1884 it had been decided that in such endeavours Canadian negotiators would be accorded the status of full plenipotentiaries and would play the major role in discussions with foreign states. Although a treaty was not concluded under this arrangement until 1893, it was a vital concession of principle.

The remaining steps which led to the Dominions gaining an exclusive control over external affairs were not to be taken until after the cataclysm of World War I. Thus only when the Empire had been transformed into the modern Commonwealth was it possible to declare that Canadian autonomy was at last unabridged. That this was so was due principally to the conviction that the diplomatic unity of the Empire was the strongest cement binding England and her colonies and that to disrupt this tie would be to shatter the whole imperial structure. Among the departments of Whitehall it was the Foreign Office which, naturally enough, held this faith with the most passionate determination. Even the Colonial Office, so often prepared to make concessions to the autonomous colonies for the sake of imperial harmony, approached the subject of diplomatic freedom for the dependencies with this belief in mind. It would have been remarkable if it had been otherwise, in that period of unchallenged Austinian theory in the conception of the state. But although the Colonial Office shared with its sister Department an adherence to the idea of the diplomatic unity of the Empire, it proved much more sympathetic to Canadian desires in the realm of commercial diplomacy than did the Foreign Office. Consistently throughout the period under discussion the Office supported the Canadian point of view in these matters and many times interceded with the Foreign Office on behalf of the Dominion. In addition the Department took the initiative in devising an arrangement by which the autonomous colonies would be exempted from the stipulations of new British commercial treaties, and successfully pressed it upon an unwilling Foreign Office. Thus, although the period 1867-87 was one of necessarily limited achievement in the establishment of Canadian autonomy in foreign affairs, the advances gained were an essential foundation to the more significant developments of the twentieth century. That these Victorial precedents were recorded without serious controversy or misunderstanding was primarily due to the conciliatory role which the Colonial Office assumed in interpreting Canadian aspirations to the heads, both permanent and political, of the British foreign service.

I

Since the earliest days of the French settlements on the St. Lawrence, Canada has lived by foreign trade. The Canadian economy, dominated by the production of export staples, has always been dependent on the existence of large, industrialized markets, such as Great Britain. The natural economic forces which inspired the trade to the British Isles from North America were assisted by the preferences and privileges which the mother country offered to imports from her colonies. Thus, when protection was abandoned in England in the middle of the nineteenth century, the economic order of British North America suffered a severe dislocation. Canadian goods were suddenly forced to compete with products from all over the world in securing British buyers, and Canadian shipping no longer enjoyed a favoured position in the Atlantic carrying trade. Eventually the economy of British North America underwent the necessary adjustments to these new realities but the process was a prolonged and disturbing one. The first reaction to the shock of 1846 was to find other markets for the staples of the Province of Canada, and the agreement of 1850 with the Maritime colonies for intercolonial reciprocity was an obvious response to the changed conditions. A second, and more significant, response was the conclusion with the United States of the celebrated Reciprocity Treaty of 1854. This arrangement constituted the first essay by Canadians in the enlargement of their external trade and gave rise to the introductory steps in the long advocacy by the Colony for the power to conduct commercial negotiations with foreign countries.

The movement for reciprocity of trade with the United States was largely inspired and organized by W. H. Merritt, a miller from the Niagara district of Canada West. It was Merritt who, in reviving the old dream of using the St. Lawrence system as a highway into the heart of North America, saw in reciprocity an essential preliminary to the achievement of this plan. It was Merritt who persuaded Lord Elgin of the soundness of the proposal and through Elgin brought the scheme under the consideration of the Imperial Government. In 1846 the Assembly of Canada first expressed a desire for a reciprocal commercial arrangement with the United States.[1]   The Legislature's address requested Great Britain to open discussions on this matter with the American Government. It contained no suggestion that colonial representatives be associated with the Imperial authorities in these negotiations. Nor did a similar request from the Canadian Executive Council two years later which urged that the British Minister at Washington be allowed to communicate freely with the Governor-General on the progress of commercial talks with the United States. This procedure was essential, the Minute went on, because of the necessity of gaining the consent of the Canadian Legislature for any agreement that might be proposed.[2] It is apparent that the problem of the precise role of Canadians in trade discussions affecting the Colony was still not resolved, however, and when, later in 1848, Merritt and another member of the Canadian Government visited Washington to confer with the British Legation, their status was entirely unofficial. Merritt, however, received marked attention from J. F. Crampton, the Chargé d'Affaires, and called on the State Department in company with Crampton in July, 1849.[3] But in the end it was Elgin who, by forceful proselytizing and astute diplomacy, won over the Pierce Administration and the United States Congress. The Reciprocity Treaty was concluded in June, 1854.

During the negotiations Great Britain had recognized, in a practical manner, the

---

1. For references to chapter VII see pages 241-52.

desire of the Province of Canada to be consulted, and even to take part, in the preliminary stages of commercial discussions affecting the Colony's interests. That the Imperial Government was unwilling to accept such participation as an inherent right was shown by its response to similar requests from New Brunswick and Nova Scotia. New Brunswick was moved to ask for greater consideration from the mother country in the negotiations with the United States because of the fear that her economic interests would be sacrificed to those of Canada. The Chamber of Commerce of Saint John protested to the British Government in 1850 that the Colony was being overlooked in the reciprocity arrangements and the Executive Council asked the Governor to allow one or more members of the Administration to proceed to Washington "in order to advise [the British Minister] fully as to the present condition of this Province, and the vital importance to our commercial interests of obtaining ... a reciprocal trade with the United States."[4] Sir Edmund Head declined to grant permission for this undertaking and Grey approved his decision. The Colonial Secretary stated that the Imperial Government could be trusted to promote to the full the interests of New Brunswick and that by showing such obvious eagerness for reciprocity the Colony would tend to defeat its own ends.[5] Thus the second request of a British colony to participate in commercial negotiations was given short shrift by the Imperial authorities.[6] Nova Scotia received an even more peremptory reply when it made the same suggestion three years later. The Duke of Newcastle, at the Colonial Office, supplied only a formal answer to an address of the Nova Scotia Assembly insisting on the right to be consulted in the reciprocity negotiations, and Nova Scotia delegates were not invited to help with the preparation of the Treaty. There were, therefore, protests in the Nova Scotia House when legislation to give effect to the Reciprocity Treaty came before it. Joseph Howe and others spoke strongly in favour of the principle that a colony must be consulted when a treaty affecting its domestic interests was being drawn up.[7] Howe's claim was completely conceded in 1857 by Henry Labouchere, in a case concerning Newfoundland. A convention between Great Britain and France, planned in that year to regulate the fisheries on the Newfoundland coast, was rejected by the Island Legislature. Labouchere accepted the adverse verdict as decisive, and abandoned the agreement. In transmitting this information to Newfoundland the Colonial Secretary enunciated two principles on which, he stated, the decision had been based:

> ... namely that the rights at present enjoyed by the community of Newfoundland are not to be ceded or exchanged without their assent and that the constitutional mode of submitting measures for that assent is by laying them before the Colonial Legislature.
>   ... the consent of the community of Newfoundland is regarded by H. M.'s Government as the essential preliminary to any modification of their territorial or maritime rights.[8]

After 1854, when the Reciprocity Treaty was signed, there was frequent examples of Canadian representatives being present in Washington to advise the Legation on commercial subjects. These agents were accorded full co-operation by Sir John Crampton, the British Minister, who recognized their value in specialized discussions and in lobbying among members of Congress. With Crampton's recall in 1856 this situation changed. The new British Minister, Lord Lyons, proved distinctly less willing to have Canadian agents associated with him in negotiations with the United States Government. With the fastidiousness of a professional diplomatist, Lyons distrusted the entrance of amateurs into his work, and felt that it was pretentious for a colony, which possessed as yet neither army nor navy, to claim a share in its foreign relations. He complained to the Governor-General and to Lord Russell at the Foreign Office when it was proposed that delegates from Canada visit Washington in an effort to secure the renewal of the Reciprocity Treaty.

> I cannot have a Canadian here supposed to be peculiarly in my confidence on the subject. This would impose on me a responsibility which I cannot undertake. Directly there was the least appearance of a Canadian being here in any such position, I should feel bound to take decisive steps to show that the appearance was false. My own opinion is that the Canadians will only do themselves harm by coming lobbying here; but, if they choose to do so, they must do it entirely independently of me; and I would suggest that any who come for this purpose should not be furnished with letters of introduction to me, and should be advised not to call upon me. [9]

Lyons left Washington in 1865, and succeeding Ministers, like Bruce and Thornton, failed to share his distaste for colonial assistance in negotiations. His departure enabled Canada to assume greater responsibilities in the determination of her relations with the United States.

In March, 1865, the United States Government gave the stipulated one year's notice for the abrogation of the Reciprocity Treaty. The attempt, which followed this announcement, to secure a renewed or modified form of the Treaty aroused once more the claim of the North American colonies that they possessed the right to be consulted before a treaty touching their interests was concluded. On this matter of the time of consultation the "Labouchere dispatch" had not been specific. Obviously, however, it was more satisfactory for a colony to be considered during the preparation of a treaty than to be presented with the finished instrument and then asked to approve or reject it.

The British Minister in Washington had no sooner been instructed to open a discussion on the question of reciprocal free trade between British North America and the American union before the colonies were clamouring for an opportunity to tender advice. Nova Scotia asked to be allowed to provide her views on the forthcoming negotiations and the Canadian Government made the more radical request that it be permitted to establish immediate communication on the reciprocity question with the British Minister to the United States, Sir Frederick Bruce. [10] The Colonial Office supported the latter suggestion and proposed to the Foreign Office that the four provinces be enabled to deal directly with Bruce. [11] This innovation was too much for the latter Department, however, which put forward the alternative plan of convening a conference at which the

Imperial Government could be apprised of the views of all the North American colonies on commercial topics. The Colonial Office speedily fell in with this scheme (which had much to commend it over the original request), and in July, 1865, Lord Monck, the Governor-General, was instructed to summon the meeting.[12]

The group which assembled at Quebec for three days in September--a conference designated the Confederate Council of Trade--represented an interesting prelude to later developments. Not only did the Council constitute one of the first formal examples of joint colonial action in British North America, but it marked an important stage in the progress of the North American colonies towards the exclusive determination of their external policy.[13] The delegates to Quebec, who came from Canada, New Brunswick, Nova Scotia, Prince Edward Island, and Newfoundland, showed from the first a remarkable unanimity in their commercial aspirations. The Reciprocity Treaty, either in its existing form or with reasonable modifications, remained the basis of the most profitable economic alignment for British North America. To that end, in the event that negotiations for the renewal of the Treaty were continued, the Council considered it desirable that its members, or a committee of them, be authorized "to proceed to Washington, ... in order to confer with the British Minister there, and afford him information with respect to the interests of British North American Provinces." But the possibility had also to be faced that the United States would not renew the Treaty. In this case, the Council resolved, "all the British North American Provinces should combine cordially together in all Commercial matters, and adopt such a common Commercial policy as will best advance the interests of the whole." More specifically, the question of trade with the West Indian islands and the mainland of Central and South America might usefully be investigated as a substitute for the loss of the American market. Here again it was desirable that representatives of British North America should be allowed to conduct the inquiries and furnish assistance in any diplomatic negotiations which might ensue.[14]

The Reciprocity negotiations dragged on throughout the autumn of 1865 and the early months of 1866. In the meantime the colonial governments had pressed forward their request for a trade delegation to visit the West Indies and explore the possibility of increased economic intercourse with that region. In September Canada asked that the Imperial authorities in the West Indies be instructed to recognize and aid such a commission and that the British Ministers in the adjoining foreign countries provide similar services.[15] Cardwell sanctioned the plan and willingly promised assistance, although he carefully refrained from commenting on the important question of the commissioners' status in the inquiry. To Canada the Secretary of State wrote,

I request you will assure the Provincial Government that H.M. Govt. cordially approve the suggestion they have made, and will support it by all the means in their power. The scheme is of course not applicable to Canada alone, but to the British N. American Colonies collectively.

On that understanding I shall request the Secretary of State for Foreign Affairs to recommend the object in view at the requisite Foreign Courts and to introduce to the British Ministers abroad those gentlemen who shall be selected for the Mission.

I, on my part, shall be happy to instruct the Governors of the British Colonies to afford them every assistance they can. [16]

The Foreign Office supplied Cardwell's omission with a description of the procedure by which colonial interests in diplomatic negotiations could be reconciled with the exclusive Imperial authority to conclude foreign engagements. The mode of conducting negotiations laid down by the Earl of Clarendon in 1865 remained for the next twenty years the authoritative pronouncement on the subject.

His Lordship concludes that, as regards foreign Countries, the Agents who may be sent from the British North American Colonies will not assume any independent character, or attempt to negotiate and conclude arrangements with the Governments of foreign Countries, but will only ... be authorized to confer with the British Minister in each foreign country, and to afford him information with respect to the interests of the British North American Provinces.

... Lord Clarendon ... will be ready to authorize Her Majesty's Minister at Madrid as regards the Spanish West Indies, and Her Majesty's Ministers on the continent of America, to communicate with these Colonial Delegates, and in the first instance to assist them in their enquiries as to what openings there may be for extending the Trade of the British Colonies, and afterwards to ascertain how far any overtures for that object would be likely to be well received by the Governments to which those Ministers are accredited.

Having thus obtained grounds for further proceedings, Her Majesty's Government might in the next place consider ... how far any proposals might be made to foreign countries in behalf of the Colonies, consistently with the general Treaty engagements of the British Crown: and this point being satisfactorily ascertained, instructions might be framed in this Country for Her Majesty's Ministers in the Countries in question, and Full Powers issued to them by Her Majesty, under which they would endeavour to bring into the shape of International engagements such arrangements as might be ultimately considered acceptable not only to the Colonies themselves but also to the foreign Powers with whom they were contracted. [17]

Although the Colonial Office immediately transmitted this "very useful statement of the course to be pursued"[18] to Canada, misunderstandings over the question of the delegates' powers had already arisen. A. T. Galt, the Canadian Minister of Finance, envisaged a wider range of responsibility for the representatives from Canada than the Foreign Office could have possibly accepted. His Instructions to the three Canadian agents directed them to gather information about the economy of the West Indies and to approach the authorities of the area with a view to removing obstructions on Canadian trade with the islands. The commissioners were also authorized to offer reductions in the customs duties of Canada in return for similar concessions on commerce from British North America. Galt continued his charge with a passage that must have chilled the collective spine of the Foreign Office. "The Government cannot at this time auth-

orize you to conclude any absolute Convention--but they trust you may be able to arrive at such conditional agreement with one or more of the Colonial and Foreign Governments as may form the basis for obtaining the sanction of Parliament to conclude
direct and positive engagements. "[19]   The source of the legislative sanction to which
Galt referred is not clear, but even if the Imperial Parliament was intended, the pre-
sumption contained in the extract can hardly be equalled in nineteenth-century imperial history. Elliot frankly repudiated the "erroneous" assumption that the Canadian
agents were to deal directly with foreign powers. "This is plainly out of the question.
Of course the most that can or ought to be done for them is to recommend them to our
foreign Minister where we have one, and at other places to our Consul. "[20]

But Galt's words had confirmed the worst suspicions of the Foreign Office about
Canada's intentions in commercial negotiations. It is just possible that this episode of
1865 coloured the Department's approach to the entire question of the colonies and the
treaty-making power for the next two or three decades. "The course proposed by the
provincial Government must lead to confusion and disappointment, as no Foreign Government in amity with England would enter into direct negotiation with dependencies
of the British Crown as if they were independent States, " the Foreign Office crushingly
remarked. Lord Clarendon's directions, on the other hand, constituted "the only course
that can be taken with regularity and in accordance with International usage. "[21] These
rules were rather ostentatiously impressed upon the North American commissioners when
they arrived in London to collect their credentials before proceeding to the West Indies.[22]
There was a further misunderstanding when the Canadian Government, without securing
the approval of the Colonial Office, directed one of its agents to visit France and Spain,
but the plan was fortunately altered before the Foreign Office found occasion to remon-
strate.[23]   The trade commissioners spent the early months of 1866 in touring the West
Indies and South America, presenting their report later in the same year. It recommended improvements in transportation and certain adjustments in the tariff rates of the West
Indian islands and the British North American colonies. Nothing developed from these
suggestions, however, and sporadic attempts to increase trade with the area and with
southern Europe continued during the next few years.

The negotiations with the United States over reciprocity were similarly fruitless.
Galt spent the early months of 1866 in Washington where he worked smoothly with Bruce
in keeping the American Government informed of the Canadian position.[24]   Although
he possessed no official diplomatic status Galt's role in the discussions with the United
States was of vital importance. In the end it became apparent that the Administration
and Congress were not prepared to modify their decision to abrogate the Treaty of 1854.
At one of the final meetings with the American authorities Galt declared that his country would now proceed to develop other markets in the West Indies and the Mediterranean
countries. In a sturdy assertion of colonial self-reliance he implied that never again
would Canada find it necessary to depend on the advantages of reciprocal free trade with
the American republic. British North America, inspired by the approaching federal union,
stood on the threshold of an era of confident economic nationalism.

In spite of these failures, in the West Indies and in the United States, the signifi-

cance of the Confederate Council of Trade cannot be over-estimated. For the first
time the British Government had promoted a conference made up of a group of colonies
to discuss trade relations with foreign countries and had not balked when that conference
trespassed within the bounds of diplomacy. The right of colonial consultation in the
making of treaties had been distinctly conceded by the Office before it called the conference, but the meeting achieved great strides towards gaining for the colonies the privilege of direct participation in the early stages of commercial negotiations. The decision
to call the Confederate Council of Trade, and the support furnished its recommendations
marked an important advance over the principles laid down in Mr. Secretary Labouchere'
dispatch of 1857.

II

The creation of the Colony of Canada brought no immediate change in the
limited right of the North American colonies to enter into commercial agreements. The
British Government, however, used as one of its arguments for promoting the union of
the provinces the fact that a single authority in North America would allow commercial undertakings on behalf of the colonies to be reached more easily. In all trade
negotiations, it was pointed out, "the Union of the Provinces would ... afford the best
hope of bringing such arrangements to a speedy and satisfactory conclusion."[23] Several attempts were made in the first years of Confederation to gain a new reciprocity
treaty with the United States, and John Rose, the second Minister of Finance in the Dominion, made a notable visit to Washington for this purpose in the summer of 1869. Rose
held no official status as a plenipotentiary although he enjoyed the fullest confidence of
Thornton, the British Minister, at whose suggestion he made the journey.

In accordance with the suggestion which you offer in the last of these Desps. the Canadian Ministers have decided on sending one of their number to Washington on the
8th inst.
          This gentleman's visit will be of a private and non-official character, but he,
in concert with you, will be prepared to discuss the various matters upon the carpet
between the U.S. and the Dominion of Canada.[26]

In spite of the fact that Rose was prepared to offer reciprocal free trade in some manufactured articles, the American Government was clearly unenthusiastic about the scheme,
and the venture failed. Direct participation by a colonial Minister in the negotiation of
a foreign treaty had to wait two more years, until 1871, for its realization. In that year
Sir John Macdonald was invited to become one of the British representatives on the Joint
High Commission appointed to resolve the differences between the United States, Great
Britain, and Canada arising from the Civil War. Macdonald's role on the Commission
was a very difficult one, for he had to reconcile the interests of the Dominion with the
Imperial Government's desire to negotiate, at all costs, a comprehensive agreement
with the United States. The Treaty of Washington,[27] although it had to be made more

palatable to Canadians by separate concessions from Great Britain,[28] represented a significant contribution towards a settlement of North American problems. Among other advantages it gained for Canada for about fifteen years a free entrance into the United States market of fish and fish products. The important fact for the theme with which this chapter is concerned, however, was that in the Washington Conference a colonial Minister was not simply employed as an adviser to the British diplomatic service, but was accredited with full powers, as an official plenipotentiary. For the first time in the history of the Empire a colonial representative was formally authorized to share in the task of making a treaty, and for the first time that colonial representative signed the completed instrument.

The early years of the Colony of Canada were marked by considerable discussion of the treaty-making power as it affected the young state. In 1870 the Canadian Parliament debated the commercial prospects of the country at great length, in commenting upon a motion calling for complete free trade between the United States and the Dominion.[29] In the course of this debate, A. T. Galt, who had broken with Macdonald after serving as Canada's first Minister of Finance, proposed an amendment in which he advanced the claim that the Colony should be allowed to engage in commercial negotiations with foreign states.

> ... great advantage would result from placing the Government of the Dominion in direct communication with all British Possessions and Foreign States, which might be willing to negotiate for commercial arrangements tending to this result.
> ... it is expedient to obtain from the Imperial Government all necessary powers to enable the Government of the Dominion to enter into direct communication for such purpose, with each British Possession and Foreign State.
> ... in all cases such proposed commercial arrangements should be subject to the approval of Her Majesty.[30]

Galt's enthusiasm for this object was not surprising, in view of his memorable advocacy of Canadian fiscal autonomy in 1859 and 1865. What was noteworthy was the favour with which the amendment was received on both sides of the House. Macdonald, of course, poured scorn on the notion that Canada could bargain with foreign states independently of Great Britain; the outside world would simply ignore the Dominion if she appeared without the sanction of her connection with the mother country. Galt's motion was disloyal because it placed the interests of one part of the Empire before the welfare of the whole.[31] But yet was Macdonald's conception of a desirable relationship between the United Kingdom and Canada in the negotiation of commercial treaties very different from Galt's? It involved the fullest recognition of the Canadian point of view in any commercial discussion, a close association between Canadian representatives and the British diplomatic service in negotiating the treaty, and an unlimited freedom for the Dominion Parliament to accept or reject the completed instrument. Macdonald's "concurrent action" of the mother country and the Colony in framing commercial treaties envisaged the maximum of Imperial assistance exerted to secure the maximum satisfaction for Canadian interests. It was an amendment based on these considerations, drawn up by Macdonald with wily skill to cut the ground from under Galt's demands and at the same time proclaim the diplomatic unity of the Empire, which was finally approved by the House.[32] If the debate had advanced no concrete suggestions for improving the machinery of colonial diplomacy, it had at least showed the solid core of support which existed in Canada for the principle of consultation and participation in commercial negotiations.

Four years later the Canadian National Association, a group which attempted to carry over the principles of the "Canada First" movement into the political life of the Dominion, incorporated a demand for the treaty-making power into the first section of their platform. "British Connection, Consolidation of the Empire, and in the meantime a voice in treaties affecting Canada" ran this sweeping profession of faith.[33]   It was linked with a proposal for closer trade relations with the British West Indies, a step which it was hoped would lead ultimately to political union. The substantial approval which for a time greeted this manifesto revealed that the "Canada First" group had gauged accurately the temper of English-Canadian feeling on certain subjects of imperial concern The prosperity of the Dominion was closely bound up with the need for foreign markets, which in turn was associated most intimately with the power to conclude commercial treaties.

The commercial depression which came upon Europe and the United States in 1873 resulted in a diminution of Canada's export trade. The period of distress coincided with the advent to power in Canada of the Liberal party, which had for long supported the idea of a low tariff and a restoration of reciprocity with the United States. Stimulated by unfavourable economic conditions, the Mackenzie Government determined to make yet another attempt at a trade agreement with the republic. The veteran editor of the Toronto Globe and mentor of the party, George Brown, was sent to Washington early in in 1874 as a "confidential agent," from whence he reported that the Grant Administration seemed sympathetic to the prospect of a commercial treaty with Canada. Mackenzie immediately made plans for a formal negotiation, securing for Brown the status of a commissioner, a rank not inferior to that which Brown's rival Macdonald had held in 1871. It was stipulated that the Canadian was to conduct negotiations in association with Sir Edward Thornton, although both men were granted full plenipotentiary powers from the British Government.[34] Brown offered Hamilton Fish, the American Secretary of State, a comprehensive plan for reciprocal free trade in natural products and certain manufactured goods, together with an entrance for American fishermen in the Canadian inshore fisheries and some navigation privileges. On the basis of these proposals a draft treaty was drawn up, but it was rejected by the United States Senate when it appeared for consideration in 1875. Thus another attempt at Canadian-American reciprocity came to naught.

The failure turned the attention of the Mackenzie Administration and the Macdonald Administration, which followed it, to plans for extending Canadian trade with other areas. The West Indies (British, French and Spanish), regarded ever since the French régime as a market capable of development, were, towards the end of the seventies, made the object of earnest endeavours to secure this result. Steamship communication was subsidized by the Government to Brazil and the Caribbean area and efforts put in hand to conclude trade agreements with Spain and France applying to their North American empires. It was for the latter purpose that Sir Alexander Galt, who probably possessed a fuller knowledge of Canadian commercial policy than any other statesman in the Dominion, was dispatched to Paris and Madrid late in 1878. Galt was originally instructed simply to negotiate with the Spanish Government for a reciprocal trade arrangement and to explore means of increasing Canadian commerce with the British West Indies.[35] The Colonial Office accorded Galt full co-operation: wrote to the Foreign Office on his behalf, secured him an interview with Lord Salisbury, and provided him with letters of introduction. While in London Galt received word that he was also to undertake negotiations with France in an effort to obtain a remission of the duties on certain Canadian imports.[36] The Foreign Office accepted Galt as a representative of the Canadian Government authorized to discuss these questions, but maintained that any formal negotiations would have to be conducted by the British ambassadors in Paris and Madrid. Although Galt might consult with the foreign governments, he was to confine himself, once negotiations had commenced, to the task of furnishing advice on points of detail to the British representative concerned. It was left to the United Kingdom to approve, together with Canada, any convention which might arise out of the discussions.[37]

Lord Lyons, who had been British Ambassador to France since 1867, presented the chief obstacle to the smooth working of this procedure. He showed almost at once that his estimation of the usefulness of colonial diplomats had not changed since his days at Washington. When Galt endeavoured to commence the negotiations he found the Ambassador hostile and discourteous. Sir Alexander then appealed to Lord Tenterden, the Permanent Under-Secretary at the Foreign Office, writing what Lyons called "a huffy letter," based on "the supposition either that your Lordship's [Salisbury's] instructions to me were insufficient or that I misinterpreted them."[38] Tenterden soothed the rather sensitive Galt and it was significant that Lyons extended the fullest co-operation, both diplomatic and social, to the Canadian agent during the remainder of his mission to Paris. Thus "no inconvenience ensued" from the episode in spite of its rather alarming possibilities of repercussion.[39] Galt's efforts to reach an agreement with the French Government were thwarted when the signature of a trade treaty with Austria-Hungary caused the French to abandon the discussions. A later attempt to gain a minor concession for Canada in the French tariff was defeated in the Chamber of Deputies. In Madrid Sir Lionel Sackville-West received Galt cordially and the two men worked on excellent terms in approaching the Spanish Government. The Spanish negotiations also failed, however, this time because of a change of government, and Galt returned to Canada with no tangible results to show for his venture.[40]

From the point of view of procedure the negotiations of 1878-9 had not been entirely satisfactory. Galt had been accorded a definitely subordinate position which differed little from that held by the trade delegation to the West Indies in 1866. There is evidence that the Canadian found his role in the negotiations restricted, and chafed under what Dr. Skelton has called "the humble hodman task of gathering materials."[41]

Many years later Sir Charles Tupper quoted Galt as saying of his work in Paris and Madrid "that he found himself greatly hampered in discharging the duties imposed upon him by the Government of Canada, because he only stood in the position of a commercial commissioner, and it was necessary that all negotiations with the Government of Spain should be filtered through Her Majesty's Minister at the Court of Madrid."[42]   The formula which had barely satisfied the Colony of Canada in 1865 was hardly likely to meet the expanded requirements of the new Dominion in 1879.

The Foreign Office throughout this period showed itself extremely reluctant to admit representatives of the Canadian Government to a share in the negotiation of commercial treaties except under narrowly defined conditions. One of these conditions was, understandably enough, that the existence of a Canadian agent engaging in discussions should not prejudice any negotiations which Great Britain might be pursuing with the same foreign power. Practically, this consideration was interpreted by the Foreign Office to mean that it would be undesirable to allow Canada to associate herself with the United Kingdom in concurrent negotiations in which each country had special interests. The rule was most frequently invoked by the Foreign Office in the case of France, with whom both Great Britain and the Dominion attempted to conclude commercial agreements during the years under review. The Cobden Treaty, acclaimed ever since its signing in 1860 as an unequalled example of the liberal commercial spirit, formed the basis of Great Britain's trade relations with France. It did not, however, except for a few specialized items, apply to the British colonies. Later instruments, concluded in 1873 and 1874 by the two nations, also failed to include the possessions of each country.[43]   This was a source of irritation to Canada, for the Dominion felt that, along with Great Britain, she should receive "most-favoured-nation" treatment in the French customs duties. Canada's export trade with France was featured by large sales of paper and wooden ships, a fact which made her interest in securing particular concessions quite different from that of the mother country.

The problem of conducting joint negotiations came to a head in 1879, when France announced that she wished to terminate all her commercial treaties with the United Kingdom by January 1 of the following year.[44]   The Colonial Office thereupon circularized the colonies, asking them to put forward their views respecting a new agreement with France. Canada replied by asking that a Canadian commissioner be allowed to participate in the forthcoming negotiations to represent the Dominion's interests.[45] The Colonial Office passed this request on to the Foreign Office in a manner which suggests clearly that it thought the Colony's proposal was reasonable and not subject to Imperial objections.[46]   There was some delay in receiving the Foreign Office answer as that Department at first refused to make a definite decision on the application.[47] Finally, after the Office had re-phrased the question, explaining that unless strong reasons existed the Colonial Secretary considered it inexpedient to refuse the Canadian request for a commissioner with at least limited powers,[48] the Department supplied a precise reply. The Office was informed that because of the great divergence between the views on financial policy held by Canada and Great Britain, the Foreign Secretary did not feel there would be any purpose served in associating a Canadian agent with the

British negotiators during the discussions with France. Lord Salisbury would be prepared to receive proposals from Canada on what she would like to obtain in a new commercial treaty, but nothing more.[49]

The immediate reaction of the Colonial Office to this communication was that it was a rather high-handed action by a sister Department which might be misunderstood in Canada. Pennell, the clerk in charge of the North American Division, wrote, with some force, "The reason alleged by the F. O. for declining to receive a representative from Canada when negotiations with France are resumed appears to me to be hardly adequate, the same reason would equally apply in regard to any negotiations on behalf of Canada founded on a statement of what they desire." He considered that the Foreign Office should be pressed to accept the Canadian request, as it would be "highly undesirable ... to do anything which may tend to cause ... irritation in the Dominion." To this end he suggested that Hicks Beach speak personally to Salisbury on the matter.[50] Bramston felt that the Foreign Office had misunderstood the Canadian request. The Dominion had not desired to become a partner with Great Britain in the negotiations with France; it had simply wished to place the English Government in possession of its views before the discussions began and "to prompt" the negotiators on Canadian interests.[51] His remarks stimulated Herbert to suggest an expedient which might overcome the difficulty. The Canadian Government should be asked to send a person possessing its confidence to confer with the Foreign Office on the pending discussions with France; this would allow the Colony's views to be advanced in a manner to which the Foreign Office could hardly find objection. The Canadian agent could later advise on points affecting the Dominion which arose during the course of the negotiations.[52] Herbert's proposed course of action was accepted by Downing Street and Ottawa without qualification.[53] The efforts during the eighties to secure a commercial treaty with France proved abortive, but it is significant that the Colonial Office compromise formed a basis of procedure which satisfied both parties in the matter. The presence of specifically Canadian objectives in trade with France made it necessary, however, that the Dominion should continue to press for a separate agreement with the Third Republic.

It was partly as a result of this episode and Galt's experiences in 1878-9 that the Canadian Government asked the United Kingdom to receive a permanent representative in London, who would be concerned, among other things, with the conduct of commercial negotiations.[54] This proposal was ultimately sanctioned by the Imperial Government, which insisted, however, that the status of the new agent in treaty discussions would have to be left to be determined by the Foreign Secretary as the need for such negotiations arose. The Macdonald Ministry accepted this arrangement, deliberately vague as it was, and the first High Commissioner of Canada in London was appointed early in 1880. The significance of commercial negotiations in the work of the new officer was indicated by the fact that Galt, the principal Canadian diplomat in this formative period, was selected to fill the post. Galt's instructions were specific on the question of commercial treaties. He was to watch over the interests of Canada in any commercial discussions which might be carried on by the mother country, and thus ensure that the Dominion was not adversely affected by the operation of British trade treaties. In addition he was to endeavour to secure commercial arrangements favourable to Canada through direct action with foreign powers, undertaken in association with the British diplomatic service. After Galt's time it was the successive High Commissioners who carried out the principal part of the Dominion's commercial negotiations abroad.

As High Commissioner Galt continued his efforts, in London, Paris, and Madrid, to conclude commercial arrangements with France and Spain, but with a singular lack of success. The Colonial Office realized that conditions in Europe were not conducive to Galt's objects in these negotiations, but it did nothing to dampen his enthusiasm for the extension of Canadian trade.[55] For its part the Foreign Office allowed Galt a free hand in these overtures, only stipulating that he keep the Colonial Office informed of the progress of his discussions. If he reached the stage where a convention was contemplated he was to show the proposed agreement to the Foreign Office. This would provide an opportunity for the Department to test the arrangement for its effect on British treaty obligations.[56] Galt took advantage of the Foreign Office's knowledge of the European scene by consulting with the Department over such matters as a feasible time at which to initiate or to resume negotiations with foreign powers. These approaches were apparently not entirely gratuitous on Galt's part, for the Department had suggested that it would be very desirable that he should have its approval before beginning conversations.[57]

A curious little episode which occurred during the course of the British negotiations with France in 1881 showed that Canada still dutifully respected the diplomatic unity of the Empire. In June the French Consul-General at Quebec, either immediately before or after he had retired from his post, remarked to one of the Canadian Cabinet Ministers that the time was opportune for Canada to approach France regarding a commercial agreement. The incident was reported in the press and resulted in the Foreign Office sending a strong letter to the Colonial Office, protesting the irregular nature of this procedure.[58] The Office felt that such a mild little overture was unlikely to lead to significant results and criticized the other Department for raising what seemed to be a storm in a tea-cup. However Macdonald, who was in England during that summer, was informed and promptly told the French Consul that any communication on trade matters must be made through Her Majesty's Government. The Foreign Office applauded this declaration and proceeded to make representations to France over the unauthorized action of its Consul. Of course the episode was completely fruitless except to afford evidence that Canada was prepared to adhere to the rules of diplomatic practice laid down for the Empire.[59]

The role of Canada in the making of commercial treaties was defined in 1883 by the two parties most chiefly concerned in the process--the Colonial Office and the High Commissioner. Their expositions of Canadian fiscal autonomy in international affairs were called forth by an error made by the Governor-General in discussing the question. In May, 1883, on the conclusion of his term in Ottawa, Lord Lorne, in a reply to an address of the Parliament of Canada, reviewed the development of the Dominion since Confederation. In the course of his remarks he told Canadians that "you have the power to make Treaties on your own responsibility with foreign Nations, and your High Commissioner is associated for purposes of negotiation with the Foreign Office. "[60] Bramston minuted dryly on this dispatch that he had always thought that Canadians were British subjects.[61] Herbert provided a fuller account of the procedure as he saw it, recognizing the possibility that divergent policies might be pursued simultaneously under the arrangement.

> It was a considerable mistake, and apparently a gratuitous one. It is exactly contrary to the fact to say that Canada has the power to make Treaties on its own responsibility with foreign nations. Canada has no powers or responsibilities of the kind but H.M. Govt. have recognized the convenience of allowing and assisting Canada to do what it pleases in such matters, and to that end undertakes to carry out Treaties and arrangements between Canada and foreign countries entirely opposed to the fiscal principles and policy of this country.[62]

The Permanent Under-Secretary wondered if the assertion should be left to pass unnoticed, for fear that might give rise to the impression that Great Britain endorsed it.   To Ashley the mistake deserved to be overlooked, since it was only partly incorrect. "Canada does make (though it cannot conclude) treaties of commerce on its own responsibility, --that is to say we do not control the terms of the treaty. "[63]   Derby's comment, "let it alone," meant that the Colonial Office did nothing to correct Lord Lorne in his well-meaning misapprehension.[64]

In the next month, Galt, returning to North America after three years' service as High Commissioner, provided a more accurate description of the limits of the Canadian position in treaty negotiations. Speaking at Halifax he stated that the freedom of the Dominion to undertake trade negotiations was "practically absolute. " He went on to discuss Lorne's observation.

> The Governor-General in one of his parting addresses had stated in very distinct terms that Canada did possess these powers, and he wished to take this opportunity, which was the first opportunity since he had returned to corroborate that statement of His Excellency. As a matter of legality a treaty had to be made between the sovereign executives of any two countries. The Queen of England, the Emperor of Germany or the President of France must be parties to treaties. But this was a mere question of form. The question of absolute interest was whether the right was accorded to us to decide the points upon which we were willing to agree with a foreign country. And he was prepared to say that in that respect every possible concession had been made by Her Majesty's Government. No difficulty had ever been raised by them with regard to the terms upon which Canada desired to enter into any negotiations with France or any other country. They did not pretend to exercise any control over the terms upon which the government of Canada had instructed him to negotiate....[63]

Sir Charles Tupper, who succeeded Galt as High Commissioner in 1883, inherited the negotiations with France and Spain which his predecessor had unsuccessfully initiated.

Tupper, who was of a more determined and aggressive nature than Galt, soon showed that he was not prepared to act merely in an advisory capacity in the conduct of negotiations affecting Canada. When, in the year 1884, the Canadian Government instructed him to attempt to secure modifications in the Spanish tariff in favour of Canada, Tupper pressed on the Imperial Government the demand that he be accorded plenipotentiary powers in this mission. Soon after the Colonial Office had transmitted the substance of Tupper's instructions to the Foreign Office, [66] Tupper himself wrote directly to the Foreign Secretary requesting coequal status with the British Minister in Spain in the negotiations. [67] The Foreign Office, which did not encourage direct communication with the Colonial Agents unless it had been specially authorized, made its reply to the High Commissioner through the Colonial Office. After laying down certain reservations regarding the principle of differential duties (a subject mentioned in the Canadian proposals), the Department gave its assent to Tupper's wishes.

> If the Spanish Government are favourably disposed, a Full Power for these negotiations will be given to Sir R. Morier and Sir C. Tupper jointly. The actual negotiations would probably be conducted by Sir Charles Tupper; but the Convention, if concluded, must be signed by both Plenipotentiaries, and be entered into between Her Majesty and the King of Spain, with the special object of regulating Canadian trade with the Spanish territories specified in the Convention. [68]

It was a month before Tupper received news of this decision, [69] because of a delay caused by the intermediate correspondence, but his jubilation over the extent of the concession was unconfined. Writing to Macdonald he characterized the principle of equal representation in commercial negotiations as "a very important point, and in the light of Galt's reports a very important one scored for Canada."[70] The Prime Minister agreed, "You certainly have scored a great point in securing your being united with the British Ambassador, not only in the negotiation but the completion of the Treaty."[71]

In the light of subsequent events, the Foreign Office decision of 1884 was indubitably a vital step in the gradual transformation of the old imperial treaty system. It was true that Macdonald and Brown had been granted full powers in their discussions with the United States a decade earlier, but special circumstances rendered those precedents much less significant. The long record of Canadian participation in reciprocity negotiations with the United States made the concession of plenipotentiary authority to the Dominion's agents in 1871 and 1874 almost inevitable. In addition, Macdonald's role in the Treaty of Washington discussions was that of a single Canadian representative in a delegation which also comprised four British commissioners. His was hardly the dominant voice in the negotiations, and similarly, Brown, in his bargaining, had often to give way to the wishes of Sir Edward Thornton. In the conversations which Tupper and Morier conducted with Spain in 1884, however, Morier's role was purely formal. Tupper functioned as the actual negotiator, being given a free hand by the British Minister to undertake the venture in the manner he thought best. The position was almost exactly reversed in 1884 from what it had been in 1879, for the British representative abroad had now been relegated to a secondary capacity. Tupper's discussions with Spain were, much to his sorrow, unsuccessful and it was not until 1893 that he was able to conclude, and sign, a commercial treaty with France which vindicated the principle enunciated nine years earlier.

The Spanish negotiations marked the final stage in the evolution of the procedure of Canadian diplomacy in the period under examination. It remains but to notice that during the eighties Canadian representatives participated in several international conferences. The first international gathering which Canada attended in her own right was probably a Monetary Conference held in Paris in May, 1881. Galt and Tupper, who were both in London at the time, asked to be allowed to take part in this meeting with "limited powers," in order that the Dominion would not be pledged by the result of the discussions. There was at first some difficulty about their recognition, since the delegates had to receive invitations from the United States and France, the sponsoring countries, but the Colonial Office strongly pressed the Foreign Office to obtain this approval. [72] The invitations were finally granted, and the British Embassy in Paris instructed to afford the Canadian representatives assistance and "all proper facilities" during their stay in the French capital. [73] They were not, however, issued with formal letters of credence for the Conference.

A more significant opportunity for the expression of the Canadian point of view in an international gathering came two years later, when Tupper attended an International Conference for the Protection of Submarine Telegraph Cables. Twenty-five powers were represented at this meeting, to which Tupper received credentials on behalf of Canada. In his Recollections Tupper records that once during the discussions he took up a position independent of the British delegation and voted against all his colleagues. The next day, when the question was reconsidered, the British delegates changed their stand and supported Tupper's point of view. One of them informed the High Commissioner later that the reversal had occurred after they had consulted the Foreign Office. "We were all of the same opinion as yourself at the first discussion, but voted in accordance with the views of Lord Lyons," Tupper was told. [74] When the draft convention for the protection of submarine cables was forwarded to London, the Colonial Office noted that the article applying it to the autonomous colonies was more liberal than had been anticipated. This, it appeared, was due to Tupper's efforts, for the Canadian had pointed out that unless Canada and Newfoundland accepted the convention, the major Atlantic cables, which landed in those colonies, would be outside its jurisdiction. He had by this argument secured a colonial article in the agreement which was more favourable to Canadian interests. In addition he had gained the point that the colonies should be allowed to withdraw from the treaty in the same manner as a sovereign power. [75] The High Commissioner returned to London well pleased with the role which Canada had played in the meeting. To Macdonald he wrote, "I feel some pride in the fact that Canada took her place in the international conference and on an equal footing with all the other Powers, and I may add that nothing could exceed the kindness and courtesy with which I was treated by all present."[76] It was the statement of a man who had seen his country move forward in the short space of twenty years to a position in which she exercised a substantial share in the determination of her foreign relations. If the achievement was due mainly to the efforts of men like Galt and Tupper, it had also been promoted by the sympathetic manner in which the Colonial Office had received Canadian requests for participation in commercial negotiations.

III

The claim of Canada for an expanding share in the conduct of commercial negotiations with foreign states was but one aspect of the Dominion's nascent confidence in fiscal matters. It represented a positive action on the part of the Colony; an attempt to enlarge Canadian external trade and to enhance the new community's status in the world. It was essentially an out-reach of Canadian interests. But the commercial independence that was being created during the years following Confederation had another facet, a negative approach. Before the Dominion could properly regard the control of her fiscal policy as being a quite indigenous responsibility it was necessary that the country be released from the operation of commercial treaties binding the whole Empire. For if she were forced to extend preferential treatment to every state which happened to possess a "most-favoured-nation" treaty with the United Kingdom then it was obvious that full liberty to determine tariff policy had not been attained. Successive Canadian ministries were driven by the logic of events to consider this problem and to endeavour to adjust it in conformity with Canadian fiscal requirements. It was deemed essential, first of all, that Canada should be able to withdraw from existing British commercial treaties in which her interests were not respected, and secondly, that she should be entitled to decide for herself whether she wished to adhere to future agreements. The first of these principles was enunciated by the Canadian Government and partly accepted by the United Kingdom during the twenty years included within the limits of this study; the second, inspired through the constructive imagination of the Colonial Office, became a feature of the administrative machinery of the imperial relationship at the same time.

Until at least a decade after the achievement of British North American federation it could be said with absolute authority that commercial treaties made by the United Kingdom irrevocably bound all the parts of the Empire. Todd has claimed that the application of Imperial treaties to the autonomous colonies was dependent upon those colonies passing the necessary measures to implement them, but this view is surely incorrect. It appears to be based on a sentence used by Lord Kimberley when repudiating a New Zealand claim that the Colony possessed the power to conclude commercial treaties on her own responsibility: "Her Majesty's Government apprehend that the constitutional right of the Queen to conclude treaties binding all parts of the Empire cannot be questioned, subject to the discretion of the Parliament of the United Kingdom or of the Colonial Parliaments, as the case may be, to pass any laws which may be required to bring such treaties into operation."[77] The operative word in the qualifying clause is clearly "discretion," which suggests that the United Kingdom's readiness to allow the colonies to implement Imperial treaties by legislation was simply a matter of convenience. Although the problem of requiring a self-governing colony to fulfil obligations imposed on it by a British treaty did not rise in an acute form during the period, it was a constant source of worry to several departments in Whitehall. For as long as the Imperial Parliament remained legally sovereign over the entire Empire, that Parliament was compelled to ensure the observance of treaties by every colony of the Crown.

The theory upon which this responsibility was based had been laid down many years before any of the British dependencies had been granted local autonomy. Treaties concluded by the mother country had bound the whole Empire without exception since the beginnings of British overseas settlement. It was not until the middle of the nineteenth century that such treaties, particularly commercial ones, began to impinge upon the awareness of some of the larger colonies. The aspect of them which excited the greatest criticism in the colonial Empire was the increasing prevalence of "most-favoured-nation" clauses in British trade agreements. The object of these provisions, that of bringing about the progressive reduction of commercial barriers all over the world, though no doubt salutary, conflicted violently with the protectionist aims of many of the larger British colonies. In 1879, according to a return furnished the Canadian Parliament, there were about forty commercial treaties between Great Britain and foreign countries which applied to the British colonies. About half contained "most-favoured-nation" clauses.[78] Not all, of course, were objectionable, although two, those with Belgium (1862) and the German Zollverein (1865), applied to the trade relations between Great Britain and her colonies and thus prevented the establishment of any system of imperial preference.

The attempt to adapt Imperial commercial treaties to the changed conditions of the British Empire was initiated by Sir Robert Herbert at the Colonial Office. It arose during the eighteen-seventies in connection with the interminable negotiations with France for the conclusion of a new trade agreement. Each time the discussions were resumed the Colonial Office was asked to supply information respecting the interests of the colonies in trade with France. On one of these occasions, in 1876, Herbert complained that the Office was frequently placed at a disadvantage in having to provide the colonial view-point at short notice. It was often impossible to draft a general provision which would satisfy the divergent requirements of all the colonies; consequently "we are in danger of doing what an important Colony may object to." Since each colony could not hope to conclude its own commercial undertakings, it might be advisable to allow the more important colonies the freedom to adhere separately to British commercial treaties after they had had time to study them. The Permanent Under-Secretary therefore suggested that the Foreign Office should be invited to consider the insertion of the following qualification in future commercial treaties.

> It is agreed between the two High Contracting Powers that except as hereinafter provided this treaty shall not apply to the Colonies or Foreign Possessions of either power; but upon a notification from either Power that it is desired that any Colony or Foreign Possession shall be admitted to the operation of this Treaty the Treaty shall from and after a date to be agreed upon not later than six months from the date of such notification become as fully applicable to such Colony or Foreign Possession as if it had been mentioned by name in the Treaty and then made subject to its provisions.[79]

The other members of the staff of the Office felt that the clause suggested would " amply meet the difficulty"[80] and it was thus sent on for examination to the Foreign Office. A powerful argument for the principle of separate adherence was provided in the Colonial Office communication. "The Dominion of Canada and the Colonies having Responsible Government would unquestionably claim to be consulted before this Country entered into any stipulations binding upon them. "[81]

The Foreign Office was not enthusiastic over Herbert's suggestion. It refused to discuss the usefulness of the plan as a general rule of action and simply stated that it might be applied in special circumstances where there was insufficient time to consult the colonies. [82]   To the Colonial Office this answer was hardly adequate. It was true that the Foreign Office had promised to keep the Secretary of State informed on the progress of negotiations which concerned the colonies, but this was not a new departure. It was precisely the practice which had caused the Office inconvenience in the past. Herbert, however, knew better than to attempt to force his scheme upon an unwilling sister Department. He noted that the Foreign Office had not objected to the form of the proposed clause, which could always be put forward again. In the meantime the Office would have to continue under the old method of procedure, although there might be an improvement if the Foreign Office could be induced to supply a notice as early as possible of any alteration in a British commercial treaty. [83]

Thus the matter slumbered until the end of the year. The French negotiation lapsed and there was no further occasion to test the procedure of consultation until the Foreign Office suddenly announced that it was necessary to conclude a temporary trade convention with Austria-Hungary within the course of a few weeks. [84]   The news provided Herbert with an admirable opportunity to bring forward again his general article covering the admission of the autonomous colonies. He felt that no purpose would be served by consulting the colonies before Great Britain possessed a draft treaty with Austria-Hungary, and there would probably be insufficient time to do this after a copy of the treaty had been received. He therefore pressed his suggestion on the Foreign Office again as being the only course free from difficulty. [85]

The Foreign Office replied in a manner which revealed that it had at last seriously taken up Herbert's proposal. A modified form of the colonial article, which it was felt would be more practicable than Herbert's draft, was returned, and the Office was invited to consider it.[86]   The chief innovation in the Foreign Office clause was the provision that colonies which had previously signified their willingness to be included in a treaty were to be named in the article. Herbert had proposed that all the colonies should be automatically excluded from the operation of British commercial treaties until they announced individually a desire for admittance. The Foreign Office would have included some and excluded others, while giving the latter group the freedom to declare their adherence to a trade instrument at a later date. The reasons for a dual classification of the colonies are obscure, for it does not appear that the Foreign Office necessarily considered the Crown Colonies as falling logically within the group named in the first part of the article. It became the invariable practice later, to include en bloc in a commercial treaty all but the self-governing colonies but this was a decision of the

Colonial Office and not the Foreign Office. It is conceivable that the Foreign Office under-estimated the time required to consult the more important colonies on the question of their admittance into a trade treaty. At any event the point did not trouble the Colonial Office, which expressed itself as perfectly satisfied with the revised form. [87] The clause was transmitted to the colonies for their information, in a circular informing them of the pending arrangement with Austria-Hungary. [88]   The Foreign Office article was not, however, used in 1877, for it was found impossible to conclude the Austro-Hungarian treaty in that year. In its place the old convention was simply prolonged indefinitely, the Hapsburg Empire indicating that it was not prepared to offer concessions to the British colonies unless those areas reciprocated in tariff reductions. [89]

In the meantime the perennial French negotiations had begun again. In March, 1877, the Foreign Office, believing that the conclusion of a treaty was almost in sight, pressed the Colonial Office for its views as to the wishes of the Empire regarding trade with France. [90]   The Office felt that the colonial article presented the most satisfactory solution to the problem occasioned, in this case, by the necessity for haste and decided to communicate on the matter with the Agents-General in London rather than with the governments of the colonies. Once again, therefore, the article was forwarded to the responsible government colonies for their approval. [91]   Once again the colonies expressed themselves as favourable to its use and once again the Foreign Office was informed that the draft article would meet the requirements of the moment. [92] But the progress of the French negotiations went its torturous way. In June the Foreign Office wrote to ask whether the colonies would grant France "most-favoured-nation" treatment in a new commercial agreement. [93]   This was too much, protested the Colonial Office. It had repeatedly told the other Department that the most suitable manner of dealing with the colonies in a French treaty was by means of the special colonial article, and yet the Foreign Office persisted in the old course. It was quite impossible for the Office to speak for the responsible government colonies before hearing their views, and out of the question to accede to any stipulations which might bind them. Very patiently Malcolm explained the Department's position for his superiors.

> I am inclined to think that the power of making supplementary articles suggested to the F.O. by Mr. Herbert ... would be the most satisfactory way of dealing with the colonies. They could thus see what the terms of the treaty (wh. is primarily and principally made in the interests of the U.K.) are and they could suggest such modifications as their circs. might demand without being impelled to accept or reject 'en bloc' whatever is put before them. [94]

Herbert agreed, his temper not having been improved by what he considered unreasonable features in the French proposals. "It seems pretty clear that it will not be safe for us to commit any Colonies to participation in the Treaty until we know what it will contain." [95]   This answer was returned to the Foreign Office, combined with a renewed request for the use of the colonial article. [96]

The struggle for the acceptance of the colonial article was at this point almost over, although, ironically, it was not to be resolved on the basis of the commercial treaty with France. The Foreign Office now changed the form of the article to provide for a "Supplementary Convention" between the High Contracting Parties in order to make the stipulations of the treaty applicable to those colonies approving them.   They also suggested that a two-year limit be fixed for the admittance of the colonies to any treaty. [97] The Office did not favour a convention, feeling that it would be easier to admit colonies en bloc by a simple notification after the opinion of all the dependencies had been canvassed. The two-year limit for signifying approval was also questioned, on the grounds that the procedure for admitting colonies might be prolonged, especially if modifications were desired in a treaty. The Department did not press the first point, however, in discussing the new wording with the Foreign Office. [98] The definitive form of the colonial article was finally settled early in January, 1878. It was essentially the same as the one the Foreign Office had proposed exactly a year earlier, except that the self-governing colonies were to be admitted to the operation of commercial treaties through a supplementary convention:

<u>Draft Article applying Commercial Treaties</u>
<u>to British and Foreign Colonies</u>

The stipulations of the present Treaty shall be applicable to the Colonies and Foreign Possessions of the two High Contracting Parties named in this Article.

(Here insert names of those Colonies, etc. to be included in the Treaty).

The stipulations of the present Treaty shall be also applicable to any Colony or Foreign Possession of the two High Contracting Parties not included in this Article, upon the conclusion by the High Contracting Parties of a Supplementary Convention to that effect.

In the latter case, the stipulations of the present Treaty shall, subject to such modifications as may be agreed upon by the High Contracting Parties, from and after a date to be agreed upon, not later than six months from the date of the notification of such Supplementary Convention, become as fully applicable to such Colony or Foreign Possession as if it had been mentioned by name in the present Article. [99]

There was much confusion regarding the initial use of the new article. In fact it was not brought into consistent operation until three years after it had been agreed upon by the Colonial Office and Foreign Office. The first commercial treaty to be drawn up after Carnarvon's circular dispatch of January 22, 1878, announcing the change of procedure, was one with Rumania. A draft of this agreement, which included a number of non-commercial features, was sent to the Colonial Office in May. [100] The Foreign Office had inserted the colonial article in the draft treaty, but Malcolm decided that another course was desirable on this occasion. There was little in the Rumanian treaty to which the colonies could take objection, and it would be a definite advantage to have some of its non-commercial aspects adopted by the principal colonies. He therefore suggested that the treaty be made applicable to <u>all</u> the colonies, with the safeguard that any colony might withdraw from it if it gave notice within six months after the ratification of the instrument.[101]   Should this proposal be unsatisfactory, he continued, then the new colonial article might be used.[102]   The Foreign Office approved this suggestion,[103] the colonies were circularized about the treaty[104] (with the result which the Office had anticipated), and the replies were sent to the Foreign Office early in 1880.[105]   The convention with Rumania was not signed in a final form until April, 1880, when the colonies were again asked whether they wished to claim exemption from its provisions.[106]   Canada, which had remained silent in response to the first request from London for information, now indicated that it desired to withdraw from the treaty.[107]   Her Majesty's Minister at Bucharest was instructed to arrange this exemption, and the formalities were finally completed by January, 1881.[108]

A second commercial treaty in this early period inspired a quite different procedure.   The Colonial Office was informed, in March, 1880, that a trade treaty, applicable to the British colonies, had been signed with Serbia in the previous month.[109] This announcement took the Office completely by surprise, for there had been no preliminary notice that negotiations were being undertaken with Serbia.   In view of the long discussions which had occurred with the Foreign Office over the colonial article this action of the sister Department seemed hardly courteous.   Herbert, when asked whether the previous correspondence should be brought to the attention of the Foreign Office, made the restrained rejoinder, "I would notice the point."[110]   The point was therefore noticed[111] and drew from the Foreign Office the admission that because there had been no colonial objections to the first reference over the Rumanian Treaty the Department had considered that a similar treaty with Serbia would also be acceptable to the colonies.   In future negotiations, however, the wishes of the Colonial Office would be faithfully carried out.[112]   To the Office this was an attempt "to gloss over" the fact that a treaty had been concluded without consulting the autonomous colonies and without inserting the special article for exemption.   The Foreign Office explanation failed to justify improper conduct in the matter.   But the damage was done and the Department could only trust that the colonies would not raise any objections to the Serbian agreement.   In the circular informing them of it, the colonial governments were told quite frankly that the treaty had been "inadvertently concluded" by the Foreign Office without considering their interests.[113]   Canada again proved an intransigent element in the Empire's attitude to the Serbian Treaty.   The High Commissioner and the Government both wrote to request immediate exemption for the Dominion and the Foreign Office had to be asked to obtain this concession.[114]   In the end the confused state of politics in the Serbian Legislature rendered withdrawal impossible and Canada was obliged to adhere to the treaty for the time being.[115]

The new procedure was at last successfully applied in 1881.   It is probable that a commercial convention with Ecuador was the first instrument to contain the colonial article in its agreed form.[116]   The autonomous colonies were circularized and asked to indicate their wishes in regard to the Ecuador Treaty in July, 1881.[117]   Canada neglected to reply and had to be prodded again for an answer in the autumn of the following year.[118]   This produced a response, which was that the Dominion did not desire to be included in the agreement.[119]   The dilatory attitude of Canada was exasperating to the Colonial Office, which favoured making a single communication to the Foreign Office listing all the colonies to be associated in a particular treaty.   On this occasion it was not possible to provide the Foreign Office with this information until the spring of 1883.[120]   A convention with Montenegro formed the subject of a circular to the autonomous colonies in June, 1882,[121] a further reminder to Canada early in 1883,[122] and, ultimately, a dispatch stating that Canada wished to be excluded from its operation.[123]   Veritably, the wheels of Olympus ground exceeding slow.

The treaties with Ecuador and Montenegro showed that the Colonial Office procedure for allowing the autonomous colonies to withdraw from British commercial undertakings had finally reached a state of consistent operation.   From 1878, when the principle had been accepted by the Foreign Office, three methods had been used to work out the mechanics of the arrangement.   There had been the example, in the Serbian Treaty, of the automatic inclusion of all the colonies (the last survival of the old type of British commercial engagement binding the whole Empire); in the Rumanian convention there had been automatic inclusion coupled with a proviso allowing for easy exemption; and finally, in the Ecuador instrument, there had been the wholesale exclusion of the self-governing colonies until their wishes could be made known.   The sequence of these various methods revealed no orderly evolution, only an empirical adaptation to the circumstances of each case.   In the future, Imperial treaties came increasingly to be applied to the autonomous colonies in accordance with the Colonial Office principle of automatic exclusion.   For instance, an agreement with Egypt was referred by the Canadian Government to Galt, who reported that there were no Canadian interests which required the Dominion to become a party to the treaty.[124]   The Macdonald Administration also turned down on behalf of Canada a treaty with Italy, negotiated in 1883.[125]   An agreement with Morocco, which had more limited obligations than the other treaties, seems to be one of the few British engagements which received the adherence of Canada at this time.   When Canada informed the Colonial Office that she had no objection to being included in the treaty, the usual colonial article was apparently not inserted.[126]

The modus vivendi of 1878, allowing the more important colonies to withdraw from the operation of British commercial treaties, was determined upon without the stimulus of colonial pressure.   It proved, however, less easy for Canada to obtain the sanction of the Imperial Government to the proposition that the same colonies had a right to be excluded from British trade treaties.   Galt first raised the latter question in 1880, after he had assumed the office of High Commissioner.   He requested, in a letter to Kimberley, that no treaty of commerce be made by the United Kingdom that would have the effect of impairing the freedom of the Canadian Parliament to control the customs and excise of the Dominion.   As a corollary to this principle he also submitted that Canada should be given the option of accepting or rejecting trade engagements applying to the whole Empire.   Finally, and this request concerned him personally, he asked that the High Commissioner be consulted and allowed to participate in any commercial negotiations that might affect Canada.[127]   The Colonial Office noted that the first two of Galt's wishes had already been conceded by the arrangements of 1878 and that it was probably the final request which the High Commissioner put forward with the most zeal. Herbert recommended that this point be urged upon the Foreign Office with all emphasis.[128] In the letter that was eventually sent to the sister Department, the Office added that in its view it would be desirable for the High Commissioner to communicate directly with the Foreign Office on the subject of commercial negotiations.[129]

The Foreign Office refused to commit itself on Galt's request for participation in trade discussions. The wishes of the Canadian Government would, of course, be kept constantly in view in all negotiations, and Galt would be notified as soon as any conversations began. Beyond those assurances the Office would not go.[130] It was a vague and inadequate reply but nothing would be gained by pursuing the question, the Colonial Office felt. This was not the view of the Macdonald Government, however. In a long and forceful Minute the Canadian Privy Council gave strong support to the High Commissioner's representations. Parts of Galt's letter were quoted with approval, and the statement that the British North America Act made over the entire control of the customs and excise of the Colony to the Canadian Parliament was stressed as a justification for Galt's claims. The Minute concluded by recommending that a dispatch, expounding the views of the Dominion Government on the matter, be prepared for the information of the Colonial Secretary. The communication was to urge that "it is the wish of the Canadian Government to be relieved as soon as conveniently can be of the obligations connected with any treaties now in existence: - that it is the desire of the Canadian Government to be informed of the inception of any new treaty --and that in future no stipulation binding upon the Commerce of Canada be introduced into any treaty without reserving to the Canadian Government the option of acceptance or refusal."[131]

Bramston, the Assistant Under-Secretary who dealt with the Canadian correspondence, felt that to exempt the Colony from the workings of British treaties would require new treaties limiting the operation of the old ones. This would be a considerable labour and one which was perhaps not warranted by the intent of the Canadian request. It should be sufficient to consult Canada when new treaties were contemplated, and to exclude her from them at her own wish.[132] To the Foreign Office, however, it appeared that the Canadian Minute contained a stronger representation than the Colonial Office had apprehended. Was not the Canadian Government, in asserting an "exclusive" power to control the customs and excise of the Dominion, trespassing on the Imperial power to conclude treaties binding on the whole Empire? It was true that the word "exclusive" was used in sections 91 and 92 of the British North America Act, but there it referred to the division of powers between the Dominion and the provinces and not to any delimitation of Imperial authority.[133] The Colonial Office received this communication with some amusement. It seemed as if the Foreign Office was raising a "bogey" simply to have the satisfaction of demolishing it. The Department was perfectly correct in pointing out that Great Britain had not abdicated any of the functions of sovereignty by passing an Act which purported to give the Dominion Parliament certain "exclusive" powers of legislation. But this was hardly the question at issue. The treaty-making power of the Imperial Parliament had not been affected by the British North America Act, although that measure had certainly delegated considerable legislative authority to Canada. It was extremely doubtful, however, whether Canada had ever put forward a claim of right upon this point, Herbert believed.[134]   Lord Kimberley inclined to the view that the Dominion had simply meant that it would be desirable for her to be excluded from existing treaties. He did not feel that it would be wise to enter into a controversy regarding this question, which could be so easily passed over.[135] Thus the Foreign Office was told that Canada had not intended the word "exclusive" to be interpreted in the wider sense suggested by the Department. The phrase had merely been used to support a claim for special consideration in the making of commercial treaties; a claim which the Office felt was justified.[136]   This vague and rather comforting assurance was also transmitted to Canada, in answer to the Privy Council Minute.

The more practical considerations connected with the Dominion's request for relief from the stipulations of existing commercial treaties proved very difficult to arrange. The most burdensome of these commitments to Canada were the two agreements with Belgium and the Zollverein, permitting those countries access into the Canadian market on the same terms granted Great Britain or her possessions. These provisions, unusual in British trade engagements, were exceedingly objectionable to Canada, not because the Dominion disliked the idea of extending "most-favoured-nation" treatment to Belgium and Germany, but because she did not favour the prospect of giving to those two countries the special concessions offered to the United Kingdom. Once granted, those concessions would, of course, have to be accorded to every country having a "most-favoured-nation" relationship with Belgium or Germany. In 1881 the two treaties had run their full term and could be denounced by the contracting parties at one year's notice. Galt therefore wrote in the autumn of the year to the Colonial Office, pointing out that the agreements affected the fiscal freedom of Canada and asking the Foreign Office to seek the cancellation of the clauses referring to the British colonies.[137]

The Foreign Office received this request with poor grace. It appeared that Galt was repeating the claim that Canada had a right to be excluded from Imperial commercial engagements. This claim could not be allowed and could be easily disqualified legally by a reference to the Law Officers. Moreover, the Canadian proposal would be extremely difficult to accomplish, for it was impossible to terminate a single article of a treaty without destroying the whole instrument. The only solution which presented itself to the Department was to ask Belgium and Germany informally if they would consent to a modification of the treaties in order to withdraw Canada from their operation.[138] To the Colonial Office the question presented itself as one of policy rather than of law. It was hardly necessary to refer the subject to the Law Officers since Canada had not made the claim which the Foreign Office criticized. The important issue in the problem was clear: should Great Britain do all that was possible to assist Canada to escape from a vexatious position? In Herbert's view there could only be one answer to this question.

But it is none the less important to understand clearly, and face, the present position, which is that Canada <u>demands</u> that H.M. Government shall take the necessary measures to relieve her from the operation of any Treaty which she desires to be no longer bound by. If we will not, at whatever diplomatic inconvenience, do for her what she would do for herself if independent, we shall at once bring into discussion as a practical matter the question of her independence: which is now being rather frankly discussed in the abstract.

I do not therefore think it will suffice to promise to "sound" ... Germany and Belgium as to their willingness to relieve Canada from the existing Commercial Treaties: but that we shall have to make a direct request for supplementary treaties to this end.[139]

On this occasion, however, the Permanent Under-Secretary was overruled by his parliamentary counterpart, Leonard Courtney, who stated that, "to sound" the foreign governments informally would be all that was required.[140] This was eventually done, but the Belgian and German Governments proved unwilling to allow any modifications in the treaties. They pointed out the impracticability of abrogating individual clauses and declared that only through denunciation, followed by the negotiation of new treaties, could the Canadian request be achieved.[141] In the end it was to take stronger representations from a more determined figure than Galt; the joint action of all the autonomous colonies; and an example of unprecedented commercial magnanimity on the part of Canada before the last restriction on the fiscal freedom of the British Dominions was removed.[142]

REFERENCES

1. The early episodes in the Canadian attempt to be associated with Great Britain in the reciprocity negotiations are described in Porritt, The Diplomatic Freedom of the British Dominions, 161-86.

Extracts from the address of the Legislative Assembly of Canada favouring reciprocity, 1846, are provided in ibid., 438-40.

2. Minute of the Executive Council of Canada and memorandum by Francis Hincks, Inspector-General, May 12, 1848: PP, 1847-8, LIX, no. 405.

Porritt states that this Minute urged the Colonial Office to sanction direct communication between the Province of Canada and the United States on the subject of reciprocity (Porritt, The Diplomatic Freedom of the British Dominions, 163). This would appear to be an overstatement of the Canadian position, however.

3. R. B. Stewart, Treaty Relations of the British Commonwealth of Nations (New York, 1939), 51-2.

4. Minute of the Executive Council of New Brunswick, May 16, 1850, enclosed in Head to Grey, no. 30, May 20, 1850: CO 188/112.

5. Grey to Head, confidential, June 7, 1850: ibid. See also Grey to Head, no. 193, June 7, 1850: ibid.

6. Extracts from a resolution of the New Brunswick House of Assembly, April 24, 1850, urging that the colonies be allowed to negotiate with foreign countries for the purpose of enlarging their trade are printed in Porritt, The Diplomatic Freedom of the British Dominions, 167-8.

7. The Nova Scotia request of 1853 for a share in the reciprocity negotiations is discussed in N. M. Rogers, "Notes on the Treaty-Making Power," Canadian Historical Review, VII (March, 1926), 27-33. The relevant portions of the address are given in ibid., 27.
Rogers calls the address the first claim on the part of a British colony to the right of participation in the negotiation of a treaty in which its interests were vitally affected, but this statement is surely unjustifiable. Even if Hincks's memorandum of 1848 be not accepted as a strong expression of this position, there still remains the New Brunswick request of 1850.

8. Labouchere to Governor of Newfoundland, no. 10, March 26, 1857: CO 195/22. This dispatch is briefly discussed in Rogers, "Notes on the Treaty-Making Power," 30-3.

9. Lyons to Monck, Jan. 28, 1864, quoted in Lord Newton, Lord Lyons: A Record of British Diplomacy (London, 1913), I, 124.
There is a similar expression of Lyons's feeling towards Canadian negotiators in Lyons to Russell, Feb. 9, 1864, in ibid., I, 125-6.

10. See Cardwell to Monck, no. 95, June 17, 1865: CO 43/154. Printed in PP, 1865, XXXVII, no. 3535, 1-3.

11. Colonial Office to Foreign Office, July 6, 1865: CO 43/132.

12. Cardwell to Monck, no. 122, July 22, 1865: CO 43/154.

13. The significance of the Confederate Council of Trade in the movement towards diplomatic autonomy for the British colonies is well brought out in N. M. Rogers, "The Confederate Council of Trade," Canadian Historical Review, VII (Dec., 1926), 277-86.

14. Monck to Cardwell, no. 185, Sept. 23, 1865: CO 42/650.

15. Reports of the Executive Council of Canada, Sept. 23, 1865, enclosed in Monck to Cardwell, no. 187, Sept. 23, 1865: ibid.

16. Cardwell to Officer Administering the Government of Canada, no. 154, Oct. 28, 1865: ibid.

17. Foreign Office to Colonial Office, Nov. 11, 1865: CO 42/652. Printed in PP, 1873, XLIX, no. C-703, 14.

18. Minute by Rogers, Nov. 13, 1865, on Foreign Office to Colonial Office, Nov. 11, 1865: CO 42/652.

19. Instructions to the Canadian trade commissioners from the Minister of Finance, Nov. 17, 1865, enclosed in Monck to Cardwell, no. 19, Nov. 20, 1865: CO 42/650.

20. Minute by Elliot, Dec. 4, 1865, on Monck to Cardwell, no. 19, Nov. 20, 1865: ibid.

21. Foreign Office to Colonial Office, Dec. 11, 1865: CO 42/652.

22. Colonial Office to Foreign Office, Dec. 18 and 27, 1865: ibid. Colonial Office to William McDougall (leader of the Canadian delegation), Dec. 19, 1865: ibid.
The Imperial Government placed a naval vessel at the disposal of the commissioners to convey them from place to place in the Caribbean area.

23. Masters, The Reciprocity Treaty, 239-40.

24. By 1866 the American Government was aware of the consideration which Great Britain had given Canada in the conduct of the reciprocity negotiations. Thus Charles Francis Adams, the United States Minister in London, commented to Secretary of State Seward on a procedure for the reciprocity discussions which he had devised in consultation with Lord Clarendon: "This had been thought the better course, as the latter--the provincial authorities--had now substantially reached such a position of independence as to make it unadvisable for the Government here to attempt to act without regard to them." Adams to Seward, May 10, 1866, quoted in Porritt, The Diplomatic Freedom of the British Dominions, 186.

25. Cardwell to Officer Administering the Government of Canada, no. 159, Nov. 24, 1865: CO 43/154.

26. Copy of Young to Thornton, no. 27, July 1, 1869, enclosed in Foreign Of-

fice to Colonial Office, July 20, 1869: CO 42/680. See also Foreign Office to Colonial Office, July 14, 1869: ibid.

27. The best study of the Treaty of Washington is Goldwin Smith, The Treaty of Washington, 1871: A Study in Imperial History (Ithaca, 1941).

28. See above, chapter III, 87-8.

29. Debates of the House of Commons (Canada), 1870, I, 449-94 (March 16, 1870) and 558-654 (March 21, 1870).

30. Ibid., 560 (March 21, 1870).

31. Ibid., 575-83.

32. Ibid., 653-4. See Macdonald to Rose, March 25, 1870, in J. Pope, ed., Correspondence of Sir John Macdonald (Toronto, 1921), 132.

33. Quoted in W. S. Wallace, "The Growth of Canadian National Feeling." Canadian Historical Review, I (June, 1920), 155.

34. Glazebrook, Canadian External Relations, 145.
The decision to send Brown to Washington, and his reception there, are the subjects of the correspondence collected in PP, 1874, LXXV, no. C-1060.

35. Officer Administering the Government of Canada to Hicks Beach, no. 18, Nov. 15, 1878: CO 42/754.

36. Tilley to Hicks Beach, Dec. 3, 1878, in SP, 1880, no. 104, 2-3. Tilley to Galt, confidential, Dec. 9, 1878: ibid., 3-4.

37. Salisbury to Lyons, no. 167, commercial, Dec. 5, 1878: ibid., 3.

38. Copy of Lyons to Salisbury, private and secret, no. 194, May 11, 1879, enclosed in Foreign Office to Colonial Office, confidential, May 13, 1879: CO 42/758.

39. Ibid. See also Foreign Office to Colonial Office, Dec. 27, 1878: CO 42/755 and Glazebrook, Canadian External Relations, 157.

40. The correspondence relating to Galt's French and Spanish negotiations is found in SP, 1880, no. 104.

41. Skelton, "General Economic History, 1867-1912," 175.

42. Quoted in Sir C. H. Tupper, "Treaty-Making Powers of the Dominions," Journal of the Society of Comparative Legislation, XVII (Jan., 1917), 7-8.

43. Foreign Office to Colonial Office, March 21, 1874: CO 323/319.

44. Foreign Office to Colonial Office, Jan. 15, 1879: CO 323/340.

45. Lorne to Hicks Beach, telegram, March 27, 1879: CO 42/756.

46. Colonial Office to Foreign Office, May 1, 1879: ibid.

47. Foreign Office to Colonial Office, May 14, 1879: CO 42/758.

48. Colonial Office to Foreign Office, May 24, 1879: ibid.

49. Foreign Office to Colonial Office, June 3, 1879: ibid.

50. Minute by Pennell, June 4, 1879, on ibid.

51. Minute by Bramston, June 5, 1879, on ibid.

52. Minute by Herbert, June 7, 1879, on ibid.
The Permanent Under-Secretary's proposals were sent to the Foreign Office in a communication dated June 14, 1879: CO 42/758.

53. Foreign Office to Colonial Office, June 25, 1879: ibid., Hicks Beach to Lorne, secret, June 26, 1879: ibid., and Report of the Privy Council of Canada, Nov. 12, 1879, enclosed in Lorne to Hicks Beach, secret, Nov. 14, 1879: ibid. At this time Canada promised to appoint a representative to confer with the Imperial Government as soon as the negotiations were resumed.

54. The establishment of the post of Canadian High Commissioner in London is treated separately as chapter VIII of this study.

55. See minute by Herbert, Aug. 29, 1879, on Lorne to Hicks Beach, no. 225, Aug. 9, 1879: CO 42/757.

56. Foreign Office to Colonial Office, Dec. 21, 1880: CO 42/765.

57. Foreign Office to Colonial Office, Jan. 29, 1881: CO 42/769.

58. Foreign Office to Colonial Office, June 29, 1881: ibid.

59. There was a question in Parliament over this incident. (<u>Hansard</u>, Third Series, CCLXIII, 840 [July 14, 1881].) See also Foreign Office to Colonial Office, Oct. 25, 1881: CO 42/769, and Colonial Office to Foreign Office, Oct. 26, 1881: <u>ibid.</u>

60. Lorne to Derby, no. 119, May 28, 1883: CO 42/774.

61. Minute by Bramston, June 14, 1883, on <u>ibid.</u>

62. Minute by Herbert, June 14, 1883, <u>ibid.</u>

63. Minute by Ashley, June 14, 1883, <u>ibid.</u>

64. Minute by Derby, June 19, 1883, <u>ibid.</u>

65. Lorne to Derby, no. 162, July 9, 1883: CO 42/774.

66. Tupper's Instructions were contained in Lansdowne to Derby, no. 122, June 5, 1884, and no. 134, June 19, 1884: CO 42/777.

67. Copy of Tupper to Foreign Office, July, 1884 (precise date not provided), enclosed in Foreign Office to Colonial Office, July 26, 1884: CO 42/779.

68. Foreign Office to Colonial Office, July 26, 1884: <u>ibid.</u>

69. Colonial Office to Tupper, Aug. 28, 1884: <u>ibid.</u>

70. Tupper to Macdonald, Sept. 11, 1884, quoted in Glazebrook, <u>Canadian External Relations</u>, 164.

71. Macdonald to Tupper, Sept. 24, 1884, quoted in Saunders, ed., <u>Life of Sir Charles Tupper</u>, II, 39. See also Sir C. Tupper, <u>Recollections of Sixty Years in Canada</u> (London, 1914), 174-5.

Although Macdonald could applaud, in private, Tupper's achievement in securing for Canada a larger share of the treaty-making power, in Parliament he deprecated any suggestion that the Dominion be given an independent right to conclude commercial treaties. In 1882, for instance, Edward Blake introduced a resolution into the Dominion House urging that the necessary powers be accorded Canada to enable her to open direct negotiations with foreign governments on trade matters. He claimed that the British diplomatic service had been inadequate in promoting Canadian interests; in fact, that its history as far as Canada was concerned had been one of "error, blunder, wrong and concession" (<u>Debates of the House of Commons</u> [Canada], 1882, I, 1068-75 [Apr. 21, 1882]). To this outburst Macdonald stoutly replied that the Foreign Office had been of great assistance to Canada in past negotiations, and that the Dominion would be "penny wise and pound foolish" if it dispensed with the aid of British diplomats in order to secure a mere advance in status (Debates of the House of Commons [Canada], 1882, I, 1075-8). Blake's motion was eventually negatived after the topic had been thoroughly discussed by the House (ibid., 1080-95).

The explanation of Macdonald's position lies, of course, in the fact that in all matters touching the constitutional development of Canada he was a complete prag-matist. To him the logical extension of Canadian autonomy was a consideration of far less importance than the responses to particular problems and situations as they arose from day to day.

72. Colonial Office to Foreign Office, immediate, April 23, 1881, and Foreign Office to Colonial Office, April 20, 1881: CO 323/349.

73. Granville to Lyons, commercial, April 16, 1881, enclosed in Foreign Of-fice to Colonial Office, April 26, 1881: ibid.

74. Tupper, Recollections, 175.

75. Minute by Bramston, Nov. 15, on Foreign Office to Colonial Office, Nov. 9, 1883: CO 323/355. See also Tupper to Colonial Office, Nov. 27, 1883: CO 323/354.

76. Tupper to Macdonald, Oct. 31, 1883, quoted in Glazebrook, Canadian Ex-ternal Relations, 164.

77. Kimberley to the Governors of the Australian Colonies, circular, April 19, 1872, printed in PP, 1872, XLII, no. C-576, 7.

78. SP, 1880, no. 26. See also Foreign Office to Colonial Office, Feb. 27, 1879: CO 42/758.

79. Minute by Herbert, April 17, 1876, on Foreign Office to Colonial Office, March 9, 1876: CO 323/328.

80. Minute by Pauncefote, April 18, 1876, on ibid.

81. Colonial Office to Foreign Office, May 17, 1876: CO 323/328.

82. Foreign Office to Colonial Office, June 3, 1876: ibid.

83. Minute by Herbert, July 1, 1876, on ibid. His remarks were sent to the For-eign Office in a dispatch of July 6, 1876: CO 323/328.

84. Foreign Office to Colonial Office, Dec. 11, 1876: ibid.

85. Colonial Office to Foreign Office, Jan. 3, 1877: CO 323/328.

86. Foreign Office to Colonial Office, Jan. 19, 1877: CO 323/333.

87. Colonial Office to Foreign Office, Jan. 26, 1877: ibid.

88. Carnarvon to Governors of the Colonies, circular, Feb. 5, 1877: ibid.

89. Foreign Office to Colonial Office, Dec. 4, 1877: ibid.

90. Foreign Office to Colonial Office, immediate, March 8, 1877: ibid.

91. Carnarvon to Agents-General of the Colonies and Sir John Rose, circular, March 14, 1877: ibid.; Carnarvon to Governors of the Colonies, circular, March 15, 1877: CO 323/337.

92. Colonial Office to Foreign Office, March 15, 1877: CO 323/333.

93. Foreign Office to Colonial Office, June 13, 1877: ibid.

94. Minute by Malcolm, June 22, 1877, on ibid.

95. Minute by Herbert, June 30, 1877, on ibid.

96. Colonial Office to Foreign Office, July 24, 1877: CO 323/333.

97. Foreign Office to Colonial Office, Aug. 6, 1877: ibid.

98. Colonial Office to Foreign Office, Aug. 14, 1877: ibid.

99. Draft Article for the Admission of the Colonies to Commercial Treaties, enclosed in Foreign Office to Colonial Office, Jan. 11, 1878: CO 323/337.
The Colonial Office concurred in this form of the article in a letter to the Foreign Office dated Jan. 19, 1878: ibid., and it was transmitted to the colonies in a circular from Lord Carnarvon, Jan. 22, 1878: ibid. In the circular the explanation was given that the clause had been approved for insertion in all future treaties of commerce.
Todd, Parliamentary Government, 265-8, states that the colonial article was devised to meet the needs of the Italian and French treaty negotiations of December, 1877, and January, 1878. Keith, Responsible Government, III, 1108-9, closely follows Todd's version of the adoption of the clause. The most recent writer on the treaty system of the British Empire, R. B. Stewart, puts the date of the formulation of the colonial article at July, 1880 (Stewart, Treaty Relations, 96-101). This is an understandable error, arising from the inconsistency with which the article was applied in the years immed-

iately after 1878 (see above, 236-8). The account provided in this chapter will have made clear that the clause originated in a suggestion put forward by Herbert in April, 1876, and that it already possessed a long history before the resumption of the Italian and French discussions in December, 1877.

100. Foreign Office to Colonial Office, pressing, May 4, 1878: CO 323/337.

101. Minute by Malcolm, May 8, 1878, on ibid.

102. Colonial Office to Foreign Office, immediate, May 17, 1878: CO 323/337.

103. Foreign Office to Colonial Office, May 27, 1878: ibid.

104. Carnarvon to Governors of the Colonies, circular, June 5, 1878: ibid.

105. Colonial Office to Foreign Office, March 8, 1880: ibid.

106. Foreign Office to Colonial Office, July 26, 1880: CO 323/345.
The colonies were circularized again on Aug. 5, 1880: ibid. Printed in SP, 1883, no. 89, 13.

107. Report of the Privy Council of Canada, Oct. 28, 1880, enclosed in Lorne to Kimberley, no. 304, Oct. 30, 1880: CO 42/763. Printed in SP, 1883, no. 89, 20.
Canada was the only colony which asked for exemption.

108. Foreign Office to Colonial Office, Jan. 26, 1881: CO 323/349.
The notes exchanged between the British and Rumanian governments about the exclusion of Canada from the treaty are in PP, 1881, XCIX, no. C-2765; and in SP, 1883, no. 89, 20-2.

109. Foreign Office to Colonial Office, March 5, 1880: CO 323/345.

110. Minute by Herbert, March 12, 1880, on ibid.

111. Colonial Office to Foreign Office, April 2, 1880: CO 323/345.

112. Foreign Office to Colonial Office, April 13, 1880: ibid.

113. Kimberley to Governors of the Responsible Government Colonies, circular, July 22, 1880: ibid. Printed in SP, 1883, no. 89, 7-8.
Stewart states that this circular of July 22, 1880, in which the promise was made to the colonies that they would not be bound by future British commercial treaties unless it was their wish, marks the change of policy in this matter (Stewart, Treaty Rela-

tions, 97-9). It will be obvious, however, that the dispatch simply re-enunciated a principle laid down in Carnarvon's earlier circular of Jan. 22, 1878.

114. Galt to Colonial Office, Sept. 10, 1880; Report of the Privy Council of Canada, Oct. 28, 1880, enclosed in Lorne to Kimberley, no. 303, Oct. 30, 1880 (printed in SP, 1883, no. 89, 8); and Colonial Office to Foreign Office, Nov. 20, 1880: CO 42/763.

115. Foreign Office to Colonial Office, confidential, April 6, 1881: CO 323/349. The correspondence with the British Minister in Belgrade on this subject is given in SP, 1883, no. 89, 8-10.

116. Keith says that the first treaty to include the colonial clause was one with Montenegro, signed in January, 1882 (Keith, Responsible Government, III, 1109). The Ecuador agreement was signed in October, 1880, and most of the colonies had indicated their views on it by the end of 1882. The Foreign Office was given a definitive statement of the colonial response towards it a month before a similar statement could be prepared about the Montenegro instrument.

117. Kimberley to Governors of the Responsible Government Colonies, circular, July 8, 1881: CO 323/349. Printed in SP, 1883, no. 89, 22.

118. Kimberley to Lorne, general, Oct. 14, 1882: CO 323/349. Printed in SP, 1883, no. 89, 28.

119. Report of the Privy Council of Canada, Nov. 10, 1882, enclosed in Officer Administering the Government of Canada to Kimberley, no. 77, Nov. 16, 1882: CO 42/772. Printed in SP, 1883, no. 89, 28-9.

120. Colonial Office to Foreign Office, April 27, 1883: CO 323/349.

121. Kimberley to Governors of the Responsible Government Colonies, circular, June 14, 1882: CO 323/352. Printed in SP, 1883, no. 89, 32.

122. Derby to Lorne, general, Feb. 8, 1883: CO 323/352. Printed in SP, 1883, no. 89, 37.

123. Report of the Privy Council of Canada, March 1, 1883, enclosed in Lorne to Derby, no. 48, March 3, 1883: CO 42/774 (printed in SP, 1883, no. 89, 37), and Colonial Office to Foreign Office, May 16, 1883: CO 323/352.

124. Foreign Office to Colonial Office, confidential, July 30, 1881; Kimberley to Governors of the Responsible Government Colonies, circular, Aug. 20, 1881: CO 323/349; and Report of the Privy Council of Canada, July 24, 1882, enclosed in Lorne

to Kimberley, no. 216, July 29, 1882: CO 42/772. The communications relating to this treaty are printed in SP, 1883, no. 89, 30-2. It was some time before the instrument was concluded.

125. Foreign Office to Colonial Office, July 17, 1883; Derby to Governors of the Responsible Government Colonies, circular, July 21, 1883: CO 323/355; and Report of the Privy Council of Canada, Sept. 15, 1883, enclosed in Lorne to Derby, no. 252, Sept. 18, 1883: CO 42/774.

126. Foreign Office to Colonial Office, July 21, 1881; Kimberley to Lorne, general, Aug. 2, 1881; Colonial Office to Foreign Office, Aug. 30, 1881: CO 323/349. The correspondence is printed in SP, 1883, no. 89, 29-30.

In 1886 Canada asked that conventions which the United Kingdom had signed with Paraguay and San Salvador be not made applicable to her, while in 1887 she acceded to a British commercial treaty with Uruguay (Reports of the Privy Council of Canada, Dec. 27, 1886, enclosed in Lansdowne to Stanhope, nos. 311 and 312, Dec. 30, 1886: CO 42/785, and Report of the Privy Council of Canada, Dec. 27, 1886, enclosed in Lansdowne to Stanhope, no. 4, Jan. 4, 1887: CO 42/790; Foreign Office to Colonial Office, Jan. 29, 1887 (3 dispatches): CO 323/369). These treaties concluded the list of Imperial commercial instruments upon which Canadian action was taken, until the end of the year 1887.

127. Galt to Colonial Office, June 11, 1880: CO 42/764.

Canada later asked that her advice be taken before any Imperial extradition treaties were applied to her (Colonial Office to Foreign Office, May 12, 1885: CO 323/361).

128. Minute by Herbert, June 16, 1880, on Galt to Colonial Office, June 11, 1880: CO 42/764.

129. Colonial Office to Foreign Office, June 24, 1880: CO 42/764.

130. Foreign Office to Colonial Office, June 28, 1880: CO 323/345.

131. Report of the Privy Council of Canada, March 26, 1881, enclosed in Lorne to Kimberley, confidential, March 28, 1881: CO 42/766. Printed in SP, 1883, no. 89, 13.

132. Minute by Bramston, April 26, 1881, on Lorne to Kimberley, confidential, March 28, 1881: CO 42/766.

133. Foreign Office to Colonial Office, May 21, 1881: CO 42/769.

Precisely this point had been settled in the case of Smiles v. Belford ([1876] 23 Gr. 590, 1 O.A.R. 436) where the Ontario Court of Appeal held that the word "exclusive" referred to the jurisdiction of the Dominion vis-à-vis the provinces and did not imply any diminution of the sovereign authority of the Imperial Parliament. For an excellent discussion of this subject see A. H. F. Lefroy, The Law of Legislative Power in Canada (Toronto, 1897-8) 208-31.

134. Minute by Herbert, July 21, 1881, on Foreign Office to Colonial Office, May 21, 1881: CO 42/769.

135. Minute by Kimberley, July 22, 1881, on ibid.

136. Colonial Office to Foreign Office, Aug. 9, 1881: CO 42/769.

137. Galt to Colonial Office, Nov. 12, 1881: CO 42/768. Printed in SP, 1883, no. 89, 10.

138. Foreign Office to Colonial Office, Nov. 28, 1881: CO 42/769.

139. Minute by Herbert, Dec. 6, 1881, on ibid.

140. Minute by Courtney, Dec. 7, 1881, on ibid.

141. Foreign Office to Colonial Office, Feb. 22, 1882: CO 42/773. Some of the correspondence relating to this episode is printed in SP, 1883, no. 89, 11-12.

142. See Appendix C, "A Note on the Later Development of Canadian Fiscal Autonomy," 324-5, for a brief account of the eventual solution of this problem.

CHAPTER EIGHT

A CANADIAN "RESIDENT MINISTER" IN GREAT BRITAIN

"Our relations to Canada have been and are political rather than colonial." Lord
Carnarvon, 1870

THE CHANGING CHARACTER of the relations between Great Britain and Canada in the
years after Confederation is nowhere better typified than in the transformation of the post
of resident Canadian agent in London. Beginning as a specialized office dealing exclusively with emigration promotion, the Canadian mission to England exercised, for a decade after the creation of the Dominion, only insignificant political responsibilities. The
latter function, the proper concern of a resident representative, was undertaken during
the period by an unofficial agent who was linked closely by personal ties with the Macdonald Cabinet. Later when a combination of circumstances rendered it desirable to
set up a more conventional establishment in the United Kingdom, the agency was re-
organized under a prominent Canadian who was given a unique quasi-diplomatic relationship with the Imperial Government. Thus the first colonial High Commissionership
was founded in London in 1880, inaugurating a new pattern of association within the British Empire. Through the personalities and influence of the later holders of the office,
and in response to the political growth of the autonomous colonies, the post became invested with an importance far beyond even that which its architects had anticipated.

Inevitably the appointment of a resident Canadian representative in the United
Kingdom modified the old channel of communication between Ottawa and London. The
Governor-General, as the Imperial Government's agent in Canada, was, of course, the
officer chiefly affected by the new arrangement. At first an uneasy compromise was
maintained by keeping the two channels open; by supplying the Governor-General with
all the correspondence relating to the tasks entrusted to the High Commissioner by the
Canadian Government. As the Governor-General's status changed, however, and he
emerged as a Viceroy heading a constitutional monarchy, it became imperative that he
relinquish the role of representing the Imperial Government in Canada. The administrative channel which had existed between Rideau Hall and Downing Street was thus permitted to become obstructed through time and neglect. The High Commissioner in London increasingly assumed the responsibility of interpreting the wishes of the Government
of Canada to the United Kingdom. In 1879, when it had asked the Imperial Government to receive an agent in London, the Macdonald Ministry had stated that the relations between Great Britain and her most important Colony were, in effect, diplomatic
in character. This conception the British authorities refused to accept, thus denying the
new agent a position in the Corps Diplomatique. In time, however, it became apparent that they had withheld merely the shadow, and not the substance, of diplomatic recognition. From the beginning the Canadian High Commissioner performed duties that

were of a diplomatic nature; a fact which was soon realized by discerning students of the imperial relationship. Sir Frederic Rogers (Lord Blachford), writing in 1885, noted this development with some satisfaction, seeing in it a powerful argument against schemes for imperial consolidation.

> [The] actual position [of the Agents-General] is one which, originally viewed with some jealousy in Downing-street, has been of late cordially accepted and studiously raised in dignity and influence. Everything seems to be done and to be doing by the Imperial Government to give Agents-General, relatively to the Colonial Minister, a status analogous to that which is held by the representatives of foreign States of equal importance in relation to the Minister for Foreign Affairs. [1]

The appointment of a Canadian High Commissioner concerned two departments of the British Government, the Colonial Office and the Foreign Office. They spoke with one voice in refusing a diplomatic status for the new agent. The Colonial Office, although it saw the usefulness of the proposed arrangement and was not unsympathetic to the Canadian request that its agent assume a definite share in commercial negotiations, was adamant on the point of diplomatic recognition. This opinion the Foreign Office approved, although with less emphasis than might have been expected. In both departments the conviction that the diplomatic unity of the British Empire would be impaired by such a concession was too strongly held in 1880 to admit of any other decision. Even today, when the post of High Commissioner in London has become one of the most important diplomatic appointments at the disposal of the Canadian Government, the office does not enjoy strict ambassadorial rank. This status, impossible under the Empire, is still impossible under the Commonwealth. For the High Commissioner of Canada is not the representative of the head of a state but merely of the Canadian Government; he cannot both represent and be accredited to the same Sovereign. Thus in a relationship which is legally dominated by the common Crown, his position is unique. It is, however, not unfavourable, for it allows him, unhampered by the protocol of conventional diplomatic practice, to approach the British Government with the assurance of an intimate. He enters the Foreign Office, so to speak, by the staff door, while other representatives are forced to approach by the main entrance. As High Commissioner for Canada in London he undertakes the functions of an ambassador, while at the same time speaking to the British Government as a trusted friend who is not a foreign representative. It is a de facto recognition of status which would have been immensely appreciated by Macdonald and the other founders of the office seventy years ago.

The earliest Canadian representatives abroad were stationed in the United Kingdom, where they were charged with the promotion and supervision of emigration from the British Isles to Canada. In 1866 the old Province of Canada appointed William Dixon as emigration agent in Liverpool, and in 1868 he was transferred to London, to head

---

1. For references to chapter VIII see pages 270-5.

a Dominion Agency of Immigration. In succeeding years branches of the Agency were established in European countries and in other port cities in the United Kingdom. Dixon's office in London became a general headquarters for Canadians in Great Britain, and the emigration agents located around the British Isles soon gained a semi-consular status in representing Canadian interests in the mother country. Besides vigorously advertising Canada as a home for emigrants, these officers attempted to foster English trade with Canada by supplying commercial information to merchants and manufacturers on both sides of the Atlantic. The origins of the existing organization of Canadian Trade Commissioners can be found in these efforts, although agents with specifically commercial functions were not appointed until 1886.[2]

With one exception there was, however, no attempt during this period by the Canadian Government to establish an office of Agent-General, such as had been created by the Australian colonies.[3] On Dixon's death in 1874 the Mackenzie Government took the injudicious step of appointing a member of the British Parliament, Edward Jenkins,[4] as General Resident Agent and Superintendent of Colonization for the Dominion in London.[5] Jenkins was not unknown in Canada, where he had lived for some years, and where his father was a prominent Presbyterian minister in Montreal. His appointment as Agent-General was made privately (and apparently rather frivolously) by Mackenzie, without consulting his Cabinet or the Governor-General.[6] The new title seemed to suggest a wider range of duties for the Canadian representative: a supposition which inspired in the Colonial Office some concern. Carnarvon noted that Jenkins's credentials were "inconveniently vague," and confessed that he did not know "what are the recognized functions of a Canadian 'agent' if indeed there are any."[7] He directed a confidential enquiry to the Governor-General about the responsibilities of the new officer. The Canadian Cabinet replied that Jenkins was to occupy himself chiefly with emigration matters and the establishment of a centre for Canadians visiting Great Britain. If any specific political duties were intrusted to him (which was unlikely) the Colonial Office would be informed of their nature. The Privy Council went on to state that the establishment of a general agency in London was to be regarded as an experiment, which would be "continued, extended or restricted" as experience determined.[8]

Under Jenkins's leadership, the experiment of an agency in London proved signally unsuccessful. Soon after his appointment Jenkins took occasion to ask several provocative questions on Canadian subjects in the House of Commons.[9] The Colonial Office expressed considerable displeasure over this mode of proceeding. Not only was it highly irregular, but it gave an impression that in seeking the information Jenkins was representing the Government of Canada. Holland remarked that Jenkins could hardly expect to receive confidential treatment from the Office if he persisted in such an anomalous course.[10] Herbert agreed, recommending a private note to Lord Dufferin to have Jenkins disciplined.

I agree in ... Sir H. Holland's opinion that much inconvenience may arise from an Agent General acting independently of this Department in Parliament. The question which Mr. Jenkins now asks should, if the present Dominion Ministers require an answer to it, be asked confidentially by the Governor General. It would be well if it were explained to Mr. Jenkins (through Canada or otherwise) that if the mode of transacting business between the two Governments which has hitherto been followed is departed from, it may become very difficult (with every desire to show him consideration) for this Department to communicate with him as freely as with an Agent General who does the business of his Government in the usual confidential manner. [11]

It is apparent that Jenkins was representing nobody but himself in these enquiries. Had he persisted in playing simultaneously the hardly compatible roles of member of Parliament and Canadian Agent, his usefulness to the Mackenzie Government in dealing with the Colonial Office would have been brought to an end. As it was, he occupied the Agent's post for only two years, for a disagreement with the Minister of Agriculture (to whose Department the office was attached) caused his resignation early in 1876. [12] Thus the experiment of a general Canadian agency in London proved a disappointment. The establishment was consequently reduced in size and placed under a chief clerk in the Canadian civil service. [13] The Colonial Office regretted this step, being very conscious of the burden of correspondence and enquiries which a general agency took from its shoulders. It was realized that Jenkins had been indiscreet in his public utterances and insubordinate to the responsible Canadian minister but it was hoped, nevertheless, that his shortcomings would not jeopardize the project of a permanent Canadian organization in Great Britain. [14]

The principal reason why the Canadian Government did not appoint an Agent-General in the United Kingdom during the seventies lay in the fact that it already had an extremely capable unofficial representative in London. Sir John Rose (he was knighted in January, 1870), the second Minister of Finance of the Dominion, had resigned from his post in the autumn of 1869 to come to London as a partner in a firm of investment bankers. His financial and diplomatic experience, his friendship with English public men of all parties, and particularly his intimate relations with Sir John Macdonald, made him an ideal person to represent Canadian interests in England. At his own request Rose had not been appointed a formal Canadian agent, but had simply been "accredited to Her Majesty's Government as a gentleman possessing the confidence of the Canadian Government with whom Her Majesty's Government may properly communicate on Canadian affairs." [15] Rose soon developed a close and respected connection with the Colonial Office. [16] During the next decade he carried out services which were of incalculable benefit to Canada in her relations with the other countries of the "North Atlantic triangle." He was an important intermediary in arranging the transfer of Rupert's Land from the Hudson's Bay Company in 1869-70; he rendered extremely valuable assistance to Anglo-American accord by preparing the way for the negotiations which led to the Treaty of Washington in 1871; he superintended the raising of many Canadian loans on the London money market and he promoted Canadian interests in emigration and commercial matters. [17] Working to a great extent in the half-light that must inevitably surround the man of business who is also a diplomat, and keeping himself scrupulously aloof from British party politics, Rose became a trusted adviser to successive Colonial Secretaries on all Canadian topics. The Mackenzie Government retained his services, giving him in 1875 the title of "Financial Commissioner for the Dominion of Canada." Rose was the real predecessor of the first High Commissioner, because, more than any other Canadian representative of the period, he acted as a quasi-diplomatic agent of Canada in Great Britain. It is also true that by functioning so usefully as a resident agent in the United Kingdom, Rose convinced Macdonald and his second Ministry that the appointment of a full-time minister in London would be of decided advantage.[18]

When Macdonald returned to power in 1878 he was not slow to bring this proposal before the attention of the British Government. In the summer of 1879 the Prime Minister and three of his associates, Sir A. T. Galt, Sir Charles Tupper, and Sir Leonard Tilley, journeyed to London in an endeavour to obtain a guarantee for a railway loan from the Beaconsfield Administration. They met with no success in this venture, but their visit was not entirely fruitless. Before they sailed for home they left at the Colonial Office, late in August, a memorandum containing their views on the subject of a resident Canadian agent in the United Kingdom. This memorandum, one of the important state papers in the development of Canadian autonomy in external affairs, although signed jointly by Macdonald, Tilley, and Tupper, bore the strong stamp of Macdonald's convictions. The desire for a Canadian agent which the paper demonstrated was based on a premise of which Macdonald had never lost sight: that British North America, by the act of federation, had become a distinctive and superior form of colony. Here was the "auxiliary Kingdom" of 1867 given full and dynamic expression: "Canada has ceased to occupy the position of an ordinary possession of the Crown. She exists in the form of a powerful Central Government, having already no less than seven subordinate local executive and legislative systems, soon to be largely augmented by the development of the vast regions lying between Lake Superior and the Rocky Mountains."[19] The Dominion, the document continued, had maintained relations of the most delicate nature with the United States ever since 1867, and, in addition, had carried out the occupation of vast territories in western North America. In this work Canada had acted as a trustee for the Empire and had sought to administer her charge for the benefit of all the British people. She had accomplished these difficult tasks by means of purely formal communication with the British Government, either through the Governor-General, or directly with the Colonial Office. On some occasions this communication had been supplemented by visits of members of the Canadian Cabinet to England. Intercourse of this manner was at best both inefficient and inadequate. Indeed the Canadian Ministers were convinced that actual dangers existed in the consultative machinery of the present imperial relationship.

It appears to the Canadian Government eminently desirable to provide for the fullest and most frank interchange of views with Her Majesty's Government, and for the thorough appreciation of the policy of Canada on all points of general interest. Otherwise there appears to be danger of a feeling growing up of indifference if not of actual antagonism and irritation, upon both sides. The idea must be avoided

that the connection of Canada with the British Empire is only temporary and un-
abiding, instead of being designed to strengthen and confirm the maintenance of
British influence and power.[20]

In 1879 there were additional reasons to suggest that the current means of communication had outlived their usefulness. For instance, the paper remarked, the following subjects were under consideration by the English and Canadian Governments at
the present time: the Pacific Railway, the negotiation of treaties of commerce with
France and Spain, the military defence of Canada, the construction of a graving dock
at Esquimalt, and the extension of the fishery and commercial clauses of the Treaty of
Washington. All these topics required personal consultation between Canadian Ministers and the appropriate departments in Whitehall, yet it would be a serious inconvenience to the administration of Canada if the Ministers concerned had to absent themselves for long periods from the Dominion. The negotiation of trade treaties was a continuing problem which received inadequate attention under the mechanism of the old
relationship. Because of a variety of circumstances it was becoming exceedingly difficult for Great Britain to promote Canada's commercial interests. The Dominion at
the moment needed trade conventions, based on her own requirements, with several
countries; these could be arranged expeditiously and without misunderstandings with foreign powers, if she were granted the authority to negotiate them. Since 1878 the colonies had been given the right to express their adherence to pending British commercial
treaties, but information about these conventions was often much delayed in reaching
the Canadian capital.

The document concluded, therefore, by urging the British Government to receive
a permanent official representative from Canada, who would be prepared to voice the
views of the Canadian Administration, and who could be accredited to foreign courts
for commercial negotiations. This representative would also be "specially entrusted with
the general supervision of all the political, material, and financial interests of Canada
in England, subject to instructions from his Government." He would be a person chosen
from the Canadian Privy Council and provided by the Government with all the assistance
necessary to fulfil these responsible duties. A representative of this character would require a more dignified title than "Agent-General" and the memorandum therefore suggested that he be designated "Resident Minister," or some similar name. Attaching
much importance to this matter, the Canadian Government trusted that the United Kingdom would "see no insuperable difficulty in giving the Canadian representative a quasi-
diplomatic position at the Court of St. James, with the social advantages of such a rank
and position."[21]

The Colonial Office response to this first request for a permanent Canadian agent
in London was characteristic of the attitude which the Office assumed throughout the
discussions on the subject. The appointment of a representative from the Dominion
would be of great advantage in the work of the Department. The difficult question of
affording the agent quasi-diplomatic status was, however, another matter. It would have
to be referred to the Foreign Office together with the suggestion that the Canadian agent

be called a "Resident Minister," which, to some members of the Office, was a title "suggestive of the Representative of a Foreign Power."[22] Herbert, in directing that the memorandum be transmitted to the Foreign Office, drafted a covering letter which revealed that he was in substantial accord with the proposal for a Canadian agent in London. His only reservation concerned the request for diplomatic status.

[The Foreign Office might be told] that there would be many advantages in having resident here a Canadian gentleman of high standing enjoying the confidence of the Dominion Government and competent to conduct on its behalf the important and delicate negotiations which frequently arise. But that Sir M. Hicks Beach does not see how it would be possible to assign to such representative the diplomatic position [and] title wh. the Minister of a [foreign] state wd. enjoy though he would be glad if some rule could be laid down under wh. the social advantages to wh. the minute points could be accorded to him.[23]

The Permanent Under-Secretary took an unusually violent objection (for Herbert) to the suggested title of "Resident Minister" for the new agent. This proposal was much "less admissible" than the other points the memorandum raised. As a designation it was open to great misapprehension; "Privy Councillor in London" or "Dominion Commissioner" would be preferable, although he admitted it was difficult to find a precise name to describe the post. The incident revealed Herbert's strong belief in the essential unity of the British Empire, whether regarded from a legal, constitutional, or diplomatic aspect.[24] Hicks Beach approved Herbert's minute but suggested that the matter should go before the Cabinet.[25]

The Canadian proposal was dealt with in the Foreign Office by Sir Julian Pauncefote, who had left the Colonial Office three years earlier to become the Legal Assistant Under-Secretary in the other Department. His experience with the colonial point of view enabled Pauncefote to fall in easily with Herbert's observations that the presence of a trusted agent of the Canadian Government in Great Britain would be useful. Like Herbert also, he felt a distaste for the proposal of diplomatic status for the new officer.[26] Lord Salisbury, the Foreign Secretary, curtly approved these opinions, which were returned to the Colonial Office for the purposes of the later discussion with Canada. The Foreign Office communication also stated that it would be impossible, at this stage, to grant the Canadian agent any regular position in forthcoming commercial negotiations in which Canada might be interested. The prospect of independent Canadian participation was not to be ruled out, but the Department reserved to itself the right to decide the extent of Canadian activity in each particular case.[27] The core of the Canadian representations had thus been accepted by the two departments of the Imperial Government most chiefly concerned, although with important qualifications. It now remained for the Canadian Cabinet to take up the specific objections advanced by the Colonial Office to the plan of a permanent representative in England.

In a dispatch dated November 1, 1879, the Secretary of State provided an official reply to the memorandum by the Canadian Ministers. Hicks Beach welcomed the proposals which the paper contained and was enthusiastic in listing the advantages of oral and personal communication with an agent over the old method of triangular correspondence. But (and it was a vital hesitation) "looking ... to the position of Canada as an integral portion of the empire, the relations of such a person with Her Majesty's Government would not be correctly defined as being of a diplomatic character, and while Her Majesty's Government would readily accord to him a status in every way worthy of his important functions, his position would necessarily be more analagous to that of an officer in the home service, than to that of a Minister at a Foreign Court."[28] The Canadian agent would be expected to communicate in the majority of instances with the Colonial Office although it would be the responsibility of the Foreign Secretary to decide on the precise capacity in which his services could be used in commercial discussions with foreign powers. The agent might, for instance, be requested to remain in London to advise Her Majesty's Government on Canadian interests, or he might be asked to go abroad in order to assist British representatives in foreign negotiations. The title for the new representative was a subject over which the Colonial Office was anxious there should be no misunderstanding. It was therefore proposed that he be called "Dominion" or "Canadian Commissioner." These forms would reveal to the public the importance of his work but would have the advantage of affording no suggestion of diplomatic status. Significantly the Colonial Office dispatch made no reference to the alleged inadequacy of the existing means of intra-imperial communication.

The Department's views on the subject of a Canadian agent were considered by the Dominion Cabinet late in December. In a resulting dispatch to Whitehall the Privy Council expressed satisfaction over the manner in which its request had been received by the Imperial authorities. The Ministers were aware that the Dominion could not maintain relations of a strictly diplomatic character with foreign countries because of the fact that she was still an integral part of the Empire. But in their view Canada's position vis-à-vis Great Britain was of a different character.

> But they respectfully submit that while this is true as respects Foreign Nations it does not accurately represent the actual state of facts in regard to the United Kingdom. Her Majesty's Government is unquestionably the Supreme governing power of the Empire but, under the British North America Act, self-governing powers have been conferred upon Canada in many most important respects, and Her Majesty's Government may on these points be more correctly defined as representing the United Kingdom than the Empire at large.[29]

In all matters of domestic concern Great Britain had transferred to Canada an independent control. This meant that the settlement of questions affecting these topics could only be arranged through mutual consent. In such proceedings Her Majesty's Government represented Great Britain per se, while the Canadian Government acted solely in response to the interests of Canada. These circumstances produced, in effect, a relationship that was of a quasi-diplomatic character.

The Canadian estimate of the imperial relationship in 1879 was substantially correct when applied to most subjects over which power was vested in the Canadian Parliament by the British North America Act and its amendments. Certainly in matters of imperial significance like the determination of fiscal policy, the construction of public works, and the organization and settlement of the Western territories, Canadian legislative authority was undisputed. But there were other subjects, many of them enumerated in the British North America Act, over which Canadian control was not absolute. For instance the regulation of merchant shipping was vested in the Canadian Parliament by virtue of the British North America Act, [30] but this did not mean that the Imperial Parliament had abdicated its right to legislate for the Colony's merchant shipping. The lack of extraterritorial authority by the Canadian Government rendered Imperial participation in the field of merchant shipping quite indispensable. Other topics, such as copyright, extradition, naturalization, and the preservation of neutrality were subject to legislation from both the Imperial and Canadian Parliaments. [31] On all these matters, which can be described as imperial in scope, it was erroneous to suggest that Canada and Great Britain occupied towards each other the position of sovereign countries. The Colonial Office would have been quite justified in refusing to accept this rather misleading definition of the connection between Great Britain and Canada in 1880. The Canadian statement was a forecast, and a remarkably accurate one, of the relations which were to be established between Great Britain and Canada after the passage of the Statute of Westminster. It was a vivid anticipation of conditions in the 1930's, but it was hardly valid fifty years earlier.

The Canadian Cabinet went on to discuss the subject of the proposed agent's interest in commercial negotiations. Here they were at pains to point out that they did not desire an independent status for their negotiator; on the contrary they were perfectly aware that such success as they had obtained in commercial discussions had resulted from the support and influence provided by the British diplomatic service. They had sought an official sanction for their representative simply to reveal to foreign powers the Colony's separate identity in commercial matters. They were, in fact, content to leave the definition of the Canadian agent's position to the Foreign Office, asking only that he be associated with a British Minister in negotiations whenever his presence was considered of value. The Privy Council Report ended by reaffirming Macdonald's conviction that the proposed officer would have duties more closely resembling those undertaken by the diplomatic rather than the home service. It was declared, however, that Canada would leave the question of his precise status to the determination of the Imperial Government. The Cabinet merely ventured to hope that he would be given privileges and honours worthy of his responsible functions. There was a reminder here that the delegates from British North America who had attended conferences in London in 1865 and 1866 had been granted an informal position in the Corps Diplomatique, with precedence immediately behind foreign ministers. On the question of title the Privy Council favoured the designation, "High Commissioner of Canada in London." The word "commissioner" was often applied to persons engaged in special public services of a comparatively minor importance, and the Government felt that the distinctive status of its agent entitled him to a more signal mark of respect. Incidentally this title would prove of great value to the agent in his dealings with foreign governments. [32]

Before the Colonial Office had received this dispatch, it was learned that the Macdonald Government proposed to appoint Sir Alexander Galt as Canada's first permanent representative in London. In this selection there was much justification, for there was no one in the Dominion who had been more active than Galt in the promotion of Canadian external trade. In addition his missions to Spain and France in 1878 and 1879, in an endeavour to obtain commercial concessions, had provided Galt with unique training (for a Canadian) in the techniques of international bargaining. In a very real sense the former Minister of Finance had filled roles which gave him a claim to the title of the Dominion's most experienced diplomat. In 1880 Galt was a widely known figure in Canada, respected for his independence of mind, trusted by Macdonald for his financial ability, and familiar with every aspect of the Canadian economy. He was, therefore, an obvious and desirable choice to establish a Canadian general agency in England.

The Colonial Office studied these additional observations of the Canadian Government with less sympathy than had been shown to Macdonald's original request. Although they were reticent in their comments on the proposal, it is possible to surmise that the heads of the Office did not take kindly to the references to the "quasi-diplomatic" character of the relations between Great Britain and Canada. Bramston described the Privy Council Minute as "very grandiloquent" and thought it simply meant that the Government wished to have Galt fully accredited to Great Britain immediately, in order that the appointment might be made before the statute creating the position was passed. [33] Herbert thought (and the source of his information was possibly Rose) that Galt's accession to the post was to be connected with some special request made to the British Government by Canada.

> This arrangement, which is based in a great degree of personal-political considerations, and may probably be reversed on a change of Government in Canada, will, I fear, be of little value, and may possibly prove mischievous.
>
> I do not however think we can with advantage criticize closely, or object to, this Report, except that I doubt very much whether the title "High Commissioner" is permissible to any functionary whose office is not specially created by Letters Patent under the Great Seal.
>
> "Special Commissioner" is quite fine enough for Sir A. Galt. [34]

The Permanent Under-Secretary recommended that the objections he entertained to the designation of "High Commissioner" should be referred to the Foreign Office for consideration, and that Lord Lorne should be instructed not to allow the title to be used in Canada until the Imperial Government had come to a decision on the matter. On this course of proceeding he was overruled by the Secretary of State, who thought that the Foreign Office should be simply asked whether it approved the form, "High Commissioner," without being given the benefit of Herbert's specific objections to the term. If the other Department rejected the title he agreed with Herbert that "Special Commissioner" would be a suitable alternative. [35]

These references to another Department inevitably consumed time, which meant that the Office was soon subjected to a familiar style of pressure from Canada in the form of telegraphic requests for a decision. On January 23 the Governor-General cabled asking for an immediate answer regarding the status of the new agent, since it was intended that the subject should be mentioned in the Speech from the Throne at the opening of the Dominion Parliament early in February.[36] The Office ignored this telegram until a reply had been received from the Foreign Office. To Herbert's intense surprise that Department accepted without demur the proposed Canadian title.[37] In addition the Foreign Office letter stated that Lord Salisbury had no views on the question of precedence for the Canadian agent so long as his insertion into the Table of Precedence did not interfere with the standing of foreign representatives.[38] Herbert persisted in his opposition to the use of the term "High Commissioner" even after receiving the Foreign Office reply.

> The title "High Commissioner" may be sought by Sir Julius Vogel (who on hearing that a "Resident Minister" for Canada was in contemplation at once suggested to his Govt. that New Zealand should also have a Resident Minister) and by the other Australian Agents General, if given to Sir A. Galt, but as the F. O. do not object I do not know that we can further resist: though I still have doubts whether there can properly be a High Commissioner not commissioned under the Great Seal.[39]

He directed that the Governor-General be informed that the Office favoured the use of the term "Special Commissioner" to describe the Canadian agent and would insist on it unless the Canadian Ministers attached great importance to their own proposal.[40] The answer might have been expected: the Cabinet did not like "Special Commissioner"; the Prime Minister strongly recommended the term "Resident Minister"; and Lorne urged a thorough concession in the form of "Resident Minister and High Commissioner"![41] In the face of this unanimity the Colonial Office obviously had to give way. On the following day the answer was returned to Canada that Galt would be recognized as "High Commissioner," his appointment to be made under the Great Seal of Canada.[42]

That Macdonald and his colleagues had failed to modify their original conception of the quasi-diplomatic relationship existing between the United Kingdom and Canada was made abundantly clear in the debates on the Act creating the post of High Commissioner.[43] Macdonald, in introducing the bill, dwelt glowingly on the evidence it provided of the new status of Canada. It was necessary that Canada's representative in London should be accorded a quasi-diplomatic position; anything less would be inconsistent with the Dominion's role as an "auxiliary kingdom, if I may use the expression."[44] For the Prime Minister of the senior British Colony was jealous of that Colony's leadership and pride of place among the various dependencies of the Empire:

> We have preferred, instead of sending Sir Alexander T. Galt home as a mere agent, telling him to follow such instructions as might, from time to time, be sent to him,

to give him such a position that he can speak with greater authority than as a mere agent for a Crown Colony, or any other colony, whether it has representative institutions or not. I am proud to believe that the Dominion is assuming the position of an auxiliary kingdom of the Empire, and from our population and wealth and probable future, we have a right to say that we ought to be taken out of the category of mere dependencies, like the West India Islands, having Crown agents, and looking after their little interests at the beck of a Colonial Minister. I have no doubt that [hon. gentlemen are] aware, by experience, that the prestige that attaches to a Canadian Minister is no inconsiderable matter, and we desired to give our agent the full prestige of such a Minister. [45]

The Liberal party's qualms about appointing a protectionist like Galt to deal with a free trade British Government Macdonald brushed aside impatiently. It was obvious that the Opposition had no confidence in their country or they would not be attempting to jeopardize a step which would indubitably advance its interests abroad. The Bill passed with a comfortable Government majority, for it was plain that few Liberals possessed objections to the principle which it embodied. [46]

The question of precedence for the new High Commissioner was a very delicate subject. With magnificent understatement the Foreign Office pointed out that if he were given a place immediately behind the foreign ministers, he would have precedence over nearly everyone else in England, "which may lead to difficulties." [47] The Lord Chamberlain's Office was convinced that the Canadian delegates of 1865-6 had not been granted any formal precedence, in spite of the fact that on one occasion they were listed in the Court Circular following the Corps Diplomatique. It appeared that the delegates had been received by the Queen before an official reception, an expedient designed to avoid just this question of precedence. [48] Herbert also was inclined to the view that the agent could not be accorded precedence after ambassadors since this would place him before certain members of the Privy Council. Such a decision would be "objectionable in principle" and would certainly raise complaints from the gentlemen concerned. He felt that Galt's precedence as the holder of a G.C.M.G. was quite sufficient for the Canadian agent. [49] Hicks Beach suggested that Galt might be presented immediately after the Privy Councillors, and the Lord Chamberlain's Office agreed to this arrangement, provided that it remained a temporary and informal right. [50] Thus this question, which in the period under discussion was capable of arousing strong and irreconcilable sentiments, was laid at rest by an empirical expedient. [51]

At this stage, with the office of High Commissioner in London approved by the British Government, it is important to examine the functions which were to be exercised by the Canadian agent. Galt had his own view of the responsibilities of the new representative and Macdonald and the Government had theirs, with the result that the official Instructions issued to Galt represented a blending of two conceptions of the position. Galt's ideas were embodied in a memorandum[52] drawn up for the Prime Minister early in March, 1880, and in a speech[53] which he delivered later in the month at Montreal on the eve of his sailing for England. Galt stated in his address that the principal duties he would undertake as High Commissioner related to questions of finance, immigration, and diplomacy. It was in the last of these subjects that his primary interests lay, and he was moved by the enthusiasm of the moment to indulge in an inflated definition of the current state of the relations between Great Britain and Canada. He was on sounder ground when he emphasized the importance of discussion and consent in the joint Anglo-Canadian task of implementing a commercial policy for the Dominion.

> I think ... I am justified in saying that the passage of [the British North America] Act has placed us quoad commercial questions, although British subjects, in the same position as regards the Imperial Government, as we stand in towards any foreign Government. Whatever we do has to be made the subject of negotiation, and being the subject of negotiation, it is clearly a negotiation to which we must be an assenting party as well as the Imperial Government. ... [54]

In both his speech at Montreal and in his memorandum for Macdonald Galt was concerned to make one point absolutely clear. He felt very strongly that the impression should not be formed that the High Commissioner would be occupied solely by emigration and financial arrangements. It was vital that there should be several important questions under discussion between Canada and England when the new representative took up his duties. This would emphasize the political aspect of the mission, which to Galt was its chief feature. The High Commissioner went on to enumerate a group of subjects which he felt were of common interest to the Dominion and to the United Kingdom and which might form the basis of official conversations in the future. There was, for instance, the question of imperial defence, then arousing attention, in which Canada might assist Great Britain in a more positive manner. There was also the important topic of the settlement of the North West territories, in which both countries had complementary interests. Canada wished the area peopled and consolidated within the Dominion, while Great Britain required as keenly a safe source of foodstuffs for her industrial population and a home for her unemployed. A scheme of joint development seemed the obvious solution to both problems. Finally there was the vital question of the future relationship between the mother country and Canada. The events of the forties had reduced the imperial tie to a mere "common allegiance in exchange for the burden of defence,"[55] a relationship which could hardly endure any prolonged strain. In fact the separatist opinions of the sixties had been such a severe test for the connection that it would be unwise to allow it to be subjected to such an onslaught again. Happily anti-colonial sentiment was declining in Great Britain (here Galt commended the imperial views of Beaconsfield and the Conservative Government) and a good opportunity existed to attack the whole negative policy of free trade. The imperial tie might be reconstituted on a basis of preferential commercial arrangements within the Empire, utilizing the enormous and varying resources of all the dependencies. In time such an imperial customs union would help to bring about a substantial alliance between Great Britain and her colonies. To Galt the moment was now opportune to press these views on the Government and people of the United Kingdom. In addition, proposals of this magnitude coming from the newly appointed High Commissioner would serve to emphasize the importance in which Canada held the post. Thus the old policy of Imperial advocacy of free trade principles was to be replaced by an attempt on the part of the senior Colony to convert the mother country in economic matters.

There is no record of Macdonald's reply to the Galt memorandum, but it is significant that the official Instructions to the High Commissioner, although silent on the vision of a grand alliance between Great Britain and Canada, contained many of the specific proposals which Galt had advanced for increasing co-operation between the two countries.[56] The Instructions, dated May 20, 1880, reveal that the new agent was to be responsible to three departments of the Canadian Government in carrying out his duties. In financial affairs, where he would manage all transactions concerning loans and the public debt of Canada (thus superseding Messrs. Baring Brothers and Glyn, Mills and Currie, and taking over most of Rose's work) he was to communicate directly with the Minister of Finance at Ottawa. His emigration duties, in which he was to be assisted by the present staff in Great Britain, were to be conducted in consultation with the Department of Agriculture. On general matters he was to correspond with the Secretary of State. It was under this latter heading that the Instructions become quite detailed. He was required to lay before the British Government the Canadian point of view on all Imperial treaties of commerce extending to Canada. Where possible he was to seek release for the Dominion from existing engagements which limited the fiscal freedom of the Canadian Parliament. He was instructed to assist Great Britain in any foreign negotiations in which the interests of Canada might be affected and to continue his earlier commercial discussions with France and Spain whenever a favourable opportunity presented itself. More generally, he was to broach the subject of an Imperial Zollverein with the British Government and to keep Canada informed of the state of public opinion on that topic in the mother country.

The new High Commissioner's most important task, however, was to secure the development of the North West territory. Here, to put it bluntly, he was directed to endeavour to obtain British support in the immense project of opening the western plains for settlement. The Instructions remarked that the burden of this responsibility was too great for Canada to shoulder. In addition Great Britain was morally committed to aid the scheme because of the financial guarantee she had provided for the Rupert's Land transfer and because of the fact that she had borne most of the expense of quelling the Red River rebellion in 1870. Help from the mother country could be usefully employed in a number of ways, the Instructions continued. The costs of the North West Mounted Police might be shared, the expenses of the system of presents to the Indian tribes divided, the Pacific Railway subsidized, and a scheme of planned emigration set on foot. Here was the crux of the matter. If the United Kingdom would but contribute towards assisting emigrants from the mother country to the Canadian West, then the development of the whole region would be expedited. Such a scheme of systematic colonization might be organized on a joint basis, with Canada absorbing the costs of civil government and the preservation of law and order in the West, and the United Kingdom helping with the extension of railway communication and with assisted emigration. Just as in the case of the imperial preferential tariff no definite instructions regarding tactics were given the Canadian representative on this point; except that he was to test the metropolitan reaction. [57]

From this review it will be noted that the Instructions which Galt received resembled on many heads his own conception of the functions of the High Commissioner, and indeed were more specific than he had been on some aspects of the agent's work. To say, as one commentator has done, that the Instructions were but the "palest reflection" of the comprehensive scheme outlined in Galt's memorandum to Macdonald[58] is to under-estimate the scope of the former document. It is true that the alliance which Galt hoped would develop from a revision of the tariff structure of Great Britain was not mentioned in the Instructions, but that object had been put forward by Galt as the last step in a series of far-reaching changes. The success of the earlier part of the program was in no way dependent upon its achievement. Tariff adjustment was initially a more significant topic and the Instructions were clear in requiring the High Commissioner to press the proposal of an imperial trading unit upon the British Government. In his memorandum Galt favoured approaching the Imperial authorities for help with the construction of the Pacific Railway, and this suggestion was repeated with only slightly less precision in the Instructions. It is plain that the first High Commissioner strongly influenced Macdonald in the drafting of the Instructions for the new office and that the creation of the post was intended by both of them to herald important developments in Anglo-Canadian relations. Thus the "personal-political considerations," which Herbert had foreseen as irrevocably bound up with the post when it was originally mooted, were reflected in the instruments accompanying Galt to England. It is perhaps a matter of gratification that these considerations were soon subordinated to the more truly constructive (although less spectacular) aspects of the work of the Canadian agent in London.

The Instructions, important to the Colonial Office because they foreshadowed the policy of the Canadian Government on a number of topics, were received with interest in Whitehall. On the whole the Department felt that Galt had set himself a sizable task in proposing to induce Great Britain to support the colonization of the Canadian North West. Bramston minuted that if Canada's means were insufficient for the project, then it must wait. [59] Herbert, for his part, showed that he had come to accept more easily the pretensions of a Canadian High Commissioner since the time when the subject had been first disclosed to him. He noted on Lord Lorne's dispatch, "Looking to the importance of the questions raised in these instructions, and to the quasi-diplomatic position of the High Commissioner I would send a copy of the whole confidentially to the Foreign Office."[60]

The attitude of the Governor-General towards the establishment of a permanent Canadian agency in Great Britain also requires brief consideration. Lord Lorne showed a spirit of co-operation in facilitating Galt's appointment that is rather surprising. In a confidential letter to the Colonial Secretary he stated that he thought the reasons provided for the creation of a Canadian agency were valid, and that he hoped the British Government would accord Galt every consideration in endeavouring to secure suitable commercial agreements for the Dominion. It was extremely desirable that the differences of opinion between the United Kingdom and Canada on tariff policy should not prejudice the Colony's chances of obtaining as favourable terms as possible from foreign countries. In the long run the appointment of a Canadian agent to look after the Dominion's commercial requirements would probably turn out to be a blessing, for it would forestall complaints that British diplomats were not sufficiently mindful of the interests of the Colony. As well, it would mean that any consequences resulting from the success or failure of negotiations would, in the future, have to be borne exclusively by the Canadian representative abroad. While expressing a complete endorsement of the new departure, Lorne took the natural precaution of requiring his Ministers to submit to him copies of all the correspondence transmitted to the High Commissioner. [61]

Galt arrived in England in April, 1880. After the bold and imaginative program sketched in the Instructions, his tenure of office as High Commissioner proved somewhat of an anticlimax. In part the explanation for his virtual failure lay in his own characteristics and activities; in part in circumstances over which he had no control. While he was on the Atlantic on his way to assume office, the general elections of 1880 were held, with disastrous results for the Beaconsfield Ministry. This was a great disappointment, for Galt's background, his Canadian party connections, and his ideas on tariff preference made him much more sympathetic to the English Conservatives than to the Liberals. He made no secret of his liking for the Conservative party, joined the Carlton Club, and spoke freely in favour of the imperial federation movement. These proceedings naturally handicapped him in dealing with the Gladstone Government. At the Colonial Office he found Lord Kimberley distinctly cool when he attempted to broach his plans for imperial assistance in emigration. [62] Another difficulty existed in the fact that through the Governor-General all the official correspondence sent to Galt from Ottawa found its way into the Colonial Office. Galt was frustrated by this course of action, which, as he said, "shows Lord K. all my hand."[63] Thus it became impossible for him to carry out his intention of pressing his proposals on the British Government by degrees. There were other obstacles, social and financial, which prevented Galt from attaining the influential position which he felt should belong to the Canadian High Commissioner. In 1883, therefore, after three years spent in representing Canada in London, Galt resigned with little to show for the ambitious program he had once outlined to Macdonald. He had failed to obtain diplomatic status for the new Canadian envoy, he had made little headway in his discussions with France and Spain on commercial questions, he had been unable to interest the British Government in subsidizing emigration to North America, and he had been quite unsuccessful in attempting to convert the Imperial authorities to a system of tariff preferences. To the masterful Galt it was a disappointing experience which left him bitter towards the metropolitan outlook. Writing to Macdonald in 1881 he complained that until the Canadian agent was given diplomatic rank his work could not adequately be carried out. "I think you should insist now on your Representative being recognized as a member of the Corps Diplomatique. It is really the only proper definition of his rank, and the only way to ensure proper respect due. As a Colonial these "arrogant insulars" turn up their noses at us all."[64]

The diplomatic status which Galt so desired in 1881 was accorded later, practically and then formally, to his successors in the office of Canadian High Commissioner. The respect in which the position was held in the mother country steadily increased as the nineteenth century merged into the twentieth and Canada grew in political maturity and material importance. Although these factors were fundamental to the
development of the post it is also true that its enhancement was substantially aided by
the individuals who served as High Commissioners during the formative years before the
First World War. Sir Charles Tupper and Sir Donald Smith (Lord Strathcona), both men
of marked ability, distinction, and wealth, raised the prestige of the office to a level
of "ambassadorial importance." Tupper in particular, during his thirteen years in London (most of which period he was also a member of the Canadian Government), made
both Whitehall and Westminster plainly aware of the presence in Great Britain of a permanent representative of the senior Colony. His most outstanding achievements in the
office Tupper considered to be the concession of equal plenipotentiary powers which he
obtained from the Foreign Office in the Spanish trade negotiations of 1884, and his at-
tendance, on behalf of Canada, at the International Cable Conference in Paris. In addition Tupper's experience and dominant personality entitled him as of right to speak
as the recognized leader and doyen of the colonial Agents-General in England. Thus
in almost every discussion between the self-governing colonies and Great Britain in the
years between 1883 and 1896 it was possible to discover the commanding figure of Sir
Charles Tupper. He himself testified that "all important questions affecting the colonies were settled in the Canadian Office after discussion and presented to the Imperial Government afterwards."[65] Among the many illustrations of this course of proceeding was Tupper's direction of the movement for the denunciation of the Belgian
and German trade treaties in the nineties.

Throughout these years of vigorous activity and advocacy the usefulness of the
position of High Commissioner was ever more clearly recognized, especially by a Colonial Office which had good reason to be appreciative of its services. This tendency
brought its rewards, for within a decade after the first appointment had been made the
Canadian High Commissioner had achieved, whatever his constitutional position, a de
facto diplomatic status. Macdonald, describing the functions of the Canadian agent to
a new Governor-General, noted, almost in passing, this significant circumstance:

By degrees the colonial ministers [i.e. Colonial Secretaries] have begun to
treat the colonial representatives as diplomatic agents, rather than as subordinate
executive officers and to consult them as such.

Canada has found it advantageous on several occasions to have Sir Charles
Tupper dealt with as a quasi member of the corps diplomatique and I have no doubt
the colonial secretary has been assisted by his experience which Sir Charles gained
during his service as a cabinet minister in Canada. We do not desire, however,
to give him "a free hand" on any subject in discussion with the Imperial Government. He must take his instructions from the government here, as much as Sir
Julian Pauncefote from Lord Salisbury and cannot travel out of "the four corners"
of any minute on which his name is mentioned.[65]

It was plain that the premise underlying the Prime Minister's memorandum of 1879 had been abundantly borne out in yet another aspect of intra-imperial relations.

REFERENCES

1. Lord Blachford (Sir Frederic Rogers), in Pall Mall Gazette, Jan. 19, 1885, quoted in Blachford, Letters, 427.

2. The work of the Canadian emigration agents in this early period is described in H. G. Skilling, Canadian Representation Abroad: From Agency to Embassy (Toronto, 1945), 1-22.
    See also the annual reports of the Minister of Agriculture, under whom the agencies were administered, especially those for 1874, 1875, and 1878: SP, 1875, no. 40, iii-xix and 71-93; SP, 1876, no. 8, viii-xxii and 118-55; SP, 1879, no. 9, xxii-xxxvi and 131-5; Journals of the House of Commons (Canada), 1879, Appendix no. 1.

3. It is apparent that by 1870 most of the self-governing colonies had dispensed with the services of the Crown Agents and had appointed special "agents" to manage their interests in Great Britain. Honduras, Victoria, New South Wales, South Australia, Western Australia, Queensland, New Zealand, and several of the New Zealand provinces, as well as Canada, maintained agents in London in 1870. Colonial Office List, 1871, 13.
    The term "Agent-General" was first used in the Colonial Office List for 1875, when Canada, New South Wales, Victoria, South Australia, Queensland, and New Zealand were described as having "Agents-General" in London. Ibid., 1875, 12. When Canada raised her agent to "High Commissioner" in 1880, the Australasian colonies still remained the only other parts of the British Empire possessing Agents-General. Ibid., 1881, 16.

4. M.P. for Dundee, 1874-80. An advanced Liberal in politics. Lawyer, editor, and writer of fiction. An early exponent of the idea of imperial federation. Author of the celebrated nineteenth-century satire, Ginx's Baby.

5. Report of the Privy Council of Canada, Feb. 16, 1874, enclosed in Dufferin to Kimberley, no. 48, Feb. 19, 1874: CO 42/727.
    The experiment of a Canadian agent who was also a member of the British Parliament did not originate with Jenkins. From 1835-7 J. A. Roebuck, the Radical M.P., was the agent in Great Britain for the House of Assembly of Lower Canada. In the preceding century some of the colonies in the West Indies maintained agents in London who held seats in Parliament.

6. Dufferin to Carnarvon, private, April 2, 1874: PRO 30/6/26.

7. Minute by Carnarvon, March 17, 1874, on Dufferin to Kimberley, no. 48, Feb. 19, 1874: CO 42/727.

8. Report of the Privy Council of Canada, April 17, 1874, enclosed in Dufferin to Carnarvon, confidential, April 23, 1874: ibid. Technically Jenkins was not to be styled "Agent-General," but "General Agent of Canada."

9. See Hansard, Third Series, CCXVIII, 493 (April 13, 1874), in which Jenkins asked whether there had been any divergence of opinion among the Law Officers in recommending the disallowance of the Canadian Oaths Bill in the previous year. The action taken on this advice had become a controversial political issue in Canada, the Liberal party asserting that it had favoured the Conservative Administration of Sir John Macdonald by delaying the parliamentary investigation of the corruption charges levied against the Government. (The practical effect of disallowance had been to save Macdonald from an unpleasant situation, but the Bill was undoubtedly ultra vires of the Canadian Parliament.)

Arising out of this question was a motion which Jenkins endeavoured to discuss in the House of Commons in June, 1874. He suggested that when the constitutionality of colonial acts was in doubt they should be referred to the Judicial Committee of the Privy Council, a proceeding which would allow the colonies to appear and defend their legislation. (Ibid., CCXIX, 1560-2 [June 12, 1874]).

Later in the same month he asked if a scurrilous article in a London newspaper, impugning the loyalty of the Government of Canada, represented the views of Her Majesty's Government. (Ibid., CCXX, 606-7 [June 29, 1874].)

10. Minute by Holland, March 31, 1874, on notice of question by Edward Jenkins, March 31, 1874: CO 42/731.

11. Minute by Herbert, March 31, 1874, on ibid.
Carnarvon subsequently informed Dufferin that he proposed to treat Jenkins with more reserve in the future. (Carnarvon to Dufferin, private, April 1, 1874: PRO 30/6/26.)

12. There was a hint of Jenkins's retirement in the autumn of 1874, when the quarrel with the Minister of Agriculture occurred. See Dufferin to Carnarvon, private, Oct. 2, 1874: PRO 30/6/27.

13. Reports of the Privy Council of Canada, Dec. 17 and 22, 1875, enclosed in Dufferin to Carnarvon, no. 10, Jan. 12, 1876: CO 42/741.

14. Minute by Blake (Colonial Office), Jan. 26, 1876, on Dufferin to Carnarvon, no. 10, Jan. 12, 1876: ibid.

15. Report of the Privy Council of Canada, Oct. 2, 1869, enclosed in Young to Granville, no. 98, Oct. 4, 1869: CO 42/677.

16. Rose considered that in organization and personnel the Colonial Office was satisfactorily constituted to handle the relations with the autonomous colonies. He also rebutted the charge that the Office was not responsive to colonial opinion: "It is but simple justice to say, as I can do, after an experience of many years, that, whichever of the great parties in the State controlled it, I am aware of no instance in which indifference, or in which a full measure of consideration for the concerns and interests of any colony, or toward any colonist personally, was wanting." (The Times, Jan. 18, 1870.) "The Colonial Office may, with great propriety, be left to deal with all matters of administration and with any modification in the relations of any colony to the empire which its changed condition may call for." (Ibid., Jan. 20, 1870.)

The Department, for its part, expressed its appreciation of Rose's co-operation on more than one occasion. See Long, "Sir John Rose and the High Commissionership," 29-30, 33.

17. Rose's achievements in London from 1869 to 1880 are lucidly described in Long, "Sir John Rose and the High Commissionership," 23-43.

18. Skilling, Canadian Representation Abroad, 88.

19. Confidential memo. by Macdonald, Tilley, and Tupper on the subject of a resident Canadian agent in Great Britain, Aug. 20, 1879: CO 42/759. Printed in SP, 1880, no. 105, 2-4.

20. Ibid.

21. Ibid.

22. Minute by Pennell, Aug. 27, 1879, on ibid.

23. Minute by Herbert, Aug. 28, 1879, on ibid.

24. This point is more fully discussed in chapter II, 44, of this work.

25. Minute by Hicks Beach, Sept. 1, 1879, on confidential memo. on the subject of a resident Canadian agent in Great Britain, Aug. 20, 1879: CO 42/759.

26. Minute by Pauncefote, Sept. 8, 1879, on Colonial Office to Foreign Office, confidential, Sept. 6, 1879: FO 83/585.

27. Foreign Office to Colonial Office, confidential, Sept. 15, 1879: CO 42/758.

28. Hicks Beach to Lorne, secret, Nov. 1, 1879: ibid. Printed in SP, 1880, no. 105, 1-2.

29. Report of the Privy Council of Canada, Dec. 22, 1879, enclosed in Lorne to Hicks Beach, secret, Dec. 24, 1879: CO 42/758. Printed in SP, 1880, no. 5, 4-6.

30. 30 and 31 Vict., c. 3, s. 91, subs. 10.

31. For a fuller discussion of this topic see below, 302.

32. Report of the Privy Council of Canada, Dec. 22, 1879, enclosed in Lorne to Hicks Beach, secret, Dec. 24, 1879: CO 42/758.

33. Minute by Bramston, Jan. 5, 1880, on Lorne to Hicks Beach, secret, Dec. 24, 1879: ibid.

34. Minute by Herbert, Jan. 12, 1880, on ibid.

35. Minute by Hicks Beach, Jan. 14, 1880, on ibid.
The communication to the Foreign Office is Colonial Office to Foreign Office, confidential, Jan. 24, 1880: CO 42/758. The letter stated that nothing had been found in the official records of the Department to give credence to the Canadian assertion that the delegates of 1865-6 had been accorded precedence after foreign ministers.

36. Lorne to Hicks Beach, telegram, Jan. 23, 1880: CO 42/760.

37. This decision was suggested by George E. March (Superintendent of the Treaty Department of the Foreign Office) in a memorandum, "Title and Precedence of the Representative of Canada in London," Jan. 29, 1880, appended to Colonial Office to Foreign Office, confidential, Jan. 24, 1880: FO 83/611. It was approved by Salisbury without hesitation.

38. Foreign Office to Colonial Office, confidential, Jan. 30, 1880: CO 42/765.

39. Minute by Herbert, Jan. 31, 1880, on ibid.

40. Hicks Beach to Lorne, telegram, Jan. 31, 1880: CO 42/760.

41. Lorne to Hicks Beach, telegram, Feb. 6, 1880: ibid.

42. Hicks Beach to Lorne, telegram, Feb. 7, 1880: ibid. Printed in SP, 1880, no. 105, 6.

43. The discussion of the Act is found in Debates of the House of Commons (Canada), 1880, I, 977 (April 1, 1880), and ibid., II, 1857-78 (April 29, 1880). The subject was mentioned, in very general terms, in the Speech from the Throne: ibid., I, 3 (Feb. 12, 1880).

See also Debates of the Senate (Canada), 1880, I, 469 (May 1, 1880); 495-8 (May 3, 1880); and 500 (May 4, 1880).

44. Debates of the House of Commons (Canada), 1880, II, 1859 (April 29, 1880).

45. Ibid., 1872.

46. An Act for the Appointment of a Resident Representative Agent for Canada in the United Kingdom (43 Vict., c. 11) received the Royal Assent on May 7, 1880.

The measure provided that the High Commissioner should act as Resident Agent of the Dominion in the United Kingdom, with supervision over the Canadian immigration offices. Under instructions he was also to concern himself with "the commercial, financial and general interests" of Canada in the United Kingdom and elsewhere.

See Lorne to Kimberley, no. 161, June 1, 1880: CO 42/761, for the Order in Council appointing Galt and for a copy of Galt's commission, both dated May 11, 1880. These documents are printed among the purely formal correspondence which is contained in PP, 1880, XLIX, no. C-2594.

47. Memo. by George E. March, "Title and Precedence of the Representative of Canada in London," Jan. 29, 1880, appended to Colonial Office to Foreign Office, confidential, Jan. 24, 1880: FO 83/611.

48. Lord Chamberlain's Office to Foreign Office, Jan. 29, 1880: ibid.

49. Minute by Herbert, Jan. 31, 1880, on Foreign Office to Colonial Office, confidential, Jan. 30, 1880: CO 42/765.

50. Lord Chamberlain's Office to Colonial Office, Feb. 18, 1880: ibid.

51. Galt was also accorded the right of the "entrée" to all royal palaces. (Lord Chamberlain's Office to Colonial Office, May 26, 1880: ibid.)

The Lord Chamberlain did not wish the subject of Galt's precedence to be discussed in public. Thus when a member of Parliament gave notice of a question about the social precedence of the new High Commissioner the Colonial Office was requested not to allow the enquiry to be put. (Notice of question by E. R. Wodehouse, June 21, 1880: CO 42/764.)

52. Galt to Macdonald, March 11, 1880, printed in Glazebrook, Canadian External Relations, 159-61.

53. Montreal Gazette, March 26, 1880. A copy of this speech is enclosed in Lorne to Hicks Beach, confidential A, March 27, 1880: CO 42/760. There is a summary of the speech in O. D. Skelton, The Life and Times of Sir A. T. Galt (Toronto, 1920), 528.

54. Montreal Gazette, March 26, 1880.

55. Ibid.

56. Galt's Instructions were transmitted to the Colonial Secretary in Lorne to Kimberley, no. 153, May 24, 1880: CO 42/761.

57. Instructions for the High Commissioner of Canada in London, May 20, 1880, enclosed in ibid.

58. Glazebrook, Canadian External Relations, 161.

59. Minute by Bramston, June 7, 1880, on Lorne to Kimberley, no. 153, May 24, 1880: CO 42/761.

60. Minute by Herbert, June 10, 1880, on ibid.

61. Lorne to Hicks Beach, confidential A, March 27, 1880: CO 42/760.

62. Galt's report to Macdonald on one of his interviews with Kimberley is found in Skelton, Life of Sir A. T. Galt, 529-30.

63. Galt to Macdonald, June 10, 1880, quoted in ibid. , 531.

64. Galt to Macdonald, March 13, 1881, quoted in ibid. , 547.
Representatives of Commonwealth countries in other Commonwealth countries have now been given the same diplomatic and consular immunities as the envoys of foreign powers. The British Act conferring these immunities is 15 and 16 George VI and 1 Elizabeth II, c. 18 (1952). Canada accorded the same privileges in 1954 (2 and 3 Elizabeth II, c. 54).

65. Tupper to R. L. Borden, Dec. 5, 1913, quoted in Sir C. H. Tupper, ed., Supplement to the Life and Letters of the Rt. Hon. Sir Charles Tupper (Toronto, 1926), 112.

66. Macdonald to Lord Stanley, Aug. 15, 1890, quoted in Skilling, Canadian Representation Abroad, 99-100.

CHAPTER NINE

THE IMPERIAL RELATIONSHIP IN OPINION AND PRACTICE, 1867-1887

"The greatest gift that the Crown and Parliament of England have bestowed upon [Canada] seems to me to be this: that they have given [it] absolute, unqualified, unstinted freedom in self-government ... combined with a union with the ancient monarchy of England. " Lord Carnarvon, 1883

THE TWENTY YEARS which elapsed between the consolidation of Canada and the call-ing of the first Colonial Conference were years of transition for the British Empire. In no sphere was this transition more marked than in the realm of ideas, particularly as they related to the political connection between Great Britain and her autonomous col-onies. The federal union of British North America took place at a time when anti-col-onial doctrines had gained their greatest ascendancy in the mother country. Indeed the creation of the Dominion was regarded as a convincing illustration of the validity of the separatist viewpoint, for it was popularly assumed that further political advance for the new state could only be in the direction of complete independence. The early years of the first Gladstone Government witnessed many dramatic occurrences and countless ex-pressions of sentiment which seemed to presage the dismemberment of the Empire. Long before this prospect was even remotely realized, however, a gradual reaction had set in. A desire to preserve the unity of the British Empire, at first vaguely expounded but later translated into political and economic terms, became the prevailing tendency in the dis-cussion of the imperial question. Founded in 1884, the Imperial Federation League sym-bolized the new spirit and served as a powerful agent in propagating the new ideas. Through the League's efforts the first Colonial Conference was convened and the way prepared for what was to prove a momentous departure in the technique of intra-imper-ial communication. Consultation emerged as the key-note of the mother country's re-lations with her autonomous colonies; the Empire was set in the process of being trans-formed into the Commonwealth.

An examination of the climate of opinion surrounding the imperial relationship in the two decades after 1867 is essential for an understanding of the British Govern-ment's attitude towards Canada during this period. Policy may, for the most part, have been distinct from opinion, but it was none the less influenced by the latter's vagaries and enthusiasms. The statesman and even the administrator was generally a child of his age. The officials of the Colonial Office reflected the changing moods which charac-terized British public sentiment concerning the imperial tie. Although the permanent heads of the Department usually preserved a discreet reticence in commenting on broad subjects like the destiny of Canada, some, like Rogers, were refreshingly outspoken in their views. Secretaries of State rarely found the occasion or the need to discuss ques-tions of this type, but when they did their observations are useful in explaining specific policies.

As important as these abstract reflections on the imperial relationship was the working conception of the Empire which the Colonial Office formulated during these years. The principles by which an autonomous colony could be supervised from Downing Street, although seldom discussed in vacuo, were obviously of considerable significance for the work of the Department. Once defined they might be applied to the lengthy list of problems which it seemed to be the Department's fate to have continually on hand. How, for instance, was colonial self-government to be reconciled with the legal and diplomatic unity of the Empire; how were the Crown's prerogative rights to be exercised in a colony with responsible government? These questions were rarely capable of a general or long-term solution. The British Empire had been, and remained, essentially an empirical creation, "not ... built up on constitutional theory, [but developing] in accordance with the actual needs of the hour and the conditions which faced its people in different quarters of the globe."[1] Nevertheless, out of the innumerable devices and expedients which went to make up the amalgam that is called "policy," various broader considerations can be discerned. Upon the foundation they provided, the Colonial Office constructed a realistic and manageable conception of the British Empire in the last half of the nineteenth century.

I

It has been said that throughout the course of British imperial history in the Victorian age the idea of separation remained always an opinion and never a policy.[2] The assertion is, no doubt, substantially correct, although there was at least one occasion in the century in which separatist principles very nearly formed the basis of Great Britain's official attitude towards her autonomous colonies. This was in the early months of Gladstone's first Government, shortly after the creation of the Canadian union. Representing as it does the climax of the anti-imperial movement in the United Kingdom the incident furnishes a convenient starting point for a short survey of the British attitude towards the colonial tie prior to 1887.

The culminating phase (as it turned out to be) of "Little England" sentiment has always been associated with the advent to power of the first Gladstone Administration in 1868. Gladstone's Government, a Liberal as distinct from a Whig ministry, based on the support of the middle classes and the industrial community, strongly influenced by the philosophy of the Manchester School, was popularly believed to have radical views regarding the relations between Great Britain and the Empire. The Administration was committed to the extension of colonial autonomy and to the promotion of freer trade. It proposed to reduce expenditure on overseas defence; it was hostile to the acquisition of new territories; it might even accept the dismemberment of the Empire with equanimity. Although exaggerated by popular discussion, this viewpoint nevertheless found credibility in the separatist opinions expressed by leading members of the new Government. Gladstone himself had become a moderate separatist by this time, looking to the eventual independence of the larger settlement colonies as the final stage

1. For references to chapter IX see pages 310-18.

in their political evolution. He would probably have subscribed to the following definition of the aim of British statesmen in their dealings with the dependencies: "To ripen those communities to the earliest possible maturity--social political and commercial--to qualify them, by all the appliances within the reach of a parent State, for present self-government, and eventual independence is now the universally admitted object and aim of our colonial policy."[3] If Gladstone was not a strong separatist, some of the other members of his Ministry were. Robert Lowe, the Chancellor of the Exchequer; Lord Clarendon, the Foreign Secretary; Lord Granville, the Colonial Secretary; and the veteran John Bright, the President of the Board of Trade, had all declared in vigorous language that independence for the colonies would be the most desirable destiny for both partners in the imperial connection.

The opening years of the Gladstone Government were marked by a succession of misunderstandings which lent substance to the charge that the new Administration would welcome the secession of the more important British colonies. Whatever the motives behind the policies of the Government, there is no question that its actions caused grave concern in the colonies and alienated large numbers of its British supporters. It has been observed, and with truth, that "relations between England and her colonies have seldom been more strained than in 1869-70, when Lord Granville ... was Colonial Secretary."[4] The most disturbing indication of the new Government's intentions seemed to be contained in the policy which Lord Granville pursued towards New Zealand. The harsh confiscatory measures adopted by that Colony had brought about a formidable uprising of the Maoris in North Island. In spite of this fact, the Imperial Government continued to implement the Cardwell principles of withdrawing the British garrisons from the self-governing parts of the Empire. The Colony's Ministers thereupon appealed for a suspension of the military evacuation and for a loan to be used for defence purposes. To these requests Lord Granville gave a peremptory refusal. He went on to suggest, in a frankly discourteous manner, that the native trouble had been caused by the land hunger of the white settlers and that the Colony must restore order by its own efforts. Insofar as there was any obligation involved, it was not a claim which New Zealand could press against the United Kingdom, "... but the reverse-- ... a very heavy claim on the part of the Mother Country against the colony."[5]

A communication of this nature was bound to cause indignation in New Zealand. There was an immediate outcry, the strength of which can be gauged by the fact that some sections of the community advocated the annexation of the Colony to the United States. In England the repercussions of Granville's attitude were hardly less sensational. Lifted from its place as part of the policy of successive governments towards New Zealand, the episode was made to appear, by the critics of the Liberal Administration, as a deliberate attempt to provoke New Zealand into an act of separation. The Spectator declared with vehemence, "It is clear that Mr. Goldwin Smith's colonial 'policy,' the policy, that is, of shaking off the colonies as too burdensome ... has not only been accepted by the existing Government, but that they are acting on it."[6] In the House of Commons the redoubtable Viscount Bury, who had been a separatist less than a decade earlier, opened a debate on New Zealand affairs with a bitter attack on Granville's attitude towards the Colony. [7] Lord Carnarvon, a thorn in Granville's side during the whole time in which he held the seals of the Colonial Office, demanded that a special commissioner be sent to New Zealand to report on the Colony's grievances. [8]

It is now apparent that Granville's response to the New Zealand requests was to a large extent the response of Sir Frederic Rogers. With his implicit confidence in Rogers, Granville tended to leave even the most important decisions in the hands of the Permanent Under-Secretary. It was but natural that Rogers, fervently believing in the Cardwell policy, deploring warfare against native peoples, and interested in reducing Imperial expenditure, should have proved hostile to the Colony's aspirations. In addition Rogers seems to have suspected that some of the New Zealand indignation was for domestic political purposes, an impression which incensed him to such a degree that later he could hardly trust himself to reply to New Zealand dispatches. [9] Much of the blame for the "harsh terms" and "severe logic"[10] which Carnarvon noted as characterizing the dispatches sent from the Colonial Office to the Colony during these months must be assigned to Rogers's inflexible style. By the spring of 1870 an accommodation had been reached in the dispute with New Zealand. The military evacuation was carried through to completion while in recompense for the withdrawal of the troops the Colonial Office agreed to provide a guarantee on a New Zealand loan for immigration and public works. With the aid of this compromise relations with the Colony passed into a happier phase.[11]

An immediate result of the Imperial policy towards New Zealand was an attempt to unite the autonomous colonies in a movement of protest against the Colonial Office.[12] The originators of this plan were self-styled "influential Colonists in England," who in the summer of 1869 convened several meetings in London to discuss the subject of imperial relations. The group was convinced that Granville's attitude towards New Zealand had caused a crisis in British imperial history, for in effect the Colonial Secretary had repudiated any obligation on the part of the mother country to assist in the development and protection of the settlement colonies. If not renounced this principle would eventually lead to the severance of the imperial connection. Such a consequence was unthinkable and the colonies were urged, therefore, to send representatives to London to consider the whole subject of imperial relations. In the missive extending this invitation the responsible government colonies were informed that their interests were not being served adequately under the present system of imperial administration. The Colonial Office was "ill adapted for carrying on friendly intercourse with Colonial Governments" and the British Parliament was too absorbed in domestic questions to be an effective legislature for the Empire. [13]

Not unnaturally, the Colonial Office at once placed the seal of official disapproval upon this project. The colonies were told curtly that Her Majesty's Government was at all times ready to consider the wishes and interests of every part of the Empire. There was no jealousy of combined colonial action in the Department but rather every desire to encourage such a development. On this occasion, however, no useful purpose would be served by convening a meeting of colonial representatives in London. The interests of the various colonies were so diverse, and the particular problems arising from their relationship with the United Kingdom so individual, that little common ground existed on which a conference could be conducted. The present system of com-munication through the responsible Ministers of a colony and through the Governor was not unsatisfactory and possessed many advantages over a scheme in which colonial in-terests would be entrusted to a group of private gentlemen in London.[14] The colonial expatriates in England, refusing to be daunted by this condemnation of their plan, ap-pointed a delegation to wait upon the Colonial Secretary. Granville proved distinctly hostile to their request for an official conference and at later meetings of the group held throughout the winter of 1869-70, the general discussion of the colonial question which had characterized the first sessions degenerated into partisan attacks directed against the Liberal Secretary of State.

The replies from the colonies showed that there was little interest in this agitation outside the metropolitan power. All the self-governing colonies, together with the Cape and Natal, returned unqualified rejections to the invitation to take part in the confer-ence.[15] Canada was emphatic in her desire to have nothing to do with the scheme,[16] although Macdonald confessed that he was reluctant to pronounce on the question until a full Cabinet council could be held. Writing to his friend Rose in November, 1869, he stated,

> When the Cabinet is full, we shall have a solemn discussion as to what our pol-icy is to be with respect to the proposed Colonial Conference in February next.   I am, at present, strongly inclined to believe that we ought to have nothing to do with it. We have no wrongs to complain of; we are quite satisfied with our position and relations with the mother country, and we have had a special understanding, since 1865, on all matters connected with those relations. Unless convinced to the con-trary, I shall oppose sending any delegation, or having any representatives at the Con-ference. If H.M. Government should ask the Colonies, it would be another matter. This question however is so serious a one, affecting our future policy, that until the Cabinet is full, I shall refrain from pressing the subject in Council.[17]

The Canadian Prime Minister was certainly not happy with Lord Granville at the Col-onial Office but his dissatisfaction was more a matter of party prejudice than valid con-stitutional complaint.[18] By the end of the year it was apparent that the idea of an un-authorized meeting of the larger colonies had proved a complete failure. Rogers, who had written the dispatch designed, as he expressed it, "to turn the flank of some fellows who are trying to set up an anti-Downing Street Colonial Conference," was jubilant at this result. He noted that the group was still agitating fiercely in the London newspapers, but observed complacently, "I think we shall beat them...."[19] The events of 1870 confirmed this impression of a minor revolution whose failure was perhaps never really in doubt. The unofficial colonial conference, in spite of its signal lack of success, was not without significance in later British imperial history. It foreshadowed, and may even have initiated, the reaction in favour of the consolidation of the Empire which began to gain force in the years after 1870. At the conclusion of an era of indifference to the colonies the malcontents in London directed English opinion to the pressing problem of

imperial organization, and offered tentative suggestions for its solution. The growth of
the Royal Colonial Society and the propaganda for "United Empire" are closely associated with the heated meetings of the ex-colonists in Cannon Street in the winter of 1869.

Canada also received unsettling communications from the Colonial Secretary of
the Gladstone Administration. The exchange occurred in connection with the celebrated episode in which A. T. Galt, a confessed advocate of Canadian independence, received a knighthood from Granville in 1869. Galt, the author of the financial terms of
Confederation, was indubitably one of the most capable figures in public life in British
North America. His views on the imperial tie were, however, distinctly radical, for he
was the first major politician in the Dominion to advocate independence as the logical
culmination of colonial autonomy. Galt saw in Confederation a significant precursor to
full sovereignty, and regarded the Imperial Government's emphasis on colonial self-reliance as a mark of encouragement to those urging an independent status. His outlook
was well known in Canada, although he deliberately refrained from organizing a party
or conducting any campaign in support of his views. In the spring of 1869 Granville,
through the Governor-General, approached Galt with the offer of a K.C.M.G. Galt
was gratified but he felt that as an honourable man he must place his convictions square-
ly before the Colonial Secretary before accepting the award. To Sir John Young he therefore sent an exposition of his separatist principles.

> I regard the Confederation of the British North American provinces as a meas-
> ure which must ultimately lead to their separation from Great Britain.
> The present connection is undoubtedly an embarrassment to Great Britain in
> her relations to the United States, and a source of uneasiness to the Dominion owing
> to the insecurity which is felt to exist from the possibility of a rupture between the
> two nations. [20]

The British Government clearly did not desire to force Canada into the American union,
but there was still a real danger that annexation might occur. The best way to forestall
it was to foster a national spirit in Canada, so that when membership in the Empire ended the Dominion would be able to take up a separate existence without strain. [21]

Granville was, however, not to be dissuaded from his intentions by Galt's explanation and the knighthood was bestowed. Later, in February, 1870, the matter was given
wide publicity in both Canada and England. In the Dominion Parliament some members
of the Macdonald Government characterized Galt as disloyal, which brought from Sir
Alexander the strong rejoinder that he shared the same attitude towards the connection
as Ministers of the Crown in England. He was thus forced to refer to his correspondence
with Granville. Writing to the Secretary of State later Galt explained that he had not
declared that Her Majesty's Government approved his views but simply that it did not
consider them the sentiments of a disloyal man. [22] Granville expressed himself as perfectly satisfied with Galt's conduct in the Canadian House and declared that he still saw
no reason why Galt's convictions should preclude him from receiving an honour from
the Crown.

When informed by you confidentially of certain opinions which you held respecting the possible future of the Dominion as a result of the confederation, I thought they constituted no reason for recommending Her Majesty to withhold the honour from a distinguished and loyal statesman like yourself.

I am not aware of anything which has since occurred which should modify that opinion. . . . [23]

The circumstances providing the greatest support for the charge that certain members of the Gladstone Administration entertained separatist opinions date also from the first years following the confederation of Canada. In a series of letters addressed to Sir John Young in 1869-70 it is possible to discern clearly the vision, so fervently held by Lord Granville and Sir Frederic Rogers, of a transient imperial tie. The letters in question stem from the period when the closest confidence prevailed between the two men and appear to have been composed and dispatched without reference to any other person in the Office. It is an interesting speculation whether Gladstone saw and approved them; there is no evidence available that he did. Although he would have agreed with the tone of Granville's dispatches to the Governor-General of Canada, the Prime Minister would hardly have committed himself to some of the expressions contained in them.

The origins of the correspondence with Sir John Young are obscure. The first of the series in the Colonial Office records is dated June, 1869, and appears to have been written in reply to a private letter from the Governor-General. In this dispatch Young had transmitted to the Colonial Secretary the opinions of a number of the leading Canadian statesmen on the future destiny of the Dominion. It was Granville's intention, apparently, to comment on these observations with a view towards defining, for the use of the Governor-General, the attitude of the Imperial Government on the question. Before attempting the task the Colonial Secretary wrote to Gladstone to ask for suggestions.[24] The Prime Minister's reply was to refer Granville to the letter which he (Gladstone) had written to Lord Cathcart in Canada in 1846, at the time of the dissatisfaction in the Colony caused by the changes in England's commercial policy. This communication, although almost a quarter of a century old, still contained his basic attitude towards the colonial tie. The letter had, he said, "distinctly enough laid down that we did not impose British connection upon the Colony, but regarded its goodwill . . . as an essential condition of the connection."[25]

Granville accepted unreservedly the Gladstone interpretation of the imperial relationship in framing his dispatch to Young. He went further, and built his communication to a large extent on the actual phrases used by Gladstone in 1846.[26] It was on "the free and loyal attachment of the Canadians" that the connection rested; it could not and should not be maintained by "coercion or through any vexatious thwarting of the social tendencies of the communities" overseas. Today, Granville noted, the principles of "freedom and voluntaryism" still governed, as they had done ever since 1846, the policy of the mother country towards the Dominion. The result had been salutary for both Canada and the United Kingdom. The Colony remained willingly within the Empire, its very freedom to withdraw strengthening the bond which connected it to the British

Crown. "Her Majesty's Government value the existing relation as the symbol and support of that attachment. They value it while it is valued by the Canadians, and while
it is useful to the Canadians. They have no desire to maintain it for a single year after
it has become injurious or distasteful to them."[27] With Gladstone, Granville believed that the true greatness of the British Empire existed in the spirit which united all its
peoples, rather than in geographical or material factors. This spirit could best be promoted by retaining Canada as a friend and ally, and not as a "half-hearted Dependency."
The way to gain Canadian friendship was to provide at all times a just consideration to
the interests of the Dominion, as those interests were defined by the people of the Colony. The Secretary of State then passed on to other and more original reflections. Her
Majesty's Government would not judge a colonial statesman disloyal because he questioned the wisdom of continuing indefinitely the present relationship, or proposed measures "to facilitate its modification or dissolution." The whole subject was one which
was open to constructive suggestion and Young was directed to discuss it fully with his
Ministers, encouraging them to be frank with him in their comments. In addition, he
was to keep the Colonial Office informed of the currents of opinion regarding the imperial connection in the Dominion. Then followed the hint that separation might be a
desirable goal for future endeavour. "You will also be good enough to bring to my notice any line of policy, or any measures which without implying on the part of Her Majesty's Government any wish to change abruptly our relations, would gradually prepare
both Countries for a friendly relaxation of them."[28]

Granville's dispatch embodies perhaps the most forthright expression of separatist
opinion that can be found in nineteenth-century official correspondence.[29] The word
"overture," which was used in the penultimate paragraph, is significant, for the whole
tone of the communication suggests that its author was advancing a proposal, albeit in
very general terms, for the consideration of the Canadian Government. Young was to
"sound out" the Government and people of Canada on the subject of the imperial connection; the response to his enquiries would determine the attitude which the United
Kingdom would assume towards the topic. This assessment of Granville's intentions is
borne out by a provocative speech on imperial questions which the Governor-General
made at Quebec shortly after receiving the dispatch. Young's address was delivered at
the time when the Imperial troops were being withdrawn from Canada, and was a rejoinder to the critics of the evacuation policy, who had seen in it a sign of the mother
country's desire to get rid of her colonies. The Governor-General, after explaining the
reasons for the concentration of military forces in the United Kingdom, indulged in some
general observations on the position of Canada. The Colony was now "in reality independent," so that it was for Canadians to decide whether they wished to maintain the
connection with Great Britain "or in due time of the maturity of the Dominion to change
it for some other form of alliance."[30] These words caused widespread comment at the
time and earned Young bitter rebukes from many quarters in both England and Canada.[31]
In fact, the speech was probably more directly inspired by the remarks of the Colonial
Secretary than its critics would have cared to imagine. Young, with his Liberal tendencies, probably possessed mild anti-imperial views of the Gladstone variety, but he

was definitely encouraged to go further and loose this "trial balloon" by the suggestions of his chief. The unfavourable reception which the speech earned impelled the Governor-General to qualify his remarks in a later address at Halifax. Thus the Secretary of State's probing had at least isolated the facts that on the whole Canadians were satisfied with the existing imperial connection and that there was little desire to modify it, either in the direction of greater freedom for the Dominion or towards the goal of a more centralized Empire. Unless the Colonial Office were prepared to embark on the advocacy of imperial dismemberment, or events were to take a form which might result in grave irritation at the connection in the larger colonies, it seemed as if separatist opinions possessed no attractions for British North America. Granville lacked the temperament and the interest in colonial affairs to have become a crusader for the first course of action, and the permanent heads of the Office after Rogers's day devoted their best efforts to avoiding the emergence of the second possibility. Thus Lord Granville's delicate overture of 1869 met a quick death and left no consequences.

The state of feeling in Canada on membership in the Empire was well described in a letter which Granville received from Young, written after the latter had passed a summer touring in the Dominion. There had been many loyal addresses presented to him, Young remarked, and none had been ambiguous in their expressions of friendship to the mother country. Among the Dominion's population only the Fenians were actively disloyal and their influence was of no account except among some of their own countrymen. There was a larger group indifferent to the British connection, constituted mainly of people with economic links with the United States, but it was not significant. "The sum of my impressions is, taking the Dominion as a whole, the people are perfectly satisfied with the institutions they possess and with their present position. They value and are proud of their connection with the Mother Country, and uniformly express themselves averse to any change either of alliance or allegiance but [are] simply anxious to remain as they are."[32]

This dispatch Granville claimed to find completely satisfactory. He directed that the Governor-General be told that his impressions were "a remarkable proof of the wisdom of the principles which have been adopted of late years by successive Cabinets in their relations with British North America." He continued: "It gives strong encouragement to believe that whether the present connection with Great Britain continue in precisely the same form, or whether at some future time the strong but elastic bond between them shall be further relaxed, that there will continue to exist between the two Countries feelings of the strongest attachment and mutual respect."[33] Finally, the Colonial Secretary expressed approval for the way in which Young had carried out his instructions of June 14, and particularly for the circumspection he had observed. Then followed a cancelled section of the minute which provides a more precise indication of the Secretary of State's views on Anglo-Canadian relations. "The friendly separation of Canada from this country, and a declaration of its independence would relieve Great Britain and the Dominion from some present embarrassment, and from future risks. But I should regret that this country should appear to adopt any abrupt proceeding which would alienate the Canadians.... "[34]

The subject of imperial organization was several times explored in the British Parliament during the course of the year 1870. It is doubtful, in fact, whether in mid-Victorial times Parliament ever gave more sustained consideration to the problem of the colonial relationship than during the troubled eighteen months when Lord Granville headed the Colonial Office. A long debate in the House of Commons, significant because it brought out the views of Gladstone and his Government on the general question of separation, occurred in April, 1870. The discussion was initiated on a motion proposed by R. R. Torrens, Liberal member for Cambridge, who is chiefly remembered as the first Premier of South Australia and the author of an important reform in the law relating to the registration of land. Torrens asked that a Select Committee be appointed "to inquire into the political relations and modes of official inter-communication between the self-governing Colonies and this Country, and to report whether any or what modifications are desirable, with a view to the maintenance of a common nationality cemented by cordial good understanding."[35]

In bringing forward this motion Torrens, who was one of the leading exponents in Parliament of the nascent imperial spirit, stressed the dissatisfaction and uncertainty that existed at the moment over the Government's policy towards the autonomous colonies. The parliamentary heads of the Colonial Office were ignorant of colonial conditions and did not appreciate the innate loyalty to Great Britain that existed in the colonies, Torrens claimed. This meant that control was left to the permanent heads of the Office, who pursued a "traditional policy"[36] well suited to the needs of dependent areas but intolerable to the colonies of white settlement because of its tacit assumption of British superiority in political wisdom. Much of the trouble lay in the "unsuitableness of departmental machinery,"[37] and in the practice of communicating on colonial problems mainly with the Governor, who as an agent of the Imperial power could not properly voice the wishes of the colonists. Torrens went on to show that he desired a revision of this machinery of government, although not in the direction of reducing colonial autonomy. He proposed instead that the Imperial veto over colonial legislation be limited to specific acts inconsistent with Great Britain's treaty obligations, and that a new system of communication with the colonies be established by allowing the parts of the Empire to send "envoys" to London. This plan offered no danger to the imperial tie, because "the alternative lay between ultimate separation and the recognition of those Colonies on the same footing as foreign States in alliance as far as regards this matter of diplomatic relations."[38]

The Government was assisted, in replying to Torrens's motion, by the support of one of the most prominent advocates of the continued unity of the Empire, Viscount Bury. Bury had renounced his separatist views soon after writing the Exodus of the Western Nations, for in 1868 he established and became the first president of the Colonial Society, later to grow into the Royal Colonial Institute. Although he held no office in the Gladstone Ministry it appears probable that Bury was authorized to reply to Torrens's motion. This possibility arises through Bury's use of a memorandum defending the existing conduct of imperial relations which had been commissioned by the Government. When notice had originally been given of Torrens's resolution the Colonial Office was naturally asked to provide relevant information about Great Britain's relations with her autonomous colonies. To aid in this assignment the Office called in the services of Sir John Rose, who in the previous year had been appointed the permanent agent of the Dominion in London. With his extensive experience in Canadian administration and diplomacy Rose was well fitted to discuss the adequacy of the existing channels of intra-imperial communication. He complied with the Colonial Office request in a memorandum setting out his views on the questions raised in Torrens's motion.[39] It was Rose's general opinion that the political relations between Canada and the United Kingdom were satisfactory and that the Colonial Office managed them in a commendable manner. Bury quoted this conclusion, the observation, as he said, of "a distinguished Canadian,"[40] to scout the impression that discontent existed in the colonies over the imperial connection.

> On that part ... which may be embraced in the words "political relations" I make no other observation than that I believe the great body of the Colonists are satisfied with them, that it is their earnest desire to continue them and that they will not readily part with the prestige or advantage which is their birthright as British subjects, but if time and altered circumstances require it they will be ready to readjust the condition of the relation so as to adapt them to any new requirements.
> In reference to ... "the mode of carrying on communication with this Country" I do not think that any serious dissatisfaction exists or that there is any ground for it. Some party or individual in a Colony may occasionally from personal disappointment or for political purposes complain of the Colonial Office but those who have had the responsibility of conducting affairs have rarely if ever had occasion for dissatisfaction, and I can suggest no machinery by which the varied, delicate and often difficult questions claiming the consideration of the Colonial Department could be better or more speedily dealt with.[41]

The colonies were a source of strength and prosperity to England, Bury continued, the value of the relationship outweighing any sums the mother country might expend on their defence. Continue to maintain the connection with the colonies in its present form, elastic but firm, he declared. The motion before the House would accomplish no useful purpose and should be rejected, for, he added scathingly, the appointment of a parliamentary committee to survey the imperial relationship would be like asking "a short-hand writer ... to take down the gossip of the smoking room."[42]

Later in the debate the Parliamentary Under-Secretary for the Colonies, William Monsell, rose to answer Torrens's charges. The colonies entertained no sense of grievance, he said, and were not interested in the idea of separation. The answers which Lord Granville had received in response to his circular about the unofficial conference proved beyond a shadow of a doubt that the existing modes of communication between Downing Street and the Empire were satisfactory. The colonies had no desire to have ambassadors in London.[43] After defending the Government in its New Zealand policy and on its reaction to the Red River insurrection, Monsell ended on a note that could not have reassured the imperial enthusiasts about the colonial intentions of the Gladstone Government.

> ... no British statesman desires the continuance of the connection on any terms but those of free goodwill. [The colonies] are bound to us by no cords but those of affection and of interest. So sure as children become men, so surely will the day come when these great communities will develop into independent States. The desire of Her Majesty's Government, and he believed, of every party in the State, was to postpone that inevitable hour--to make the ties that bind us together so elastic that they may not burst, and, avoiding those abstract questions the hon. Gentleman's proposal would be sure to raise if it were adopted, to leave to each Colony the fullest control over its internal concerns. [44]

Monsell was followed by his chief, who was moved to speak, as he said, because of the serious charges made against the Government. Gladstone admitted the present uneasiness in the colonies, but claimed it had existed for the last thirty years; ever since, in fact, responsible government had been granted to some parts of the Empire. The Government was not introducing any new policy, but simply applying "admitted principles," of which the basic one was the extension of colonial autonomy. Then followed the notable aphorism: "When you are involved in a bad system you cannot pass even to a better without feeling some inconvenience in the transition."[45] Echoing Burke's prescription, he declared the Government's policy to be one of "freedom and voluntaryism."[46] In withdrawing the military forces from the self-governing colonies the mother country was encouraging colonial self-reliance, and not merely economizing in a manner likely to prove hazardous to imperial interests. What changes were proposed for the imperial constitution, Gladstone asked; what modifications were suggested in the methods of consultation that would not abridge colonial freedom? All the schemes he had examined for imperial consolidation were visionary and impracticable. Then he reiterated one of his favourite ideas regarding the relationship with the colonies: that if separation should come, it should be "a peaceable and friendly transaction." "Surely it is a great object to place, if possible, our colonial policy on such a footing, not for the purpose of bringing about a separation, but of providing a guarantee that, if separation should occur, it should be in a friendly way. That is the sense, the principle, and the secret of our policy with regard to colonial reform."[47] Taken by itself, this statement would suggest unequivocally that Gladstone was prepared to acquiesce in the loss of the colonies, but he immediately followed it with the panegyric claim that the policy of the Government "does not, in my opinion, tend to weaken the relations between the mother country and the Colonies, but, on the contrary, while securing the greatest likelihood of a perfectly peaceable separation, whenever separation may arrive, gives the best chance of an indefinitely long continuance of a free and voluntary connection. That is the footing on which we ... have endeavoured to found our colonial policy."[48]

In the face of this admirable exposition of principles, so satisfactory to the wishes

of all groups in the House, is it any wonder that Torrens's plea for "a consistent, uniform and rational"[49] policy towards the self-governing colonies was rejected by a handsome majority of forty-three votes?

The statements made in the Commons by Gladstone and Monsell represented the
most radical views which the new Administration was to express in public on the question of colonial emancipation. They also marked one of the final illustrations of anti-
imperial sentiment in official declarations. For even as the current of separatist opinion reached its flood the tide gradually turned. From about the year 1870 can be discerned the first faint evidences of a new movement in the British attitude towards the
colonies, a movement which has been aptly described as the "rebirth of imperialism."[50]
The new body of opinion was inspired by a desire to preserve the unity of the British Empire, to counteract the centrifugal tendencies of a previous age and consolidate the existing imperial relationship. This was the original "imperialism," before the concept
became widened to connote a score of meanings ranging from territorial expansion and
Caesarism to the civilizing mission of the white race. In its essentials it reproduced
the simple faith of Durham and Elgin: the conviction that it was in the interests of both
the mother country and the colonies that the intangible ties between them be kept viable
and spontaneous. The "Little England" attitude gave way slowly to the new spirit and
it was probably not until the late eighties that "imperialism" can be said to have become dominant in English thinking about the Empire.

The factors stimulating the late Victorian interest in imperial unity are complex
and reach back into the preceding era. In the main they are associated with the momentous transformation that convulsed the Western world in the second half of the nineteenth century. "It was, in short, the changed economic and political balance of power
in the world at large, rather than the growing consequence of the settlement colonies,
which gave impetus to the new imperialism. The year 1870 lifted the curtain on a new
and vaguely disturbing scene."[51] The forces agitating Europe and North America in
1870 were those of nationalism, militarism, and protection: unfamiliar concepts destined to produce catastrophic results. The German victory of 1871 had created a powerful national state in the heart of Europe. In Italy and Austria-Hungary a new national
consciousness was stirring, foreshadowing the eventual overthrow of the dynastic organization of Europe. In the New World the United States had asserted its solidarity at the
cost of civil war, and stood, an aggressive mature nation, more than ever dominant in
North America. To the political nationalism of these states was added industrial growth,
tariff protection, and the ambitious cult of militarism. The long Pax Britannica was
drawing to a close. For the first time since the days of Napoleon Great Britain began
to feel her position challenged and vulnerable. The Empire was not now a luxury to be
sloughed off without ceremony; it possessed resources, people, and skills that might
prove of immeasurable strength to the mother country. As the skies darkened the children might repair to the defence of the home they had once left. As the markets of the
world shrank, and the sources of food became limited, the Empire might still allow the
United Kingdom to exist as "the workshop of the world." As the rivalry with foreign
countries increased in intensity, the overseas possessions would serve to enhance the im-

portance of the little island in the North Atlantic. In a world of large powers, Great
Britain and her colonies would remain a giant among giants. This was the challenge;
the response was the new imperialism.

There were other causes that helped to explain the change in the attitude of the
mother country towards her colonies. Through all the discouragement of the separatist
period the colonies had remained loyal; surely their attachment to the metropolitan
power ought to be recompensed? Was it not time, as Disraeli asked in 1872, to respond "to those distant sympathies which may become the source of incalculable strength
and happiness to this land"?[52]   The aristocratic leadership of government, with its narrow emphasis on the London scene, was passing away. The Second Reform Bill had en-
franchised large sections of the middle class, and the working men were soon to be admitted into the ever widening circle of the rulers of the state. To these classes the colonies represented objects of encouragement and promise rather than liabilities. The influence of the new voting groups could not help but revise England's traditional outlook
towards her Empire. "It was colonial loyalty to the English people, joining hands with
English loyalty to their overseas kin, that brought to an end the period of doubt."[53] In
addition, the Empire was becoming physically manageable. It was no longer a vast ambiguous geographical expression but a compact unit, knit together by the undersea cable
and telegraph, and made accessible by steam navigation.

Much, of course, was still obscure in the early seventies. The general conversion
of the powers to imperialism could hardly be forecast in the exact way in which it
was actually to happen. It could not be clearly foreseen that, through her existing
monopoly and her prior claims, Britain was to invite the common opposition of all
the new colonial powers.... Nevertheless, it is striking how much was, after all,
forecast thus early. Enough, indeed, to force a revision of accepted views of empire.[54]

It is in these circumstances that the explanation of the outcry raised over the colonial policies of the Gladstone Government must be sought. It was precisely because
Lord Granville's anti-colonial views coincided with the first signs of the new imperial
sentiment that they aroused so much controversy. A decade before they would have
passed practically unnoticed; a decade later their appearance would have been unthinkable. But coming as they did at a time of transition when attitudes towards the Empire
were in a state of flux, they had the effect of contributing substantially to the general
discussion. The formation of the Colonial Society in 1868 furnished the earliest evidence of the new spirit in the United Kingdom. Planned as a club for the use of those
interested in the British possessions overseas, this organization was modelled on the Royal
Geographical Society. Later, after it had received a royal charter and become the Royal
Colonial Institute, it was turned into a medium for dispensing the new doctrines. It is
no accident that the motto of the Society, "United Empire," served also to express the
essential credo of the imperialist movement. From 1870, when W. E. Forster identified himself with the new outlook (the first prominent public man so to do) there began

a steady current of advocacy in its favour. Edward Jenkins expounded in the Contemporary Review in 1871 the idea of imperial federation, and in the same year de Labil-
lière, most fervent of imperial enthusiasts, lectured on the subject in London.   When
Disraeli took up the theme at the Crystal Palace in 1872, it was already a topic of public interest. His words on that notable occasion revealed him as an enlightened oppor-
tunist who was prepared to use the concept of imperial unity as a means of attacking the
Liberals.

> But self-government, in my opinion, when it was conceded, ought to have
> been conceded as part of a great policy of Imperial consolidation. It ought to have
> been accompanied by an Imperial tariff, by securities for the people of England for
> the enjoyment of the unappropriated lands which belonged to the Sovereign as their
> trustee, and by a military code which should have precisely defined the means and
> the responsibilities by which the Colonies should be defended, and by which, if nec-
> essary, this country should call for aid from the Colonies themselves. It ought, fur-
> ther, to have been accompanied by the institution of some representative council in
> the metropolis, which would have brought the Colonies into constant and continuous
> relations with the Home Government. [55]

The Conservative victory of 1874 drove separatism from the field of practical politics.
"Who talks now of casting off the colonies? What more popular cry than the preservation of our colonial empire?" exclaimed Forster in the following year.[56] The new faith
had indeed begun to take hold.

    The rise and development of the movement for imperial unity are admirably il-
lustrated in the debates on colonial policy held in the British Parliament in the years
immediately following 1870. A subject which occasioned much alarm in circles favourable to the continuance of the colonial connection was the withdrawal of the garrisons from the autonomous parts of the Empire. This theme inspired a series of discussions in the Lords during 1870, most of them originated by Lord Carnarvon, who joined
with a faith in colonial self-government a perceptive interest in the neglected subject
of imperial defence.[57]   In Carnarvon's eyes the military organization of the Empire
constituted one of the principal bonds of the whole structure. It was natural, therefore,
that he should regard the implementation of the Cardwell policy with the utmost apprehension. His initial alarm over the decision to withdraw the regulars from New Zealand
was increased by the news of the Fenian attacks on Canada in the summer of the year.
It was unjust to Canada, who wished the troops to remain, he declared, to recall them
at this critical juncture. Great Britain had encouraged the federation of the colonies in
British North America; was it proper that she should abandon the new nation to an un-
certain future within three years after the union had been accomplished? Canada was
the only Colony of the Crown which bordered a foreign country; her relations with the
United States were at all times difficult; it was vital that she be treated by the United
Kingdom with sympathy and consideration.

    The discussions which Carnarvon inaugurated in the Lords provided Granville with

a timely opportunity to expound his views on current imperial issues. He performed
this task in a pleasant and cultivated manner typical of the style of a great Whig magnate who was also the Liberal party's chief intermediary with the Sovereign. His bearing induced Carnarvon to observe at one point that if the Secretary of State had exercised the same courtesy towards the colonies as he did in dealing with the Lords there
would be little dissatisfaction existing in the colonial Empire! Granville disputed Carnarvon's claim that the military relations between Great Britain and the autonomous
colonies formed an important cement of the imperial connection. He tended to see in
the "intangibles" stressed by Gladstone a more durable aspect of the colonial tie.

> I do not agree with the noble Earl that the great bond between the colonies and this
> country is the military protection afforded to the former; for I am of opinion that
> the ties which bind us together are loyalty to the Crown, goodwill between the col-
> onies and the mother country, and a reciprocity of mutual advantages. When this
> state of things shall cease to exist, the idea of compelling by force any great and
> self-governing colony to remain connected with this country is an idea which no
> statesman would entertain; though no statesman should take too seriously any light-
> ly expressed wish on the part of a colony for separation from this country.[58]

On another occasion the Colonial Secretary revealed a certain impatience with the critics
of his New Zealand policy. He protested that the principle of withdrawing Imperial
troops from the self-governing colonies had been accepted by Carnarvon and Buckingham before him (which was true) and that it was hardly fair to accuse him of following
a revolutionary and disruptive policy when he was merely continuing in the footsteps of
an earlier government. He believed the strategic advantages of military concentration
in Great Britain were indisputable, and declared that he had no intention of making a
special exemption for New Zealand in the application of the policy.[59]

It was not until the excitement over the New Zealand affair had begun to subside
and the details of the settlement had been made known that the Gladstone Government
proceeded to offer reassurances about its colonial intentions. The first avowal of the
Ministry's faith in the Empire was not given until the summer of 1870, but even at this
advanced date it produced a settling effect. Issued earlier, perhaps in the Torrens debate, it would have been even more beneficial. In July, 1870, Lord Kimberley succeeded Granville at the Colonial Office, a fact which in itself caused the imperial enthusiasts to breathe a little more easily. Speaking in reply to Carnarvon's remarks on
the Fenian raids in May, Kimberley provided the most specific assurances that had yet
been given of the Government's intention to retain and defend all parts of the colonial
Empire. No member of the Administration had ever said that England would abandon
Canada, he declared. On the contrary, the Imperial Government possessed a most sol-
emn obligation to protect every corner of the Empire. Although a concentration of
troops at home had been decided on that did not mean a relinquishment of military commitments in the overseas territories. The Cabinet felt that the major share of the defence of Canada should properly fall to the Canadians themselves, and that to develop

a "military spirit" in the Dominion was the surest means of making the Colony secure. It was assumed without question, however, that in a crisis the mother country would come to the aid of Canada. [60]

The most emphatic rejection of separatism from an official spokesman occurred in the following year. In May, 1871, a resolution, almost identical with that of Torrens's, was moved in the House of Commons by R. A. Macfie, an early propagandist for the scheme of imperial federation. There was little of consequence said in the debate until Knatchbull-Hugessen, the new Parliamentary Under-Secretary, rose to give the Government's views on the subject. In his opening remarks Knatchbull-Hugessen brushed aside Macfie's proposals as unnecessary and quickly launched into an enthusiastic recital of the advantages accruing to Great Britain as an imperial power. Clearly this was to be a different type of speech on a colonial topic than had been heard from the ministerial benches for several years. The Colonial Office was constantly endeavouring to work out new arrangements for the more harmonious conduct of imperial relations, the Under-Secretary stated, and in its daily routine performed all the services which a parliamentary investigation might be expected to recommend. An efficient and capable Department, the Office was manned by a group of as "able and industrious public servants" as it was possible to find in Whitehall. [61] In fact, the policy of the Government found its purest expression "through the agency of the Colonial Office." And what was that policy? "[It] was to retain and preserve the connection between the mother country and the Colonies, basing always that connection on the sure and sound foundation of mutual good and the promotion of mutual interests."[62] A strong element in the Administration's attitude was the encouragement of self-reliance in the autonomous communities. In no sense did this imply the hope or the prospect of a termination of the connection with these colonies, in spite of Governor Wodehouse's assertions.

> Self-reliance did not mean separate existence, for a Colony might be great and self-reliant, and still maintain an intimate connection with the mother country. The Government wished to retain the Colonies; but they wished to retain them bound to this country by ties of kindred and affection....
>
> Let them [the great colonies] feel that there was nothing to be gained by separation; let them have nothing to complain of; let them see that we regarded them as brethren, made their interests our own, and viewed their increasing power and prosperity not only without jealousy, but with real and cordial satisfaction, and he believed their hearts would be more and more closely knit to us, and they would still make it their boast to rank with us as fellow subjects of the same Sovereign and citizens of the same Empire. This was the policy of the Government: it was no new policy; it was no party policy. [63]

These sentiments were received with gratification by the Commons, not least of all by the groups favouring schemes of closer imperial unity. In the course of his address Knatchbull-Hugessen had stated that the plan of a confederation for the Empire was personally attractive to him, although he realized that the project might have to be postponed for some years. It was indicative of the gathering strength of the new imperial attitude that such a remark could now draw applause from members on both sides of the House.

The Gladstone Ministry left office in February, 1874. Before doing so it had not only reaffirmed the value of the colonial connection but had envisaged the possibility of permanent co-operation between Great Britain and the self-governing colonies. The latter sentiment was expressed in 1873, in response to a motion urging colonial contributions for the defence of the Empire. The fact that the suggestion came from a Conservative member gave Knatchbull-Hugessen the opportunity to brand it as the Tory colonial policy, but he was careful not to be too hard on the scheme. The Government was interested in proposals through which the colonies would assume a fair share of the burdens of the imperial tie, and was naturally concerned that the people of England should not have to shoulder expenditures that might properly be borne by others. But it was a very delicate matter to apportion financial charges and no British administration could take the responsibility of embarking on a course which might prove distasteful to the great colonies. It was a fact that United Kingdom expenditure on the Empire had been decreasing in recent years and it could be safely said that at the present time more of it was allotted for general imperial purposes than for the benefit of particular colonies. In the latter case such assistance as was awarded was usually justified by the extraordinary expenses incurred by a territory in the early stages of its development. The Government could not support the motion, although Ministers recognized the justice of the claim which it contained.[64] Gladstone, in the same debate, went a little further than Knatchbull-Hugessen in exploring this concept of co-operation within the Empire. There was no real difference of opinion between the Government and the proponents of the motion, he declared, but the question was essentially one of degree. To attempt suddenly a revision of the burden of expenses for the Empire would be to court disaster. The pace towards imperial co-operation could not be quickened; the goal could only be reached by the processes of a "free and natural growth."[65] It would be no solution of the problem to force the colonies to grant grudging contributions towards the costs of imperial membership. Far better to allow them freedom, until eventually the stage might be reached when they would become eager to share in the responsibilities of empire. It was his earnest hope that some day the principle underlying imperial relations could be described as co-operation through the "spontaneous action" of mother country and colonies.[66] It was not an unimaginative glimpse of the transformed British Empire-Commonwealth of half a century later, with the Gladstonian principle of voluntaryism animating the entire organization.

By 1873 it was apparent that the new attitude towards the Empire was passing from the defensive to the offensive. At first the movement had spent its energies in combating separatism, Knatchbull-Hugessen's speech of 1871 furnishing a good example of this type of activity. Two years later plans for consolidating the Empire were being explored and Gladstone was able to advance the principle of co-operation as a basis for future action. The difference between the Prime Minister's remarks in 1870 on the Torrens motion and his utterances in 1873 provide an excellent indication of the progress which the nascent imperialist movement had made. Gladstone, on this as on other topics, was an accurate articulator of the currents of public feeling in the mother country. During the latter part of the period before 1887 the desire for the unity of the Empire became the most stimulating mode of thought in the discussion of the colonial question. Over the years it expressed itself in many forms--political federation, economic integration, social intercourse, military co-operation, and innumerable variants. Except in the sphere of imperial defence the British Government refrained from committing itself to any of these separate routes leading to the common goal. Thus the official discussion of the future of the Empire during the early years of the re-invigorated imperialism tended to be confined to generalities, or, occasionally, to be the product of an individual whim. It was also repetitive, for the same end was seen by successive governments and officials and the same obstacles to its realization noted by each passing generation.

In these circumstances it will be sufficient, therefore, to indicate the character of official opinion on the imperial connection by examining the views of one man. Lord Dufferin was an individual who was completely caught up in the imperialist fervour of his time. He considered that his most important duties in assuming the Governor-Generalship of Canada were to prevent the annexation of the Dominion by the United States and to preserve the Colony's relationship with Great Britain. For these ends he laboured during his years in the Dominion with discernment and with appreciable success. If the problems he encountered in Canada's relations with the United States were not as serious as those faced by his predecessor, he had graver obstacles to surmount in maintaining the harmonious working of the Canadian federal system. Dufferin was wise enough to notice that the consolidation of the Dominion and the creation of a genuine national sentiment were the surest foundations for stable relations with the United Kingdom. In a long letter to his intimate friend Carnarvon in 1874 he discussed the general destiny of the senior Colony. Dufferin observed that in his journeys throughout Canada he had discovered little support for the project of annexation. There was, however, a vague sentiment at large in favour of independence; a sentiment which he did not feel should be discouraged. For it was but an expression of a healthy self-assertion on the part of the Canadian people.

I [do not] think that this novel mode of thought will be devoid of benefit, provided it remains for the next twenty or thirty years a vague aspiration, and is not prematurely converted into a practical project. Hitherto there has been a lack of self-assertion and self-confidence amongst Canadians in forcible contrast with the sentiments which animate our friends to the South of us:--now however, the consolidation of the Provinces, the expansion of their Maritime interests, and above all the reduction to their sway of the great North West, has stimulated their imagination, and evoked the prospect of a National career far grander than as Nova Scotians, New Brunswickers, or Upper and Lower Canadians they would have dreamt of a few years ago.

If then this growing consciousness of power should stimulate their pride in the resources and future of their country, nay even if it should sometimes render them jealous of any interference on the part of England with their Parliamentary autonomy,

I do not think we shall have any cause of complaint. On the contrary, we should view with favour the risk of a high-spirited, proud, national feeling amongst them. Such a sentiment would neither be antagonistic to our interests, nor inimical to the maintenance of the tie which now subsists between us.[67]

The creation of a national spirit in Canada would, however, make more delicate the conduct of Anglo-Canadian relations, Dufferin felt. It would require that there be no exhibition of jealousy nor "capricious exercise of authority" from Great Britain, since these would tend to drive national aspirations into anti-British channels. If this eventuality should occur and lead to the independence of Canada, it would constitute a disaster for the Empire. The separate existence of Canada would be but a temporary phenomenon, for "the forces of gravitation, unbalanced by the influence of the British connection which now overcome it, would drag her straight into the bosom of the great Republic."[68]

What, then, was to be done to maintain and strengthen the connection between England and Canada? Dufferin's answer was plain: to continue the present loose relationship, anomalous as it was, neither binding Canada by commitments for imperial purposes nor exasperating her by shows of official unconcern. "Our chief object should be to keep things pretty much as they are for the next twenty years, and although in time of course, some change is inevitable, it may then be expected to be of a nature, and to take place under conditions which will reward us for our wise and temperate government."[69] It was a statement which several generations of administrators in the Colonial Office could be expected to endorse. To preserve the unity of the Empire was the aim of Imperial policy towards the autonomous colonies, and that aim could best be fulfilled by following Dufferin's fundamental rule of action. Superficially the rule might appear simple, but its application raised problems as complex as any produced by the relations between Great Britain and foreign states.

The organization which typified, and in many respects led, the early movement for imperial unity was the Imperial Federation League. The concept of imperial consolidation through political federation was not new in 1880 (it had been in the air since the middle of the nineteenth century) but the birth of an association devoted to its attainment was dependent on the existence of a body of sympathetic public opinion. The latter did not materialize until the early years of the eighties,[70] and the League was not formally launched until 1884. The aim of the new body was boldly set forth: to secure "by Federation the permanent Unity of the Empire." It promised to work for a federal system which would not "interfere with the existing rights of local Parliaments in local affairs." In addition, it proposed to draft a plan to combine the resources of the Empire, "on an equitable basis," for the achievement of common objectives and for the defence of common rights.[71] It was an ambitious programme which revealed even in its formulation a considerable difference of opinion among its adherents. For the plain truth was that the title of the new association did not accurately represent the views of its founders. In its early days the League never committed itself precisely to the idea of a political federation for the British Empire, and in fact included members

who were quite opposed to such a plan. The name was a pleasant euphemism, designed
to conceal the wide divisions in the new imperialist movement. In its activities the
League merely advocated the general concept of imperial unity, thus managing to include within itself strict federalists (some of whom were believers in free trade), a military group which hoped to see colonial contributions to the British army and navy, and
a preferential trade element which wanted to develop Empire solidarity by means of
tariff arrangements. The historian of the League has written,

> The League was intended to attract, as it did, the sympathies of men of varying
> shades of opinion, and in such circumstances harmony was most likely to be pre-
> served whilst it was content to work along general lines for the general object fav-
> oured by all instead of elaborating precise schemes for a new imperial constitution.
> It was certainly when the League endeavoured to elaborate an approved plan that its
> break-up became inevitable, clear proof that it was never unanimously in favour of
> any one in particular. [72]

The most outstanding achievement of the Imperial Federation League was the call-
ing of the Colonial Conference of 1887. That this meeting, the first of its kind in British imperial history, should have been successfully urged upon the Salisbury Government
within three years after the founding of the League, testifies in no small measure to the
vigour and influence of the organization in its early days. It also speaks convincingly
for the rapidity with which ideas of imperial consolidation had taken hold among the
people of Great Britain. It is significant that all the delegates to the Conference, from
both the autonomous colonies and the mother country, accepted without question the
assumption that their purpose at the meeting was to strengthen imperial ties. Although
Stanhope deliberately excluded the topic of political federation from the agenda of the
Conference, there was a desire on the part of most of the representatives from the colonies to make imperial unity more of a functional reality. The invitations to the meeting, sent out in November, 1886, stressed two aspects of the organization of the Empire
as worthy of discussion. One was the question of defence; the other the provision of the
so-called "peace interests"--postal and telegraphic communication and related services.
To the majority of the eleven autonomous colonies who were represented at London in
1887, as to the British Government, the defence issue was the paramount business of the
Conference. In his opening speech Lord Salisbury drew the attention of the delegates
to the project of a _Kriegsverein_, "a Union for purposes of mutual defence," and the Conference subsequently spent over half its time in discussing this proposal. [73]   In the end
a limited achievement was recorded in the field of naval defence, where the creation
of an Australasian squadron was planned, to be subsidized by contributions from the Antipodean colonies but to remain under Imperial control. To the surprise of the British
Government, the question of the future commercial policy of the Empire proved the topic
which excited the greatest colonial interest. A Cape delegate advanced the spectacular suggestion of a common tariff levied on goods coming into the British Empire from
outside, the revenue from it to be devoted to defence purposes. This plan was designed

to solve the problem of apportioning the burden of imperial defence and to emphasize the solidarity of the Empire. It was but the first of many schemes of imperial preference which the protectionist colonies were to put forward.

Jan Hofmeyr's suggestion of an imperial tariff in 1887 marked the fact that a powerful force was threatening to capture the leadership of the movement for imperial unity. The belief in the consolidation of the Empire through economic means--the concept of an Imperial Zollverein--was a sentiment which began in the colonies and forced itself upon the consciousness of the British people. Colonial opinion had advanced further in this respect than that of the mother country for several reasons. In the first place, most of the colonies were already protectionist, and imperial preference meant simply an extension of present tariff practices. In addition, the Empire represented to the colonies the chief trading unit, whereas at this time Great Britain undertook three-quarters of her trade with nations outside the imperial structure. Thus the project necessarily involved a far greater readjustment of English commercial policy than of colonial. It was not without support in the mother country, however. The National Fair Trade League, a protectionist body founded in 1881, favoured a tax on food coming from outside the Empire as the first step towards the establishment of a uniform tariff system. The campaign for imperial preference received a powerful stimulus in 1887, through Hofmeyr's advocacy at the Colonial Conference, and through the events in Canada in that year, where preferential arrangements were advanced as an antidote to Commercial Union. As the movement grew in strength it made more incompatible the position of the various groups forming the Imperial Federation League. Under Sir Charles Tupper, the protectionist wing in the League began to draw apart from the main body, a weakening tendency which finally brought about the dissolution of the organization in 1893. The League, unable to put forward a specific plan for the federation of the Empire and declining to submit to the control of the tariff reformers, preferred disintegration to continued impotence.

Thus the early movement for imperial unity came to an end. The second phase was to be dominated by schemes of commercial and economic union, until they too were rejected in the Liberal victory of 1906. The digressions assumed by the later expressions of imperial sentiment should not, however, obscure the importance of the decade of the seventies in the development of the new attitude. From this period dated the underlying principle of all subsequent imperialism--the conviction that the Empire should be maintained, and that it was desirable to establish reciprocal relations with the great settlement colonies. In the end these ideas marked the chief contribution of the mid-Victorian age to the solution of the perplexing problem of reconciling autonomy with empire.

II

The evolution of the British Empire into the Commonwealth of Nations has been influenced compellingly by the progress of Canada towards more extended autonomy. In the achievement of the freedom of each self-governing colony to shape its own fiscal policy the Canadian experience was decisive; it was none the less important in other aspects of imperial growth. The pre-eminent position of the Dominion among the autonomous British colonies enabled her to take the lead in asserting colonial aspirations, the concessions which she obtained serving in turn to emphasize her special and individual status. It was but natural that as the other dependencies of the Crown came to claim the rights of maturity, they should ask for constitutional equality with Canada, the senior Colony. As the first "Dominion," Canada gave her own designation to the new status which the autonomous colonies were accorded in the twentieth century. This position was ultimately to be as anomalous and as incapable of precise definition as that which she had enjoyed ever since the primary concessions of 1848-9.

The factors producing the important estimation in which British North America was held by the mother country in the latter half of the nineteenth century are not difficult to isolate. In 1860 the mere physical size of the seven colonies, with their enormous hinterland, gave promise of the emergence of a state holding sway over a magnificent domain. The combined area of the colonies, together with the vast territories controlled by the Hudson's Bay Company, exceeded that of the continental United States; might not some day the resources and achievements of the British colonies outstrip those of the neighbouring republic? Of all the parts of the Empire British North America was the closest geographically to the mother country, bound to her by the strong economic links of the North Atlantic community, and principally settled by people of British stock.

By 1860 the North American colonies formed the most populous, the most enterprising, and the most valuable possessions of the Crown of Great Britain. Politically the colonies were easily the most advanced in the Empire. Legislative assemblies had been in existence in the Canadas since 1791; in Nova Scotia since before the American Revolution. It was in these territories that the dynamic principle of responsible government had been first elaborated and applied, and afforded the opportunity of development. The North American colonies had been, after 1784, the only portion of the British Empire to see the advantages of union, and to possess the courage to undertake this momentous project. The first colonial state had resulted; confederation had followed self-government in the logical sequence of overseas nation-building. The political structure set up under the British North America Act provided additional evidence of Canada's increasing "status and weight" in the assemblage of the colonies.[74] The Dominion became a miniature "empire" in herself, with the undeveloped western region as her own colonial domain. In the words of one of her leading patriots, Canada assumed through Confederation a number of major responsibilities which entitled her to the fullest measure of confidence and consideration from the Imperial power.

Canada is not merely a Colony or a Province: she is a Dominion composed of an aggregate of seven large provinces federally united under an Imperial Charter, which expressly recites that her constitution is to be similar in principle to that of the United Kingdom. Nay, more, besides the powers with which she is invested over a large part of the affairs of the inhabitants of the several provinces, she enjoys absolute powers of legislation and administration over the peoples and territories of the north-west, out of which she has already created one province, and is empowered to create others with representative institutions.

These circumstances, together with the vastness of her area, the numbers of her free population, the character of the representative institutions and of the responsible Government which as citizens of the various provinces and of Canada her people have so long enjoyed, all point to the propriety of dealing with [her] in a manner very different from that which might be fitly adopted with reference to a single and comparatively small and young Colony.

Besides the general spread of the principles of constitutional freedom there has been, in reference to the Colonies, a recognized difference between their circumstances, resulting in the application to those in a less advanced condition of a lesser measure of self-government, while others are said to be invested with "the fullest freedom of political government;" and it may be fairly stated that there is no dependency of the British Crown which is entitled to so full an application of the principles of constitutional freedom as the Dominion of Canada. [75]

Understandably, the new status of Canada was but imperfectly realized in the mother country in the first years after North American consolidation. Sir John Macdonald's suggested designation of "Kingdom of Canada" for the young federation was rejected for fear it "would wound the sensibilities of the Yankees"; [76] Governor-General Monck's project of a special colonial order of knighthood, the "Order of St. Lawrence, " to commemorate the achievement of Canadian union, was condemned as too unconventional a step. [77]   Nevertheless, British statesmen and administrators who were in touch with the temper of the new Canadian nation were convinced that in North America a unique type of colony had been established within the imperial structure. Typical of the holders of this view was Viscount Monck, who wrote the Colonial Office in 1868 to urge that the members of the Canadian Privy Council be granted the same style as English Privy Councillors. "For the first time in the Colonial history of Great Britain a portion of her Colonial Empire has been elevated by Her Majesty from the rank of a 'Province' to that of a distinct 'Dominion,'" he asserted. [78]   Monck's statement was a plea for the recognition of the nascent Canadian nationhood as well as a justification for the ceremonial pretensions of the Colony.

Administratively, during these years, the Colonial Office came increasingly to look upon the Dominion as a virtual foreign country rather than as a colony. Sir T. F. Elliot, who had surveyed from Downing Street the whole span of Canadian development since the thirties and who was certainly unprepared to recognize more than the realities of a situation suggested, was in the habit, after 1867, of using terminology illustrative of this distinction. Writing to Sir Henry Taylor in 1868, he noted, "... you are doubtless aware that we now treat [the] Dominion pretty nearly as an independent Country. It consists of nearly four million inhabitants and we have to leave to them the whole responsibility and power of managing their own affairs. "[79]   Sir Frederic Rogers used the same mode of address, although in his case the wish may perhaps have been father to the thought. Arguing in 1871 that the War Office should continue to pay the salary of the Military Secretary to the Governor-General of Canada, he compared the post to that of a military attaché at an embassy abroad. "Canada is almost a foreign country, and we cannot expect to escape some expense in keeping up our relations with her in that capacity. For our ambassador--who is the Governor--she pays:--The Military Secretary to the Govr. occupies ... a position somewhat analogous to a military attaché at Paris or Berlin. And it seems to me that we might pay."[80]

The importance of Canada was stressed by the Imperial Government on various occasions to support two propositions: first, that the salary of the Governor-General should not be reduced below the sum of £10,000 fixed in 1867, and secondly, that it was desirable that his rank and precedence be established above that of other colonial Governors. Dufferin urged once that the Governor-General of Canada should not receive an emolument less than that paid an officer administering the government of any other (and therefore subordinate) colony in the Empire.[81] Similarly, in 1875 Dufferin suggested to Lord Carnarvon that the title of the Governor-General of Canada be changed to that of "Viceroy." This alteration, he said, would tend to elevate unmistakably the Dominion Government above the provinces, and would prove a most acceptable innovation in American eyes. It would also reflect the current state of the relationship between Great Britain and Canada.

I think the time has arrived when it would be well to consider whether it might not be desirable to erect the Dominion of Canada into a Vice-royalty. Such a change would undoubtedly be very popular with the Canadian people. It would be regarded as a fresh intimation of the intention of this country to maintain her connection with her Colonies. It would be accepted as a tribute of consideration paid by Great Britain to the growing importance of the Dominion, and as a recognition of the stability of Confederation.[82]

Carnarvon gave the concept of Canada as the senior Colony of the Empire full and frequent expression. His personal knowledge of the Canadian scene influenced him in forming this opinion, which was revealed in both his official correspondence and in his public speeches. For instance, it was more than a desire to compliment the inhabitants of the Dominion which caused the former Secretary of State to preface an address at Montreal in 1883 with this remark: "Canada is no ordinary possession of the Crown; none ranks entirely beside her, even in the group of noble nationalities which England, the mother of nations, has planted abroad."[83] The new definition had its useful aspects as well, for it could be employed to justify concessions to Canada which could not be granted to the other autonomous colonies. Thus a request for an Imperial subsidy for a line of Atlantic steamers was proffered in 1875 by Cartwright on the grounds "that Canada is a Confederation with a very broad basis and good security and engaged on many Imperial works." Carnarvon applauded this reasoning, seeing its value in the solution of the wider problem of dispensing Imperial financial assistance. "I have no doubt that politically it has advantages.... It is possible that this argument may enable us to withstand the similar applications which will come in from other Colonies for a time."[84]

By the decade of the eighties, the position of Canada had been officially recognized as pre-eminent among the self-governing colonies. When Chamberlain placed Laurier at his right hand for the group photograph of the Colonial Conference of 1897 it was no more than a formal acknowledgement of an assumption which had influenced Imperial policy for many years.

The British Empire, as it existed in the two decades after 1867, possessed a unity which gave a valid significance to the word "Empire." For in this period the self-governing colonies were still part of an "Empire"--one which in many respects had changed but little since the years following the American Revolution. Juridically, the Empire retained its characteristic elements of a sovereign power and a number of dependencies in varying stages of political evolution. The realities might have become altered, but the forms called to mind an older and more uncomplicated age. Habits and patterns of thought are sometimes clung to long after they have lost their original meaning, to influence men's outlook in a later era for which they may have no special relevance. It is for this reason that the forms by which the unity of the British Empire was secured in the second half of the nineteenth century are important to a discussion of intra-imperial relations at this time. The Colonial Office, like most other administrative institutions, tended to place a reliance in methods of procedure and basic mental attitudes that had been developed in earlier years. The Office's outlook towards the aspirations of the self-governing colonies was inevitably influenced by these considerations. This is not to suggest that the Department became atrophied in its dealings with the autonomous colonies (nothing could be further from the truth) but merely to submit that it obeyed a natural inclination to approach these problems bearing in mind the requirements of a united Empire.

In the first place among the factors contributing to the formal unity of the Empire was the legislative supremacy of the British Parliament. Omnipotent throughout the dominions of the Crown in 1766, Parliament remained legally omnipotent a hundred years later. Nothing in the British North America Act or in the constitutions of the other self-governing colonies affected the right of the United Kingdom Parliament to legislate for the colonies. Sir Charles Adderley, when President of the Board of Trade in 1876, made this fundamental point clear in repudiating a claim that the Imperial Parliament had renounced some of its legislative authority over Canada. "Imperial Acts bound Canadian subjects as much as all other British subjects. It was a total mistake to suppose that the Act of 1867 ... in any way altered the relation of Canadian subjects to the Imperial Parliament."[85] A commentator agreed, pointing out, however, that this explanation furnished only half the story.

> The whole question of the relations of the Imperial authority to the representative Colonies is one of great difficulty and delicacy. It requires consummate prudence and statesmanship to reconcile the metropolitan supremacy with the worthy spirit of colonial independence. As a matter of abstract right, the Mother Country has never parted with the claim of ultimate supreme authority for the Imperial Legislature. If it did so, it would dissolve the Imperial tie and convert the Colonies into foreign and independent States.[86]

Aside from the legal right of the United Kingdom Parliament to legislate on all subjects throughout the entire Empire, there existed also the duty of that Parliament to make laws in certain fields that were of common concern or of overriding imperial importance. Merchant shipping was one of the most vital of these areas, as well as perhaps the most difficult in which to enact satisfactory measures. There were, in addition, topics like copyright, extradition, the maintenance of a state of neutrality, the provision of vice-admiralty courts, the apprehension of fugitive offenders, naturalization, and others, which normally were considered subjects for action by the Imperial Parliament.[87] This usage was necessary either because the colonies did not possess extraterritorial powers or because it was considered desirable to adopt a uniform procedure for the regulation of these subjects. In most of the acts applying to the autonomous colonies in the period under review, the intention to extend to the colonies was clearly expressed. It is also true that in the majority of these instances the self-governing colonies were consulted and their wishes learned before the proposed measures were made applicable to them. Consultation and discussion were coming to be the usual practice in the drafting of imperial legislation, just as they were to emerge as the essential rules in the deliberations of the Commonwealth.

The other fundamental unity of the British Empire existed in the common executive, symbolized by the Crown, which surmounted the entire imperial structure. The prerogative rights of the Crown were most significant for the autonomous colonies in the field of the treaty-making power. Without securing full authority from the Imperial Crown the colonies were unable to appoint plenipotentiaries, conduct negotiations, or conclude binding instruments. In the same way the judicial unity of the Empire was secured through the system of appeals by special leave to the Judicial Committee of Her Majesty's Privy Council. Regulated in some colonies, the appeal to the Sovereign in Council nevertheless constituted a bond throughout the British dependencies. More specifically the Sovereign dispensed honours and titular distinctions, appointed and dismissed colonial Governors, and made possible the exercise of the prerogative of mercy by her representative in each colony. Finally there remained the Crown's power of disallowance of colonial legislation, and the Governor's authority to reserve local measures for the consideration of the Secretary of State. The exercise of the right of disallowance, designed to safeguard Imperial interests, was an effective limitation on the representative government colonies in the latter part of the nineteenth century. In Canada, however, disallowance was never used after the early years of Confederation, and reservation only occasionally, so that two vital aspects of Imperial control passed into abeyance. The fate of disallowance as it affected Canadian acts was typical of the manner in which the various manifestations of Imperial executive authority were transformed with the progress of colonial autonomy. In time these forms were divested of every suggestion of British supremacy and continued merely as symbols of the unity of the Empire. This process was, of course, not complete by 1887, but as far as Canada was concerned the ultimate meaning of the externals of imperial unity was plain.

It is precisely in this distinction between "legal power" and "constitutional right" that the primary importance of these forms lay during the period under discussion.[88]

Throughout the nineteenth century the unity of the British Empire was being undermined, fatally and persistently, by the principles of colonial autonomy. The whole period can be interpreted in terms of the devolution of the functional authority of a sovereign state. The Austinian theory of sovereignty, which had ruled so triumphantly throughout the century, could be described by 1900 as still valid in a strictly legal sense, but its real force had long since gone. As in the time of the American Revolution, the legal definition of the Empire had failed to keep pace with the course of constitutional practice. With the creation of the Canadian Dominion the divergence between the legal omnipotence of the Imperial Parliament and its constitutional right of legislation became unmistakably pronounced. It was at all times legally possible for the Parliament of Great Britain to repeal, without consultation with Canada, the British North America Act, but such a step would have been clearly contrary to the established usage and convention of the age. The great problem which faced Imperial statesmen in maintaining the unity of the Empire was to distinguish between what was possible and what was practicable. All might, in theory, be attempted, but could something, in particular circumstances, be achieved? This was the dilemma which confronted the heads of the Colonial Office as they dealt with Anglo-Canadian relations in the latter half of the nineteenth century. It was well stated in 1876 by Lord Carnarvon, who stands out among the Colonial Secretaries of his generation in his understanding of the complexity of the problem.

> But the power of the Imperial Parliament over every part of the Empire has not been, and cannot be, in any degree curtailed or superseded by the grant of local self-Government. Whether, and in what way the responsibility of using this power should at any time be exercised, is a separate question, the difficulty and delicacy of which, from a political point of view, is, and will always I cannot doubt be, fully recognized by Her Majesty's Advisers, of whatever party; and I am very confident that [the Canadian] Ministers appreciate the desire which has ever been shown to respect to the full the Constitution of Canada, and to leave to the Ministers and Parliament of the Dominion the most complete authority over persons and things within their jurisdiction. [89]

Simply expressed, the problem can be reduced to the need to reconcile the legitimate demands of the individual colony with the requirements of an indivisible Empire presided over by an omnicompetent authority. How then, in the case of British policy towards Canada in the two decades 1867-87, was this formidable administrative antithesis approached? It is possible to isolate a number of desiderata which, although never elevated into guiding principles, nonetheless influenced the political and permanent heads of the Colonial Office in their attitude towards Canadian problems after 1867. In the first place, it was readily recognized by everyone in authority that the United Kingdom's relations with Canada were incapable of precise definition and not subject to the lessons of earlier colonial experience. The Department's supervision of them had of necessity to be based on the conclusions drawn from a strictly empirical study. Sir Edmund Head, one of the wisest of colonial Governors, had offered this counsel as early as 1858:

It may be said that ... the line which separates the duty of the Mother Country and that of the Colony is vague and undefined. It would be singular if it were
otherwise; for the present relation of Great Britain to her freely governed Colonies
is, I believe, new and unprecedented in the history of the world, and political duties
and relations can only be rendered definite by experience and practice. [90]

There were thus no charts to assist the navigators responsible for guiding the imperial
connection into an unknown future. There were only hints to be gained during the course
of the voyage and attitudes to be formed in the light of particular circumstances. The
most immediately useful of these observations was the one provided by Lord Dufferin in
1876 when pressing Canadian constitutional problems were awaiting settlement: "... I
should be inclined to think that the safest line to adopt would be that of recognizing Canada as endowed with full powers of self government, qualified only by a due exercise of
the Queen's Prerogative. "[91]   On another occasion he cautioned that, whatever the inconvenience, Canadian questions must be taken up with the prospect of an empirical
solution kept steadily in view. "Under any circumstances a discussion on the limits of
Colonial autonomy is a very thorny and barren topic ... ," he noted. [92]

Another consideration to which the Colonial Office paid respectful attention was
closely related to this concept of colonial autonomy. It was that Great Britain must be
prepared to acquiesce in the internal decisions made by Canada, no matter how improper or objectionable they might appear. This was Gladstone's contribution to the discussion of the imperial question, apart from the colonial utterances of his early years (almost entirely superseded), and, except for a few isolated cases later, he applied it with
perception in all his dealings with the autonomous colonies. Self-reliance was the goal
which it was hoped would be realized from the operation of this principle. The defence
of Canada, for instance, was a responsibility falling primarily on the Canadians; Great
Britain's share in it was the secondary one of providing advice and assistance.

We do not think it is our function with regard to Canada, considering the position
and development of Canada, to insist on this or that particular measure with respect
to the defence of Canada, as we recognize the full competency and capacity of Canada, and have no doubt of the inclination of Canada to perform what the Dominion
Government may think to be its proper duties, and as we believe it to be the best
judge of those duties. Our office has been to offer the Dominion every reasonable
assistance; that duty we have fulfilled. ... [93]

The good or bad government of a particular colony might well be a matter of significance to the Empire and to the Imperial power, but it was a fact of much greater importance to the colony concerned. It was better for the parts of the Empire to develop
spontaneously than to impose, even with the most laudable intentions, a uniformity upon the whole structure. For colonial self-government, which encouraged the free expression of the national life of the various dependencies, could contribute substantially
to the cohesion of the imperial system. "The real life of the Empire might well fail

entirely to survive artificial uniformity, for the Empire is an organism in which the development of the whole is dependent on the free growth of the several parts. "[94] Independence produced diversity, but it also produced strength.

Accompanying these assumptions was the supplementary one that, in any community, responsibility must always be associated with authority. Herbert, as Permanent Under-Secretary, declined to recommend the sanctioning of a Canadian Bill on one occasion because he felt insufficient notice had been given the parties affected by the measure. In this instance the trust imposed in a legislative body had clearly been abused. But this was not to say that the Imperial Government should act as a perpetual arbiter in disputes arising out of the legislative capacities of the autonomous colonies.

It is within the competency of Canada to legislate as its Parliament thinks fit upon a matter of internal interest.... For H.M. Govt. to consent to be made a court of appeal from the Legislature of Canada in such a question would be to withdraw from the Dominion the rights and responsibilities of self-government. Any person who may deem themselves aggrieved by the action of the Dominion Legislature in such a case must look to that Legislature for redress. [95]

Sometimes, however, there did exist substantial Imperial interests above and beside those of a more distinctly colonial nature. How were they to be maintained? Attempting to answer this question, Edward Blake in 1876 suggested a course of proceeding, novel and seemingly ineffectual, which yet offered the hope of constructive cooperation in an Empire composed of autonomous parts. There was, Blake argued, no lasting protection for British interests in constitutional safeguards, in reserve powers, in the provisions of a Governor's Instructions, or in any other "form of words." In the final resort Imperial interests could only be preserved through the good sense of a responsible colonial Ministry.

The truth is, that Imperial interests are, under our present system of government to be secured in matters of Canadian executive policy, not by any such clause in a Governor's instructions (which would be practically inoperative, and if it can be supposed to be operative would be mischievous); but by mutual good feeling, and by proper consideration for Imperial interests on the part of Her Majesty's Canadian advisers.... [96]

The Colonial Office acquiesced in this view of the question when it was originally propounded and used it later to govern its appreciation of this formidable (and delicate) problem.

It is not an unwarranted statement to claim that the assumptions which have been enumerated here made possible the peaceful transformation of the British Empire into the modern Commonwealth. Obviously in order to have achieved this spectacular result it was necessary for these principles to be translated into British official policy. That this translation ultimately took place over the whole range of departments in Whitehall can be explained mainly through the influence of the Colonial Office. For it was that Department which absorbed most conscientiously the implications of the new rules of action. The Colonial Office's long experience with the administration of overseas territories in every stage of political maturity; its position as the Department which maintained the original and primary liason with Canada; and the wisdom and insight displayed by its heads combined to produce within its precincts a climate exceedingly sympathetic to an understanding of the new principles. This is not to apportion undeserved credit to the work of the Office. For it too had its moments of doubt and discouragement, when it seemed as if the game had been played out, as well as the other and more frequent moments of exhilaration. As the nineteenth century moved spaciously to its close the Colonial Office came to display an increasing assurance in the application of these salutary principles. They assumed a general character and thus succeeded in interweaving themselves with more conventional aspects of the Department's approach to the administration of the Empire.

The function of the Office at this time can be considered to have possessed a dual significance. Clearly the Department's first responsibility, its raison d'être, lay in the maintenance of sound and mutually satisfactory relations with the great settlement colonies such as Canada. In order to fulfil this role it had to convince the other departments in Whitehall that it was competent to express their attitudes and interests to the Canadian Government. The first duty could not be adequately carried out without the achievement of a large measure of success in the second. Conversely it would have proved impossible to secure co-operation from the other public departments if the Office had not demonstrated its ability to look after Imperial interests while at the same time maintaining a cordial connection with Canada. Thus the two aspects of its work were really but one task: the momentous problem of defining the organization of an Empire whose very foundations appeared to be dissolving.

The goals which the Office held before it in managing relations with Canada were gained, on the whole, with creditable success. The extent of that success can best be measured by a detailed examination of Anglo-Canadian interaction in the years following 1867. It has been the purpose of this work to explore aspects of these relations during a limited but formative period, for it is only through a number of "case studies" that the full magnitude of the task of the Colonial Office can be appreciated. The specialized subjects discussed in these pages do not, of course, include all the issues which went to make up the fabric of Anglo-Canadian relations in the two decades after Confederation. They can, however, be considered as representative of the types of problem which arose and of the administrative techniques devised to meet them. For the purposes of an investigation of British imperial policy, the methods of procedure used by the Colonial Office are naturally of consummate importance.

Several courses of action were pursued by the Department in taking up Canadian subjects in the period between 1867 and 1887. Sometimes there was a full recognition of the rightness or expediency of the Canadian position. The episodes which fell in this category were usually unaffected by the presence of any legitimate interest relating to the United Kingdom Government. Occasionally these cases were slightly concerned with matters of Imperial significance, which however were not considered of sufficient importance to justify an interference into Canadian domestic affairs. The triangular controversy in which the Department found itself in 1869-70 and again in the later years of the seventies over the provision of Imperial guarantees is an admirable example of such a situation. It illustrates in a striking manner the fact that on occasion the Office went to battle for the Canadian point of view, regardless of the circumstance that Imperial interests were involved. From the moment when the news of the Canadian appropriation of the Intercolonial loan funds was received in Downing Street, Rogers's direct "I go very much with the Colony" typified the role assumed by the Department. The Treasury attacked the Canadian action; the Office discreetly modified the subsequent communication of Treasury opinion to Canada. The dissatisfaction felt by the Lords of the Treasury impelled them to propose impossible safeguards for future guarantees; in rejecting these provisions the Office formulated other arrangements adaptable to the peculiar circumstances of each guarantee. Through the entire discussion the principle that Canada must be allowed the management of guaranteed funds was tacitly recognized by the Department. In later brushes with the Treasury this principle was defended more confidently. Thus in the comedy of errors which characterized the Treasury's handling of the Public Works guarantee the Office emerged as a pillar of vigorous and assertive virtue. Finally, when the implications of the question were seen to be political rather than financial, the Department's attitude towards the Canadian claims was vindicated.

Roughly the same position was assumed by the Office in the interminable discussions with the Board of Trade over Canadian commercial policy. Here, after 1867, the endorsement of the right of Canada to frame an indigenous tariff system was virtually unqualified. Not only did the Department decline to follow the pointed recommendations of the Board of Trade in regard to particular tariff measures of the Dominion, but it decided to renounce its old function of being the vehicle by which English commercial protests were transmitted to Canada. It reserved to itself the right to make representations against the Canadian tariff in special circumstances, but these statements were to be no more than the usual observations tendered by one country when it is injured by the tariff policy of another. Differential duties were in a different category than protection, since they affected the United Kingdom's treaty obligations, but here again the Department showed itself prepared to accept a large measure of exclusively Canadian control. Preferential trade agreements between the Dominion and neighbouring colonies and between Canada and the United States were allowed by the Colonial Office without opposition. The principle that these arrangements were capable of indefinite extension to other colonial or even to foreign areas was in turn approved by the middle of the eighties. With the exception of the operation of a limited number of existing British trade treaties upon the Canadian tariff, the freedom of the Dominion to construct its own commercial policy was complete by 1887. The manner in which the Department had accepted the Canadian aspirations and campaigned for them in Whitehall was an important factor in achieving this state of affairs.

Canadian questions required a somewhat different handling when extensive Imperial interests were at stake. In these cases the Office had the dual task, in seeking agreement with Canada, of safeguarding the essential aims of the United Kingdom and at the same time modifying the too liberal assessment of these interests often made by other departments. To reconcile the demands of Canadian autonomy with the obligations of imperial unity was a duty which provided the Office with its most complicated problems. The discussions with Canada and with the Lord Chancellor over the Supreme Court Act of 1875 represent an appropriate illustration of these difficulties. The Office saw the expediency of assenting to the Canadian insistence that she possessed an unqualified right to limit appeals, but was conscious of the desirability of preserving the leave to appeal as a bond of empire. By suggesting regulations designed to bridge the gap between the opposing views, by interpreting Canadian aspirations to the Lord Chancellor, by arranging personal conferences among the leading figures in the controversy, by using all the devices of accommodation and suasion that are at the call of a public department, the Office managed to settle this vexed question in a satisfactory fashion. The compromise which was finally produced lasted for almost three-quarters of a century, a notable achievement in an era of rapid constitutional change such as that which has characterized the development of the British Empire since 1875. Over the appointment of a Canadian agent in London the same role was attempted by the Colonial Office, although on this occasion its own convictions closely resembled those held by the Foreign Office. While welcoming a Canadian representative in the capital of the Empire the Department could not bring itself to grant him the quasi-diplomatic status which the Macdonald Government felt the nature of the new agent's functions warranted. The Department was perfectly willing to conduct relations with Canada on what amounted to a diplomatic basis, but it did not favour translating this indefinite modus operandi into a conventional form, dignified by official nomenclature. The diplomatic unity of the Empire lasted into the twentieth century, although long before its passing the Office had accepted a de facto ambassadorial status for the Canadian High Commissioner. In this instance the substance had been conceded while the shadow was retained.

Finally, there is a third example of the work of the Department in arranging compromise settlements in the discussions with Canada over the commercial treaty-making power. During the period 1867 to 1887 the Department went a long way in urging Canadian freedom of action in this field upon the Foreign Office, but was unable to accept the last stage of an independent colonial plenipotentiary, armed with full powers from the Crown. Its efforts, however, helped to raise the Canadian share in commercial negotiations from that of a distinctly advisory capacity to one of equal importance (and greater practical significance) with the representatives of the British foreign service. The Office took the lead in securing for Canada and the other autonomous colonies the right to withdraw from new British commercial treaties. This step constituted an important working advance which gave support to the later request of the self-governing parts of the Empire that older imperial agreements, which prejudiced their commercial autonomy, should be abandoned by Great Britain. Thus indirectly the Colonial Office made possible the surmounting of the final obstacle faced by the greater British Dominions in their movement towards fiscal independence.

Occasionally the Office adopted an attitude towards Canada that was not directly influenced by the views of other English departments. On a constitutional point, for instance, legal advice would naturally be taken, but the final decision was for the Office to pronounce. The period 1867-87 provided an interesting illustration of this type of independent action by the Department in the case of the Canadian disallowance question. Here the Canadian Government and the Colonial Office held contrasting and incompatible views. Both approached the subject with an intelligent conception of the nature of Canadian federalism, expounded with earnest conviction. But the Office committed tactical errors which hampered the presentation of its case and displayed a subsequent disingenuousness which was hardly commendable. After a stubborn fight the Department was forced to concede the Canadian interpretation, which, after all, was in conformity with the new spirit animating the Empire at the time.

There was a tendency in British official relations with Canada during the period 1867-87, for the views of the various departments in Whitehall to come together. It was a trend propelled as much by the logic of events as by any conscious pressure on the part of the Office. For just as the Department valued its own independence in the formation of policy, it respected the autonomy of other divisions of government. Herbert minuted wisely in 1885 on a communication from the Foreign Office, "Unless Lord Salisbury's personal attention to this matter can be obtained it may perhaps as well stand over indefinitely. We are powerless as a Department, to induce other departments to give any consideration to Colonial wishes."[97] The separate responsibilities of the great public departments did not, however, prevent their gradual adoption of a common policy towards the self-governing colonies. In the main that policy was based on the lessons which the Colonial Office had learned through its relations with British North America following responsible government and Confederation. It was a policy strictly empirical in temper, liberal, magnanimous, and exhibiting a salutary consistency. Fundamentally it was constructed on the realization that the national evolution of the larger settlement colonies had created an Empire in which the most profound issue was a problem of "international government." Great Britain's relations with Canada, and with the other autonomous colonies, were, as Lord Carnarvon once observed, "political rather than colonial,"[98] diplomatic rather than administrative. The acceptance of this principle in Whitehall made possible the transformation of the British Empire into the unique fraternity of nations that is the modern Commonwealth. Thus the Colonial Office, through its response to Canadian aspirations in the crucial twenty years that followed the emergence in North America of the first colonial state, deserves to assume a distinguished place among the architects of the Commonwealth of Nations.

1. N. W. Rowell, The British Empire and World Peace, quoted in Skilling, Canadian Representation Abroad, xvi.

2. E. A. Benians, "Colonial Self-Government, 1852-70," in Cambridge History of the British Empire, II, 701.
In passing, it should be pointed out that separatism was never an unmixed evil. Some historians of the Empire, in fact, have seen the separatists as helping to create the modern Commonwealth through their emphasis on colonial self-reliance and independence. By encouraging these qualities in the colonies and by persuading Great Britain to approve them, the separatists may have rendered a powerful service to the concept of the Commonwealth. (C. A. Bodelsen, Studies in Mid-Victorian Imperialism [Copenhagen, 1924], 57-9; H. D. Hall, The British Commonwealth of Nations: A Study of its Past and Future Development [London, 1920], 52-3.)

3. Arthur Mills, Colonial Constitutions, quoted in Bodelsen, Mid-Victorian Imperialism, 44.

4. W. T. Waugh, "The Development of Imperial Relations," Report of the Canadian Historical Association, 1927, 83.

5. Granville to Sir G. F. Bowen (Governor of New Zealand), March 21, 1869, printed in A. J. Harrop, England and the Maori Wars (London, 1937), 351.

6. Spectator, July 24, 1869, quoted in Harrop, England and the Maori Wars, 16.

7. Hansard, Third Series, CXCVIII, 456-93 (July 22, 1869).

8. Ibid., 778-83 (July 27, 1869).

9. Hall, The Colonial Office, 232.

10. Hansard, Third Series, CXCIX, 199 (Feb. 14, 1870).

11. In some of the Australian colonies there was also dissatisfaction with the Colonial Office during these years. For instance in Victoria demands were voiced for a personal union with the mother country and in 1869 there was a furious attack in the Legislative Assembly upon the Office. A number of resolutions were moved protesting interference by the Department in the domestic affairs of colonies and claiming that the Colonial Secretary had violated the principles of responsible government by venturing to tender advice in certain local issues in Victoria. Rogers, who was singled out for criticism by the sponsor of these resolutions, suggested a dispatch explaining the Department's views on the subject of imperial organization. The dispatch was not sent, however, since the resolutions were never officially brought under the notice of the Colonial Sec-

retary. (Hall, The Colonial Office, 265. See also the same author's Australia and England: A Study in Imperial Relations [London, 1934], 185-93.)

12. The details of the scheme for an unofficial colonial conference in 1870 are to be found in PP, 1870, XLIX, nos. C-24 and C-51.

13. Messrs. J. A. Youl, H. Sewell and H. Blaine to Responsible Government Colonies, Aug. 13, 1869: PP, 1870, XLIX, no. C-24, 1-2.

14. Granville to Responsible Government Colonies, circular, Sept. 8, 1869: ibid., 3.

15. These replies are found in PP, 1870, XLIX, no. C-24, 4-15 and PP, 1870, XLIX, no. C-51, 1-5.

16. Young to Granville, no. 166, Dec. 30, 1869: CO 42/678. Printed in PP, 1870, XLIX, no. C-24, 12-13.

17. Macdonald to Rose, Nov. 16, 1869, printed in Pope, Correspondence of Sir John Macdonald, 104.
The same sentiment was expressed by most Canadian newspapers. The Montreal Gazette's "Our present relations with the Empire, if let alone by agitators, either upon this side of the water or the other, are satisfactory," was typical. (Montreal Gazette, Jan. 5, 1870, quoted in Glazebrook, Canadian External Relations, 113.)

18. See Macdonald's letter to Carnarvon, expressing his worry over the policies of the Gladstone Government.

> We are glad to know that we have in you a friend. I may almost say a friend in need--for we greatly distrust the men at the helm in England, who can not, I fear, be considered as appreciating the importance of maintaining the Empire as it is, intact.
> We indulge the belief here, however, that Messrs. Bright, Lowe, and Gladstone (shall I add Lord Granville?) are not true exponents of the public opinion of England. We may perhaps be obliged to appeal from the Government to the people of England.

(Macdonald to Carnarvon, April 14, 1870, quoted in Hardinge, Life of Carnarvon, II, 21.)

19. Rogers to Lady Rogers, Nov., 1869, quoted in Blachford, Letters, 279.

20. Galt to Young, May 15, 1869, quoted in Skelton, Life of Sir A. T. Galt,

452. The correspondence between Galt, Young and Granville over this episode is re-produced in Life of Sir A. T. Galt, 451-6.

21. Galt wrote to Cardwell about the same time, expressing his apprehension over the fact that American intentions were directed towards propelling Canada towards an early separation from Great Britain. His fears were caused by the feeling that Can-adian national sentiment would still be in an immature state when the break occurred, he explained. (Galt to Cardwell, May 17, 1869, ibid., 453.)

22. Galt to Granville, Feb. 25, 1870, quoted in ibid., 453-4.
Galt's remarks in the Canadian Parliament are found in Debates of the House of Commons (Canada), 1870, I, 141-5 (Feb. 21, 1870).

23. Granville to Galt, May 18, 1870, quoted in Skelton, Life of Sir A. T. Galt, 456. See also Granville to Galt, March 15, 1870: ibid., 454-5.
When the subject was raised in the British House of Commons Monsell read Gran-ville's letter of March 15 to a somewhat startled House. (Hansard, Third Series, CC, 324-5 (March 21, 1870). There was a supplementary question on March 24: ibid., 574-5.)

24. Professor Knaplund states that there is no trace of this letter in the Gladstone correspondence, nor of any communication between the two men on the subject. (Knap-lund, Gladstone and Imperial Policy, 100.) Fortunately the Granville correspondence yields Gladstone's reply.

25. Gladstone to Granville, May 29, 1869: PRO 30/29/57.
Rogers, who composed the early drafts of Granville's dispatch to Young, confes-sed that he was unable to find any other pronouncements on the imperial tie similar to that of Gladstone's. On the contrary, he noted, other expressions of opinion "look rather in a difft. direction. Secretaries of State seem rather desirous of urging that the con-nexion is in fact for the common interest, than that it ought to be dissolved if it is not so." (Minute by Rogers, c. June 7, 1869, on draft of Granville to Young, confidential, June 14, 1869, appended to Young to Granville, confidential, Nov. 11, 1869: CO 42/678.)

26. Most of the dispatch is simply a long extract from Gladstone to Cathcart, no. 14, Feb. 3, 1846: CO 43/146.

27. Granville to Young, confidential, June 14, 1869: CO 42/678. (The word-ing of the dispatch is now Granville's.)

28. Ibid.
Granville offered more than a hint of his own separatist preferences in a letter

SIR ROBERT HERBERT, THE BUST BY SIR GEORGE FRAMPTON
(By permission of the Commonwealth Relations Office)

written to Lord Russell later in the same summer: "Our relations with North America are of a very delicate character. The best solution of them would probably be that in the course of time and in the most friendly spirit the Dominion should find itself strong enough to proclaim her independence." (Granville to Russell, Aug. 28, 1869, quoted in Fitzmaurice, Life of Granville, II, 22.)

This viewpoint was not uncommon among statesmen and diplomatists concerned with Anglo-American relations in the disturbed period after the Civil War. Lord Lyons, writing to Clarendon in 1870, noted, "I never feel comfortable about Canada and our North American possessions.... In fact it seems to be in the nature of things that the United State's prestige should grow and ours should wane in North America, and I wish we were well and creditably out of the scrape." (Lyons to Clarendon, 1870, quoted in Newton, Life of Lyons, I, 291-2.) Clarendon wholeheartedly agreed. "I ... wish that [our possessions in North America] would propose to be independent, and to annex themselves. We can't throw them off, and it is very desirable that we should part as friends." (Clarendon to Lyons, June 1, 1870, quoted in ibid., 292.)

29. An examination of the successive drafts of the dispatch shows that it was primarily the work of Rogers (whose separatist views are well known) but the significant last paragraph was added by Granville. (The drafts are found in CO 42/678.)

30. Sir John Young as reported in the Toronto Globe, July 16, 1869, quoted in Stacey, Canada and the British Army, 218.

31. In 1870 Sir Philip Wodehouse, the Governor of the Cape, made a speech which had a similarly disturbing effect. Wodehouse deplored the general trend towards self-government in the settlement colonies, declaring that it was entirely opposed to the continuance of a colonial existence. In his view Canada and the Australian colonies were heading directly towards independence. (Egerton, British Colonial Policy, 1606-1909, 358.) His attitude was therefore very different from Young's, who although he probably did not favour separation, was not alarmed by its prospect. In the popular imagination, however, the speeches by the two Governors were regarded as utterances expressing sympathy with the idea of colonial independence.

32. Young to Granville, confidential, Nov. 11, 1869: CO 42/678.

33. Minute by Granville, Nov. 30, 1869, on ibid.

34. Ibid. The dispatch based on these observations is Granville to Young, confidential, Jan. 10, 1870: CO 42/678.

35. Hansard, Third Series, CC, 1847 (April 26, 1870.)

36. Ibid., 1825.

37. Hansard, Third Series, CC, 1833 (April 26, 1870.)

38. Ibid., 1835.

39. See my article, "Sir John Rose and Imperial Relations," for a discussion of the circumstances surrounding the writing of this memorandum. The memorandum itself is reproduced in ibid., 25-8. The original version is found in CO 42/694.

40. Hansard, Third Series, CC, 1853 (April 26, 1870.)

41. Ibid., 1854.

42. Ibid.

43. The duties of Sir John Rose, although not strictly those of an "envoy," were probably very similar to what Torrens had in mind in moving his motion. Monsell made no attempt to concede this point, nor to enlighten the House on the informal modes of communication and advice that were used by the Colonial Office in dealing with the autonomous colonies.

44. Hansard, Third Series, CC, 1890 (April 26, 1870.)

45. Ibid., 1900.

46. Ibid., 1902.

47. Ibid., 1901.

48. Ibid., 1902.

49. Ibid., 1907.

50. S. C. Cheng, Schemes for the Federation of the British Empire (New York, 1931), 32.

51. D. G. Creighton, "The Victorians and the Empire," Canadian Historical Review, XIX (June, 1938), 148.

52. Monypenny and Buckle, Life of Disraeli, V, 195.

53. Hall, The British Commonwealth of Nations, 55.

54. J. E. Tyler, The Struggle for Imperial Unity, 1868-1895 (London, 1938), 18-9.

55. Monypenny and Buckle, Life of Disraeli, V, 195.

56. Tyler, Imperial Unity, 6.

57. The debates occurred on Feb. 14, March 7, and July 22, 1870. Hansard, Third Series, CXCIX, 193-233 (Carnarvon: 193-213); ibid., 1324-62 (Carnarvon: 1324-34); ibid., CCIII, 703-29 (Carnarvon: 703-13). Lord Russell also initiated a discussion on imperial defence on June 20: ibid., CCII, 451-85 (Russell: 451-60).

58. Ibid., CXCIX, 216-7 (Feb. 14, 1870).

59. Granville's defence of his colonial policy in these discussions is found in ibid., 213-21 (Feb. 14, 1870); ibid., 1334-46 (March 7, 1870); ibid., CCII, 481-5 (June 20, 1870). See also a revealing minute relating to New Zealand, dated March 25, 1870, quoted in Harrop, England and the Maori Wars, 373.

60. Hansard, Third Series, CCIII, 713-7 (July 22, 1870). Granville endorsed these views in a more guarded manner in the same debate: ibid., 723-5.

61. Ibid., CCVI, 764 (May 12, 1871).

62. Ibid., 766.

63. Ibid., 766-7. Knatchbull-Hugessen's speech is found in ibid., 760-8.

64. Ibid., CCXIV, 1526-30 (March 7, 1873).

65. Ibid., 1534.

66. Ibid. Gladstone's remarks are found in ibid., 1532-4.

67. Dufferin to Carnarvon, private, April 25, 1874: PRO 30/6/26.

68. Ibid.

69. Ibid.

70. Sir John Seeley's Expansion of England was published in 1883, and W. T. Stead, a major propagandist for empire, assumed the editorship of the Pall Mall Gazette in the same year. The literature of imperialism grew prodigiously from about this time.

71. Tyler, Imperial Unity, 108.

72. Tyler, Imperial Unity, 110-11.

73. R. Jebb, The Imperial Conference: A History and Study (London, 1911), I, 18-9.

74. The phrase and the opinion are Rogers's. See Blachford, Letters, 300.
Hicks Beach gave this concept more definite expression in 1879: "... the North America Act of 1867 may be considered to have bestowed on Canada greater powers of independent legislation than are possessed by other Colonies under responsible Government...." (Minute by Hicks Beach, Oct. 14, 1879, on Privy Council Office to Colonial Office, Oct. 7, 1879: and Colonial Office to Privy Council Office, Oct. 30, 1879: CO 42/759.)

75. Blake to Carnarvon, c. July 1, 1876, printed in SP, 1877, no. 13, 4.

76. Macdonald to Knutsford, confidential, July 18, 1889, printed in Pope, Correspondence of Sir John Macdonald, 451.

77. C. P. Stacey, "The Knighting of Francis Hincks: A Communication," Canadian Historical Review, XXXII (Sept., 1951), 300-1.

78. Monck to Buckingham, confidential, Aug. 11, 1868: CO 42/670.

79. Elliot to Taylor, private, June 26, 1868: CO 42/669.

80. Minute by Rogers, March 15, 1871, on Lisgar to Kimberley, no. 45, Feb. 20, 1871: CO 42/696.

81. Dufferin to Carnarvon, private, Oct. 22, 1875: PRO 30/6/28.

82. Confidential memo., "Vice-royalty," by Lord Dufferin, 1875, enclosed in Dufferin to Carnarvon, July 24, 1875: ibid.

83. Quoted in Sir Robert Herbert, ed., Speeches on Canadian Affairs by the Fourth Earl of Carnarvon (London, 1902), 286.

84. Carnarvon to Northcote, Oct. 26, 1875: PRO 30/6/7. See also Northcote to Carnarvon, private, Nov. 4, 1875: ibid.
For another illustration of Carnarvon's view that the British North America Act conferred a "more advanced political condition" on Canada see the important dispatch on the subject of imperial legislative powers, Carnarvon to Dufferin, secret, Oct. 19, 1876, Confidential Print, "North America No. 90": PRO 30/6/88.

85. Hansard, Third Series, CCXXIX, 1334-5 (May 26, 1876).

Herbert was also strongly of this opinion. "... we must, I think, face in clear and courteous terms the fallacy that by the 'British North America Act, 1867' or in any other way the power of the British Parliament to legislate for any and every part of the Empire is or can be limited. " (Minute by Herbert, July 23, 1876, on Board of Trade to Colonial Office, July 17, 1876: CO 42/745.)

86. Letter to the Editor of The Times by "Historicus": The Times, June 1, 1876. Todd identifies "Historicus" as Sir W. Vernon Harcourt. (Todd, Parliamentary Government, 29). See also the leader in the same issue of The Times for the opposite view.

87. Imperial legislation applying to the autonomous colonies can be seen for the period in the following Acts: Colonial Laws Validity Act, 1865 (28 and 29 Vict., c. 63); Colonial Shipping Act, 1869 (32 and 33 Vict., c. 11); Coinage Act, 1870 (33 and 34 Vict., c. 10); Foreign Enlistment Act, 1870 (33 and 34 Vict., c. 90); Naturalization Act, 1870 (33 and 34 Vict., c. 14); Extradition Act, 1870 (33 and 34 Vict., c. 52); Copyright Act, 1875 (38 and 39 Vict., c. 53).

The list is not exclusive, but it includes the majority of the subjects which the Colonial Office considered of imperial significance.

88. The phrases in quotation marks are taken from R. L. Schuyler, Parliament and the British Empire (New York, 1929), 214-24, which contains a good discussion of the relationship between law and convention in the British Empire.

89. Carnarvon to Dufferin, secret, Oct. 19, 1876, Confidential Print, "North America No. 90": PRO 30/6/88.

90. Head to Labouchere, Feb. 8, 1858, quoted in Stacey, Canada and the British Army, 89.

91. Dufferin to Carnarvon, private, June 1, 1876: PRO 30/6/29.

92. Dufferin to Carnarvon, private, Feb. 2, 1876: ibid.

93. Hansard, Third Series, CCXII, 1365-6 (July 18, 1872).

94. Keith, Responsible Government, I, 284.

95. Minute by Herbert, Sept. 1, 1874, on Chairman, Direct United States Cable Company, Limited to Colonial Office, Aug. 14, 1874: CO 42/734.

96. Blake to Carnarvon, c. July 1, 1876, printed in SP, 1877, no. 13, 8.

97.   Minute by Herbert, July 8, 1885, on Foreign Office to Colonial Office, June 20, 1885: CO 42/781.

98.   Hansard, Third Series, CCIII, 712 (July 22, 1870).

APPENDIXES

APPENDIX A

THE ORGANIZATION OF THE COLONIAL OFFICE, 1867-1887

1. Political Staff

Ministry	Colonial Secretary	Parliamentary Under-Secretary
14th Earl of Derby, III July 1866-Jan. 1868 B. Disraeli, I Jan.-Dec. 1868	Lord Carnarvon July 1866-March 1867 Duke of Buckingham and Chandos March 1867-Dec. 1868	* C. B. Adderley July 1866-Dec. 1868
W. E. Gladstone, I Dec. 1868-Feb. 1874	Lord Granville Dec. 1868-July 1870 Lord Kimberley July 1870-Feb. 1874	* W. Monsell Dec. 1868-Jan. 1871 E. H. Knatchbull-Hugessen Jan. 1871-Feb. 1874
B. Disraeli (created Lord Beaconsfield, August, 1876), II Feb. 1874-April 1880	Lord Carnarvon Feb. 1874-Feb. 1878 Sir M. Hicks Beach Feb. 1878-April 1880	J. Lowther Feb. 1874-Feb.1878 Lord Cadogan March 1878-April 1880
W. E. Gladstone, II April 1880-June 1885	Lord Kimberley April 1880-Dec. 1882 15th Earl of Derby Dec. 1882-June 1885	M. E. Grant Duff April 1880-Aug. 1881 L. H. Courtney Aug. 1881-May 1882 E. Ashley May 1882-June 1885
Lord Salisbury, I June 1885-Feb. 1886	F. A. Stanley June 1885-Feb. 1886	Lord Dunraven June 1885-Feb. 1886
W. E. Gladstone, III Feb.-Aug. 1886	Lord Granville Feb.-Aug. 1886	G. O. Morgan Feb.-Aug. 1886
Lord Salisbury, II Aug. 1886-Aug. 1892	E. Stanhope Aug. 1886-Jan. 1887 Sir H. Holland (created Lord Knutsford, Feb. 1888) Jan. 1887-Aug. 1892	Lord Dunraven Aug. 1886-Feb. 1887 Lord Onslow Feb. 1887-Feb. 1888

* Denotes superintending Under-Secretary, North American Department.

320

2. Permanent Staff

Permanent Under-Secretary	Assistant Under-Secretary	Chief Clerk North American Department
* Sir F. Rogers May, 1860- May, 1871	* Sir T. F. Elliot November, 1847- December, 1868	A. J. Blackwood c. August, 1840- May, 1867
	* Sir F. R. Sandford December, 1868- January, 1870	W. Dealtry May, 1867- January, 1879
	Sir R. G. W. Herbert February, 1870- May, 1871	
Sir R. G. W. Herbert May, 1871- February, 1892	* Sir H. Holland March, 1870- August, 1874	
	Sir R. Meade May, 1871- February, 1892	
	* W. R. Malcolm July, 1874- June, 1878	
	Sir J. Pauncefote September, 1874- June, 1876	
	* Sir J. Bramston June, 1876- November, 1897	
	E. Wingfield July, 1878- March, 1897	E. B. Pennell May, 1879- March, 1895

321

APPENDIX B

A NOTE ON THE LATER HISTORY OF APPEALS TO
THE PRIVY COUNCIL FROM CANADA

THE SUBJECT OF APPEALS to the Privy Council from Canada has had a chequered history since it was first raised in 1875-6. The Mackenzie Government, immersed in increasing political difficulties, was unable to consider the question further after Blake's visit to London in the summer of 1876. Blake himself retired as Minister of Justice in the following year. The practical effect of the Canadian Act of 1875 was to abolish the appeal as of right from the Supreme Court to the Privy Council, but the latter body continued to exercise the power to grant leave to appeal in certain classes of actions and under certain circumstances. Appeals as of right went normally from the provincial superior courts to the Judicial Committee and were governed by local statute (as in the case of Ontario), by Order in Council (Manitoba), or by Imperial Act (British Columbia).

The Conservative Administration of Sir John Macdonald in 1888 enacted a new section in the Criminal Code of Canada which abolished the appeal in criminal cases (51 Vict., c. 43, s. 1). Since the Crown's prerogative right to hear appeals existed on a statutory basis, this Act would seem to have contravened the provisions of British legislation and, under the Colonial Laws Validity Act, to have been null and void. The conflict was not noticed, either unconsciously or deliberately, until 1926, when the Judicial Committee, in the case of Nadan v. The King, held that the Canadian law of 1888 was invalid ([1926] A.C. 482). The judgment was received unfavourably in Canada, but nothing was done until the passage of the Statute of Westminster, which repealed the Colonial Laws Validity Act and gave the Dominions extraterritorial powers, solved the difficulty. Then the section abolishing criminal appeals was re-enacted (23 and 24 Geo. V, c. 53, s. 17) and subsequently upheld by the Judicial Committee (British Coal Corporation v. The King, [1935] A.C. 500).

In 1938 and 1939 a private member of the Canadian Parliament introduced bills to prohibit the appeal from the Supreme Court and from provincial courts in all civil cases. The principle received wide support in the Dominion and was ultimately endorsed by the Government, who requested that the question be held over while the opinions of interested groups were obtained and a reference was made to the Supreme Court to discover whether the Dominion Parliament possessed the right to legislate on the matter. The Supreme Court of Canada decided that the bill abolishing appeals was intra vires and leave to appeal against this decision was granted by the Privy Council in 1940, but it was agreed to postpone the hearing because of the Second World War. The appeal was heard in January, 1947, when the Judicial Committee held that the Parliament of Canada, without consulting the provinces, was competent to abolish appeals to the Privy Council in civil cases. No other alternative but to give the Supreme Court of Canada ultimate jurisdiction, the Board declared, was "consonant with the status of a self-governing Dominion." (Attorney-General, Ontario and Others v. Attorney-General, Canada and Others, [1947] A.C. 127.)   The Judicial Committee's decision was embodied in an Act passed in 1949 amending the Supreme Court Act (13 Geo. VI, c. 37, s. 3).

APPENDIX C

A NOTE ON THE LATER DEVELOPMENT OF CANADIAN
FISCAL AUTONOMY

THE BROAD LINES on which the development of the fiscal autonomy of Canada had proceeded during the period after Confederation were followed in later years. The Colony's
claim to shape its own tariff policy was asserted after 1887 without encountering resistance from British sources, and Macdonald declared in 1890 that he felt the Imperial
Government would willingly sanction any arrangement for differential duties between
various parts of the Empire. (Debates of the House of Commons (Canada), 1890, II,
3684, [April 21, 1890].) Macdonald's conviction that differential treatment should not
be extended to countries outside the Empire if it injured the trading prospects of other
British colonies, was confirmed in the same year when he managed to secure the rejection by Great Britain of the Blaine-Bond treaty between the United States and Newfoundland. Great Britain's practice of consulting the self-governing colonies when new trade
agreements with foreign countries were being drawn up was continued, and Canada gradually withdrew from British commercial treaties containing "most-favoured-nation"
clauses. The prohibition of differential duties in favour of foreign countries was removed from the constitutions of the Australian colonies in 1895 (58 and 59 Vict., c. 3).

    As the movement for imperial preference grew in strength, the obstacles to the
scheme contained in the commercial treaties with Belgium and Germany came to be
more clearly realized. The Agents-General in London protested the agreements in 1890,
the Canadian Parliament adopted an address against them in 1892, and the Ottawa Conference of 1894 strongly pressed for their denunciation. Finally, in 1897, after the benefits conferred on Great Britain by the Canadian preferential tariff of that year were extended through the treaties to many other countries, it was seen that the situation had
become intolerable. A year later the two treaties were denounced and the last restriction on the freedom of Canada to frame its own tariff was removed. The episode unfortunately brought about a tariff war between Germany and Canada, but it enabled other
colonies to follow the Dominion in establishing preferential rates for Great Britain and
the Empire in their tariff structures.

    The senior Colony similarly continued to lead the way towards the attainment of
authority to negotiate treaties with foreign countries. The promise of joint powers in
the making of commercial treaties, secured by Tupper in 1884 for his Spanish discussions, was confirmed in 1888. In that year Tupper served as a joint plenipotentiary with
Joseph Chamberlain and the British Minister at Washington in the drafting of a treaty between Great Britain and the United States settling fisheries and boundary problems. The
treaty failed, however, to be ratified by the United States Senate. Five years later the
principle was effectively established when Tupper negotiated an instrument for reciprocal tariff concessions between the Dominion and France, signing it in association with

the British Ambassador. The High Commissioner played the leading part in these negotiations, with the British representative acting in a purely formal capacity. The treaty
was later ratified by the Canadian Parliament. As Colonial Secretary, in 1895, Lord
Ripon endeavoured to halt the movement of the larger colonies in treaty negotiations
by stating that unless they were prepared to accept a subordinate capacity in such discussions, the diplomatic unity of the Empire would be disrupted. These instructions,
which would have had the effect of turning the clock back to 1879 and Galt's status at
Madrid, were never applied. The opening of new negotiations with France in 1907 provided an opportunity to repudiate the Ripon policy, and this was done when Sir Wilfrid
Laurier and two other Canadian Ministers were authorized to confer directly with the
French Government, merely keeping the British Ambassador "informed of their progress."
The resulting treaty was signed by two Canadians and Sir Francis Bertie, the Ambassador. The precedents of 1884 and 1893 had now received formal approval, and there
were no further advances in the treaty-making powers of the colonies before the outbreak of the First World War. Only three British colonies--Canada, Newfoundland, and
the Cape--had made commercial treaties before 1914. Imperial control over treaties
of a political character was not so easily relinquished. The procedure of approach and
negotiation remained the same as for commercial treaties but in general the British representative tended to assume a more effective role in the discussions.

The First World War resulted in a rapid succession of significant advances in the
constitutional position of the larger colonies. The creation of the Imperial War Cabinet, the representation of the Dominions at the Paris Peace Conference, their membership in the League of Nations, and the various Imperial Conferences of the period pre-
saged changes in the treaty-making power of the Dominions. Canada had been promised distinct diplomatic representation at Washington in 1920 and a Legation was established there in 1927. Even before this date the first treaty to be exclusively negotiated
and signed by a Canadian agent had been concluded. The Halibut Convention of 1923
was drawn up with the United States by Ernest Lapointe as "Canadian" plenipotentiary,
the Dominion requesting specifically that the British Ambassador in Washington should
not sign the instrument. By this step the old era of Imperial diplomatic control came
to an end: Canada had progressed in treaty negotiations from a subordinate role to an
associated role and on to an independent and responsible capacity.

BIBLIOGRAPHY

A NOTE ON SOURCES

THIS STUDY has been mainly constructed from the original records of the Colonial Office and other departments of the British Government in the Public Record Office, London. In particular the great CO 42 series, "the most important single file of documents in the Public Record Office relating to Canada," has been intensively examined. It is from the marginal notes, comments, and memoranda contained in this series that the views of the staff of the Colonial Office on Canadian questions have been learned. Without the opinions of the permanent officials it would have been impossible to describe Imperial policy towards Canada in the period after 1867. Many of the documents in series CO 42 are to be found in the "Q" series in the Public Archives of Canada, although the prohibition by the Record Office of the transcribing of minutes meant that for many years this supplementary material was not readily accessible to Canadian historians. The project to microfilm series CO 42, which is now under way, will eventually result in a copy of the entire series being available in Ottawa, while the original remains in London.

In addition other records of the Colonial Office, such as series CO 323, dealing with commercial topics, have been consulted; and letters of the Foreign Office and the Treasury have been used for particular subjects. Great assistance has been obtained from the Carnarvon Papers, especially from Lord Carnarvon's correspondence with Lord Dufferin, 1874-8, and with members of the British Government. A limited group of letters has been drawn upon in the Granville Papers which, together with those of Lord Carnarvon, are held in the Public Record Office.

Some use has been made of material in the Public Archives of Canada, Ottawa: notably several of the volumes in the Macdonald Papers (e.g. Macdonald's correspondence with Sir John Rose) and selected records of the Canadian Privy Council. If the work has been chiefly based on British sources the obvious justification lies in the fact that it is primarily a study in Imperial administrative history. The policy of the Colonial Office towards Canada was devised almost entirely from the dispatches and other papers which came into the Department from Ottawa and from other offices in Whitehall. This material is found in England; it may not have told the whole story in particular instances, but it normally constituted all that the Colonial Office knew on any Canadian problem.

GUIDES AND CHECK LISTS

Giuseppi, M.S., A Guide to the Manuscripts Preserved in the Public Record Office (London, 2 vols., 1923-4).

List of Colonial Office Records in the Public Record Office (London, 1911).
[Original correspondence to 1837, Sessional Papers of Canada, and other printed material to 1899.]

List of Colonial Office Records in the Public Record Office, 1838-1860, Public Record Office (typescript).

List of Colonial Office Records in the Public Record Office, 1861-1885, Public Record Office, 1930 (typescript).

List of Colonial Office Original Correspondence in the Public Record Office, 1886-1902, Public Record Office, 1948 (typescript).

Supplementary List of Colonial Office Records, Public Record Office, 1950.

Colonial Office, Indexes to Correspondence, 1815-1870, Public Record Office, 1949 (typescript).

List of Colonial Office Registers, 1886-1902, Public Record Office, 1948 (typescript).

List of Confidential Prints, Public Record Office (typescript).

List of Foreign Office Records to 1878 in the Public Record Office (London, 1929).

General Alphabetical Index to the Bills, Reports, Estimates, Accounts and Papers, Printed by Order of the House of Commons, and to the Papers Presented by Command, 1852-1899 (London, 1909).

MANUSCRIPT MATERIAL

I. Official Sources

   (a) Records of the Colonial Office (Public Record Office)

CO 42 series, North American Department
Original Correspondence: In-letters from the Governor-General of Canada, and drafts of replies from the Office. In-letters from other departments on Canadian subjects and drafts of replies. Private official correspondence on Canadian topics.
[The basic series for the preparation of this study.]

Vols. 549-52, 619, 624, 626, 650, 652, 660, 662-794 (1848-87)

CO 43 series, North American Department
Entry books of dispatches to the Governor-General of Canada and the public departments on Canadian topics.

  Vols. 132, 135-6, 138-42, 154-8 (1865-73)

CO 137 series, West Indian Department
In-letters from the Governor of Jamaica, drafts of replies.

  Vol. 505 (1882)

CO 188 series, North American Department
In-letters from the Lieutenant-Governor of New Brunswick, drafts of replies.

  Vols. 112-13 (1850)

CO 195 series, North American Department
Entry book of dispatches to the Governor of Newfoundland.

  Vol. 22 (1857)

CO 217 series, North American Department
In-letters from the Lieutenant-Governor of Nova Scotia, drafts of replies.

  Vols. 211-12 (1853)

CO 226 series, North American Department
In-letters from the Lieutenant-Governor of Prince Edward Island, drafts of replies.

  Vols. 103-5 (1867-9)

CO 318 series, West Indian Department
In-letters from the public departments on West Indian topics.

  Vol. 275 (1884)

CO 323 series, General Department
In-letters from the Foreign Office, Agents-General, High Commissioner for Canada.
Drafts of replies.
[Essential for a study of British commercial treaties and their effect on the colonies.]

  Vols. 279, 283, 286, 290, 294, 300, 305, 307, 309, 315, 319, 323, 328, 331-3,
  337, 340, 345, 349, 352, 354-5, 357-8, 361, 365, 369 (1865-87)

(b) <u>Records of the Foreign Office</u> (Public Record Office)

FO 83 series, Foreign Office
Correspondence with the Colonial Office, other departments on general topics.

Vols. 556-9, 585, 611, 614, 802 (1878-84)

(c) <u>Records of the Treasury</u> (Public Record Office)

T 1 series, Treasury
Correspondence with the Colonial Office on guarantees.

Box 6920 B, Bundle no. 19614; 6299 A, 19904; 6938 C, 21140; 7655 A, 229; 7720 A, 21033 (1869-78)

(d) <u>Records of the Privy Council of Canada</u> (Public Archives of Canada)

Privy Council Despatches
Dispatches from the Colonial Office, etc., and other material that came before the Canadian Privy Council. Canadian interdepartmental correspondence arising from these references.

Vols. 1-37 (1867-80)

II. <u>Private Sources</u>

(a) <u>Carnarvon Papers</u> (Public Record Office)

PRO 30/6 series (formerly GD 6)
Letters received and drafts of letters written by Lord Carnarvon. Memoranda, Confidential Prints, Cabinet reports.
[Carnarvon's correspondence with Dufferin, Cairns, Northcote, and Blake was especially useful for this study.]

Vols. 6	Cairns, 1874-7	Vols. 42-7	Miscellaneous Colonial Correspondence, 1874-8
7	Northcote, 1874-8		
9	Lord President of the Council, etc., 1874-7	50-1	Miscellaneous Memoranda on Canadian topics, 1874-8
11	Prime Minister, 1874-8	70	Confidential Prints, 1866-7
16	Speaker, Law Officers, etc., 1874-8	72	Cabinet Memoranda (Canada), 1874-8
17	Under-Secretaries, Treasury, Foreign Office, etc., 1874-8	87-9	Confidential Prints (North America) 1874-8
22	Miscellaneous Official, 1874-8	97-8	Confidential Prints (Miscellaneous), 1874-7
26-31	Dufferin, 1874-8		

(b) Granville Papers (Public Record Office)

PRO 30/29 series
Letters received and drafts of letters written by Lord Granville. Memoranda, Confidential Prints, etc.
[Some correspondence with Gladstone found useful, also some Foreign Office prints.]

Vols. 55   Clarendon, Kimberley,   Vols. 68 Memoranda on North American topics,
               1869-74   1869-71
         57-8 Gladstone, 1869-70   213 Cabinet Correspondence, 1885-6

(c) Macdonald Papers (Public Archives of Canada)

Letters received and drafts of letters written by Sir John Macdonald. Memoranda and other material.
[Correspondence with Sir John Rose used.]

Vols. 258-9 Rose to Macdonald, 1864-87 Vols. 511, 514-28 Macdonald to Rose, 1865-89

PRINTED SOURCES

I. Official Publications

(a) Great Britain

(i) Parliamentary Papers, House of Commons

1847-8, LIX, no. 405: Dispatch from the Governor-General of Canada, transmitting memorandum from his Executive Council, and the Inspector-General of Canada, on the operation of the Navigation Laws upon the Province of Canada.

1856, XLIV, no. 431: Correspondence between the Colonial Office and the Governors of the North American and West Indian colonies on the subject of a proposal for the mutual abolition of customs duties upon the productions of Canada and the West Indies.

1864, XLI, no. 400: Correspondence between the Colonial Office and the authorities in Canada on the subject of the reduction of duties charged on British goods entering Canada.

1865, XXXVII, no. 3426: Correspondence relative to a meeting at Quebec of delegates appointed to discuss the proposed union of the British North American provinces.

1865, XXXVII, no. 3535: Correspondence relating to the conferences between the United

Kingdom Government and the deputation from the Executive Council of Canada on subjects of importance to the Province.

1867, XLVIII, no. 160: Correspondence between the Colonial Office and the Treasury respecting the proposed guarantee of the Intercolonial Railway loan.

1867, XLVIII, no. 3769: Correspondence respecting the proposed union of the British North American provinces.

1868-9, XLIII, no. 272: Statement and account of proceeding under the Canada Railway Loan Act.

1868-9, XLIII, no. 272-1: Further papers relating to the Intercolonial Railway loan.

1870, XLI, no. 219: Return of all loans to foreign countries and British colonies, and of all loans raised by foreign countries and British colonies, of which the capital or interest have been guaranteed by Act of Parliament, from 1820 to 1868 inclusive.

1870, XLIX, no. C-24: Correspondence respecting a proposed conference of colonial representatives in London.

1870, XLIX, no. C-51: Further correspondence respecting a proposed conference of colonial representatives in London.

1870, XLIX, no. C-185: Dispatch from Earl Granville to the Rt. Hon. Sir John Young, respecting the recent Fenian raid into Canada.

1870, XLIX, no. 244: Dispatches from the Colonial Office to the Governor-General of Canada respecting the investment of money raised under the authority of the Canada Railway Loan Act.

1870, XLIX, no. 315: Statement of proceedings taken by the Treasury to give effect to the guarantee of a loan for £300,000 authorized by 32 and 33 Vict., c. 101.

1871, LXX, no. 262: Correspondence respecting the appointment of a Joint High Commission to consider the various questions affecting the relations between Great Britain and the United States.

1871, LXX, no. 344: Dispatch from Her Majesty's High Commissioners at Washington, May 8, 1871, with copy annexed of the Treaty of Washington.

1871, LXX, no. 346: Instructions to Her Majesty's High Commissioners at Washington, February 9, 1871, and protocols of conferences at Washington.

1872, XLII, no. C-576: Correspondence with the Australian colonies with reference to proposals for intercolonial tariff arrangements.

1872, XLIII, no. C-539: Correspondence with the Government of Canada in connection with the appointment of a Joint High Commission and the Treaty of Washington.

1872, XLIII, no. C-541: Further correspondence with the Government of Canada in connection with the appointment of the Joint High Commission and the Treaty of Washington.

1873, XLVIII, no. 36: Return of all loans raised by British colonies which the Treasury has been authorized by the present Parliament to guarantee.

1873, XLIX, no. C-702: Further correspondence with the Government of Canada in connection with the Treaty of Washington.

1873, XLIX, no. C-703: Further correspondence with the Australasian colonies with reference to proposals for intercolonial tariff arrangements.

1873, XLIX, no. C-750: Further correspondence with the governments of Canada, Prince Edward Island, and Newfoundland, respecting the Treaty of Washington and the Canadian Pacific Railway.

1873, XLIX, no. C-774: Further correspondence with the governments of Canada, Prince Edward Island, and Newfoundland, respecting the Treaty of Washington.

1874, LXXV, no. C-1060: Correspondence relating to the negotiations for a Reciprocity Treaty between Canada and the United States.

1875, LIII, no. C-1202: Correspondence relating to the exercise of the prerogative of pardon in New South Wales.

1875, LIII, no. C-1248: Further correspondence relating to the exercise of the prerogative of pardon in New South Wales.

1877, XLIX, no. 274: Return of all outstanding loans raised by British colonies and by foreign governments which the Treasury has been authorized to guarantee.

1878-9, LI, no. C-2305: Dispatch from the Governor-General of Canada respecting the new customs tariff.

1878-9, LI, no. C-2369: Dispatch from the Governor-General of Canada respecting the new customs tariff. (In continuation of no. C-2305.)

1880, XLIX, no. C-2594: Correspondence between the Imperial and Canadian Governments relative to the appointment of Sir A. T. Galt as High Commissioner to represent Canada in England and to reside in London.

1881, XCIX, no. C-2765: Notes exchanged between the British and Rumanian Governments recording the exclusion of Canada from the operations of the treaty of commerce and navigation of 1880.

1884, LXXXIII, no. C-3927: Correspondence respecting the commercial convention concluded between Spain and the United States relative to the West India trade.

1884-5, LXXI, no. C-4340: Correspondence respecting the negotiation of a treaty regulating trade between the British West India colonies and the United States.

1887, LVIII, no. C-5179: Correspondence respecting the Canadian tariff.

    (ii) Hansard's Parliamentary Debates, Third Series

    (iii) Public General Statutes of the United Kingdom

    (iv) Confidential Prints (Colonial Office)

"North America No. 72," Correspondence respecting the renewal of the Reciprocity Treaty with the United States: CO 807/2.

"North America No. 74," Correspondence respecting the Canadian Pacific Railway Act and British Columbia, 1873-5: CO 807/5.

"North America No. 75," Correspondence on Marine Electric Telegraph Act, 1873-4: CO 807/6.

"North America No. 84," Correspondence respecting the establishment of the Supreme Court of Canada, 1875-6: CO 807/13.

"North America No. 84a," Further correspondence respecting the establishment of the Supreme Court of Canada, 1876: CO 807/14.

"North America No. 86," Blake's memorandum on the Governor-General's Commission and Instructions, 1876: CO 807/16.

"North America No. 90," Carnarvon to Dufferin, secret, October 19, 1876, on Imperial legislative powers: CO 807/20.

"North America No. 96," Memorandum by Carnarvon on Canada Guaranteed Loan, 1877: CO 807/26.

"North America No. 99," Correspondence on revision of Instructions for the Governor-General, 1875-9: CO 807/29.

"North America No. 103," Correspondence on the Canadian tariff, 1880: CO 807/31.

"North America No. 106a," Letter in The Times on Imperial shipping legislation, 1876: CO 807/35.

"North America No. 106b," Letters in The Times on Imperial shipping legislation, 1876: CO 807/36.

"North America No. 131," Dispatch from the Governor-General of Canada on Commercial Union, 1887: CO 807/60.

(b) Province of Canada and Dominion of Canada

(i) Sessional Papers of the Province and Dominion of Canada

1863, no. 14 (Province of Canada): Dispatches and other documents on the subjects of the Intercolonial Railway and reciprocal free trade among the British North American colonies.

1869, no. 5: Correspondence on the Intercolonial Railway loan.

1869, no. 18: Correspondence with provincial governments in regard to the disallowance of local legislation.

1869, no. 47: Correspondence between Canada, Great Britain, and the United States on the subject of the renewal of the Reciprocity Treaty with the United States.

1870, no. 13: Correspondence between Imperial and Canadian Governments, touching the Intercolonial Railway loan and the application of the proceeds thereof.

1870, no. 35: Correspondence with the Imperial Government and provincial governments touching provincial legislation.

1872, no. 18: Messages, dispatches, and minutes of the Privy Council relating to the Treaty of Washington.

1872, no. 36: Correspondence relating to the school act passed by the legislature of New Brunswick.

1873, no. 44: Correspondence relating to the common school act of New Brunswick, passed in 1871.

1874, no. 25: Correspondence between the Imperial and Canadian Governments, and between the federal and provincial governments since 1873 on the subject of provincial legislation.

1875, no. 40: Report of the Minister of Agriculture for the Dominion of Canada for 1874. (Reports of immigration agents in Great Britain.)

1876, no. 8: Report of the Minister of Agriculture for the Dominion of Canada for 1875. (Report of Agent-General in London.)

1876, no. 116: Correspondence with the Colonial Secretary on the subject of the exercise of the power of disallowance of provincial statutes.

1877, no. 13: Report of the Minister of Justice on certain public matters--extradition, maritime jurisdiction on inland waters of Canada, Governor-General's Commission and Instructions, Supreme Court Act.

1877, no. 89: Correspondence between the federal and provincial governments and the Imperial and Canadian Governments since the establishment of Confederation concerning the disallowance of provincial legislation.

1879 (Journals of the House of Commons, Appendix no. 1): Report of the select standing committee on immigration and colonization.

1879, no. 9: Report of the Minister of Agriculture for the Dominion of Canada for 1878. (Annual report of the London agent.)

1879, no. 155: Dispatch and enclosures addressed by the Governor-General to the Secretary of State for the Colonies, on the subject of the tariff recently introduced to the Legislature.

1880, no. 26: List of treaties of commerce and navigation between Great Britain and foreign powers, containing most-favoured-nation clauses, and showing whether they apply to the British colonies.

1880, no. 75: Return showing the terms on which Dominion loans were negotiated in London.

1880, no. 104: Correspondence with the Canadian Commissioner and with the Imperial Government on the subject of negotiations with France and Spain.

1880, no. 105: Correspondence between the Imperial and Canadian Governments relative to the appointment of Sir A. T. Galt as High Commissioner to represent Canada in England.

1883, no. 89: Correspondence respecting the negotiations for commercial arrangements
with France, Spain, or other countries, and reports by the High Commissioner on the
subject.

1884, no. 67: Statement of the amount of Canadian trade with Brazil and the British
and foreign West India islands.

1887, no. 43: Report on trade relations between Canada and the West Indies.

  (ii) Debates of the House of Commons (Canada)
       Debates of the Senate (Canada)

  (iii) Statutes of the Province of Canada
        Statutes of Canada

II. Newspapers

The Times

III. Directories, Office Lists, Biographical Dictionaries

Colonial Office List (London, 1862 -).

Foreign Office List (London, 1852 -).

Stephen, Sir L., Lee, Sir S., and others, eds., The Dictionary of National Biography
    (1885 -).
    [Contains the only published biographical data for many civil servants.]

Wallace, W. S., ed., The Dictionary of Canadian Biography (Toronto, 1926).

Dod's Parliamentary Companion (London, 1838 -).

Morgan, H. J., and others, eds., The Canadian Parliamentary Companion (Montreal,
    1862 -).

IV. Printed Collections of Documents

Bell, K. N., and Morrell, W. P., eds., Select Documents on British Colonial Policy,
    1830-60 (Oxford, 1928).

Doughty, Sir A. G., ed., The Elgin-Grey Papers, 1846-52 (Ottawa, 4 vols., 1937).

Houston, W., ed., Documents Illustrative of the Canadian Constitution (Toronto, 1891).

Keith, A. B., ed., Selected Speeches and Documents on British Colonial Policy, 1763-1917 (Oxford, 2 vols., 1918).

Kennedy, W. P. M., ed., Statutes, Treaties and Documents of the Canadian Constitution, 1713-1929 (Toronto, 2nd ed., 1930).

Madden, F., ed., Imperial Constitutional Documents, 1765-1952: A Supplement(Oxford, 1953).

V. Books and Articles

(a) Contemporary or Nearly Contemporary Works

Blachford, Lord (Sir Frederic Rogers), "The Causes of the Zulu War," Nineteenth Century, XXV (March, 1879), 564-74.

*------ Letters, ed. by G. E. Marindin (London, 1896).
Mainly autobiographical material and letters.

------ "Native Policy in South Africa," Edinburgh Review, CXLV(April, 1877),447-87.

------ Review of Sir Thomas Erskine May's Democracy in Europe, in Edinburgh Review, CXLVII (April, 1878), 301-33.

Burpee, L. J., ed., "Joseph Howe and the Anti-Confederation League," Transactions of the Royal Society of Canada, Series III, X (May, 1916), 409-73.

Bury, Viscount, Exodus of the Western Nations (London, 2 vols., 1865).

Coupland, Sir R., ed., The Durham Report (Oxford, 1945).

Dowden, E., ed., Correspondence of Henry Taylor (London, 1888).

Escott, T. H. S., Pillars of the Empire: Sketches of Living Indian and Colonial Statesmen, Celebrities, and Officials (London, 1879).

*Grey, Earl, The Colonial Policy of Lord John Russell's Administration (London, 2 vols.,

* Denotes works bearing a direct relationship to the subjects included in this study.

2nd ed. , 1853).
Grey's views on commercial policy are fully expressed in this work.

Grey, Earl, "How Shall We Retain the Colonies?" Nineteenth Century, XXVIII (June, 1879), 935-54.

Herbert, Sir R. , ed. , Speeches on Canadian Affairs by the Fourth Earl of Carnarvon (London, 1902).

Merivale, H. , Lectures on Colonization and Colonies (London, 1861).

Norton, Lord, "How Not to Retain the Colonies, " Nineteenth Century, XXIX (July, 1879), 170-8.

*Pope, J. , Memoirs of Sir John Macdonald (London, 2 vols. , 1894).
Useful, but eulogistic.

------ ed. , Correspondence of Sir John Macdonald (Toronto, 1921).

Rogers, Sir F. , see Blachford, Lord.

Rose, J. , Speech on the Budget by the Honourable John Rose, Minister of Finance, Delivered in the House of Commons, Ottawa, May 7, 1869 (Ottawa, pamphlet, 1869).

Smith, G. , The Empire: A Series of Letters Published in "The Daily News, " 1862, 1863 (Oxford, 1863).

Strachey, L. , and Fulford, R. , eds. , The Greville Memoirs, 1814-60 (London, 8 vols. , 1938).

Taylor, Sir H. , Autobiography (London, 2 vols. , 1885).

------ ., The Statesman: An Ironical Treatise on the Art of Succeeding (Cambridge, reprint, 1927).

*Todd, A. , Parliamentary Government in the British Colonies (London, 2nd ed. , 1894).
Remains the fullest treatment of the constitutional development of the autonomous colonies for the period before 1880.

Underhill, F. H. , ed. , The Dufferin-Carnarvon Correspondence, 1874-8, The Publications of the Champlain Society, vol. XXXIII (Toronto, 1955).

Wallace, W. S. , ed. , "Edward Blake's Aurora Speech, " Canadian Historical Review, II (September, 1921), 249-71.

(b) Later Works

Allin, C. D., and Jones, G. M., Annexation, Preferential Trade and Reciprocity (Toronto, c. 1924).

Barnes, D. G., A History of the English Corn Laws, 1660-1846 (London, 1930).

Beach, Lady V. Hicks, Life of Sir Michael Hicks Beach (London, 2 vols., 1932).

*Beaglehole, J. C., "The Colonial Office, 1782-1854," Historical Studies, Australia and New Zealand, I (April, 1941), 170-89.
An able sketch of the origins of the nineteenth-century Colonial Office.

Benians, E. A., "The Beginnings of the New Empire, 1783-93," The Cambridge History of the British Empire, II (Cambridge, 1940), 1-35.

------ "Colonial Self-Government, 1852-70," The Cambridge History of the British Empire, II (Cambridge, 1940), 677-704.

Bertram, Sir A., The Colonial Service (Cambridge, 1930).

Biddulph, Sir R., Lord Cardwell at the War Office (London, 1904).

*Bodelsen, C. A., Studies in Mid-Victorian Imperialism (Copenhagen, 1924).
An extremely important treatment of public opinion on imperial questions, 1784-1893.

Boyd, J., Sir George Etienne Cartier, Bart. (Toronto, 1914).

Bramston, Sir J., "The Colonial Office from Within," Empire Review, I (April, 1901), 279-87.

*Brebner, J. B., North Atlantic Triangle: The Interplay of Canada, the United States and Great Britain, The Relations of Canada and the United States Series (New Haven, 1945),
The first work of its kind and outstandingly successful.

Brown, B. H., The Tariff Reform Movement in Great Britain, 1881-1895 (New York, 1943).

Burn, W. L., Emancipation and Apprenticeship in the British West Indies (London, 1937).
Includes a good description of the personnel of the Colonial Office in the thirties.

Burt, A. L., "Broad Horizons," Annual Report of the Canadian Historical Association, 1950, 1-10.

------ Imperial Architects (Oxford, 1913).

Butler, J. R. M., "Colonial Self-Government, 1838-52," The Cambridge History of the British Empire, II (Cambridge, 1940), 335-87.

Cannon, L. A., "Some Data Relating to the Appeal to the Privy Council," Canadian Bar Review, III (October, 1925), 455-81.

Carrington, C. E., The British Overseas: Exploits of a Nation of Shopkeepers (Cambridge, 1950).

------ An Exposition of Empire (Cambridge, 1947).

Cartwright, Sir R., Reminiscences (Toronto, reprint, 1913).

Cecil, A., "The Foreign Office," The Cambridge History of British Foreign Policy, 1783-1919, III (Cambridge, 1923), 539-630.

Cheng, S. C., Schemes for the Federation of the British Empire (New York, 1931).

Childe-Pemberton, W. S., Life of Lord Norton, 1814-1905, Statesman and Philanthropist (London, 1909). (Sir C. B. Adderley.)

Colquhoun, A. H. U., "The Reciprocity Negotiations with the United States in 1869," Canadian Historical Review, VIII (September, 1927), 233-42.

------ "An Unpublished State Paper, 1868," Canadian Historical Review, I (March, 1920), 54-60.

Cooke, A. C., "Empire Unity and Colonial Nationalism, 1884-1911," Annual Report of the Canadian Historical Association, 1939, 77-86.

Corbett, P. E., and Smith, H. A., Canada and World Politics (London, 1928).

Creighton, D. G., British North America at Confederation (Ottawa, 1939).

------ Dominion of the North: A History of Canada (London, 1947).

------ "Sir John Macdonald and Kingston," Annual Report of the Canadian Historical Association, 1950, 72-80.

Creighton, D. G., "The Victorians and the Empire," Canadian Historical Review, XIX (June, 1938), 138-53.

Currey, C. H., British Colonial Policy, 1783-1915 (Oxford, 1916).

Dale, H. E., The Higher Civil Service of Great Britain (Oxford, 1941).

*Dawson, R. M., The Government of Canada (Toronto, 1948).
    The definitive work on the subject.

------ The Principle of Official Independence (London, 1922).

de Kiewiet, C. W., British Colonial Policy and the South African Republics, 1848-72, Royal Empire Society Imperial Studies, no. 3 (London, 1929).
    Contains a good sketch of the Colonial Office in this period.

------ The Imperial Factor in South Africa: A Study in Politics and Economics (Cambridge, 1937).
    Introduction provides a review of factors influencing colonial policy in the seventies.

Dewey, A. G., The Dominions and Diplomacy: The Canadian Contribution (London, 2 vols., 1929).

Egerton, H. E., A Short History of British Colonial Policy, 1606-1909 (London, 9th ed., 1932).

Ensor, R. C. K., England, 1870-1914 (Oxford, 1936).

Ewart, J. S., The Kingdom of Canada and Other Essays (Toronto, 1908).

------ The Kingdom Papers (Toronto, 2 vols., 1917).

Farr. D. M. L., "Sir John Rose and Imperial Relations: An Episode in Gladstone's First Administration," Canadian Historical Review, XXXIII (March, 1952), 19-38.

Fay, C. R., "The Movement towards Free Trade, 1820-53," The Cambridge History of the British Empire, II (Cambridge, 1940), 388-414.

Fiddes, Sir G. V., The Dominions and Colonial Offices (London, 1926).

Fitzmaurice, Lord E., Life of the Second Earl Granville (London, 2 vols., 1905).

Forsey, E., "Disallowance of Provincial Acts, Reservation of Provincial Bills, and

Refusal of Assent by Lieutenant-Governors since 1867," Canadian Journal of Economics and Political Science, IV (February, 1938), 47-59.

*Glazebrook, G. P. de T., Canadian External Relations: An Historical Study to 1914 (Toronto, 1942).
The best short treatment of the subject in existence. Indispensable.

Graham, W. R., "Liberal Nationalism in the Eighteen-Seventies," Annual Report of the Canadian Historical Association, 1946, 101-19.

Habakkuk, H. J., "Free Trade and Commercial Expansion, 1853-70," The Cambridge History of the British Empire, II (Cambridge, 1940), 751-805.

Hall, H. D., The British Commonwealth of Nations: A Study of its Past and Future Development (London, 1920).

Hall, H. L., Australia and England: A Study in Imperial Relations (London, 1934).

*------ The Colonial Office: A History, Royal Empire Society Imperial Studies, no. 13 (London, 1937).
A good introductory survey but discursive and sometimes careless. Canadian material is at times inaccurately assessed.

Hamilton, Sir W. A. Baillie, "Forty-four Years at the Colonial Office," Nineteenth Century, CCCLXXXVI (April, 1909), 599-613.

*Hardinge, Sir A., The Life of Henry Howard Molyneux Herbert, Fourth Earl of Carnarvon (Oxford, 3 vols., 1925).
Scanty attention to Canadian topics.

Harkin, W. A., ed., Political Reminiscences of the Rt. Hon. Sir Charles Tupper (London, 1914).

Harlow, V., "The New Imperial System, 1783-1815," The Cambridge History of the British Empire, II (Cambridge, 1940), 129-87.

Harrop, A. J., England and the Maori Wars (London, 1937).

Holland, S. (Viscount Knutsford), In Black and White (London, 1926).

Hougham, G. M., "Canada First: A Minor Party in Microcosm," Canadian Journal of Economics and Political Science, XIX (May, 1953), 174-84.

Jebb, R., The Imperial Conference: A History and Study (London, 2 vols., 1911).

------ Studies in Colonial Nationalism (London, 1905).

*Keith, A. B., Responsible Government in the Dominions (Oxford, 3 vols., 1st ed.,
    1912).
    The standard work on the subject; absolutely indispensable. Based largely on Todd
    for the period before 1879.

*Kennedy, W. P. M., The Constitution of Canada, 1534-1937 (London, 2nd ed., 1938).
    Still the best survey of the constitutional history of Canada.

Knaplund, P., The British Empire, 1815-1939 (London, 1942).

------ "Colonial Problems and Colonial Policy, 1815-37." The Cambridge History
    of the British Empire, II (Cambridge, 1940), 275-307.

*------ Gladstone and Britain's Imperial Policy (London, 1927).
    A valuable monograph, containing selections from Gladstone's writings on colonial
    topics.

------ "Intra-Imperial Aspects of Britain's Defence Question, 1870-1900," Canadian
    Historical Review, III (June, 1922), 120-42.

------ James Stephen and the British Colonial System, 1813-47 (Madison, 1953).

------ "Mr. Oversecretary Stephen," Journal of Modern History, I (March, 1929),
    40-66.

Lash, Z. A., "The Working of Federal Institutions in Canada," The Federation of
    Canada, 1867-1917 (Toronto, 1917), 77-107.

Lefroy, A. H. F., The Law of Legislative Power in Canada (Toronto, 1897-8).

Lingelbach, A. L., "The Inception of the British Board of Trade," American Histori-
    cal Review, XXX (July, 1925), 701-27.

*Long, M. H., "Sir John Rose and the Informal Beginnings of the Canadian High Com-
    missionership," Canadian Historical Review, XII (March, 1931), 23-43.
    A useful treatment of a career which merits fuller examination.

Longley, R. S., "Cartier and McDougall, Canadian Emissaries to London, 1868-69."
    Canadian Historical Review, XXVI (March, 1945), 25-41.

Longley, R. S., Sir Francis Hincks: A Study of Canadian Politics, Railways, and Finance in the Nineteenth Century (Toronto, 1943).

------ "Sir Francis Hincks, Finance Minister of Canada, 1869-73," Annual Report of the Canadian Historical Association, 1939, 112-23.

Lower, A. R. M., Colony to Nation: A History of Canada (Toronto, 1946).

MacDermot, T. W. L., "The Political Ideas of John A. Macdonald," Canadian Historical Review, XIV (September, 1933), 247-64.

MacKinnon, F., "The Establishment of the Supreme Court of Canada," Canadian Historical Review, XXVII (September, 1946), 258-74.

Manning, H. T., British Colonial Government after the American Revolution, 1782-1820 (New Haven, 1933).

Martin, C., "British Policy in Canadian Confederation," Canadian Historical Review, XIII (March, 1932), 3-19.

------ Empire and Commonwealth: Studies in Governance and Self-Government in Canada (Oxford, 1929).

------ "The United States and Canadian Nationality," Canadian Historical Review, XVIII (March, 1937), 1-11.

Masters, D. C., "A. T. Galt and Canadian Fiscal Autonomy," Canadian Historical Review, XV (September, 1934), 276-82.

------ "Reciprocity and the Genesis of a Canadian Commercial Policy," Canadian Historical Review, XIII (December, 1932), 418-28.

------ The Reciprocity Treaty of 1854 (London, 1936).

Maxwell, J. A., "Lord Dufferin and the Difficulties with British Columbia, 1874-77," Canadian Historical Review, XII (December, 1931), 364-89.

Monypenny, W. F., and Buckle, G. E., The Life of Benjamin Disraeli, Earl of Beaconsfield (London, 6 vols., 1910-20).

Morison, J. L., British Supremacy and Canadian Self-Government, 1839-1854 (Glasgow, 1919).

Morison, J. L., "The Imperial Ideas of Benjamin Disraeli," Canadian Historical Review, I (September, 1920), 267-80.

Morley, J., The Life of William Ewart Gladstone (London, 3 vols., 1903).

*Morrell, W. P., British Colonial Policy in the Age of Peel and Russell (Oxford, 1930).
An invaluable survey of a crucial period in British imperial history.

Mowat, R. B., The Diplomatic Relations of Great Britain and the United States (London, 1925).

------ The Life of Lord Pauncefote (London, 1929).

------ The Victorian Age (London, 1939).

*Neuendorff, G., Studies in the Evolution of Dominion Status: The Governor-Generalship of Canada and the Development of Canadian Nationalism (London, 1942).
Useful, but reveals in places a remarkable ignorance of the Canadian scene. Must be used with caution.

Newton, Lord, Lord Lyons: A Record of British Diplomacy (London, 2 vols., 1913).

Ollivier, M., Problems of Canadian Sovereignty, 1867-1931 (Toronto, 1945).

Oman, Sir C., Memories of Victorian Oxford (London, 1941).

Ormsby, M. A., "Prime Minister Mackenzie, the Liberal Party, and the Bargain with British Columbia," Canadian Historical Review, XXVI (June, 1945), 148-73.

Penson, L. M., "The Origin of the Crown Agency Office," English Historical Review, XL (April, 1925), 196-206.

*Porritt, E., The Fiscal and Diplomatic Freedom of the British Oversea Dominions (Oxford, 1922).
Contains much useful material but suffers from faulty organization, repetition, errors of fact, and lack of historical insight.

------ Sixty Years of Protection in Canada, 1846-1907 (London, 1908).

Rogers, N. M., "The Confederate Council of Trade," Canadian Historical Review, VII (December, 1926), 277-86.

Rogers, N. M., "Notes on the Treaty-Making Power," Canadian Historical Review, VII (March, 1926), 27-33.

*Saunders, E. M., ed., Life and Letters of the Rt. Hon. Sir Charles Tupper (London, 2 vols., 1916).
Standard life of Tupper; much autobiographical material.

*Schuyler, R. L., The Fall of the Old Colonial System: A Study in British Free Trade, 1770-1870 (New York, 1945).
A general survey based exclusively on printed sources.

*------ Parliament and the British Empire: Some Constitutional Controversies concern-ing Imperial Legislative Jurisdiction (New York, 1929).
Contains a useful discussion of Imperial legislative power in the nineteenth century.

Shippee, L. B., Canadian-American Relations, 1849-1874, The Relations of Canada and the United States Series (New Haven, 1939).

Shortt, Adam, "Economic History, 1840-67," Canada and Its Provinces, V (Toronto, 1914), 185-257.

Skelton, O. D., "General Economic History, 1867-1912," Canada and Its Provinces, IX (Toronto, 1914), 95-274.

------ Life and Letters of Sir Wilfrid Laurier (New York, 2 vols., 1922).

*------ The Life and Times of Sir A. T. Galt (Toronto, 1920).
A vigorous life, exhibiting traces of an anti-British bias.

*Skilling, H. G., Canadian Representation Abroad: From Agency to Embassy (Toronto, 1945).
Chapters on the office of High Commissioner are excellent.

Smith, G., Reminiscences (New York, 1910).

Smith, G., The Treaty of Washington, 1871: A Study in Imperial History (Ithaca, 1941).

Stacey, C. P., "British Military Policy in Canada in the Era of Federation," Annual Report of the Canadian Historical Association, 1934, 20-29.

------ Canada and the British Army, 1846-71: A Study in the Practice of Responsible Government, Royal Empire Society Imperial Studies, no. 11 (London, 1936).

Stacey, C. P., "Canada and the Nile Expedition of 1884-85," Canadian Historical Review, XXXIII (December, 1952), 319-40.

------ "Fenianism and the Rise of National Feeling in Canada at the Time of Confederation," Canadian Historical Review, XII (September, 1931), 238-61.

------ "The Knighting of Francis Hincks: A Communication," Canadian Historical Review, XXXII (September, 1951), 300-1.

Stanley, G. F. G., The Birth of Western Canada: A History of the Riel Rebellions (London, 1936).

Stewart, A. R., "Canadian-West Indian Union, 1884-85," Canadian Historical Review, XXXI (December, 1950), 369-89.

*Stewart, R. B., Treaty Relations of the British Commonwealth of Nations (NewYork, 1939).
A useful modern work, although it contains some weaknesses in interpretation.

Tansill, C. C., Canadian-American Relations, 1875-1911, The Relations of Canada and the United States Series (New Haven, 1943).

Taylor, U., Guests and Memories: Annals of a Seaside Villa (Oxford, 1924).

Trevelyan, G. M., British History in the Nineteenth Century, 1782-1901 (London, 1931).

Trotter, R. G., "Canada as a Factor in Anglo-American Relations of the 1860's," Canadian Historical Review, XVI (March, 1935), 19-26.

------ Canadian Federation, Its Origins and Achievement (Toronto, 1924).

Tunstall, W. C. B., "Imperial Defence, 1815-70." The Cambridge History of the British Empire, II (Cambridge, 1940), 806-41.

Tupper, Sir C., Recollections of Sixty Years in Canada (London, 1914).

Tupper, Sir C. H., ed., Supplement to the Life and Letters of theRt. Hon. SirCharles Tupper, Bart. (Toronto, 1926).

------ "Treaty-Making Powers of the Dominions," Journal of the Society of Comparative Legislation, XVII (January, 1917), 5-18.

*Tyler, J. E., The Struggle for Imperial Unity, 1868-95, Royal Empire Society Imperial Studies, no. 16 (London, 1938).
The best single work on the Imperial Federation League.

Underhill, F. H., "Canada's Relations with the Empire as seen by the Toronto Globe, 1857-67," Canadian Historical Review, X (June, 1929), 106-28.

*------ "Edward Blake and Canadian Liberal Nationalism," in Flenley, R., ed., Essays in Canadian History (Toronto, 1939), 132-53.
Places Blake in his Canadian setting.

------ "Edward Blake's Interview with Lord Cairns on the Supreme Court Act, July 5, 1876," Canadian Historical Review, XIX (September, 1938), 292-94.

*------ "Edward Blake, the Supreme Court Act, and the Appeal to the Privy Council, 1875-76," Canadian Historical Review, XIX (September, 1938), 245-63.
Contains much material on Blake's personal attitude to the Supreme Court Act.

------ "Political Ideas of the Upper Canada Reformers, 1867-78," Annual Report of the Canadian Historical Association, 1942, 104-15.

------ "Some Aspects of Upper Canadian Radical Opinion in the Decade Before Confederation," Annual Report of the Canadian Historical Association, 1927, 46-61.

Wallace, W. S., "The Growth of Canadian National Feeling," Canadian Historical Review, I (June, 1920), 136-65.

Waugh, W. T., "The Development of Imperial Relations," Annual Report of the Canadian Historical Association, 1927, 82-8.

Wheare, K. C., The Statute of Westminster and Dominion Status (Oxford, 5th ed., 1953).
Provides a good discussion of the question of appeals to the Judicial Committee of the Privy Council.

Whitelaw, W. M., The Maritimes and Canada before Confederation (Toronto, 1934).

*------ "Responsible Government and the Irresponsible Governor," Canadian Historical Review, XIII (December, 1932), 364-86.
A valuable article for any student dealing with the autonomous colonies in this period.

Williams, E. T., "The Colonial Office in the Thirties," Historical Studies, Australia and New Zealand, II (May, 1943) 141-60.

Williamson, J. A., A Short History of British Expansion (London, 2 vols., 3rd ed.,
    1947).

Willison, Sir J. S., Sir Wilfrid Laurier and the Liberal Party: A Political History(Lon-
    don, 2 vols., 1903).

------ "Some Political Leaders in the Canadian Federation," in The Federation of Can-
    ada, 1867-1917 (Toronto, 1917), 39-76.

Woodward, E. L., The Age of Reform, 1815-70 (Oxford, 1938).

INDEX